ANTHOLOGY O[F] WORLD SCRIPTURES: WESTERN RELIGIONS

Robert E. Van Voorst

Western Theological Seminary

THOMSON
WADSWORTH

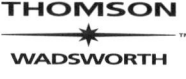

Australia • Canada • Mexico • Singapore • Spain
United Kingdom • United States

Anthology of World Scriptures: Western Religions
Robert E. Van Voorst

Publisher: Holly J. Allen
Acquisitions Editor: Steve Wainwright
Assistant Editor: Barbara Hillaker
Editorial Assistant: Gina Kessler
Technology Project Manager: Julie Aguilar
Marketing Manager: Worth Hawes
Marketing Assistant: Alexandra Tran
Marketing Communications Manager: Stacey Purviance
Project Manager, Editorial Production: Megan E. Hansen
Creative Director: Rob Hugel

Executive Art Director: Maria Epes
Print Buyer: Doreen Suruki
Permissions Editor: Roberta Broyer
Production Service: Aaron Downey, Matrix Productions, Inc.
Copy Editor: Patricia Herbst
Cover Designer: Hatty Lee
Cover Image: © G. Rossenbach/Masterfile
Cover Printer: Malloy Incorporated
Compositor: International Typesetting and Composition
Printer: Malloy Incorporated

© 2007 Thomson Wadsworth, a part of The Thomson Corporation. Thomson, the Star logo, and Wadsworth are trademarks used herein under license.

ALL RIGHTS RESERVED. No part of this work covered by the copyright hereon may be reproduced or used in any form or by any means—graphic, electronic, or mechanical, including photocopying, recording, taping, web distribution, information storage and retrieval systems, or in any other manner—without the written permission of the publisher.

Printed in the United States of America
1 2 3 4 5 6 7 09 08 07 06

Library of Congress Control Number: 2005936630

ISBN 0-495-17059-3

Thomson Higher Education
10 Davis Drive
Belmont, CA 94002-3098
USA

For more information about our products, contact us at:
Thomson Learning Academic Resource Center
1-800-423-0563

For permission to use material from this text or product, submit a request online at **http://www.thomsonrights.com**. Any additional questions about permissions can be submitted by e-mail to **thomsonrights@thomson.com**.

To Nick and Debi Lam
In Gratitude for Your Friendship

True friends stick closer than one's nearest kin.
Proverbs 18:24

Contents

Preface xiii
Acknowledgments xv

CHAPTER ONE
Western Scripture among the World's Religions 1

    A Brief History of Scripture Scholarship 2
    The Nature and Definition of Scripture 3
    The Uses of Scripture 8
    Advantages and Disadvantages of Studying Western Religions through
        Their Scriptures 10
    Western Scriptures and Modern Scholarship 14
    Western Scriptures and the World Wide Web 16
    The Plan of This Book 17
    Suggestions on How to Read Western Scriptures 18

    Glossary 19
    Questions for Study and Discussion 20
    Suggestions for Further Reading 20

CHAPTER TWO
Zoroastrianism 23

    Introduction 23
    Overview of Structure 23
    Use 24
    Origin and Development 25

    History 26
    The Call of Zarathushtra (*Yasna* 29) 26
    A Hymn of Praise to Zarathushtra (*Yasht* 24:87b–94) 27

    Teaching and Ethics 28
    Hymn to Ahura and the Purifying Fire (*Yasna* 36) 28
    Hymn to Ahura Mazda the Creator (*Yasna* 37:1–5) 28
    The Choice between Good and Evil (*Yasna* 30) 29

    Worship and Ritual 30
    The Place of the *Gathas* (*Yasna* 55:1–3) 30
    The Zoroastrian Confession (*Yasna* 12) 30

The Four Great Prayers (From the *Yasna*) 31
Disposal of the Dead (*Vendidad, Fargard* 6, section 5, 44–51) 32

Later Development of Scriptural Themes 32
Judgment of the Soul at the Chinvat Bridge (*Menok I Khrat* 2.110–195) 32

Glossary 34
Questions for Study and Discussion 35
Suggestions for Further Reading 35

CHAPTER THREE
Judaism 37

Introduction 37
Names 38
Use 38
Overview of Structure 42
Origin and Development 44

History 46
The Call of Abraham (*Genesis* 12:1–9) 46
The Call of Moses (*Exodus* 3:1–20) 46
Crossing the Red Sea (*Exodus* 14:1–31) 47
The Covenant with Israel (*Exodus* 19:1–8) 49
A Psalm for David (*Psalm* 132) 49
Ezra's Enforcement of *Torah* Observance (*Ezra* 9:1–7, 13–15; 10:1–12) 50

Teaching 51
The Oneness of God (*Deuteronomy* 6:1–9) 51
God's Creation of the World (*Genesis* 1:1–31; 2:1–9, 15–25) 52
The Revolt of Humanity (*Genesis* 3:1–24) 53
Prayer for Divine Deliverance (*Psalm* 5) 55
The Messianic King (*Isaiah* 11:1–9) 55
The Final Judgment of the World (*Daniel* 7:1–14) 56
Resurrection of the Dead (*Daniel* 12:1–3) 57

Ethics 57
The Ten Commandments (*Exodus* 20:1–14) 57
Laws on Slaves, Violence, and Property (*Exodus* 21:1–36; 22:15–26) 58
Justice for All (*Exodus* 23:1–9) 60
Holy War (*Deuteronomy* 20:1–20) 60
Sexual Love (*Song of Songs* 1:1–2:17) 61
God's Call to an Unfaithful People (*Amos* 4:1–13) 63

Two Views of Wisdom (*Proverbs* 1:1–9; 20–33; *Ecclesiastes* 1:1–9)   64
The Virtuous Wife (*Proverbs* 31:10–31)   65

Organization   66
The Ordination of Priests (*Exodus* 29:1–37)   66
A Call to Be a Prophet (*Isaiah* 6:1–13)   67
Women as Judges and Prophets (*Judges* 4:4–10, 12–16; *II Kings* 22:11–20)   68

Ritual   69
The Establishment of Circumcision (*Genesis* 17:9–14, 23–27)   69
The Establishment of the Passover (*Exodus* 12:1–19, 24–27)   70
The Observance of the Sabbath (*Exodus* 31:12–17)   71
Offerings for the Forgiveness of Sin (*Leviticus* 4:27–5:7)   71
The Day of Atonement (*Leviticus* 16:1–5, 11–19, 29–34)   72
Kosher and Nonkosher Foods (*Leviticus* 11:1–31, 41–45)   73

Later Developments of Scriptural Themes   74
The Chain of Rabbinic Tradition: "The Sayings of the Fathers" (*Mishnah, Aboth* 1.1–18)   75
The Replacement of Sacrifice by Study (*Babylonian Talmud, Minahot* 110a)   76
The Duty to Marry and Have Children (*Babylonian Talmud, Yebamoth* 61b–63)   77
Why Judaism Survives under Persecution (Maimonides, *Letter to Yemen*)   78

Glossary   79
Questions for Study and Discussion   80
Scriptures in Film   80
Suggestions for Further Reading   80

CHAPTER FOUR
Christianity   83

Introduction   83
Names   84
Overview of Structure   84
Use   87
Origin and Development   88

History   90
The Birth of Jesus the Messiah (*Matthew* 1:18–25)   90
Jesus' Miracles (*Luke* 8:26–56)   91
The Arrest, Trial, and Death of Jesus (*Mark* 14:43–50, 53–65; 15:1–41)   92

The Resurrection of Jesus (*Mark* 16:1–8)   94
The Ascension of Jesus (*Acts* 1:6–11)   94
The Coming of the Holy Spirit (*Acts* 2:1–21)   95
Persecution of the Apostles (*Acts* 5:27–42)   96
The Council at Jerusalem (*Acts* 15:1–21)   97

Teaching   98
The Parables of Jesus (*Mark* 4:1–34)   98
The Divine Word Became Human (*John* 1:1–18)   99
Nicodemus Visits Jesus (*John* 3:1–21)   99
A Sinful Woman Forgiven (*Luke* 7:36–50)   100
Results of Justification (*Romans* 5:1–11)   101
The End of Time (*Matthew* 25:31–46; *Revelation* 20:1–21:4)   102

Ethics   103
The Sermon on the Mount (*Matthew* 5–7)   103
Directions concerning Marriage (*I Corinthians* 7:1–16, 25–40)   107
Love (*I Corinthians* 13:1–13)   108
Ethics in the Christian Household (*Ephesians* 5:21–6:9)   109
Being Subject to Authorities (*Romans* 13:1–10)   110
The Fall of Rome (*Revelation* 17:1–18:5)   110

Organization   111
The Twelve Apostles and Their Mission (*Matthew* 10:1–15)   111
Matthew's Church Order (*Matthew* 18:1–10, 15–22)   112
Peter as the Rock (*Matthew* 16:13–20)   113
Qualifications of Bishops and Deacons (*I Timothy* 3:1–13)   113
Women in the Early Church (*Luke* 10:38–42; *I Corinthians* 11:2–16; *Galatians* 3:25–28; *I Timothy* 2:8–15)   114

Ritual   115
Baptism (*Matthew* 28:16–20; *Romans* 6:1–14)   115
The Eucharist (*Matthew* 26:17–19, 26–29; *John* 6:25–40, 52–59)   116
Confession and Anointing (*James* 5:13–18)   117

Later Development of Scriptural Themes   117
The Scripture Canon in Formation (Irenaeus, *Against Heresies* 1.27.2; *Muratorian Canon*)   117
Early Noncanonical Jesus Tradition (*Gospel of Thomas* 1–2, 13–14, 18, 22, 29, 42, 49–50, 53, 83–84, 99, 101, 104)   119
Gnostic Christianity and Orthodox Christianity in Conflict (*Gospel of Truth* 34–43; Irenaeus, *Against Heresies*, Preface 1.1–2, 7.1–5)   121
Women and Gnosticism (*Gospel of Mary* 7:8–18)   123
Papal Primacy Derived from Petrine Primacy (Pope Leo I, *Sermons* 4.2–4)   125

Glossary 126
Questions for Study and Discussion 126
Scriptures in Film 127
Suggestions for Further Reading 127

CHAPTER FIVE
Islam 129

Introduction 129
Name 130
Use 130
Overview of Structure 131
Origin and Development 133

History 134
The Call of Muhammad (*Qur'an* 96; 53:1–18) 134
The Mission of Muhammad (*Qur'an* 11:1–16; 93) 136
Opposition to Muhammad (*Qur'an* 52:29b–49; 63) 137
The Night Journey (*Qur'an* 17:1–2) 138
The Flight to Medina (*Qur'an* 9:40) 139
The Wives of Muhammad (*Qur'an* 33:28–40, 50) 139
The Death of Muhammad (*Qur'an* 21:34–36) 140

Teaching 141
God's Absolute Oneness (*Qur'an* 6:100–103; 112) 141
God's Names (*Qur'an* 59:22–24) 141
God's Power (*Qur'an* 24:41–46; 6:95–99) 142
God's Predestination (*Qur'an* 42:8–13; 7:177–182) 142
Jinn (*Qur'an* 72:1–15) 144
Creation (*Qur'an* 15:16–48; 16:1–17) 144
Adam, Eve, and the Fall (*Qur'an* 2:30–37) 146
The Holy *Qur'an* (*Qur'an* 42:50–53; 46:1–8; 2:87–91) 146
On Unbelievers, Jews, and Christians (*Qur'an* 9:1–7; 3:38–50; 2:111–121, 132–136) 148
Resurrection and Judgment (*Qur'an* 75:1–15; 69:14–35) 150
Heaven and Hell (*Qur'an* 76:1–22; 56:1–50; 77:1–39) 151

Ethics 153
The Conduct of Believers (*Qur'an* 17:23–38) 153
Women (*Qur'an* 4:19–22, 34–39; 2:220–223, 227–233) 154
The Different Dimensions of Struggle (Jihad) (*Qur'an* 6:16, 19–20; 48:11–21; 2:190–194, 216–218) 156
Law Codes (*Qur'an* 4:1–10) 157

Worship and Ritual 158
　The Opening of the *Qur'an* (*Qur'an* 1)　158
　Confession of Faith (*Qur'an* 57:1–7; 37:32–39)　159
　Prayer (*Qur'an* 2:142–149)　159
　Alms (*Qur'an* 107; 9:53–60)　160
　The Fast (*Qur'an* 2:183–187)　161
　Pilgrimage (*Qur'an* 2:125–129; 106; 2:196–199)　161
　The Mosque (*Qur'an* 24:36–38; 9:15–18)　163
　Against Evil Magic (*Qur'an* 113; 114)　163

Later Developments of Scriptural Themes　164
　Selections from the *Hadith*　164
　　On Innovations　164
　　On Ritual Washings　164
　　On Prayer　165
　　On Alms　165
　　On God　165
　　On the Power of Reading the *Qur'an*　166
　　On the Martyr in Jihad　166
　　On Plunder in Jihad　166
　　On Women and Children in Jihad　167
　　On the Steps for Jihad against Enemies　167
　A Sunni Creed (*Creed of Abu Hasan al-Ash'ari*)　167
　A Shi'ite Creed (Ibn Babawayh al-Qummi,
　　Risalatu'l I'tiqadat)　170
　Sufi Poetry on Love for God (*The Secret Rose
　　Garden* 1)　171

Glossary　173
Questions for Study and Discussion　173
Scriptures in Film　174
Suggestions for Further Reading　174

CHAPTER SIX
New Religious Movements　177

　Introduction　177
　Names　178
　Use　179
　Overview of Structure　180
　Origin and Development　182

The Scripture of Baha'i 183
The Essence of Baha'i Teaching and a Sketch of the Life of Baha'u'llah (Shoghi Effendi, *The Promised Day Is Come*, Preface) 183
Baha'i, Islam, and Christianity (The Bab, *Qayyumu'l-Asma* 1, 61–62) 185
Baha'i Laws (Baha'u'llah, *Kitab-I-Aqdas* 1–2, 12–14, 16, 30–34, 45, 63–65, 149–150, 189) 185
Baha'i Prayers (Short Obligatory Prayer, Medium Obligatory Prayer, Prayer for America) 188

The Scripture of the Church of Jesus Christ of Latter-day Saints 189
Joseph Smith's Story (*Pearl of Great Price, Joseph Smith—History* 1, 1–22, 25–35, 40–47, 59–62, 67–74) 189
The First Description of the *Book of Mormon* (*Book of Mormon*, original title page) 192
The Coming of Jesus Christ in 34 C.E. to the New World (*Book of Mormon, 3 Nephi* 11.1–41) 193
Destruction of the Nephites and Burial of the Golden Plates (*Book of Mormon, Mormon* 6:1–3, 6–11, 16–22) 194
Preparations for the Trek to Utah (*Doctrine and Covenants* 136.1–11, 17–24, 30–42) 195
The Essence of Latter-day Saint Teaching (*Pearl of Great Price, Articles of Faith* 1–13) 196
Church Pronouncements on Polygamy and Men of African Descent (*Doctrine and Covenants*, Official Declarations of 1890 and 1978) 197

The Scripture of Christian Science 199
Introduction to Christian Science Scripture and to the Work of Mary Baker Eddy (*Science and Health with Key to the Scriptures*, Preface) 199
The Essence of Christian Science Teaching (*Science and Health with Key to the Scriptures*, "Recapitulation") 201
Prayer and Its Role (*Science and Health with Key to the Scriptures*, "Prayer") 201
Healing Practices (*Science and Health with Key to the Scriptures*, "Christian Science Practice") 202
Interpretation of *Genesis* 1 (*Science and Health with Key to the Scriptures*, "Genesis") 203
Two Testimonials to Healing (*Science and Health with Key to the Scriptures*, "Fruitage") 204

The Scripture of the Unification Church   205
Dual Characteristics of the Universe and of Human Beings (*Divine Principle* 1.1.1.1)   205
The Purpose of the Creation of the Universe (*Divine Principle* 1.1.3.1)   206
The Spiritual Fall and the Physical Fall of Adam and Eve (*Divine Principle* 1.2.2.1–2)   207
The Restoration of Humanity (*Divine Principle* 1.3, Introduction)   208
Salvation through the Second Messiah, the True Parent (*Divine Principle* 2, Introduction)   209
The Advent of the Second Messiah as a Korean (*Divine Principle* 2.6, Introduction; 2.6.3.2–3)   210

Glossary   211
Questions for Study and Discussion   211
Scriptures in Film   211
Suggestions for Further Reading   212

Index   213

Preface

The major living religions of the West have expressed their teachings and practices in writing. Over the course of time, some of these writings gained unique standing and became scriptures. As scriptures, they continue to influence the course of their religions. To read these scriptures, therefore, is to encounter Western religions in a direct and meaningful way.

This book is designed to facilitate this encounter for the general reader and especially for the student of Western religion. Its pages contain the most notable and instructive holy writings of Zoroastrianism, Judaism, Christianity, Islam, and four new religious movements—Baha'i, Mormonism, Christian Science, and the Unification Church. The collection began with my efforts to gather the most important passages of world scripture for my students, organize them in a way helpful for teaching and learning, and include the full set of pedagogical aids that students have come to expect.

This anthology not only presents scripture readings but also sets them in the context of their application in the religions themselves, taking into account recent scholarship on the role of scriptures in religion. Moreover, it does this in one volume and in one format. Designed to be used as a secondary textbook, the anthology has an organization that is easily adaptable to a range of primary textbooks and to most of the current methods of teaching comparative religion.

Anthology of World Scriptures: Western Religions is organized as follows. The first chapter examines the general phenomenon of scripture in the world's religions, its nature, use, and place in modern scholarship. Chapter 1 also introduces the reader to the art of reading scripture and using the World Wide Web to encounter scripture.

Chapters 2 through 5 each present the scripture of a single religion and are organized as follows: Vignettes about scripture and its usage draw the reader's interest and imagination. Then an introduction sets the context by explaining the overall use, structure, origin, and development of the scripture in its religion. The first grouping of scripture passages concerns the history of the religion, especially the founder (if any) and early history of the religion. The second grouping covers main doctrinal teachings, including divine or ultimate reality, creation and the environment, human nature, and human fulfillment. The third grouping deals with ethical systems, both personal and social; topics such as war and peace, justice, and the role of women are anthologized as fully as possible here. The fourth grouping focuses on organization—the ways in which the religion orders itself and seeks to order its wider culture. The fifth grouping includes worship, devotion, ritual, and meditation. Most chapters have a final section, "Later Developments of Scriptural Themes," that shows some of the subsequent understanding and use of scriptures. Chapter 6 keeps together the scriptures of each of the four new religious movements and does not employ the five groupings described above. Each chapter has full pedagogical aids, including headnotes for each passage, full annotations to explain difficult terms and concepts in the readings (placed at the bottom of the page for easy access), a glossary with pronunciations, a brief treatment of how scriptures are treated in Hollywood films, questions for study and discussion, and suggestions for further reading.

The scriptures presented here come from the religions commonly understood to be the major living world religions in the West. By "world religion," scholars generally mean those religions that have had an impact on the world's leading cultures, not necessarily religions that are spread throughout the world. By "Western," scholars typically mean the religions that have become important in the Western world, even though Zoroastrianism, Judaism, Christianity, Islam, and Baha'i were born on the Asian continent (the "Near East," not the "Far East," but the East nonetheless) and have a significant presence there.

I am very grateful for the strong reception that my *Anthology of World Scriptures* has received. I trust that this volume on Western scriptures will continue to stimulate readers to explore the world of religion.

Acknowledgments

The editorial staff at Wadsworth have been fine partners in developing and producing this book. I especially want to thank religion editor Steve Wainwright and assistant editor Barbara Hillaker. Aaron Downey of Matrix Productions and my copyeditor Patricia Herbst also have been excellent partners in producing this book.

Scholars at other institutions offered detailed, insightful critiques at many points along the way. I thank those who reviewed the content of these chapters as it appeared in five editions of my *Anthology of World Scriptures*: David W. Aiken, Ferris State University; Vivodh J. Z. Anand, Montclair State University; Paul Bernadicou, University of San Francisco; James Cook, Oakland Community College, Orchard Ridge; Dell deChant, University of South Florida; Marianne Ferguson, Buffalo State College; Roger Keller, Brigham Young University; Richard Mahon, Riverside Community College; William K. Mahony, Davidson College; Michael McKale, Saint Francis College; Vivian-Lee Nyitray, University of California at Riverside; Patrick S. O'Donnell, Santa Barbara City College; Richard Penaskovic, Auburn University; Christopher Queen, Harvard University; Stephen J. Reno, Southern Oregon State College; Philip Riley, Santa Clara University; Roger L. Schmidt, San Bernardino Valley College; Philip Schmitz, Eastern Michigan University; Daniel Sheridan, Loyola University of New Orleans; Robert Smith, Trenton State College; Donald Swearer, Swarthmore College; James Whitehill, Stephens College; Boyd Wilson, Hope College; and Glenn Yocum, Whittier College. For their helpful review of the current book, I thank Amy DeRogatis, Michigan State University; Rodger Payne, Louisiana State University, and Dewey D. Wallace Jr., George Washington University.

The efforts of all those people made this a better book; any errors that remain are mine alone. I would be most grateful if users of this book and its Wadsworth website resources would send me your comments and suggestions for improving them. You can reach me by my postal address: Western Theological Seminary, 101 East 13th Street, Holland, MI 49423-3622; or my e-mail address: bob.vanvoorst@westernsem.edu.

Finally, this book gives me the happy opportunity to express my deep gratitude to my wife, Mary, for all her love and support. Mary and I dedicate this book to two best friends and excellent people, Nick and Debi Lam.

CHAPTER ONE

Western Scripture among the World's Religions

❖ In North Carolina, a controversy brews over a book about Muslim scripture selected for the freshman orientation seminar in the University of North Carolina at Chapel Hill—Michael Sells's *Approaching the Qur'an: The Early Revelations.* In the shadow of September 11, 2001, some North Carolina citizens charge that "impressionable freshmen" will think that Islam is a harmless, attractive faith and perhaps be drawn to it. Even the American Civil Liberties Union warns that teaching this book might be a "violation of the separation of church and state," and promises to monitor the situation closely.

❖ Near the federal prison in Terre Haute, Indiana, demonstrators gather at the execution of Timothy McVeigh. He is being punished for the 1995 bombing of the federal office building in Oklahoma City in which 169 people died. Some people protest his execution by carrying signs with words from the *Bible* of both Judaism and Christianity: "You shall not kill." Counterprotesters also carry signs with biblical words: "You shall not allow a murderer to live." In 2004, similar scenes played out at the state trial of Terry McNichols, who was convicted of participating with McVeigh in this crime but did not receive the death penalty.

❖ Outside a movie theater in Utah, crowds gather, waiting for the director, producers, and actors of a film having its premiere to arrive. Although the scene is similar to most premieres, the film is not. It is a feature-film adaptation of the *Book of Mormon,* officially sanctioned by the Church of Jesus Christ of Latter-day Saints. Beside its general release to theaters and then to video-rental outlets, it will be used in the missionary activities of the church.

The influence of Western scripture is felt throughout the world in ways both extraordinary and commonplace. Not all contemporary examples of scripture usage are as dramatic or controversial as these vignettes suggest. They do indicate, though, that the scriptures of Western religions have a continuing profound impact on life and culture. This anthology introduces these scriptures and encourages a deep encounter with them in all their variety. Scriptures of the Western world are so vast in size that some sort of sampling is necessary for all but the most expert specialist. This anthology thus offers from each tradition excerpts that faithfully reflect the history and continuing life of the tradition.

A BRIEF HISTORY OF SCRIPTURE SCHOLARSHIP

In the last 150 years the scholarly study of world scriptures has passed through three distinct stages that have strongly influenced how we read Western scriptures.[1] In the first stage, at the middle of the nineteenth century, European scholars began a vast enterprise of making critically reliable translations. They focused on the little-translated sacred literature of Asia and the scriptures of Islam and Zoroastrianism. Their concern was to translate individual texts, not to examine the general religious features of scripture. They treated scripture as a mine out of which to dig the history and doctrine of religions, with little regard for the ways scripture functioned in religious communities.[2]

The academic movement known as the "History of Religions school" dominated the second stage in the study of scriptures. This school, which continues to exert a strong influence today, analyzes the historical development of each religion. Perhaps in reaction to the earlier methodological reliance on world scriptures, scholars like Joachim Wach and Mircea Eliade relied on the study of ritual, myth, symbols, and other nontextual elements of religion. Scripture, both Eastern and Western, was largely neglected at this stage. Such a respected treatment of comparative religion as Gerardus van der Leeuw's *Religion in Essence and Manifestation* contains only a brief discussion of scripture as a feature of world religions.[3] Also, as social science methods increasingly entered the field of religious scholarship, researchers turned away from studying literary sources from the past in favor of the study of present-day living communities of faith.[4]

Although this second stage is still very influential, a third stage is emerging in which scholars are rediscovering the value of scripture. The overreliance on scripture characteristic of the first stage and the neglect of scripture in the second stage are being balanced as scholars increasingly view scripture as an important feature among the religions of the world. Now scripture is correctly seen as one religious facet

---

[1] For an excellent comprehensive discussion of the history of the academic study of world religions, with some detailed comments on scripture study, see E. Sharpe, *Comparative Religion: A History,* 2d ed. (LaSalle, IL: Open Court Press, 1987). Perhaps the best succinct presentation of this topic is by S. Cain, "History of the Study of Religion," in M. Eliade, ed., *Encyclopedia of Religion* (New York: Macmillan, 1987), vol. 14, pp. 64–83.

[2] A continuing feature of this first stage is a number of popular anthologies of world scriptures that use world scriptures as a mine for enlightenment and pay little or no attention to how scripture functions in world religious communities. For example, Robert Ballou's *The Bible of the World* (New York: Viking, 1939) and its abridgment in *World Bible* (New York: Viking, 1944) have remained in print continually, although never revised. The Unification Church has published *World Scripture: A Comparative Anthology of Sacred Texts,* ed. Andrew Wilson (New York: Paragon House, 1991). Philip Novak has edited *The World's Wisdom: Sacred Texts of the World's Religions* (San Francisco: HarperSanFrancisco, 1994).

[3] Gerardus van der Leeuw, *Religion in Essence and Manifestation* (London: Allen & Unwin, 1938; German original, 1933). One short chapter, 64, deals almost exclusively with Western scripture.

[4] For example, the widely used *Reader in Comparative Religion: An Anthropological Approach,* ed. W. A. Lessa and E. Z. Vogt, 4th ed. (New York: Harper & Row, 1997), has excellent readings in all the basic topics in the cultural-anthropological study of religion—symbol, myth, ritual, shamanism, magic—but not one essay on scripture and its uses.

among many and therefore not to be isolated from the others. Another new element is an emphasis on the actual ways in which scripture is viewed and used in world religions. To understand scripture, according to this view, we must know not just the scriptural text but also how it comes alive in the total life of the religion.

Recent research gives evidence of this emerging third stage. Large-scale studies such as Geo Widengren's *Phenomenology of Religion* and Friedrich Heiler's *Manifestations and Essence of Religion* deal extensively with the nature and use of scripture among the world's religions.[5] Ninian Smart's *Sacred Texts of the World* uses scripture to approach several different religious phenomena in each world religion.[6] Five recent books deal with scripture and its role in religion: *The Holy Book in Comparative Perspective*, by Frederick Denny and Roderick Taylor; *Sacred Word and Sacred Text*, by Harold Coward; *Rethinking Scripture: Essays from a Comparative Perspective*, by Miriam Levering; *Sacred Texts and Authority*, by Jacob Neusner; and *What Is Scripture? A Comparative Approach*, by Wilfred Cantwell Smith.[7] As a result of the research in this stage, the comparative study of scripture is today one of the leading features in the study of world religions. Smith, of Harvard University, and some of his students have had a strong influence on current scripture study. They argue for scripture study centered on the actual reception and use of scriptures. The work of William Graham on the oral dimensions of scripture has been especially influential.[8] A measure of the strength of this stage is that it is now appearing in textbooks, where several works are notable.[9] As a representative of this third stage of scripture study, the present work offers a wide range of scripture selections from the religions of the world, with introductions and annotations to set the readings in the context of their actual usage.

THE NATURE AND DEFINITION OF SCRIPTURE

At first glance, defining scripture seems easy enough. We think of scripture as the holy writing, the sacred text of a religion. All religions seem to have scriptures, and all appear to use them in the same way. As a phenomenon among religions, scripture seems on the surface to be a constant. On closer examination, however, these simple notions vanish.

---

[5] Geo Widengren, *Religionsphänomenologie* (Berlin: de Gruyter, 1969); Friedrich Heiler, *Erscheinungsformen und Wesen der Religion*, 2d ed. (Stuttgart: Kohlhammer, 1979).
[6] Ninian Smart, *Sacred Texts of the World* (London: Macmillan, 1982).
[7] F. M. Denny and R. L. Taylor, eds., *The Holy Book in Comparative Perspective* (Charleston: University of South Carolina Press, 1985); Harold Coward, *Sacred Word and Sacred Text* (Maryknoll, NY: Orbis, 1988); Miriam Levering, ed., *Rethinking Scripture* (Albany: State University of New York Press, 1989); Jacob Neusner, ed., *Sacred Texts and Authority* (Cleveland: Pilgrim, 1998); Wilfred Cantwell Smith, *What Is Scripture? A Comparative Approach* (Philadelphia: Augsburg Fortress, 1993).
[8] See especially William Graham's *Beyond the Written Word: Oral Aspects of Scripture in the History of Religion* (Cambridge: Cambridge University Press, 1983).
[9] T. W. Hall, R. B. Pilgrim, and R. R. Cavanagh, *Religion: An Introduction* (San Francisco: Harper & Row, 1985); Kenneth Kramer, *World Scriptures: An Introduction to Comparative Religion* (New York: Paulist, 1986); Roger Schmidt, *Exploring Religion*, 2d ed. (Belmont, CA: Wadsworth, 1988); Jean Holm and John Bower, *Sacred Writings* (London: Pinter, 1994); Richard Viladesau and Mark Massa, *World Religions: A Sourcebook for the Student of Christian Theology* (New York: Paulist, 1994); Ian S. Markham, ed., *A World Religions Reader* (Oxford: Blackwell, 1996).

Books that are traditionally regarded as scriptures vary in several important aspects. The first variation among scriptures is in *literary form*. People who come from religious traditions that include scriptures tend naturally to assume that the sacred texts of other religions look and function exactly like theirs. Scriptures, however, are as varied as the religions and cultures from which they come:

- Some scriptures, especially those of the three main Western religions (Judaism, Christianity, and to a lesser degree Islam), prominently feature historical **narratives.** They tell an event in story form. Scriptures from other religions, especially Eastern faiths, have few narratives or none at all.

- Some scriptures enshrine their religion's vision of a moral life in law codes, some feature more loosely bound moral precepts, and still others do not seem concerned about ethics.

- Poetry is the leading literary form of some scriptures; others feature prose.

- Some scriptural books have moral philosophy (for example, the Confucian *Analects,* the wisdom literature of the Jewish and Christian *Bible*), but many have no explicit philosophy at all.

- Some scriptures contain directions and songs for sacrifice (the Jewish *Bible*), whereas others have no developed prescriptions for rites and ceremonies (the *Qur'an*).

- Also present in scriptures are myth, legend, prophecy, sermons, love poems, divination, and magic, among many other **genres,** or literary forms.

Even this brief overview shows that Western scriptures do not take a fixed literary form. Therefore, we cannot open a book, browse through it, and pronounce it scriptural. Scripturalness is primarily a relational, not a literary, quality. As William Graham has written, the holiness of a book is not automatically accepted when the text is first written, but it is "realized historically in the life of communities who respond to it as something sacred or holy."[10] Communities shape and receive scripture, and scripture shapes the life of faith. The relation between scripture and religion is reciprocal and dynamic.

The second variation among scriptures has to do with their *number.* Within any one religion, they can range from one book to an entire library. Like the *Qur'an*, scriptures can be one unified text of moderate size between two covers. Like the Jewish and Christian scriptures, they can be collections of many short books between two covers. In Eastern religions, they range in number from one book (the *Adi Granth* of Sikhism), to the dozen or so texts of Confucianism, to the hundred or more texts of Hinduism, to the more than a thousand texts of Taoism and some forms of Buddhism.

The third variation in scriptures lies in *function*. In some religions, scripture is so central—or seems so to outsiders—that the lives of believers seem almost dictated by scripture. Zoroastrianism, Judaism, Christianity, and Islam are all properly called "religions of the book" because of the high place and powerful function of their scriptures.

---

[10] W. A. Graham, "Scripture," *Encyclopedia of Religion,* vol. 13, p. 134.

New religious movements that originate from these religions are also scripture-centered. In contrast, Eastern religions often have a more informal relationship to their scriptures, which lay devotees consult mainly for general guidance and inspiration. (Monks and nuns, however, have a more formal and developed relationship to their scriptures.)

The varying oral and textual dimensions of scripture also lead to differences in function. Some religions view the spoken word of scripture as primary. In other religions, especially in the Western world, the power and function of the book seem to depend on its written, textual nature. Muslims, for example, believe that the *Qur'an* is a transcription of a book already written in heaven. Like most Western scripture, it originated in a process of oral tradition, but its use and authority in its religion come from its written, textual nature. A later section of this chapter deals more fully with the uses of scriptures, but enough has been said here to suggest that they function in significantly different ways.

Given all this variety, is it possible to define the word *scripture* in a way that takes variety into account yet applies to all world religions? Although some scholars answer in the negative,[11] most argue that a comprehensive definition is possible and necessary. The definition we use here is this: **Scripture** *is writing that is accepted and used in a religious community as especially sacred and authoritative.* By looking closely at the key words and implications of this definition, we can discuss formal and functional aspects of scriptures—what they are and how people use them.

First, every scripture is a *writing*. Scriptures exercise much of their authority as books, and we encounter them as books. Some scholars argue that **oral tradition,** the passing down of material by word of mouth only, can be "scriptural."[12] Although oral and written traditions do have some similar characteristics and functions, strictly speaking "oral scripture" is a contradiction in terms—scripture is by definition written. (The word *scripture* comes from the Latin *scriptura,* or "writing.") The scriptures of all religions, however, do have continuing, significant oral and aural (hearing) dimensions.[13] Most scriptures originated in oral tradition and stayed in oral tradition for several generations before being put in writing. Although the writing of scripture obscures its oral dimensions, the orality of the text is still embedded in the writing, waiting to be drawn out by faithful vocalizing of the words. Scripture comes most fully alive when believers read it aloud and hear it in worship. Most believers, even those in highly literate cultures, hear scripture in worship more often and more meaningfully than they read it privately. In this book, as in any book, we encounter scriptures as texts, but these texts are meant to be spoken and heard.

According to our definition, scriptures are *especially sacred*. They have special religious significance in pointing to ultimate reality and truth. Sacredness should not be

---

[11] In *Rethinking Scripture,* for example, the essays by Coburn and Folkert reject the term *scripture* for *the Word* and *canon*. The other authors in this book keep "scripture" as a conceptual category, and it is the dominant category in the volume as a whole, as the title implies.
[12] See, for example, Schmidt, *Exploring Religion,* p. 208: "Broadly conceived, *scripture* refers to oral as well as written traditions that people regard as sacred. Each religious community has a scripture, a body of sacred oral or written traditions."
[13] See especially Graham, *Beyond the Written Word*. For a general treatment of orality, see W. Ong, *Orality and Literacy* (New York: Routledge, Chapman and Hall, 1982), and J. Goody, *The Interface between the Written and the Oral* (Cambridge: Cambridge University Press, 1982).

seen simply as being of divine origin or even as the "wholly other," Rudolf Otto's influential conception of sacredness that suits Western religions but not many Eastern faiths. For example, the sacred Tao ("Way") witnessed by the *Tao Te Ching* is not wholly other but is hidden in the universe and the self, waiting to be discovered and "tuned in to." Moreover, only a few books among world scriptures explicitly claim sacredness for themselves; the *Qur'an* is the most notable example in Western religions. Most scriptures receive their sacred status only after they have been written, circulated, and widely accepted as reflecting the faith in some special sense. The relational aspect of all scripture comes to the fore in a religious community.

Notice that scriptures are books held to be *especially* sacred. Most religions have a secondary religious literature that is also viewed as holy, instructive, or authoritative. For example, Judaism has its *Talmud,* books of religious law, and Islam its *hadith,* traditions about Muhammad. This may seem to complicate the matter of defining the idea of scripture. On what basis can we say that a certain holy book in a religious tradition is scripture but another holy book is not? The answer lies in the special reception and usage that believers give to works that they see as *especially* sacred. Most religions explicitly or implicitly hold some works to be secondary to scripture. *Talmud* is not the Hebrew *Bible; hadith* is not the *Qur'an*. Almost every religion has commentarial, devotional, or legal literature that follows up on scripture, and believers typically make a careful distinction between scripture and these works.

Another mark of special holiness is use in ritual. When believers read books aloud in worship, when they speak their words to carry out sacrifice, and especially when they venerate (pay formal respect to) books during worship, we have a sure indication that these books are especially sacred. Secondary religious literature rarely makes its way into worship. Different types of veneration are practiced in Judaism, Christianity, Islam, Zoroastrianism, and in many new religious movements. Even in everyday life, scriptures enjoy special respect: The Christian *Bible* is the only book in the West still often bound in leather; Muslims wrap the *Qur'an* in silk and store it in a special place. In the new religious movements, the key writings of the founders that function as scriptures are often printed and bound to resemble more traditional holy books.

The third element of our definition of *scripture* is the authority of the text. Just as sacredness is an aspect of every scripture, scriptures are also *especially authoritative* in their communities. Among all written texts in a community a scripture is always the most authoritative and is often the court of final appeal in religious matters. The range of this authority and the way it is exercised vary depending on the nature of the religion and the content of its scriptures. In the Western "religions of the book," scriptures are comprehensive in content and regulate much of life. In the Eastern religions, scriptures are often not authoritative in the same way as in the Abrahamic traditions. Yet Eastern scriptures often express the heart of their faith, the way of salvation. Moreover, "at least four of the six South Eastern or Far Eastern fundamentalist-like movements . . . do in fact privilege a sacred text and presume to draw certain fundamentals—beliefs and behaviors—from it."[14] The authority of scripture

---

[14] M. E. Marty and R. S. Appleby, eds., *Fundamentalisms Observed* (Chicago: University of Chicago Press, 1991), p. 820.

for most followers of a given religion is paradoxically acknowledged even when some occasionally reject it. Typically among Western religions, to receive one religion's texts as scripture is automatically to exclude the texts of other religions. For example, the presentation of Jewish *Bible* material in the *Qur'an* means that Muslims should not look directly to the Jewish *Bible* and read it. An exception to this is the Christian *Bible,* which contains all the Jewish *Bible* renamed as the "Old Testament."

The authority of scripture in both East and West is established by a special class of scholars who are the guardians of scripture and recognized experts in its interpretation. In Buddhism, monks with special training and ability teach the sacred writings to other monks and inquiring laypeople. The Jewish rabbi, the Christian pastor, and the Muslim mullah, all leaders of local congregations, are experts in interpreting and teaching their scriptures. The authority of scripture in nearly every faith, including new religious movements, therefore, is mediated largely by individuals considered to be its official interpreters. **Commentary,** a book written to explain another book, has a large role in the history of many religions and regulates how scriptures are received and used, especially at the official level. As John Henderson states, "Commentaries and commentarial modes of thinking dominated the intellectual history of most premodern civilizations. . . . Until the seventeenth century in Europe, and even later in China, India, and the Near East, thought, especially within high intellectual traditions, was primarily exegetical [text-interpretive] in character and expression."[15] We must also remember that only quite recently in the sweep of human history have mass-produced books appeared and mass literacy has become possible. This is another reason for the existence of a special class to read, comment on, and relate sacred books to a religious community. Of course, the uses of scriptures by ordinary followers of a religion are at times quite different from the official prescribed use.

Two features of scripture not directly related to our definition should be stated here. First, scriptures of every religion are often heterogeneous but are nonetheless *seen as a unity* by their communities. Modern scholarship has shown that the *Qur'an* has passed through different phases of development during and since the life of Muhammad. But neither the conclusions of scholars nor the acknowledged difficulties of the *Qur'an* call its unity into question for a Muslim. Judaism's *Bible* went through a long period of development and has dozens of books in it, but it is seen as one distinct, unified book; indeed, *Bible* means "the Book."

A second important feature of scripture is that it has *a degree of closure*. This closure is often called a **canon,** a list or collection of books recognized as scriptural. The canon is absolutely fixed in the three **Abrahamic monotheisms**—Judaism, Christianity, and Islam—and in Zoroastrianism. All the scriptures of these religions were long ago officially identified, and nothing can now be added or subtracted from their canons. In Hinduism, Buddhism, Jainism, Confucianism, and Taoism, however, the situation is quite different, for two reasons. First, their sacred literature is vast. The problems in defining a canon for a religion like Taoism, for example, which has 1,200 sacred texts, are enormous. Second, the process of producing scripture has not

---

[15] J. B. Henderson, *Scripture, Canon, Commentary: A Comparison of Confucian and Western Exegesis* (Princeton: Princeton University Press, 1991), p. 3.

officially ended. Where new scriptural revelations can be added—as Mormons added two in the twentieth century—a closed canon cannot exist.

How can believers relate to their religion's scriptures when they are so vast that no one person or group can know them all, let alone be expert in them all? In traditions with large canons, certain books are basic for almost everyone. Also, different groups in a religion attach themselves to a few select scriptures that reflect their particular interests. This tendency to choose specific books from among the total corpus of scripture results in a "canon within the canon." Most commonly it occurs in religions with very large numbers of books, but it also can be found in religions with smaller canons. In sum, scripture canons can be either completely closed or open to development and change. No matter how readily they can be altered, canonical texts are still viewed and treated as scripture.

THE USES OF SCRIPTURE

When scripture is set in the full context of the everyday life of believers, its uses become plain. How believers use scripture shows its status and role in a religion. The following chapters of this book outline the varied uses of scripture in each religion. In this section, we discuss some basic dimensions of the comparative study of scripture usage.

We begin with three uses that are primarily *cognitive,* understanding and thinking in some way about the words and their meaning. First, scripture is a source for establishing and defending key doctrines. Scriptures can be used doctrinally because they typically contain the key teachings of the faith and because believers usually see them as continuing the voice of the founders. They have primary importance as statements of the deep truths of the universe and the right way to live in it. These teachings can assume different forms: God(s) and humanity; human imperfections and salvation; beginnings and ends of the individual and the cosmos; the moral life and how to achieve it. When scripture is used to establish doctrine, its official interpreters—monks, priests, scholars, and the like—most often do this. Sometimes formal debate in councils or assemblies sets down doctrines, often within the confines of a monastery or temple. Defending doctrine occurs less often at the popular level, but even here scripture can function authoritatively. An appeal to a passage of holy writ is often the final word in any argument about religion.

Second, scripture is also prominently used in public worship. Worshippers often display and read it aloud. Although this practice is characteristic especially of the Abrahamic "religions of the book," it is also significant in religions such as Hinduism and Buddhism that are not so book oriented. The worship that goes on in a Buddhist monastery, for example, prominently features scriptures. Monks read them, chant them, meditate on them, and walk around them in solemn procession. Even when the book is not prominent in worship, its content often permeates the ceremonies of most scripturalizing religions. Prayers, sacrifices, and hymns come from and echo the language of scripture. Many lyrics of the music of worship are drawn from the scriptural text. Hymns and chants, with their emotional power, are significant vehicles for use of scripture in most religious traditions in both East and West.

Perhaps the place and function of scripture are never so prominent as when worshippers formally venerate it. Almost every religion with scripture pays it ritual respect in some way. Hindus speak the words of a *Veda* with great care. In certain Taoist and Confucian temples, the location of the scripture collection is itself holy. In Judaism, the scrolls are removed from their ark at the front center of the synagogue with great solemnity and on certain festival days are paraded around the synagogue. In many Christian churches, everyone stands for the oral reading of the gospels. **Bibliolatry** [bib-lee-AHL-ah-tree], literally, "worship of a book," results when believers give excessive veneration to their scriptures or become absolutely dependent on them.

A third typical cognitive use of scripture is in meditation and devotion. This is usually private and individual, but it can also occur in group settings, as when Buddhist monks meditate in session on sutra passages or on mantras drawn from scripture. In Western religions, the scripture books are often marked into sections for devotional reading; it is the duty of believers to read, ponder, and often memorize the words. In meditation and devotion, the scriptures teach the truth of the religion and promote the growth of the reader into the fullness of the faith.

Another important dimension of scripture use—one often overlooked—is *noncognitive*, using the words in a variety of ways without any mental attempt to understand their meaning. One noncognitive use occurs when scriptures are written in a language that followers of the faith cannot understand. This is especially the case when a religion like Islam holds that its scripture is so essentially bound to its original language that it cannot be translated and retain its sacred nature.

A second noncognitive use of scripture is decorative and iconic; the text itself is revered as a holy object. (An **icon** is a holy picture, usually of a saint.) One cannot live or travel in any Muslim area without encountering Qur'anic verses everywhere. They are displayed on private houses and public buildings, often in a stylized calligraphy that is a mainstay of art in Muslim lands. These word decorations are not meant to be read so much as to be felt, thereby exercising their holy presence for the blessing of the community. In these and other iconic usages of scripture, the appeal is typically more to the imagination and emotion than to the mind.

A third noncognitive application mixes religion and magic. The power of scripture is such that it can bring blessing and keep away evil; it has an objective supernatural power quite by itself. Scripture can be used in charms or talismans, a manifestation of the supernatural power of scripture. The mere possession of a holy book also has power to bless and to ward off evil. For example, putting a certain Taoist text in the hands of a woman undergoing a perilous childbirth is said to cause the immediate safe birth of her child. In many religions, individuals who can afford to do so will often buy a holy book for possession in the home; this practice is especially common in Judaism, Christianity and Islam.

Perhaps the most striking noncognitive use of scripture is **bibliomancy** [BIB-lee-oh-man-see], the use of holy books to foresee the future and guide one's response to it. Many religions feature the informal practice of opening a scripture book at random and reading the first passage that meets the eye. This passage, it is thought, has special power to direct the believer through an uncertain or difficult situation in life or through the difficulties of the new day. One of the most famous ancient conversions to Christianity, that of Saint Augustine, featured bibliomancy of this sort. Some printed editions of the *Qur'an* have symbols at the top of the page by which a reader opening the book at random can discern whether a planned action is advisable, inadvisable, or neutral. Sikhism has formalized bibliomancy in its "taking the word" ceremony in which Sikh scripture is opened at random and read for a special meaning. Some Taoists read the *I Ching* philosophically, but more use it in divination. All these forms of bibliomancy assume that supernatural guidance is exercised in and through the book for the blessing of the believer.

Scholars of religion have categorized scripture uses in other ways beyond cognitive and noncognitive. Perhaps the most helpful is that of Sam D. Gill, who proposed that uses of scripture are informative or performative. *Informative* means imparting information in various ways, such as in doctrine and history. *Performative,* in contrast, means doing something, as for example when scripture is used to make sacrifice, to make the laws of a religious or civil community, or to bless and curse.[16] In both its informative and its performative aspects, scripture is also used for transformation. This transformative power is a result of its sacredness and authority. Scriptures come from a sacred source and are themselves sacred. This sacred quality generally entails some power to make holy those who read or listen to them.

The transformative power of scripture occurs in both individual and communal ways—for example, to gain insight about personal or group problems and find the resources to solve them. Not all religions consider their scriptures to be divinely inspired, but all hold them to be inspiring and transformative in some way. This transformative power can be based on cognition, in which believers directly encounter the scriptures and experience their life-changing meaning. It can also happen just as often in noncognitive ways, as described earlier.

ADVANTAGES AND DISADVANTAGES OF STUDYING WESTERN RELIGIONS THROUGH THEIR SCRIPTURES

The study of Western religions through their sacred scriptures has both advantages and disadvantages. We need to be aware of the limitations of this method and work from strengths to overcome the weaknesses as much as possible.

The first disadvantage, as we saw earlier, is that the reception and use of scripture is *not uniform* across religions. Believers regard their scriptures in different ways, and scriptures function differently in each religion. As a student of world religions you must take note of these variations and learn to look at each religion's scriptures in a fresh way. Readers of scripture who come from a "religion of the book" must especially try to lay aside their preconceptions. Protestant Christians, for example, must beware of assuming that certain qualities of scripture and its function to which they are accustomed (for example, the belief that scripture is best absorbed by individual silent reading and meditation) are true of every religion's scripture. Moreover, the use of new scriptures in new religious movements in both Asia and North America often differs from usage in older, classical religious movements. The more we

---

[16] Sam D. Gill, "Nonliterate Traditions and Holy Books: Toward a New Model," in Denny and Taylor, *Holy Book,* p. 234.

genuinely encounter world scriptures in their full range of reception and use, the less likely we will be to inject our own biases into the scriptures of others. Then "scripture" itself will become a fuller, more useful category.

A second disadvantage is that we must *read translations,* which cannot fully capture the literary characteristics or meaning of the original. We can lay out four aspects of this disadvantage.

- Some of the original meaning and resonance of the words is lost or distorted in translation. For example, among Muslims, the identity and power of the *Qur'an* in its Arabic language is such that it would be unthinkable to translate it into another language and still consider it the true *Qur'an;* instead it is often called an "interpretation."

- Some languages and styles are hard to translate into English. For example, the formal Chinese style used by several Confucian and Taoist scriptures is often elusive or even cryptic. Moreover, to cross the borders of language families in translation (to go from Semitic languages of the Jewish *Bible* and the *Qur'an* into English, for example) is more difficult than staying inside a language family (to go from the Greek *New Testament* into English). These difficulties result in translations that vary widely.

- Bias creeps in. Translators inevitably cannot be fully objective and sometimes distort meaning. A leading example today is the translation of the Arabic word *jihad* in the *Qur'an.* It has a variety of meanings, but many translators (some of them Muslim) render it only as "war," "holy war," or "fighting." It can also mean "struggle" or "striving."

- Updating is needed because languages change. Some scripture translations are updated regularly; others are not, for a variety of reasons, and become more and more outmoded as time goes on.

A third main disadvantage is that scriptures tend to *reflect only the patriarchal and elite perspectives* of their traditions. They come from times and cultures that are patriarchal, where the voices of women—if they come through at all—are muted and filtered.[17] Scriptures strongly tend to embody official and elite ideas, the mainstream that feminist scholars call "malestream." Comparatively little of popular religion can be found in them. Although the contents of scripture are patriarchal and elitist, feminist scholars today in many religions are working to make contemporary understanding and use of these scriptures more equalitarian. This book offers some coverage of social justice and the role of women, but the perspective through which these scriptures are filtered is necessarily that of the elite male.[18]

Finally, and perhaps most seriously, we *lack the living context* of scripture when we encounter only its textual form. Scripture, which for most traditions (except new religious movements, of course) comes from ancient times, comes alive as it is

---

[17] See the introductory section of Serinity Young, ed., *An Anthology of Sacred Texts by and about Women* (New York: Crossroad, 1993), for good treatment of this issue.
[18] An excellent current series of books edited by Donald S. Lopez Jr., "Princeton Readings in Religions," seeks to rectify this male-elite perspective with anthologies on nearly all religions of the world, drawing on more popular writings and anthropological field reports.

appropriated in the life of religious communities. Despite growing religious pluralism, many North American readers of scripture do not have access to these communities. They cannot easily visit a mosque or see the ritual of a Jewish home or synagogue. They cannot directly see the broad ways that scripture is reflected in religious life, or the more specific ways it is used in worship, devotion, or law. What can be reproduced in a book like this is primarily the written text itself. The uses of scripture can be outlined here, but a printed book inevitably emphasizes the written, textual aspects of scripture over the oral and living.

These disadvantages might seem strong enough to cause you to give up the encounter with world scriptures. The advantages of studying religions through their scriptures are compelling, however. By working from the strengths of this approach, you can overcome the weaknesses to some extent and use scripture appropriately to enter the world of other religions.

The first advantage of this approach is that scripture is *widespread* among religions. Even though it is not fully universal, each "major" (to use a traditional but rather prejudicial term) living religion has a scripture. Scriptures naturally vary in form, content, and usage, but they are usually present in a religion. As we have seen, recent researchers emphasize that they form a distinct and important element in the life of most religions. The tendency to *scripturalize*, to make and use scriptures, is strong among religions. Indeed, almost every contemporary religion that is based in a literate culture produces and uses scriptures of some sort.[19] New religious movements also express themselves in writings that have a scriptural status.

Second, scriptures tend to be *comprehensive* for their faiths. Matters that a religion considers of great importance for its life are generally written down for the continuing community. "The sacred writings provide not only the essence of each particular religious tradition, but also the archetypal experiences which stir in the depths of all human lives: death, trust, anxiety, wonder, loyalty to a cause greater than oneself, fascination, healing, fulfillment, peace."[20] Of course, what religions view as important does vary, and scriptures reflect this variety. For example, the Jewish scriptures regulate a multitude of aspects of life considered significant, from worship to ethics to diet. What each religion considers of supreme importance is strongly reflected in its scriptures. Scriptures offer broad insight into the key characteristics of their faiths.

Third, scriptures are *authoritative* for their religions. Because they are believed to come from God or the gods, an enlightened teacher, or a wise sage, and because they bear witness to an ultimate reality, the truth contained in scriptures is recognized and lived out by believers. To read a scripture is to discover what is of primary value in the world's religions. And because scriptures are authoritative, they typically reflect the distinctive main aspects of each tradition. "Despite the variety of attitudes to scriptural works [in the world's religions], there is a continuing tendency to find

---

[19] Only Shinto does not treat its holy books as scripture in the full sense. Thus Shinto is the exception that proves the rule that religions based in literate cultures produce and use scriptures.
[20] Leonard J. Biallas, "Teaching World Religions through Their Scriptures," *Horizons* 17 (1990): 80.

in a sacred text . . . the primary source for true doctrine, correct ritual, [and] appropriate conduct."[21]

The fourth advantage of studying scriptures lies in their *ancient* or *foundational* character. They or the oral traditions on which they are based arise soon after the beginning of a religion and often signal important stages in its early development. Chinese religions call their oldest scriptures "Classics," and in a sense all world scriptures are classic treatments of their religious tradition. Where a religion has a founder or founders, scriptures usually give deep insight into the life of the founder(s) from the perspective of later followers. The foundational character of scriptures thus makes them valuable as a primary source for the history of religions. In the new religious movements that we examine in Chapter 6, scriptural books were completed and published by the founder himself or herself, at the very beginning of the movement.

Furthermore, because the traditional religions of the world have so richly influenced and been influenced by their cultures, scriptures are among the most important literary sources for the understanding of world cultures. Even though scriptures are indeed ancient and important, it is usually erroneous to argue, as does Charles Braden, that religion is somehow "founded on" scriptures.[22] This is a common misconception, especially in "religions of the book." Rather, as T. W. Hall puts it so well, "Historical investigations show that the religious communities existed prior to the writing of their scripture . . . religions produced scripture and scripture did not produce religion."[23] However, this conclusion is not as accurate when applied to new religious movements, because among them scriptures often do coincide with the beginnings of the movement.

Fifth, scriptures are *accessible* in translation to English-language readers. Most of the important religious books of the world have been translated into English, and many of those that have not are now being translated. Sometimes the translations of a certain scripture are few, but others can boast a near riot of English versions. The *Tao Te Ching*, for example, had more than twenty English versions in print in 2006; and even though the *Qur'an* cannot be translated and still retain its holiest status, new English translations are produced regularly. Although no translation can convey the full meaning and feeling of the original, a good translation can suggest it. Students of world scripture who want a closer, more accurate look at a given passage should consult at least two or three different contemporary translations of it, comparing them closely.

Finally, scriptures as literary texts are *open to critical analysis*. Both the specialist scholar and the beginning reader can analyze them directly or, better yet, enter a conversation with them. Although most religious texts range from mildly strange to completely baffling for those who come from other cultures and religious traditions, the same intellectual and scholarly skills that you use to read any other text can be put to use on world scriptures. With some effort, you can understand scriptures and use them as a pathway into other faiths.

---

[21] Richard C. Bush et al., *The Religious World: Communities of Faith,* 2d ed. (New York: Macmillan, 1988), p. 3.
[22] Charles Braden, *The Scriptures of Mankind: An Introduction* (New York: Macmillan, 1952), p. 8.
[23] Hall, Pilgrim, and Cavanagh, *Religion,* p. 109.

WESTERN SCRIPTURES AND MODERN SCHOLARSHIP

The earlier discussion of critical analysis of scripture leads us to an important but often neglected topic. How does the modern academic study of scripture influence how religions use scriptures and how we read them?

Historical and critical literary scholarship is largely Western and European in origin, stemming from various methods of interpreting literature developed in the Renaissance and the Enlightenment. Textual criticism methodically judges manuscripts to find the likely original reading; grammatical criticism analyzes the content and style of the wording of a work in its original language; literary criticism studies genres. Most important is historical criticism, in particular the **historical-critical method,** which probes the developmental genesis of works from the past, their original meaning as understood by their first audience. In the early nineteenth century this approach began to be applied to the *Bible*. Critical study of the Christian scripture has uncovered development, diversity, and even some disagreement within it. Christianity's effort to understand the *Bible* critically has suffered reversals from time to time. Yet many Protestant groups accept this critical study, perceiving that it offers a fuller understanding of scripture that is compatible with faith.

In the early twentieth century biblical criticism spread to Judaism, and today Conservative and Reform Jews widely accept it; only Orthodox Jews still oppose it. Since the Second Vatican Council (1962–1965), Roman Catholics have also embraced the historical-critical method.[24] Today the basic methods of literary study still are largely European academic methods. Scholars and students read sacred texts through Western eyes and by Western methods.

The effort to collect, edit, and publish the literature of world religions is also a Western academic enterprise. It had its roots in the eighteenth century, when the first copies of Chinese and Indian scripture made their way to Europe and were greeted with great interest, even enthusiasm, in some circles. One reason for this enthusiasm was an Enlightenment hope that these scriptures might be a religious or philosophical alternative to what some saw as the hidebound clericalism of Christianity. The *Vedas,* for example, were at first viewed as religious expressions from near the dawn of time, pristine and unspoiled by priestcraft. Gradually Europeans realized that the *Vedas* reflect a priestly system as traditional as that of Christianity. By the middle of the nineteenth century, as we saw, a more mature scholarly interest in world scriptures blossomed into a systematic effort to publish reliable translations. The editing and publishing of sacred texts continue today, especially in religions that have large canons. The methods used to edit, translate, publish, and interpret these scriptures draw generally from the Western tradition.

Scholarship in comparative religion came from a background that was largely Protestant in orientation. Thus, over the last century, an inevitable "Protestant bias" has crept into the way scholarship has looked at the scriptures of other faiths. Certain

---

[24] See G. P. Fogarty, *American Catholic Biblical Scholarship* (San Francisco: HarperCollins, 1989), and R. B. Robinson, *Roman Catholic Exegesis since* Divino Afflante Spiritu (Atlanta: Scholars Press, 1988).

mainstream Protestant ideas about the nature of scripture colored the study of the scriptures of other religions and only today are being identified and corrected. These include

- A concern with textuality to the exclusion of orality, from the Protestant emphasis on the scripture as *written*.

- An orientation that assumes that scriptures are to be read mainly by the individual, from Protestant ideas of the "priesthood of all believers" and universal literacy.

- The notion that scriptures are widely authoritative over every aspect of religious life, from the Protestant assertion that the scriptures are the sole authority in the Christian faith.

- The assumption that scriptures are best understood by objective, academically recognized methods of study, from mainstream Protestant attachment to sound academic procedures.[25]

Of course, believers of the other religions of the world do not share this bias, as we can see when we reflect comparatively on each of these assumptions. In some religions, such as Hinduism, the oral dimension dominates the written. In others, such as Islam, written and oral traditions are more in balance. Next, most religions do not share the Protestant notion that scriptures should be read by the individual; rather, their adherents speak and hear their scriptures in groups, usually in worship and ritual. Indeed, it comes as a striking realization for modern North Americans that most followers of many religions throughout history (and even today!) cannot read and therefore cannot read their sacred texts. For the typical follower of most faiths, texts must be *spoken* (often from memory) and *heard*.

We examined earlier the next Protestant assumption, that scriptures seek to regulate every aspect of religious life, and we concluded that they seek to regulate the center of religious life as their religion conceives that center. For most religions of the world, the Western academic approach to scripture goes against the grain of faith and is consequently viewed as alien. To study scripture historically and objectively is to question its sacredness because such study employs the same methods used to study other, nonsacred literature. For example, Islam discourages going behind the present edition of the Arabic text to inquire about earlier versions. Traditional, conservative Islam also forbids Muslims to study or use the *Qur'an* in such a way to question its unity or divine origin, as the Muslim writer Salman Rushdie discovered. His controversial novel, *The Satanic Verses*, allegedly committed blasphemy against the *Qur'an*. In 1989, Iranian officials put a $2 million price on his head, and he only recently—and tentatively—came out of hiding when the death threat was lifted. Each religion has some systematic study of its sacred texts, but such study usually remains devotional, meditative, and interpretive. Noncritical and unthreatening, it does not question the received beliefs about the origin and standing of the text.

When we read scriptures, then, we must always remember that the way we read is fully conditioned by our cultural backgrounds and academic enterprises. Those who

---

[25] See Levering, *Rethinking Scripture*, pp. 3–5, for more on this Protestant bias.

read from a religious background must always try to keep their own viewpoints identified and in check. Those with no religious commitments must try to suspend any doubts they may have about religion and scriptures. We read scriptures as *outsiders*, in an objective, scholarly, noncommittal way. This is altogether necessary as a first step in coming to grips with Western scriptures. A second step, more difficult than the first but equally necessary, is to read them as much as possible as *insiders*, with the eyes, minds, and hearts of those for whom these texts are much more than the object of scholarship.[26]

WESTERN SCRIPTURES AND THE WORLD WIDE WEB

The last ten years have seen the explosive growth of the World Wide Web. Much information about religion can be found on the web; it seems to be one of the leading topics of discussion and inquiry. As a part of this interest in religion, many websites feature scriptures in translation or sometimes in the original.

Many positive features of this new opportunity to encounter Western scriptures are obvious. The access is almost always free. The amount of scripture on the web is growing rapidly and may someday encompass all Western scriptures. The Internet is an appealing way for most young, computer-oriented students (but not always their professors!) to encounter scriptures. It presents different ways of studying and learning—for example, the ability to search a text electronically. The Internet by its structure encourages exploration. Some sites are fully interactive, allowing students to ask questions and participate in online discussion groups. Finally, but not least, when students explore a religion site sponsored by its followers, the perspective provided there is likely to be a bit more that of an "insider" than classroom or textbook descriptions.

The drawbacks of studying Western scriptures on the web are also obvious. Some sites are not well constructed; they may have poor layout, little eye appeal, out-of-date links, or other technical deficiencies. The translations used are too often public domain works that are out-of-date and not edited for today's readers. When representatives of a religion post that religion's writings for religious conversion or public relations purposes, the interpretations they provide may not agree with the current academic consensus about that religion. Most significantly, these electronic publications are subject to little or no scholarly control, such as editorial or peer review before publication, so their quality varies greatly. Some sites are excellent, some average, and some poor.

This mixed situation means that many students need help in finding, using, and especially analyzing critically these web-based scripture sites. Readers of this anthology may access a special website to further their use of the web in religious studies. It has links to short, helpful essays on using the Internet in an academically appropriate way. It also has links to sites useful in the study of scriptures. The listing is not comprehensive, but it does offer a starting place to surf and learn. The address is: http://religion.wadsworth.com.

---

[26] See the excellent remarks by Eric Sharpe in *Encyclopedia of Religion*, vol. 14, p. 85, on "imaginative sympathy" in reading scripture as "insiders." See also Ross N. Reat, "Insiders and Outsiders in the Study of Religious Traditions," *Journal of the American Academy of Religion* 51 (1983): 459–475.

THE PLAN OF THIS BOOK

This book contains excerpts of Western scriptures in the following order of religions: Zoroastrianism, Judaism, Christianity, Islam, and selected new religious movements. This progression keeps the religions of the West together in their family groups and goes in order of historical development. Moreover, the reader can see the relationships among religions and scriptures more easily when related bodies of texts are dealt with in succession. For example, when the Christian scriptures and then the Islamic follow the Jewish scriptures, the deep relationship among them becomes apparent. A final chapter gives excerpts from the scriptures of Western new religious movements treated in order of their time of origin: Baha'i, the Church of Jesus Christ of Latter-day Saints, Christian Science, and the Unification Church.

Each chapter except the last (where each new religious movement is treated in a separate section) is structured as follows: An introduction outlines the scriptures included, setting them in the context of the whole religion by examining briefly their name(s), overall structure, use, origin, and growth. The first grouping of scripture passages deals with the history of the religion. If the faith has a founder, special attention is given to him or her; any subsequent history of the religion that scripture reflects is also excerpted. Second are passages covering the main doctrinal teaching of the religion. These topics include divine or ultimate reality, creation and the environment, the nature of humanity, and achieving human fulfillment (salvation, release, harmony, etc.). Third are passages about the moral/ethical structure of the scriptures: good, evil, and the authentic human life. Personal morality is probably more widely treated in world scriptures, but social ethics are also prominent, especially in Western scriptures. Such topics as war and peace, violence and nonviolence, tolerance and intolerance of people of other faiths, the status of women, and a just society are represented as fully as possible. Fourth are passages about the organization of the religion, either in its internal organization (for example, bishops and deacons in Christianity) or in its attempts to organize its wider culture (such as the laws of Judaism). Last are passages about religious worship, ritual, devotion, and meditation. Of course, some religions have more in some of these categories than in others, but most religions do fit into them without significant distortion. Where they do not fully fit, this format is adapted to do justice to the particular nature of the texts.

The predominant rationale for this organization is *pedagogical*. It is meant to further the learning of students encountering Western religions. North American readers are familiar with the categories used here, and both teachers and students of world religions will recognize them as a standard paradigm for research and teaching in religion. Moreover, they are categories that seem to fit world scriptures themselves. Why not discard any attempt to use categories of organization and simply provide one or two longer excerpts from each religion's body of scripture? A rather uniform scripture like the *Qur'an* may be possible to encompass in a few long readings. Even Islamic tradition says that the whole message of the *Qur'an* is contained in each of its chapters, so to read one is in a sense to read them all! However, what Paul Muller-Ortega says about Hinduism is true of the Western religions, including the new religious movements: "It is not possible to put a single sacred text in the hands of students and expect the reading of that one text to allow students to encompass the tradition. . . . Thus, the preferred method of exposing students to the enormity of the Hindu sacred literature has been by means of anthologies."[27]

SUGGESTIONS ON HOW TO READ WESTERN SCRIPTURES

Individuals reading world scriptures for the first time often feel they are entering a strange new world. Sometimes preconceived notions of what reading a given scripture will be like turn out to be quite wrong. Students of world religion are especially susceptible to the difficulties of reading scripture. Their textbooks usually try to make scriptures easier to encounter by simplifying and summarizing the content. To encounter scriptures more directly and in their original form is a harder process. As Mortimer Adler and Charles Van Doren once wrote, "The problem of reading the Holy Book . . . is the most difficult problem in the field of reading."[28] In the end, however, it is more profitable for readers to wrestle as directly as possible with the texts. Of course, an anthology such as this does not present world scriptures in their totality but serves as a bridge to the full scripture text.

Each reader must ultimately find an individually suitable method for reading world scriptures. But these ten suggestions drawn from my experience and the experience of others may be helpful:

1. *Use your knowledge of religion to set these readings in a fuller context.* Try to relate scriptures as fully as possible to the life of the religions from which they come. For example, when you are reading a passage about ritual, visualize how the ritual is carried out.

2. *Read the introductions to each chapter before you turn to the passages.* They will provide an important background for understanding the passages.

3. *Skim the selections first.* Having a general feel for the "lay of the land" will help you when you begin to read in detail.

4. *Read the scripture passages objectively.* Use the same intellectual skills that you bring to any other text, religious or nonreligious. Remember their holy status in their religions, but don't be intimidated by it.

5. *Mark the text as you read.* Research shows that readers who mark the text, underlining or highlighting as few as three or four items per page, understand and remember more than readers who do not mark their text. Marking helps to make the text your own.

6. *Pay attention to literary genre.* The form and content of any literary passage reflects its genre. Read with a feeling for the differences among myth, poetry, narrative, law, and other literary forms.

7. *Make a personal glossary of unfamiliar terms and names as you go along.* You can do this easily by circling them in the text and writing them in the bottom margin. (Use circles or some other type of marking that will distinguish them from your other

---

[27] Paul Muller-Ortega, "Exploring Textbooks: Introductions to Hinduism," in B. R. Gaventa, ed., *Critical Review of Books in Religion, 1988* (Atlanta: Scholars Press, 1989), p. 71.
[28] Mortimer Adler and Charles Van Doren, *How to Read a Book* (New York: Simon & Schuster, 1940), p. 288.

marked material.) Then you can go back later to make a short note of their meaning, also in the margin. The unfamiliarity and difficulty of so many words, both technical terms and personal names, is a large obstacle for many students of world religions. With a little extra effort, you can minimize this difficulty.

8. *Read each selection repeatedly until you are familiar with it.* Familiarity enables you to identify any problems you have in understanding it. View these problems as opportunities for achieving greater understanding, not as roadblocks.

9. *Read the selections aloud as much as possible.* This may feel embarrassing at first because you are not accustomed to it. Listen to the sounds of the words, and try to get a sense of the oral dimensions of the text. You cannot reproduce the feeling of the original language, but reading aloud will at least remind you that the text does have an oral dimension.

10. *Put yourself, as well as you can, inside the faith of the scripture.* What could these writings mean to you if you were among those who first heard them? What could they mean to you today if you were a typical follower of that faith? By using your knowledge and imagination, you can participate in the unique use of scripture in each religion and become—partially and temporarily—an insider.[29]

GLOSSARY

Abrahamic monotheisms   Judaism, Christianity, and Islam.

bibliolatry [bib-lee-AHL-ah-tree]   Excessive veneration of a scripture book.

bibliomancy [BIB-lee-oh-man-see]   The use of scripture to foresee future events and guide one's response to them.

canon   A more or less fixed collection of books regarded as scriptural.

commentary   A book written to explain another book, often passage by passage. Many religions possess commentaries on their scriptures.

genre   A literary form, such as poetry, myth, proverb, narrative history, and philosophical meditation.

historical-critical method   The scholarly study of a text that derives meaning from the text's earliest phases and traces the text's historical development.

icon   A holy picture. Metaphorically, scripture is an icon when it is revered as a sacred object apart from its content.

narrative   The telling of an event or series of events in story form.

oral tradition   The passing down, usually through many generations, of myths, narratives, poems, and the like by word of mouth.

scripture   Text that a religious community holds to be especially sacred and authoritative.

---

[29] "By an act of historical imagination we can actually participate up to a certain point in the aspirations and devotions of other times and places. Yet this truly is only up to a certain point, for the curtain is suddenly lowered and we realize with a shock just how far away those places and times really are. That experience has been called 'the paradox of understanding.'" Jaroslav Pelikan, *On Searching the Scriptures—Your Own or Someone Else's* (New York: Quality Paperback Book Club, 1992), p. 7.

QUESTIONS FOR STUDY AND DISCUSSION

1. What does the word *scripture* mean to you?

2. "Scripture is more a Western concept than an Eastern concept." To what extent do you agree or disagree with this common statement?

3. Suppose that a new potential scripture—a new gospel book about Jesus, for example—is discovered and shown to be authentic. Would such a potential scripture actually get into the scripture canon of Christianity? Why or why not?

4. What uses of scripture seem most important or interesting to you? Why?

5. What disadvantages are posed by the ancient character of scriptures? Can these be overcome? If so, how?

6. Reflect on this description of Mohandas Gandhi's teachings about studying others' scriptures: "One should read others' scriptures with respect and reverence even to be enriched in one's own religious convictions."

7. What other advantages and disadvantages of using the Internet in religious studies occur to you, besides the ones given here?

SUGGESTIONS FOR FURTHER READING

L. J. Biallas, "Teaching World Religions through Their Scriptures." Horizons (Villanova University) 17 (1990): 76–91. Especially useful to teachers, but students can profit from it as well; focuses on narrative forms.

H. Coward, *Sacred Word and Sacred Text: Scripture in World Religions.* Maryknoll, NY: Orbis, 1988. Sound chapter-length treatments (especially of orality) of scripture in Christianity and Islam, and also Hinduism, Sikhism, and Buddhism.

H. Coward, ed., *Experiencing Scripture in World Religions.* Maryknoll, NY: Orbis, 2000. Brief, lively essays by various scholars who are also believers, on the use of scripture in Judaism, Christianity, Islam, Hinduism, Sikhism, and Buddhism.

F. M. Denny and R. L. Taylor, eds., *The Holy Book in Comparative Perspective.* Columbia: University of South Carolina Press, 1985. After an introduction by the editors, this volume features up-to-date treatments of the scriptures of nine major religions, including the Church of Jesus Christ of Latter-day Saints.

W. A. Graham, "Scripture." In M. Eliade, ed., *The Encyclopedia of Religion,* vol. 13, pp. 133–145. New York: Macmillan, 1987. This lucid article is the best short survey of its topic.

P. L. Kwok and E. Schüssler Fiorenza, eds., *Women's Sacred Scriptures.* London: SCM Press/Maryknoll, NY: Orbis, 1998. A treatment of the scriptures of several world religions with a view to a feminist reclaiming of scripture.

M. Levering, ed., *Rethinking Scripture: Essays from a Comparative Perspective.* Albany: State University of New York Press, 1989. Begins with two excellent essays by W. C. Smith, "The Study of Religion and the Study of the Bible" and "Scripture as Form and Concept: Their Emergence in the Western World." W. A. Graham also has an essay, "Scripture as Spoken Word."

W. C. Smith, *What Is Scripture? A Comparative Approach.* Minneapolis: Fortress, 1993. A full survey of its topic by the most influential researcher on world scriptures.

S. Young, *An Anthology of Sacred Texts by and about Women.* New York: Crossroad, 1993. A comprehensive selection of scriptures and other important religious writings from, among others, Judaism, Christianity, Islam, Hinduism, Buddhism, Confucianism, Taoism, and new religious movements.

Zoroastrian Ritual
With the *Avesta* lying open at his right, a Zoroastrian priest in India offers a sacrifice.
Credit: Jehangir Gazdar/Woodfin Camp & Associates.

CHAPTER TWO

Zoroastrianism

✣ In a house in Bombay, India, a seven-year-old girl is being received into the Zoroastrian religion. A priest stands behind her, guiding her hands as she ties a sacred cord around her waist. She will wear this cord, which serves as a belt, for the rest of her life, except while bathing or sleeping. Five times a day she will ceremonially loosen it, say her prayers, then retie it. The cord has seventy-two threads representing the seventy-two chapters of the chief book of the Zoroastrian scripture, the *Yasna*.

✣ As he sits on the floor in a Zoroastrian temple, a priest offers sacrifice. Before him are spread a variety of consecrated objects, mostly fruits, vegetables and herbs, and a small flame. Usually he recites the scriptural words of sacrifice from memory, but today is one of the seven great yearly festivals of the faith, so a large-print edition of the *Avesta* rests on a small stand to his right. He refers to the book from time to time to read some passages aloud and refresh his memory for the recitation of other passages.

INTRODUCTION

Begun perhaps three thousand years ago in ancient Persia (modern Iran) by the prophet Zarathushtra (also known as Zoroaster), Zoroastrianism became the state religion of the Sassanid Empire, which arose in Persia in the third century C.E. Today its numbers are severely reduced. No more than 250,000 adherents are clustered in eastern Iran and near Bombay, India, and about 15,000 in North America. The scriptures of Zoroastrianism strongly advocate a moral life and maintaining ritual purity in worship and in daily life. Because of their obscure ancient language, troubled history of transmission, and fragmentary state, these scriptures are often difficult to understand. Nevertheless, the main beliefs of Zoroastrianism are clear, and modern Zoroastrians, like earlier believers, are concerned about how the scriptural message is embodied in daily life. Most scholars believe that Zoroastrianism had some significant influence on Judaism (the existence of angels and demons, judgment at the end of time, heaven and hell, and the rest) and, through Judaism, on Christianity and Islam, but the scope of this influence is debated.

Overview of Structure

The ancient scriptures of Zoroastrianism are known as the ***Avesta.*** The meaning of the word *avesta* is uncertain. Usually translated as "injunction, command," it has also been translated as "wisdom, knowledge," as "authoritative utterance," and as "scripture." It probably derives from the Middle Persian word *avastaq*, "law." The "injunction" is that of the god Ahura Mazda, the Lord and Creator, through the prophet Zarathushtra.

The term *avesta* is broad enough to encompass all the commands of Zoroastrianism: to serve good and turn from evil; to be both morally and ceremonially pure; and to worship Ahura Mazda and the good spirits by sacrifice and praise.

The *Avesta* [ah-VES-tuh] has four major divisions, each with ritual content and orientation. The **Yasna** (Sacrifice), the first and most important part, consists of hymns for worship in seventy-two chapters. The *Visparad* (All the [Divine] Lords) has twenty chapters of hymns. Within the *Yashts* (Hymns) are twenty-one hymns of praise to sacred beings and heroic humans. The twenty-two-chapter *Vendidad* (The Law against Demons) contains myths and codes of religious law. We now examine these *Avesta* books in turn.

The earliest and most important section of the *Yasna* [YAHZ-nuh] is the **Gathas**, a collection of seventeen hymns. They now occupy five sections of the *Yasna*. Orthodox Zoroastrians believe the whole of the *Avesta* to be the work of Zarathushtra, but they hold the *Gathas* [GAH-tuhs] as especially his words. Modern scholarship agrees, using the *Gathas* as the primary source for our knowledge of Zarathushtra. The *Gathas* are distinguished from the other *Yasna* hymns by their emphasis on ethics and their lack of attention to ritual concerns. One main topic elsewhere in the *Yasna* is the haoma ritual, in which the juices of the haoma plant are ground out and mixed with milk and herbs. Also in the *Yasna* are prayers, a confession of faith, and rules for sacrifices to water. Priests daily recite all seventy-two chapters (from memory!) during Zoroastrianism's main sacrificial ceremony, the sacrifice of the haoma in fire. This sacrifice is called the Yasna, from which this part of the *Avesta* gets its name.

About one-sixth as long as the *Yasna*, the *Visparad* [VEE-spuh-rahd] contains poetic invocations, praises, and sacrifices to all the divine lords of Zoroastrianism. Words from this section of the *Avesta* are recited at various stages of the Yasna ceremony. Zoroastrians also recite the *Visparad* during their six holy days of obligation, especially New Year's Day.

The *Yashts* [yahshts] are hymns of praise to twenty-one divinities, angels, and human heroes of ancient Persia. Among the most important are hymns to Mithra and a hymn to the guardian spirits—**Fravashis** [frah-VAH-shees]—of the old saints. Much of the material in the *Yashts* is drawn from pre-Zoroastrian religion and provides an interesting glimpse of how Zoroastrianism adapted older Indo-European religious ideas to its own use. This occurred after the time of Zarathushtra himself; according to the *Gathas*, the prophet made a clean break with the older religion.

The *Vendidad* [VEN-dih-dahd] begins with two myths about the creation and a primeval flood that tell how divine law came to humans. The remaining sixteen chapters form a law code that prescribes purifications and penalties for priests. Chapters 3 and 5, for example, contain regulations for funerals; Chapter 18 deals with the difference between true and false priests. Like the *Yashts*, the words of the *Vendidad* are recited during Yasna ceremony.

Use

As their names imply, the *Avesta* books are strongly oriented to worship and sacrifice. The scriptures are the hymn texts for sacrifice, and sacrifice is done to the constant accompaniment of scripture recitation, usually from memory. The use of scripture throughout Zoroastrian history has therefore been almost exclusively performative. Priests use scripture for the enactment of ritual, not for study, meditation, or the formation and teaching of doctrine. The Avestan language used in formal worship and in the traditional main prayers of the faithful is largely unknown to some priests and to most laypersons. Thus, Zoroastrians typically have had little knowledge of what their scriptures actually "teach."

At the end of nineteenth century, a movement of reform sought to change this age-old use of the *Avesta*. Under the influence of Western religion and European methods of religious scholarship, reformers claimed that the *Gathas* are the center and only authentic part of the *Avesta* and that everything else is to be judged in light of the leading ideas of the *Gathas*. Rituals were regarded as secondary to moral teachings and were interpreted symbolically, altered, or sometimes disregarded altogether. The rational, philosophical, and moral elements of the faith were given priority. This shift from a performative to a cognitive use of scripture among a minority of Zoroastrians in India and North America is the source of one of the chief internal disagreements in Zoroastrianism.

Origin and Development

The *Avesta* begins with Zarathushtra himself. Though a date for the prophet in the sixth century B.C.E. is still accepted by most scholars, some (especially Mary Boyce) push Zarathushtra back to 1400–1000 B.C.E. The oral tradition that was later written down into the *Gathas* as we know them can be traced more or less to Zarathushtra for reasons of both style and content.

Next to arise, probably over the course of a millennium, were the other poetic sections of the *Avesta*, which scholars today call the "Younger *Avesta*." The rest of the *Yasna* and the *Yashts* are in metrical poetry. Last to be written were the prose portions of the *Avesta*. The whole process was complete and the canon of the *Avesta* was fixed by about 325 C.E.

In its original form, the *Avesta* was probably about four times larger than it is now. Besides the liturgical texts now in the *Avesta*, it probably treated cosmogony, eschatology, astronomy, natural history, the history of Zarathushtra, and several other topics. The *Zand*, a later collection of Zoroastrian literature, contains many references to a large loss of Zoroastrian scripture during the invasions of Alexander the Great (fourth century B.C.E.). What remained from these persecutions was material that was fixed in the memory of the priests—liturgical scripture. A collection was made under the Sassanid Empire in the third and fourth centuries C.E. The *Avesta* as we know it comes from this period and was probably first written down at this time. Zoroastrianism became the state religion of the Sassanid Empire, and a written text may have been viewed as a tool for promoting uniformity in religious doctrine and practice.

In the seventh century C.E. Islam began to press hard on the religion of Ahura Mazda. Although it officially tolerated Zoroastrianism as a monotheistic religion, Islam sought to end the faith by suppressing its temples and burning its scripture books. Some Zoroastrians fled Muslim intolerance for a more congenial life around Bombay in India, where they were welcomed by the dominant Hindu culture.

During this period the *Avesta* was reduced even further to its present size, preserved by the small Zoroastrian community left to continue to this day. The oldest manuscript that has survived dates to 1323 C.E.; the entire *Avesta* collection was printed for the first time in the nineteenth century.

HISTORY

The Call of Zarathushtra*

This Gatha *is a conversation among four main characters: (1) the collective soul of the cattle, which represents the means of livelihood for the people of the Zoroastrian faith; (2) Asha, or "Righteousness," one of the Immortal Holy Ones; (3) Ahura Mazda, the Lord and Creator; and (4) Zarathushtra. It closes with Zarathushtra's prayer for divine aid. Worshippers use this passage as a prayer for divine help to destroy the powers of deceit and to promote peace and truth.*[1]

The Soul of the Cattle and the people cried aloud to you, O Ahura and Asha, "For whom did you create me, and by whom did you fashion me? Assaults of wrath and violent power come upon me, with desolating blows and bold insolence. I have no other pasture-giver than you. Teach me good cultivation of the fields, which is my only hope of blessing!"

Then the Creator of the Cattle asked Righteousness: "How did you appoint a guardian for the cattle when you made her? How did you secure for her both pasture and a cattle-chief who was skilled and energetic? Did you select one who might hurl back the fury of the wicked?"

The Divine Righteousness answered in his holiness, "We were very perplexed. We could not obtain a leader who was capable of striking back their fury, and who himself was without hate. We cannot know the influences that approach and move the heavenly fires, fires which reveal the favor and the will of God. God is the mightiest of beings. Those who have performed their actions approach him with invocations. He has no need to ask!"

Zarathushtra said, "The Great Creator is most mindful of the commands that have been fulfilled in the deeds of demon-gods and good or evil men. He knows the commands that they will fulfill. Ahura is the discerning judge. It shall be to us as he desires! [5] Therefore we both, my soul and the soul of the mother cattle, are making our requests for this world and the next to Ahura. With hands stretched out in entreaty, we pray to the Great Creator with questions in our doubt. He will answer. Destruction will not come to the one who lives righteously, or to the careful farmers of the earth!"

Then the Lord, the Great Creator who understands the mysterious grace by his insight, spoke. "We cannot find a spiritual master in this way. Nor can we find a leader moved by righteousness and appointed by its spirit. Therefore I have named you as the leader of the diligent tillers of the ground!"

The Immortal Holy Ones said, "Mazda has created the inspired Word of reason that is a spoken formula of fatness for the offering. The Divine Righteousness consented to Mazda's deed. He has prepared food for the cattle and food for the eaters. He is bountiful with his saving doctrine. But who is endowed with the Good Mind, who can give those teachings by word of mouth to mortals?"

---

* *Yasna* 29.
[1] Except where noted, all passages from Zoroastrian scripture are taken, with editing, from J. Darmesteter and L. H. Mills, trans., *The Zend-Avesta, Sacred Books of the East,* vols. 4, 23, 31 (Oxford: Oxford University Press, 1880–1887).

Ahura said, "I have found one man, Zarathushtra Spitama, who alone has listened to our words! He desires to announce our mighty and completed acts of grace, for me the Great Creator, and for Righteousness. Therefore I will give him the good dwelling and the authoritative position of one who speaks for us!"

Then the Soul of the cattle lamented, "Woe is me, for I have obtained a lord who is powerless to carry out his wish! He is only a feeble and timid man. I desire one who is lord over his will, one who is able like a king to carry out what he desires." The Immortal Holy Ones said, "Yes, when shall one who brings strong help to her[2] ever appear?"

[10] Zarathushtra said, "O Ahura, O Righteousness, grant gladness to these our disciples. Grant them the sovereign kingdom of God, which is established in his Good Mind. This kingdom gives them the peaceful amenities of home and quiet happiness, instead of the terrible ravages that they suffer. O Great Creator, I have always thought You to be the first possessor of these blessings! O Great Creator and Living Lord, when shall the divine Righteousness, the Good Mind of the Lord, and his sovereign power hurry to me? When will they give me strength for my task and my mission? Without this I cannot advance or even undertake my work. Give us your aid in abundance for our great cause!"

---

[2] *her:* the (female) Soul of the Cattle.

A Hymn of Praise to Zarathushtra*

With this hymn Zoroastrians venerate the memory of Zarathushtra. Notice the recurring use of "who/he first." The end of this selection recounts a legend of the cosmic praise offered to the baby Zarathushtra.

We worship the piety and the guardian spirit of the holy Zarathushtra. He was the first who thought what is good, the first who spoke what is good, the first who did what is good. He was the first Priest, the first Warrior, the first Plower of the ground. He first knew and first taught. He first possessed and first took possession of the Bull, of Holiness, of the Word, the obedience to the Word, the dominion, and all the good things made by Mazda, the good things that are the offspring of the good Principle.

He first took the turning of the wheel[3] from the hands of the evil spirits and cold-hearted men. He was first in the material world to pronounce the praise of Asha, thus bringing the evil spirits to nothing. He confessed himself a worshipper of Mazda, a follower of Zarathushtra. He is one who hates the evil spirits and obeys the laws of Ahura.

[90] He was first in the material world to say the word that destroys the evil spirits, the law of Ahura. He was first in the material world to proclaim the words that destroy the evil spirits, the law of Ahura. He was the first in the material world to declare all the creation of the evil spirits unworthy of sacrifice and prayer. He was strong, giving all the good things of life, and he was the first bearer of the law among the nations.

In him was heard the whole Mathra, the word of holiness. He was the lord and master of the world. He was the praiser of Asha, who is the most great, most good, and most fair. He had a revelation of the Law, that most excellent of all beings.

For him the Immortal Holy Ones longed, in one accord with the sun, in the fullness of the faith of a devoted heart. They longed for him as the lord and master of the world, as the praiser of the most great, most good, and most fair Asha. He had a revelation of the Law, that most excellent of

---

* *Yasht* 24:87b–94.
[3] *turning of the wheel:* the life of the created world.

all beings. In his birth and growth the waters and the plants rejoiced. In his birth and growth the waters and the plants grew. In his birth and growth all the creatures of the good creations cried out, "Hail! Hail to us! For he is born, the great priest Spitama Zarathushtra. Zarathushtra will offer us sacrifices with drink offerings and bundles of sandalwood. The good Law of the worshippers of Mazda will come, and it will spread through all the seven parts of the earth."

TEACHING AND ETHICS

Hymn to Ahura and the Purifying Fire*

This hymn to Ahura Mazda and to the spirit of fire is set in the fire temple. Notice the emphasis on morality in thought, word, and deed. Today fire is still a symbol of moral purity and the spiritual center of every Zoroastrian temple.

[1] We desire to approach you . . . in this house of your holy Fire, O Ahura Mazda, most bounteous Spirit! If anyone brings pollutions to this flame, you will cover him with pollutions. O most friendly one, O Fire of the Lord, give us zeal! Come to us with the loving blessing of one who is most friendly, with the praise of the one most adored. Yes, come to us and aid us in this great task!

You truly are the Fire of Ahura Mazda. Yes, you are the most bounteous one of his Spirit. Therefore yours is the most potent of all names for grace, O Fire of the Lord! Therefore we come to you, O Ahura, with the help of your Good Mind that you implant in us. We come to you with your good Righteousness, and with actions and words implanted by your good wisdom!

[5] We bow before you, and we direct our prayers to you with confessions of our guilt, O Ahura Mazda! With all the good thoughts that you inspire, with all the words well said, and the deeds well done, with these we come to you. To your most beautiful body we make our deep acknowledgments, O Ahura Mazda. We acknowledge those stars that are your body, and we acknowledge that one star, the highest of the high, as the sun was called.

---

*Yasna 36.

Hymn to Ahura Mazda the Creator**

This selection is a beautiful expression of faith and devotion to Ahura Mazda the Creator and to the spirits associated with him.

We worship Ahura Mazda, who made the Cattle, Righteousness, the waters, the wholesome plants, the stars, the earth, and all existing things that are good. Yes, we worship him for his Sovereign Power and his greatness. They are full of blessing, and have priority among the Yazads who abide beside the Cattle in protection and support.

We worship him under his name as Lord, Mazda dear, the most gracious of names. We worship him with our bones and with our flesh. We worship the Fravashis of the saints, of holy men and holy women. We worship Righteousness the Best, the most beautiful, the Bountiful Immortal, who is endowed with light in all things good.

**Yasna 37:1–5.

[5] We worship the Good Mind of the Lord, and his Sovereign Power, and the Good Faith, the good law, and Piety the ready mind within your people!

The Choice between Good and Evil*

This Gatha instructs the believer in the basic teachings of Zarathushtra on good and evil. It speaks of the ancient character of good and evil, their role in creation of the world, their present struggle for domination, and their destiny at the end of history. The believer must constantly choose the good and thereby build up its power in the universe. Most scholars believe that many of these ideas had an influence on Judaism and then on Christianity and Islam.

[1] Now I will proclaim to you my observations about him who knows all things to you who are drawing near and want to be taught. I will proclaim the praises of Ahura, the sacrifices that spring from the Good Mind, and the blessed meditations inspired by Righteousness. I pray that favorable results may be seen in the lights. Hear then with your ears; see the bright flames with the eyes of the Better Mind. It is a decision about religions, man and man, each individual himself. Before taking up this cause, awake to our teaching!

The primeval spirits as a pair combined their opposite strivings, yet each is independent in his action. They have long been famous. One is better, the other worse, in thought, in word, and in deed. Let those who act wisely choose correctly between these two. Do not choose as evil-doers choose!

When the two spirits came together at first, they made life and life's absence. They decided how the world shall be ordered at its end. The wicked receive Hell, the worst life; the holy receive Heaven, the Best Mental State. [5] He who was the evil one chose the evil realm, working the worst possible results. But the more gracious spirit chose the Divine Righteousness. Yes, he who clothes himself with the firm stones of heaven as his robe made this choice. He also chose those who make Ahura happy by their actions, actions performed in accordance with the faith.

The Demon-gods and those who worship them can make no righteous choice between these two spirits, since they have been deceived. As they were questioning and debating in their council, the Worst Mind approached them that he might be chosen. They made their fatal decision. Then they rushed to the Demon of Fury, that they might pollute the lives of mortals.

Then Aramaiti, the personified Piety of the saints, approached. The Sovereign Power, the Good Mind, and the Righteous Order came with her. Aramaiti gave a body to the spiritual creations of good and of evil; she is the abiding and ever-strenuous one. O Mazda, let that body for your people be at the end like it was when you first created it! At the end the great struggle shall be fought out which began when the evil spirits first seized the Demon of Wrath as their ally, and then just vengeance shall come upon these wretches. Then, O Mazda, your Good Mind within your people shall gain the Kingdom for you. O living Lord. The Good Mind speaks his command to those who will deliver the Demon of the Lie into the two hands of the Righteous Order, like a captive is delivered to a destroyer.

May we be like those who bring on this great renovation. May we make this world progressive, until its perfection is reached. May we be like the Ahuras of Mazda. Yes, may we be like you, in helpful readiness to meet your people, presenting benefits in union with the Righteous Order. Our thoughts will be where true wisdom shall live in her home.

---

*Yasna 30.

[10] When perfection is attained, then the blow of destruction shall fall upon the Demon of Falsehood, and her adherents shall perish with her. But the righteous saints, who walk on earth in good reputation and in honor, will gather swiftly in the happy home of the Good Mind and of Ahura.

Therefore, O mortals, you are learning these religious commands that Ahura gave in our happiness and our sorrow. You are also learning the long punishment of the wicked, and the blessings that are in store for the righteous. When these begin their course, salvation will be yours!

WORSHIP AND RITUAL

The Place of the *Gathas**

This passage, which stands at the end of the Gathas, *serves to show their high place in the Zoroastrian faith.*

As our offering to the bountiful *Gathas* that rule as the leading chants within the appointed times and seasons of our ritual, we present all our riches of land, and our persons, together with our very bones and tissues. We present our forms and forces, our consciousness, our soul, and Fravashi.

The *Gathas* are our guardians and defenders, and our spiritual food. Yes, they are both food and clothing to our souls. The *Gathas* are guardians and defenders and spiritual food, both food and clothing to our souls. May they be an offering for us. May they give abundant rewards . . . for the world beyond the present world, after our consciousness and our body are separated from each other. May these Praises of the Offering come forth and appear for us with power and victory, with health and healing, with progress, with growth, with preparation and protection, and with blessing and holiness. May they abound with gifts for those who can understand. Let them appear with free generosity to the enlightened. Let them appear as Mazda, the most beneficial, has produced them. He is the one who is victorious when he strikes. He helps our communities advance, and he protects and guards the religious order of the communities; even now they are being furthered. He guards those who will bring salvation to us, and he protects the entire creation of holy and clean things.

---

* *Yasna* 55:1–3.

The Zoroastrian Confession**

This stately creed of Zoroastrianism is called the Faravane. *Recited daily by every faithful worshipper of Mazda, it outlines an important Zoroastrian doctrine: the dualism of good and evil as cosmic forces. Believers pledge themselves to Mazda and the good, and reject the evil spirits.*

I drive the evil spirits away. I confess myself a Mazda-worshipper of the order of Zarathushtra. I renounce the evil spirits and devote myself to the lore of the Lord. I am a praiser of the Bountiful Immortals. I attribute all things good to Ahura Mazda, the Holy and Resplendent One. To Him belong all things good . . . and the stars, in whose lights the glorious beings and objects are clothed. I choose Piety, the generous and the good. I loudly condemn all robbery and violence against the sacred Cattle, and

---

** *Yasna* 12.

all droughts that waste the Mazdayasnian villages. I put away the thought of wandering at will, of pitching my tent freely like a nomad. I wish to remove all wandering from the Cattle that abide steadfastly on this land. Bowing down in worship to Righteousness, I dedicate my offerings with praise. May I never be a source of decline, and may I never be a source of withering to the Mazdayasnian villages, not for the love of body or life.

I renounce the shelter and headship of the evil spirits, evil as they are. They are utterly empty of good and void of Virtue. They are deceitful in their wickedness. Of all beings they are most like the Demon of the Lie, the most loathsome of existing things. They are completely empty of good.

[5] I renounce and renounce again the evil spirits and all possessed by them, the sorcerers and all who use their methods, and every being of the sort. I renounce their thoughts, their words and actions, and the seed that propagates their sin. I renounce their shelter and their headship. I renounce sinners of every kind, who act like demons!

Thus indeed might Ahura Mazda have shown to Zarathushtra, answering every question that Zarathushtra asked, in all the consultations that they had. Thus might Zarathushtra have renounced the shelter and the headship of the evil spirits in all the questions, and in all the consultations with which Zarathushtra and the Lord conversed together. And so I myself, in whatever circumstances I may be placed, as a worshipper of Mazda and of Zarathushtra's order, also renounce the evil spirits and their shelter. The holy Zarathushtra renounced them the same way in old times.

I belong to that religious holiness to which the waters belong, to that holiness to which the plants, to that holiness to which the Cattle of blessed gift, to that religious holiness to which Ahura Mazda, who made both cattle and holy men, belongs. To that holiness I belong. I am of the creed that Zarathushtra held, which Kavi Vistaspa, Frashaostra, and Gamaspa held.[4] Yes, I am of that religious faith as every **Saoshyant**[5] who shall yet come to see us, the holy ones who do truly significant things. Of that creed, and of that tradition, am I.

I am a Mazda-worshipper of Zarathushtra's order. Thus I confess, as a praiser and confessor. I praise aloud the thing well thought, the word well spoken, and the deed well done. Yes, I praise at once the faith of Mazda, the faith that has no saying that fails, the faith that wields the deadly battle-ax, the faith of kindred marriage.[6] I praise the holy Creed, which is the most imposing, best, and most beautiful of all religions which exist, and of all that in the future shall come to be. I praise Ahura's Faith, the Zarathushtrian creed. I ascribe all good to Ahura Mazda, and such shall be the worship of the Mazdayasnian belief!

---

[4] King *Kavi Vistaspa* was Zarathushtra's royal patron and protector. *Frashaostra* was an early follower of Zarathushtra; his daughter Hvovi was Zarathushtra's third wife. *Gamaspa* was the chief counselor of King Vistaspa and a friend of the new faith.
[5] *Saoshyant* [sa-OSH-yant]: "future rescuer"; a future savior who will help purify the world.
[6] *kindred marriage*: the Zoroastrian practice of marriage between distant relatives.

The Four Great Prayers*

These four prayers are the most important in Zoroastrian worship. They are named after their first words.

Ahuna vairyo[7]**:** As is the Master, so is the Judge to be chosen in accord with truth. Establish the power of acts arising from a life lived with good purpose, for Mazda and for the lord whom they made pastor for the poor.

---

*From the *Yasna*.
[7] This prayer and the *Ashem vohu* are taken from M. Boyce, *A History of Zoroastrianism*, 2 vols. (Leiden: Brill, 1975, 1982).

Airyema ishyo: May longed-for Airyaman come to the support of the men and women of Zarathushtra, to the support of our good purpose. The Inner Self earns the reward to be chosen. I ask for it the longed-for recompense of truth, which the Lord Mazda has in mind.

Ashem vohu: Asha is good, it is best. According to wish it is, according to wish it shall be for us. Asha belongs to Asha Vahishta.

Yenhe hatam: Those Beings, male and female, whom Lord Mazda knows the best for true worship, we worship them all.

Disposal of the Dead*

This passage describes the Zoroastrian "towers of silence," in which the dead are exposed to birds of prey so that their ritually defiling bodies may not pollute the sacred earth. First, provision is made for the on-ground exposure of the dead in places where "towers of silence" cannot be built.

"O Maker of the material world, you Holy One! Where shall we bring the bodies of the dead, where shall we lay their bodies, O Ahura Mazda?" [45] Ahura Mazda answered, "On the highest summits, where you know there are always corpse-eating dogs and corpse-eating birds, O holy Zarathushtra! There the worshippers of Mazda shall secure the corpse by the feet and by the hair. They shall secure it with brass, stones, or lead, lest the corpse-eating dogs and the corpse-eating birds go and carry the bones to the water and to the trees."

"If they shall not secure the corpse, so that the corpse-eating dogs and the corpse-eating birds carry the bones to the water and to the trees, what is the penalty that they shall pay?" Ahura Mazda answered: "They shall be severely punished. They shall receive two hundred stripes with the Aspahe-astra, two hundred stripes with the Sraoshokarana."[8]

"O Maker of the material world, you Holy One! Where shall we bring the bodies of the dead, where shall we lay them, O Ahura Mazda?" [50] Ahura Mazda answered: "The worshippers of Mazda shall build a building out of the reach of the dog, of the fox, and of the wolf, and in which rainwater cannot stay. Such a building shall they build, if they can afford it, with stones, mortar, and earth. If they cannot afford it, they shall lay the dead man on the ground, on his carpet and his pillow, clothed with the light of heaven,[9] and beholding the sun."

---

* *Vendidad, Fargard* 6, section 5, 44–51.
[8] The same type of whip is probably meant here, so that the total number of lashes would be two hundred.
[9] *clothed with the light of heaven:* naked. Exposed to the birds of prey, the body will undergo the same ritual disposal as corpses put in towers of silence.

LATER DEVELOPMENT OF SCRIPTURAL THEMES

Judgment of the Soul at the Chinvat Bridge**

In Zoroastrian belief, the soul of the departed hovers near the body for three days. On the fourth day it faces a judgment on the Chinvat ("Requiter") Bridge, where the deceased's good and evil deeds are weighed. If good actions outweigh evil ones, the soul ascends to Heaven; if evil acts outweigh the good, it is dragged off to Hell. At the Last Judgment,

---

** *Menok I Khrat* 2.110–195.

at the end of time, all bodies are resurrected and reunited with their souls. Then there is a final and universal cleansing, from which all people emerge spotless and enter into Paradise. This passage is designed, like most depictions of Heaven and Hell in world scriptures, to motivate believers to live correctly in this life, body and soul.[10]

Do not put not your trust in life, for at the last death must overtake you. Dogs and birds will tear at your corpse, and your bones will be tumbled on the earth.

For three days and nights the soul sits beside the pillow of the body. [115] Accompanied by the blessed Srosh, the good Vay, and the mighty Vahram, and opposed by Astvihat (the demon of death), the evil Vay, the demon Frehzisht and the demon Vizisht, and pursued by the active ill-will of Wrath . . ., the soul on the fourth day after death will reach the lofty and awful Bridge of the Requiter. Every person whose soul will be saved and every person whose soul will be damned must come to this bridge. Many enemies lie in wait here. Here the soul will suffer from the ill-will of Wrath who wields a bloody spear, and from Astvihat who swallows all creation yet is never satisfied, and it will benefit by the mediation of Hihr, Srosh, and Rashn. [120] Then the soul submits to the weighing of its deeds by the righteous Rashn. He lets the scales of the spiritual gods incline to neither side, neither for the saved nor yet for the damned, nor yet for kings and princes. Not so much as a hair's breadth does he allow the scales to tip; he is no respecter of persons, for he deals out impartial justice both to kings and princes and to the humblest of men. And when the soul of the saved passes over that bridge, the breadth of the bridge appears to be one parasang.[11]

The soul of the saved goes on, accompanied by the blessed Srosh. [125] His own good deeds come to meet him in the form of a young woman, more beautiful than any on earth. The soul of the saved says, "Who are you? I have never seen a young woman on earth more beautiful than you." [130] She replies, "I am no woman! I am your own good deeds, O young man whose thoughts and words, deeds and religion were good. When you saw someone offer sacrifice to the demons, then you sat apart and offered sacrifice to the gods. When you saw a man do violence and theft, afflict good men and mistreat them, or store up goods wrongfully obtained, then you refrained from treating creatures with violence. Instead, you were considerate to good men; you entertained them and offered them hospitality; you gave alms both to the man who came from near and to him who came from afar; and you amassed your wealth in righteousness. [135] When you saw someone who passed a false judgment or took bribes or gave false testimony, you spoke a right and true witness. I am the good thoughts, good words, and good deeds that you said and did. . . ."

[140] When the soul departs, a fragrant breeze wafts toward him, a breeze more fragrant than any perfume. Then the soul of the saved asks Srosh, "What breeze is this, the like of which I never smelled on earth?" Then the blessed Srosh answers the soul of the saved, "This is a wind (wafted) from Heaven; therefore it is so fragrant.". . . .

[145] Then with his first step he enters the heaven of good thoughts, with his second the heaven of good words, with his third the heaven of good deeds, and with his fourth step he reaches the Endless Light where is all bliss. All the gods and good spirits come to greet him and ask him how he has been, saying, "How was your passage from those transient, fearful worlds where there is much evil to these eternal worlds in which there is no adversary, O young man whose thoughts and words, deeds and religion are good?"

[150] Then Ahura Mazda, the Lord, says, "Do not ask him how he has been, because he has been separated from his beloved body and has traveled on a fearsome road." They serve

---

[10] Taken, with editing, from E. W. West, *Pahlavi Texts*, part 3, *Sacred Books of the East*, vol. 24. (Oxford: Clarendon Press, 1885), pp. 16–26.

[11] *one parasang:* about three miles.

him the sweetest of all foods with the butter of early spring, so that his soul may take its ease after the three nights of terror on the Bridge inflicted on him by the demons. They seat him upon a throne everywhere bejeweled. . . . [157] And for ever and ever he dwells blissfully with the spiritual gods.

But when the man who is damned dies, for three days and nights his soul hovers near his head and weeps, saying, "Where shall I go and in whom shall I now take refuge?" [160] During those three days and nights he sees all the sins and wickedness that he committed on earth. On the fourth day the demon Vizarsh comes and binds the soul of the damned in most shameful ways, and despite the opposition of the blessed Srosh drags it off to the Bridge of the Requiter. Then the righteous Rashn makes clear to the soul of the damned that it is damned indeed. Then the demon Vizarsh seizes the soul of the damned, strikes it, and abuses it without pity, urged on by Wrath. [165] The soul of the damned cries out loudly, moans in terror, and makes many piteous pleas; he struggles much, although his life-breath endures no more. All his struggling and his howling prove of no avail, because no help is offered him by any of the gods or by any of the demons.

The demon Vizarsh drags him off against his will into deepest Hell. Then a young woman who does not look like a woman comes to meet him. The soul of the damned says to that ill-favored woman, "Who are you? I have never seen anyone on earth as hideous as you." [170] She replies, "I am no woman! I am your deeds—hideous deeds—evil thoughts, evil words, evil deeds, and evil religion. When on earth you saw someone who offered sacrifice to the gods, then you sat apart and offered sacrifice to the demons. When you saw someone who entertained good men and offered them hospitality . . . then you treated good men with dishonor; you gave them no alms and you shut your door to them. [175] When you saw someone who passed just judgment or took no bribes or bore true witness or spoke up in righteousness, then you passed false judgment, you gave false testimony, and you spoke unrighteously." . . .

[182] Then with his first step he goes to the hell of evil thoughts, with his second to the hell of evil words, and with his third to the hell of evil deeds. With his fourth step he lurches into the presence of the accursed Destructive Spirit and the other demons. [185] The demons mock at him and scorn him, saying, "What grieved you in Ahura Mazda, the Lord, and the Amahraspands and in fragrant and delightful Heaven? What grudge or complaint did you have against them that you should come to see the demons and this murky Hell? We will torment you and have no mercy on you for a long time!" The Destructive Spirit cries out to the demons, "Do not ask about him, for he has been separated from his beloved body, and he has come through that most evil passageway. Serve him the filthiest and most foul food that Hell can produce." [190] Then they bring him poison and venom, snakes and scorpions, and other noxious reptiles that flourish in Hell, and they serve him these to eat. Until the resurrection and the final body he must remain in Hell, suffering much torment and many kinds of punishment.

GLOSSARY

Avesta [ah-VES-tuh] variously translated as "injunction," "wisdom," and "scripture"; the name of the Zoroastrian scriptures.

Fravashis [frah-VAH-shees] guardian spirits.

Gathas [GAH-tuhs] a collection of seventeen hymns in the *Yasna*, which Zoroastrians hold to be the words of Zarathushtra.

Saoshyant [sa-OSH-yant] "future rescuer"; a future savior who will help purify the world.

Vendidad [VEN-dih-dahd] The Law against Demons; a division of the *Avesta* containing myths and codes of religious law.

Visparad [VEE-spuh-rahd] "All the [Divine] Lords"; a twenty-chapter collection of hymns in the *Avesta*.

Yashts [yahshts] "Hymns"; hymns of praise to twenty-one divinities, angels, and human heroes of ancient Persia; a division of the *Avesta*.

Yasna [YAHZ-nuh] "Sacrifice"; hymns for worship; the first and foremost division of the *Avesta*.

QUESTIONS FOR STUDY AND DISCUSSION

1. What, to judge from the *Gathas*, were the main religious ideas of the prophet Zarathushtra?

2. What sort of changes occurred in Zoroastrian religion after the passing of Zarathushtra? For your answer, compare the *Gathas* with the rest of the *Avesta*.

3. Explain how Zarathushtra is worshipped by means of these scriptures.

4. How do the striking funeral and cleanliness rituals reproduced here testify to the strong connection made in Zoroastrianism between ritual purity and moral purity?

SUGGESTIONS FOR FURTHER READING

Primary Sources

M. Boyce, *Textual Sources for the Study of Zoroastrianism*. Chicago: University of Chicago Press, 1990. A full selection of texts, with introductions but few annotations.

J. Darmesteter and L. H. Mills, *The Zend-Avesta*. In F. Max Müller, ed., *Sacred Books of the East*, vols. 4, 23, and 31. Oxford: Oxford University Press, 1880–1887. Its Victorian English often interferes, but this is the only relatively complete translation of the *Avesta* in English.

J. Insler, *The Gathas of Zarathushtra*. Leiden: Brill, 1975. Contains the Avestan text, English translation and notes, and excellent commentary.

Secondary Sources

J. Barr, "The Question of Religious Influence: The Case of Zoroastrianism, Judaism, and Christianity." *Journal of the American Academy of Religion*, 53 (1985): 201–235. A reexamination of the notion, commonly accepted in religious scholarship, that Zoroastrian teachings had a great influence on Judaism and through it on Christianity and Islam.

M. Boyce, *A History of Zoroastrianism*, 2 vols. Leiden: Brill, 1975, 1982. The standard history of Zoroastrianism, with comprehensive treatment of the *Avesta* as the main source of our knowledge of early Zoroastrianism.

M. Boyce, *A Persian Stronghold of Zoroastrianism*. Oxford: Oxford University Press, 1977. Although no explicit and extended treatment of scripture is included here, this firsthand report on the life of Iranian Zoroastrians sheds much light on present-day use of the *Avesta*.

J. W. Boyd, "Zoroastrianism: Avestan Scripture and Rite." In F. M. Denny and R. L. Taylor, eds., *The Holy Book in Comparative Perspective*. Charleston: University of South Carolina Press, 1985, pp. 109–125. An excellent discussion of orthodox versus reformist reception and use of the *Avesta*.

Celebrating Scripture
Orthodox Jews at the Western Wall in Jerusalem lift a Hebrew *Bible* scroll in its box during the Festival of Sukkot ("Booths"). This act emphasizes Jews' joy in their scripture and the obligation to keep its teachings. *Credit:* Used by permission of BiblePlaces.com.

CHAPTER THREE

Judaism

- In New York City, detective Mordacai Dzinkansky sets up a "sting" operation with unsuspecting criminals who are selling *Torah* scrolls into a worldwide black market. These scrolls—many of them worth more than $50,000 each—have been stolen from synagogues. A member of the N.Y.P.D. Torah Task Force and a Hebrew-speaking Orthodox Jew, Dzinkansky is remarkably effective at winning the confidence of criminals, bringing them to justice, and recovering the stolen *Torahs* for return to their rightful owners.

- Jewish demonstrators surround the parliament building in Jerusalem as members of parliament inside debate withdrawing Jewish settlers from predominantly Arab Gaza and giving their land to the Palestinian Authority. Several of the signs carry references to "Eretz [land of] Israel," the size of Israel promised by God to Abraham in *Genesis* 15:18–21. Some Israeli rabbis have threatened to excommunicate any soldiers who participate in transferring any part of this land to Palestinian control. The transfer goes through in 2005, but insistence by a small but politically powerful group on keeping "Eretz Israel" continues to complicate the peace process.

- In London, a prominent Jewish rabbi criticizes the pop singer Madonna's latest venture into religious practice, this time the Jewish mystical belief and practice known as the Kabbalah. Rabbi Yitzchak Schochet of London's Mill Hill Synagogue strongly objects to Madonna's use of the Kabbalah in her latest music video and in a series of books for children, arguing that it tarnishes Jewish scripture and law. Particularly objectionable to Rabbi Schochet and most other observant Jews is Madonna's new tattoo on her right shoulder of the ancient sacred Hebrew name for God. Interest in—and controversy over—her practice of the Kabbalah reaches a fever pitch on the Internet; a search of the combined terms "Madonna" and "Kabbalah" returns more than 425,000 hits in January 2006.

INTRODUCTION

Judaism is founded on a belief in one personal God who was revealed in the early history of the Jewish people, calling them to serve God and spread divine love and justice in the world. The influence of the Jewish scriptures stems directly from rigorous adherence over more than 2,500 years in ways those three vignettes can only suggest. The Jewish *Bible* is the foundation of both the Christian and the Islamic scriptures as well, and thus its teachings have carried over into the lives of the world's two largest religions. Even though some of the importance of the Jewish scriptures has been lost in the modern secularized world, their deep influence on everyday life and on patterns of Western thought and culture has abated only a little. Our seven-day week with its day of rest is an inheritance from Jewish scripture; the belief that there is only one God is a gift of these writings as well. That all people are equally human, that the human race is one family, and that each individual can fully realize the meaning of life regardless of social or economic class: These ideas have also come to the Western world from the Jewish scriptures.

Names

The most particularly Jewish name for the whole Jewish *Bible* is **Tanakh** [TAH-nahk]. It is an acronym formed from the first letters of the names of the three sections of the scriptures: *Torah* [TOH-rah], "Teaching" or "Law"; **Nevi'im** [NEH-vih-eem], "Prophets"; and **Kethuvim** [KETH-u-veem], "Writings" (see Table 3.1). The name *Tanakh* arose in the Middle Ages and is widely known among European and American Jews. It is not widely known among non-Jews, however, nor is it the commonly used academic name for the Jewish scriptures.

Many people call the Jewish scripture the *Old Testament,* but that is a Christian name (the latter part of the Christian *Bible* is called the *New Testament*). Because of the predominance of Christianity over Judaism in the West, the name *Old Testament* has become traditional even in journalistic and academic circles. Jews, however, rightly see the term and the more kindly "First Testament" as derogatory, and students of religion now avoid both of them as partisan and inappropriate. A better designation is "Hebrew scriptures." ("Hebrew" here refers to the language of the Jewish *Bible,* which is Hebrew except for one verse each in the books of *Genesis* and *Jeremiah* and several chapters in *Ezra* and *Daniel*. The exceptions are in Aramaic, a language closely related to Hebrew.) Christians and Jews accept "Hebrew scriptures" as both accurate and nonprejudicial. Its wide acceptance is indicated by its use in the *New Revised Standard Version* of the (Christian) *Bible*.

The most common name for the Jewish scriptures, the simple term **Bible** (from the Greek *biblos,* "book"), is probably its oldest. This word has its roots in the Hebrew term *Ha-Sefarim,* "The Books" (*Daniel* 9:2), which Greek-speaking Jews by the second century B.C.E. translated as *ta biblia*. The term passed into the Greek translation of the *New Testament* and then through Latin to give us the English word *Bible*. This name stresses the written, textual nature of the Jewish **revelation,** the communication of God's person and truth to humanity. (When Jews refer to the *Bible,* they mean of course *their* scripture, of which the Christian *New Testament* is *not* a part.) In sum, no single name for the Jewish scripture has ever been common to all Jews, but *Bible* is probably the most ancient and the most widely accepted, so we use it here.

Use

The Jewish *Bible* is built on the foundation of the *Torah,* the written law of God. But ancient law needs interpreting and application to new times and situations, and so arose the concept of "oral Torah." The oral Torah explains, supplements, and applies

Table 3.1
The Books of the Jewish *Bible*

Division	English Name	Hebrew Name	Chapters
Torah ("Teaching, Law")	Genesis	*Bereshith* ("in the beginning")	50
	Exodus	*Shemoth* ("names")	40
	Leviticus	*Wayiqra* ("and he called")	27
	Numbers	*Bemidbar* ("in the wilderness")	36
	Deuteronomy	*Debarim* ("words")	34
Nevi'im ("Prophets")	<u>Former Prophets</u>		
	Joshua	*Yehoshua*	24
	Judges	*Shofetim* ("judges")	21
	I–II Samuel	*Shemuel*	31, 24
	I–II Kings	*Melakim* ("kings")	22, 25
	<u>Latter Prophets</u>		
	Isaiah	*Yeshayahu*	66
	Jeremiah	*Yirmeyahu*	52
	Ezekiel	*Yehezqel*	48
	The Twelve:		
	Hosea	*Hoshea*	14
	Joel	*Yoel*	3
	Amos	*Amos*	9
	Obadiah	*Obadyahu*	1
	Jonah	*Yonah*	4
	Micah	*Micah*	7
	Nahum	*Nahum*	3
	Habakkuk	*Habaqquq*	3
	Zephaniah	*Zephanyah*	3
	Haggai	*Haggai*	2
	Zechariah	*Zekaryahu*	14
	Malachi	*Malaki*	4
Kethuvim ("Writings")	Psalms	*Tehillim* ("praises")	150
	Job	*Iyyob*	31
	Proverbs	*Mishle* ("proverbs of")	42
	Ruth	*Ruth*	4
	Song of Songs	*Shir Hashirim* ("song of songs")	8
	Ecclesiastes	*Koheleth* ("preacher")	12
	Lamentations	*Ekah* ("how")	5
	Esther	*Ester*	10
	Daniel	*Daniel*	12
	Ezra-Nehemiah	*Ezra-Nehemyah*	10, 13
	I–II Chronicles	*Dibre Hayamin* ("words of")	29, 36

the commands of the written *Torah*. It is called "oral" because it was believed by the end of the first century C.E. to have been revealed to Moses on Mount Sinai and passed down orally by experts for more than a thousand years. It was also probably kept in oral form so as not to compete in standing and authority with the *Bible*, the written *Torah*. In time, the oral Torah grew so large and authoritative that it had to be written down, first in the *Mishnah* (ca. 200 C.E.), then in its commentary, the *Gemara* (ca. 450–550 C.E.), and shortly thereafter in the combination of those two works—the **Talmud** [TALL-mood]. The *Talmud* has two versions: the short *Jerusalem Talmud* and the longer and more authoritative *Babylonian Talmud*. For almost all Jews from 500 to 1800 C.E., the scripture was understood by way of the oral Torah as written down in the *Talmud*, and Orthodox Jews still understand scripture in this way. For example, the biblical law "An eye for an eye" is not to be taken literally but means that a person who injures another must pay adequate monetary fines to compensate for the loss.

This was how the *Talmud* was used through the Middle Ages. This period of rabbinic Judaism also saw the rise of the fourfold meaning of the scripture: midrashic, philosophical, mystical, and literal. *Midrash* was the sermonic, illustrative interpretation of the *Bible*, often quite fanciful. The philosophical meaning sought by Maimonides and others yielded deep truths in the *Bible* that could be related to the teachings of Plato or Aristotle. The hidden, mystical meaning made possible a direct experience of God, emotional as well as intellectual or moral. One mystical group, the Kabbalists, found cryptic meanings in words and letters of scripture and ignored the other three types of meaning. The literal meaning emerged from the study of the diction and grammar of the text: the greatest practitioner of literalism was Rashi (Rabbi Solomon Itzchaki) of Troyes, France. Rabbis often combined the four levels of meaning in some way, but the literal meaning was prominent by the end of the Middle Ages and was most compatible with the developing historical method.

With the emancipation of Judaism from legal restrictions and official discrimination around 1800 C.E., liberalizing Jews applied the historical-critical method of studying texts to the Jewish *Bible*. Accepting the ideas of the Enlightenment, these Jews said that scripture was to be understood like any other book, with supernatural and miraculous elements largely discounted. The Dutch Jewish philosopher Baruch Spinoza (1623–1677), a pre-emancipation scholar, had already introduced and exemplified this approach. He dismissed the divine inspiration of scripture and Moses' authorship of the *Torah*, advocating a historical interpretation. At first his methods shocked and scandalized the Jewish world, but over the next three hundred years they became more common.

By the end of the 1800s, the three main groups of modern Judaism had emerged along with their distinct approaches to scripture. The Reform branch, which largely adopted the historical-critical method, approaches the *Bible* much as mainstream Protestants and Roman Catholics understand it. The Orthodox branch sticks to the traditional and Talmudic views of scripture and methods of interpreting it—for example, believing that the whole *Torah* was written by Moses, that the *Talmud* is the oral Torah, and that every law of God is to be followed literally as fully as possible. The Conservative branch lies between the other two, employing modern historical methods to understand and apply scripture but seeking to preserve much of the essential and traditional meaning.

When Muhammad called the Jews (and Christians) the "people of the book," he made an accurate assessment of the role of scripture in Judaism. For more than two thousand years the *Bible* has been read, prayed, and taught in the synagogue. It has shaped the doctrine, ethics, and worship of the Jews. Its instruction and inspiration have helped to preserve them through good times and bad, over their wide dispersion through much of the world.

As in most religions, the site where Jews have characteristically met and used their scripture is their place of worship. Synagogue worship is filled with the *Bible;* scripture saturates the prayers, chants, hymns, and liturgies. The main point of the service is the solemn reading of passages appointed for the day in the prayer books. The entire *Torah* is read at the Sabbath services during the course of each year. Special *Torah* readings are fixed for the main festivals and High Holy Days. Related readings from the prophets (called the *Haftorah*) are also fixed in the **lectionary,** or list of readings, for each Sabbath and holy day. Some passages from the *Kethuvim* section of the *Bible* (see Table 3.1) are read on five lesser festivals (Sukkoth, Passover, Shavu'ot, Purim, the Ninth of Ab) from the five scrolls known as the *Megilloth* (*Ecclesiastes, Song of Songs, Ruth, Esther,* and *Lamentations*).

The readings themselves are very musical. The worship leader chants the words in Hebrew, guided by accent marks written into the Hebrew text and also employing traditional Hebrew melodies. The place where the *Torah* scrolls are kept is the **ark.** It is a special closet or recess in the synagogue wall on the side nearest Jerusalem and is usually the focal point of the synagogue. The scrolls themselves are typically covered with richly embroidered cloth, and the upper ends of the wooden rollers are adorned with gold and silver decorations. When a scroll is removed from the ark during the service, everyone in the synagogue stands and special songs are sung. Then the scroll is placed on a reading desk, and the reader uses a special pointer, often made of solid silver, to keep track of his or her place in the text. When the reading is complete, the scroll is rolled up, its covers are put back on, and it is returned to the ark with great solemnity. Then the rabbi preaches a sermon based on the texts that were read, especially the *Torah* reading.

The *Bible,* together with the *Talmud,* is also the focus of group and individual study. Since ancient times it has been a legal obligation for every Jewish man—and often an option for women—to be able to read and understand scripture. In North America, every synagogue of substance provides after-school classes in Hebrew language and religious studies to children from elementary to high school age. Jewish parochial schools that teach both general and religious subjects, with heavy doses of scripture, can be found in cities with sizable Jewish populations. This emphasis on early education in scripture fosters Jewish adults who are able and willing to study it on an advanced level. Every Jewish home typically possesses a *Bible* in the native language of the family and often one in Hebrew as well.

The daily life of the observant Jew is also immersed in reminders of the *Bible* and its instruction. For example, fastened to the doorpost of many homes is the **mezuzah** [meh-ZOO-zah], a small box containing three short passages from the

Torah, among them the well-known words of *Deuteronomy* 6:4–9: "Take to heart these instructions with which I charge you this day. Impress them upon your children. Recite them when you stay at home and when you are away, when you lie down and when you get up . . . inscribe them on the doorposts of your house and on your gates." This passage also commands the wearing of **tefillin** [teh-FILL-in], called "phylacteries" in English. Orthodox Jews wear tefillin while praying, which they typically do three times a day. Tefillin are two small wooden boxes that contain tiny scripture scrolls. Using leather straps, the wearer binds one to his forehead and the other to his weaker arm. Outward practices of religion such as displaying the mezuzah and wearing tefillin are intended to remind every Jew of the duty to act in obedience to God during every activity night or day, at home or away.

Overview of Structure

Reduced to its most basic form, the overall structure of the Jewish *Bible*, shown in Table 3.1, may be summarized as follows (the dates provide a time line for the events narrated in the books and are not to be taken as dates of the writing of the books themselves). In *Genesis*, the first book of the *Torah*, God creates the world good, but humanity falls into sin and rebellion. After the growth of the human race through many generations, Abraham responds to God's call by migrating from Mesopotamia to Palestine (ca. 1750 B.C.E.). He and his main descendants, Isaac and Jacob, move about in the hills of Palestine; Jacob and his descendants go to Egypt during a famine. In *Exodus*, the second book of the *Torah*, Moses leads the Hebrews by God's power from Egypt into the Sinai Peninsula (between Egypt and Palestine), where they receive the law of God (ca. 1280 B.C.E.). In *Leviticus*, they receive God's instruction for worship and purity. *Numbers* relates how they wander in the wilderness until they are ready to enter the Promised Land. In *Deuteronomy*, the people receive the law a second time as Moses warns them against serving other gods. These five books are together known as the *Torah*, "Teaching" or "Law." They are the most important of the Hebrew scriptures.

Nevi'im, "Prophets," the second section of the Jewish *Bible*, is subdivided into two parts: *Former* and *Latter*, referring to the position of the books in the canon, not to the time of their composition. The books of the *Former Prophets* are *Joshua, Judges, Samuel* (volumes I and II), and *Kings* (volumes I and II). *Joshua* presents a somewhat idealized version of how the Israelites crossed the Jordan River and conquered the peoples of Palestine (ca. 1250 B.C.E.). *Judges* provides another view of how the Israelites engaged in continuing wars to maintain their possession of the land as they were led by charismatic figures against their enemies. *I Samuel* and *II Samuel* relate how a monarchy was established with Saul as the first king and David (crowned 1000 B.C.E.) as his successor. *I Kings* and *II Kings* tell how, under King Solomon, Israel grew to be a small empire then, when Solomon died, split into two nations—the northern kingdom of Israel (or Ephraim) and the southern kingdom of Judah. The northern kingdom was conquered by Assyria in 721 B.C.E., never to reappear. The southern kingdom fell to Babylonia in 590 B.C.E., and many of the

Judeans went into exile in Babylon. They considered the Exile punishment for their failure to serve God alone.

The first book of the *Latter Prophets* is *Isaiah,* a composite text that contains the words of Isaiah in the eighth century B.C.E. and the messages of "Second Isaiah" (an anonymous prophet responsible for *Isaiah* 40–55) and "Third Isaiah" (an anonymous prophet responsible for Isaiah 56–66) in the sixth century B.C.E. *Jeremiah* presents the message of the mournful prophet who foresaw the destruction of Jerusalem by the Babylonians. *Ezekiel* prophesies hope among the Jewish exiles in Babylon. The last book is *The Twelve* (known by the Aramaic name *Terei Asar*). It is a collection of short prophetic texts: *Hosea, Joel, Amos, Obadiah, Jonah, Micah, Nahum, Habakkuk, Zephaniah, Haggai, Zechariah,* and *Malachi*. The books of *The Twelve* are known as the *Minor Prophets* because of their relatively small size—each one was formerly written on one scroll. The careers of these twelve prophets extended from the 700s to the 500s B.C.E.

The third section of the Jewish *Bible* is the *Kethuvim,* "Writings." As the name suggests, within this section is a miscellaneous collection of several types of literature. It begins with the *Psalms.* A **psalm** [sahlm] is a sacred song used for divine worship. *Proverbs* and *Job* are books about wisdom. The former is a collection of wise sayings attributed to Solomon, the latter a drama about the perennial question "If God is good, why do good people suffer?" *Ruth* tells the beautiful story of how a non-Israelite woman became one of the people of God and an ancestor of King David. The *Song of Songs* is a collection of poetry that celebrates love between a man and a woman, traditionally interpreted by Jews as symbolic of the relationship between God and Israel. *Ecclesiastes* offers a bittersweet perspective on what wisdom and life have to offer. *Lamentations,* traditionally ascribed to the prophet Jeremiah, mourns the destruction of Jerusalem by the Babylonians. *Esther* is the dramatic story of how a Jewish woman delivers her people from destruction by a Persian king. *Daniel* contains visions of the end of time. *Ezra-Nehemiah* records the return of the Jewish exiles from Babylon at the end of the sixth century B.C.E., the reconstruction of Jerusalem, and the reconstitution of Judaism. Finally, *I Chronicles* and *II Chronicles* tell much the same story as *I* and *II Kings* (in the *Former Prophets* section), but from the perspective of the Jerusalem priesthood.

These, then, are the books of the Jewish *Bible*. In Jewish reckoning, they number twenty-four in all, a number obtained by counting as one book each *I* and *II Samuel, I* and *II Kings, I* and *II Chronicles, The Twelve,* and *Ezra-Nehemiah* (see Table 3.1). In ancient times they were traditionally written on twenty-four scrolls, and even after the two-volume books were physically separated at the end of the Middle Ages, this number was kept.

The order of the books of the Jewish *Bible* that is familiar to Christians is based on the Greek translation made before Christianity began. (This translation, known as the *Septuagint,* was the only scripture of early Christianity until the *New Testament* was recognized as scripture in the second and third centuries C.E. We deal more fully with the relationship of the Jewish and Christian scriptures in Chapter 4.) Table 3.2 shows the order of books in the Greek version of the Jewish *Bible*.

Table 3.2
The Books of the Greek Version of the Jewish *Bible*

Genesis	*Proverbs*
Exodus	*Ecclesiastes*
Leviticus	**Wisdom of Solomon*
Numbers	**Wisdom of Sirach*
Deuteronomy	**Psalms of Solomon*
Joshua	*Isaiah*
Judges	*Jeremiah*
Ruth	*Lamentations*
I Kings (I Samuel)	**Baruch*
II Kings (II Samuel)	**Letter of Jeremiah*
III Kings (I Kings)	*Ezekiel*
IV Kings (II Kings)	*Daniel*
I Chronicles	**Susanna*
II Chronicles	**Bel and the Snake*
*I Esdras	*Hosea*
II Esdras (Ezra-Nehemiah)	*Joel*
*Tobit	*Amos*
*Judith	*Obadiah*
Esther	*Jonah*
*I Maccabees	*Micah*
*II Maccabees	*Nahum*
*III Maccabees	*Habakkuk*
*IV Maccabees	*Zephaniah*
Job	*Haggai*
Psalms	*Zechariah*
*Odes	*Malachi*

* These apocryphal, or deutero-canonical, books are not included in the canon of the Hebrew scriptures or in the *Bibles* of most Protestant churches. They are included in the *Bibles* of the Eastern Orthodox and Roman Catholic churches, but the Catholic canon excludes *I Esdras, III and IV Maccabees, Odes,* and *Psalms of Solomon*. Some *Bibles* used by Orthodox Christians omit *IV Maccabees, Odes,* and *Psalms of Solomon*.

Origin and Development

The Jewish *Bible* had a long history of formation in oral tradition, transcription in writing, and editorial polishing. Because this process of development is shrouded in the mists of antiquity, scholarly judgments vary, but there is some agreement about the following summary description.

- ❖ The writing probably began about 1100 B.C.E., with the writing down of the oldest sections of poetry and historical narratives (e.g., the "Songs of Moses and Miriam" in *Exodus* 15; the "Song of Deborah" in *Judges* 5). In the reign of Solomon, the story of his father David began to be written (*II Samuel* 9–*I Kings* 2). One source of the *Torah*, which tells of creation and the patriarchs as a prelude to the formation of Israel, was written in southern Israel. Another source of the *Torah* was written in northern Israel from a northern religious and political perspective.

- ❖ The eighth century B.C.E. saw a flowering of literary effort. The disciples of the prophets Amos, Hosea, Isaiah, and Micah began to write down their words. When the northern kingdom of Israel fell in 721 B.C.E., the sources mentioned above were combined into the "Old Epic" narrative to give us much of our present *Genesis*. In 621 B.C.E., the finding of a law scroll in the Jerusalem temple, a scroll probably containing the substance of *Deuteronomy* 12–26, provided impetus for the writing of the rest of that book.

- ❖ The Exile in Babylon (587–539 B.C.E.) was a fruitful period of literary activity. *Jeremiah, Ezekiel,* and "Second Isaiah" (*Isaiah* 40–55) were written down by those prophets' disciples. The Deuteronomic history (*Deuteronomy, Joshua, Judges, I* and *II Samuel,* and *I* and *II Kings*) was probably completed at the end of the Exile. Priestly sections of the *Torah* were completed, and many of the *Psalms* were written down.

- ❖ After the Exile, more prophetic books were completed: "Third Isaiah" (*Isaiah* 56–66), *Malachi, Joel,* and *Haggai*. By 400 B.C.E., the *Torah* probably reached its present form as it was finished and edited by the Jerusalem priests, becoming the first and primary section of Jewish scripture. Around 350 B.C.E., the historical works *I* and *II Chronicles* and *Ezra-Nehemiah* were completed. The later wisdom books, *Job* and *Ecclesiastes,* were compiled, and two short stories, *Ruth* and *Esther,* appeared. By 200 B.C.E., the eight-book section known as *Nevi'im* was largely complete. The final texts of the Jewish scripture were in the apocalyptic mode: *Isaiah* 24–27, *Ezekiel* 38, and especially the book of *Daniel,* the last book to be written, in 160 B.C.E. The *Kethuvim* section was basically determined by about 100 B.C.E.

The full and formal canonization of the entire Jewish *Bible* as we now have it—the *Law (Torah), Prophets (Nevi'im),* and *Writings (Kethuvim)*—took place at the end of the first century C.E. No one disagreed on the books of the *Torah* and the *Prophets*—this canon had been settled for centuries. A Jewish council meeting at Jamnia (ca. 90 C.E.) seems to have ruled on the writings as we have them, but it took some years for this ruling to be widely accepted. The main criterion for canonicity was the recognition that God was revealed in these books and spoke to his people in them. Canonization did not confer scripturality on a book. Rather, scriptural status emerged from the official and formal recognition of a long-standing reception and use of these books as holy and scriptural by the Jewish community itself. Once recognition was given, canonization helped reinforce the texts' holiness and authority.

HISTORY

The Call of Abraham*

The history of the Jewish people begins with Abraham, whose name was Abram at first. God calls him to journey to Canaan (ancient Palestine) and promises that his descendants will form a great nation, will become a source of blessing to the world, and will inherit the land of Canaan. Abraham responds faithfully to God's call. Compare this passage with Genesis 17:9–14, 23–27, given later in the "Ritual" section of this chapter.[1]

The Lord said to Abram, "Go forth from your native land and from your father's house to the land that I will show you.
I will make of you a great nation,
And I will bless you;
I will make your name great,
And you shall be a blessing.
I will bless those who bless you
And curse him that curses you;
And all the families of the earth
Shall bless themselves by you."

Abram went forth as the Lord had commanded him, and Lot went with him. Abram was seventy-five years old when he left Haran.[2] [5] Abram took his wife Sarai and his brother's son Lot, and all the wealth that they had amassed, and the persons that they had acquired in Haran; and they set out for the land of Canaan. When they arrived in the land of Canaan, Abram passed through the land as far as the site of Shechem, at the terebinth[3] of Moreh. The Canaanites were then in the land.

The Lord appeared to Abram and said, "I will assign this land to your heirs." And he built an altar there to the Lord who had appeared to him. From there he moved on to the hill country east of Bethel and pitched his tent, with Bethel on the west and Ai on the east; and he built there an altar to the Lord and invoked the Lord by name. Then Abram journeyed by stages toward the Negeb.

---

* *Genesis* 12:1–9.
[1] All passages from the Jewish *Bible* are from *Tanakh: The Holy Scriptures*. Copyright © 1985 Jewish Publication Society. Used by permission of the publisher.
[2] *Haran:* the city in northern Mesopotamia (modern-day Iraq) where Abraham lived.
[3] *terebinth:* an oak tree with sacred significance.

The Call of Moses**

Speaking from a burning bush, God calls Moses to be God's prophetic agent in liberating the Hebrews from their Egyptian slavery. This passage provides insight into the personality of Moses, the most influential person in the Tanakh *and in Jewish history.*

Now Moses, tending the flock of his father-in-law Jethro, the priest of Midian, drove the flock into the wilderness, and came to Horeb, the mountain of God. An angel of the Lord appeared to him in a blazing fire out of a bush. He gazed, and there was a bush all aflame, yet the bush was not consumed. Moses said, "I must turn aside to look at this marvelous sight; why doesn't the bush burn up?" When the Lord saw that he had turned aside to look, God called to him out of the bush: "Moses!" He answered, "Here I am." [5] And He said, "Do not come closer. Remove your sandals from your feet, for the place on which you stand is holy ground.[4] I am," He said, "the God of your father, the

---

** *Exodus* 3:1–20.
[4] *Remove your sandals:* the custom in many ancient Near Eastern religions of going barefoot in a holy place, still practiced in Islamic mosques.

God of Abraham, the God of Isaac, and the God of Jacob." And Moses hid his face, for he was afraid to look at God.

And the Lord continued, "I have marked well the plight of My people in Egypt and have heeded their outcry because of their taskmasters; yes, I am mindful of their sufferings. I have come down to rescue them from the Egyptians and to bring them out of that land to a good and spacious land, a land flowing with milk and honey, the region of the Canaanites, the Hittites, the Amorites, the Perizzites, the Hivites, and the Jebusites.[6] Now the cry of the Israelites has reached Me; moreover, I have seen how the Egyptians oppress them. [10] Come, therefore, I will send you to Pharaoh, and you shall free My people, the Israelites, from Egypt."

But Moses said to God, "Who am I that I should go to Pharaoh and free the Israelites from Egypt?" And He said, "I will be with you, that shall be your sign that it was I who sent you. And when you have freed the people from Egypt, you shall worship God at this mountain."

Moses said to God, "When I come to the Israelites and say to them 'The God of your fathers has sent me to you,' and they ask me, 'What is His name?' what shall I say to them?" And God said to Moses, "Ehyeh-Asher-Ehyeh."[5] He continued, "Thus shall you say to the Israelites, 'Ehyeh sent me to you.'" [15] And God said further to Moses, "Thus shall you speak to the Israelites: The Lord, the God of your fathers, the God of Abraham, the God of Isaac, and the God of Jacob, has sent me to you: This shall be My name forever, This My appellation for all eternity."

"Go and assemble the elders of Israel and say to them: the Lord, the God of your fathers, the God of Abraham, Isaac, and Jacob, has appeared to me and said, 'I have taken note of you and of what is being done to you in Egypt, and I have declared: I will take you out of the misery of Egypt to the land of the Canaanites, the Hittites, the Amorites, the Perizzites, the Hivites, and the Jebusites, to a land flowing with milk and honey.' They will listen to you; then you shall go with the elders of Israel to the king of Egypt and you shall say to him, 'The Lord, the God of the Hebrews, manifested Himself to us. Now therefore, let us go a distance of three days into the wilderness to sacrifice to the Lord our God.' Yet I know that the king of Egypt will let you go only because of a greater might. [20] So I will stretch out My hand and smite Egypt with various wonders which I will work upon them; after that he shall let you go."

---

[5] *Ehyeh-Asher-Ehyeh:* "I am what I am," based on the holy name YHWH, probably pronounced "YAH-weh." This name both reveals and conceals God's nature. It is translated here, as in the ancient synagogues, as "the Lord."
[6] *Canaanites . . . Jebusites:* native peoples of Palestine before the Israelite conquest of the Promised Land.

Crossing the Red Sea*

The dramatic climax of the Exodus is the Israelites' escape through the sea and the destruction of the Egyptians who pursued them. This tale is told at every Passover feast.

The Lord said to Moses: "Tell the Israelites to turn back and encamp before Pi-hahiroth, between Migdol and the sea, before Baal-zephon;[7] you shall encamp facing it, by the sea. Pharaoh will say of the Israelites, 'They are astray in the land; and wilderness has closed in on them.' Then I will stiffen Pharaoh's heart and he will pursue them, that I may gain glory through Pharaoh and all his host; and the Egyptians shall know that I am the Lord." And they did so.

[5] When the king of Egypt was told that the people had fled, Pharaoh and his courtiers had a change of heart about the people and said,

---

*Exodus 14:1–31.
[7] *Pi-hahiroth, Migdol, Baal-zephon:* Egyptian fortified towns. The Israelites were trapped between the Egyptians and the sea.

"What is this we have done, releasing Israel from our service?" He ordered his chariot and took his men with him; he took six hundred of his picked chariots, and the rest of the chariots of Egypt, with officers in all of them. The Lord stiffened the heart of Pharaoh king of Egypt, and he gave chase to the Israelites. As the Israelites were departing defiantly, the Egyptians gave chase to them, and all the chariot horses of Pharaoh, his horsemen, and his warriors overtook them encamped by the sea, near Pi-hahiroth, before Baal-zephon.

[10] As Pharaoh drew near, the Israelites caught sight of the Egyptians advancing upon them. Greatly frightened, the Israelites cried out to the Lord. And they said to Moses, "Was it for want of graves in Egypt that you brought us to die in the wilderness? What have you done to us, taking us out of Egypt? Is this not the very thing we told you in Egypt, saying, 'Let us be, and we will serve the Egyptians, for it is better for us to serve the Egyptians than to die in the wilderness'?" But Moses said to the people, "Have no fear. Stand by, and witness the deliverance which the Lord will work for you today; for the Egyptians whom you see today you will never see again. The Lord will battle for you; you hold your peace."

[15] Then the Lord said to Moses, "Why do you cry out to Me? Tell the Israelites to go forward. And you lift up your rod and hold out your arm over the sea and split it, so that the Israelites may march into the sea on dry ground. And I will stiffen the hearts of the Egyptians so that they go in after them; and I will gain glory through Pharaoh and all his warriors, his chariots, and his horsemen. Let the Egyptians know that I am Lord, when I gain glory through Pharaoh, his chariots, and his horsemen."

The angel of God, who had been going ahead of the Israelite army, now moved and followed behind them; and the pillar of cloud shifted from in front of them and took up a place behind them, [20] and it came between the army of the Egyptians and the army of Israel. Thus there was the cloud with the darkness, and it cast a spell upon the night, so that the one could not come near the other all through the night.

Then Moses held out his arm over the sea, and the Lord drove back the sea with a strong east wind all that night, and turned the sea into dry ground. The waters were split, and the Israelites went into the sea on dry ground, the waters forming a wall for them on their right and on their left. The Egyptians came in pursuit after them into the sea, all of Pharaoh's horses, chariots, and horsemen. At the morning watch, the Lord looked down upon the Egyptian army from a pillar of fire and cloud, and threw the Egyptian army into panic. [25] He locked the wheels of their chariots so that they moved forward with difficulty. And the Egyptians said, "Let us flee from the Israelites, for the Lord is fighting for them against Egypt."

Then the Lord said to Moses, "Hold out your arm over the sea, that the waters may come back upon the Egyptians and upon their chariots and upon their horsemen." Moses held out his arm over the sea, and at daybreak the sea returned to its normal state, and the Egyptians fled at its approach. But the Lord hurled the Egyptians into the sea. The waters turned back and covered the chariots and the horsemen—Pharaoh's entire army that followed them into the sea; not one of them remained. But the Israelites had marched through the sea on dry ground, the waters forming a wall for them on their right and on their left.

[30] Thus the Lord delivered Israel that day from the Egyptians. Israel saw the Egyptians dead on the shore of the sea. And when Israel saw the wondrous power which the Lord had wielded against the Egyptians, the people feared the Lord; they had faith in the Lord and His servant Moses.

The Covenant with Israel*

*After the Exodus, God renews the **covenant**, or pact, made with Abraham. The familiar terms of the covenant from* Genesis *17:1–8 are present here: "I will be your God"; "You will be my people"; "You must obey me." These covenant conditions are here prefaced and founded on what God did in liberating the people from Egypt.*

On the third new moon after the Israelites had gone forth from the land of Egypt, on that very day, they entered the wilderness of Sinai. Having journeyed from Rephidim, they entered the wilderness of Sinai and encamped in the wilderness. Israel encamped there in front of the mountain, and Moses went up to God. The Lord called to him from the mountain, saying, "Thus shall you say to the house of Jacob and declare to the children of Israel: 'You have seen what I did to the Egyptians, how I bore you on eagles' wings and brought you to Me. [5] Now then, if you will obey Me faithfully and keep My covenant, you shall be My treasured possession among all the peoples. Indeed, all the earth is Mine, but you shall be to Me a kingdom of priests and a holy nation.' These are the words that you shall speak to the children of Israel."

Moses came and summoned the elders of the people and put before them all that the Lord had commanded him. All the people answered as one, saying, "All that the Lord has spoken we will do." And Moses brought back the people's words to the Lord.

---

*Exodus *19:1–8.

A Psalm for David**

The story of David's rule over Israel is told in II Samuel. *Psalm 132 portrays well the significance of David for the continuing life of Judaism. Israel hopes for the coming of its Messiah from the descendants of David to take up again the rule of David. Orthodox Jews look for a literal fulfillment of this hope; more liberal Jews look for a symbolic fulfillment.*

O Lord, remember in David's favor his extreme self-denial, how he swore to the Lord, vowed to the Mighty One of Jacob, "I will not enter my house, nor will I mount my bed, I will not give sleep to my eyes, or slumber to my eyelids [5] until I find a place for the Lord, an abode for the Mighty One of Jacob."
We heard it was in Ephrath; we came upon it in the region of Jaar.[8]
Let us enter His abode, bow at His footstool.
Advance, O Lord, to Your resting-place, You and Your mighty Ark!
Your priests are clothed in triumph; Your loyal ones sing for joy.
[10] For the sake of Your servant David do not reject Your anointed one.
The Lord swore to David a firm oath that He will not renounce, "One of your own issue I will set upon your throne.
If your sons keep My covenant and My decrees that I teach them, then their sons also, to the end of time, shall sit upon your throne."
For the Lord has chosen Zion;[9] He has desired it for His seat.
"This is my resting-place for all time; here I will dwell, for I desire it.

**Psalm *132.
[8] *Ephrath:* David's home city, also known as Bethlehem; *Jaar:* where the Ark of the Covenant was kept from Samuel's time until David moved it to Jerusalem.
[9] *Zion:* Jerusalem.

[15] I will amply bless its store of food,
   give its needy their fill of bread.
I will clothe its priests in victory, its loyal ones
   shall sing for joy.

There I will make a horn sprout for David;
   I have prepared a lamp for My anointed one.
I will clothe his enemies in disgrace, while on
   him his crown shall sparkle."

Ezra's Enforcement of *Torah* Observance*

The return of the Jews from Exile in Babylon brought a new dedication to keep the Torah, *for it was widely perceived that God had used the Exile to punish them for their sins. One way that this* Torah *observance was enforced was in the divorce of Jewish men from non-Jewish wives. Marriage only within Judaism became the rule in Jewish law and was widely followed in all branches of Judaism until modern times. (See the book of* Ruth, *perhaps also written at this time, for a more liberal view of intermarriage.)*

When this was over, the officers approached me, saying, "The people of Israel and the priests and Levites have not separated themselves from the peoples of the land whose abhorrent practices are like those of the Canaanites, the Hittites, the Perizzites, the Jebusites, the Ammonites, the Moabites, the Egyptians, and the Amorites. They have taken their daughters as wives for themselves and for their sons, so that the holy seed has become intermingled with the peoples of the land; and it is the officers and prefects who have taken the lead in this trespass."

When I heard this, I tore my garment and robe, I tore hair out of my head and beard, and I sat desolate.[10] Around me gathered all who were concerned over the words of the God of Israel because of the returning exiles' trespass, while I sat desolate until the evening offering. [5] At the time of the evening offering I ended my self-affliction; still in my torn garment and robe, I got down on my knees and spread out my hands to the Lord my God, and said, "O my God, I am too ashamed and mortified to lift my face to You, O my God, for our iniquities are overwhelming and our guilt has grown high as heaven. From the time of our fathers to this very day we have been deep in guilt. Because of our iniquities, we, our kings, and our priests have been handed over to foreign kings, to the sword, to captivity, to pillage, and to humiliation, as is now the case.... [13] After all that has happened to us because of our evil deeds and our deep guilt—though You, our God, have been forbearing, less than our iniquity in that You have granted us such a remnant[11] as this—shall we once again violate Your commandments by intermarrying with these peoples who follow such abhorrent practices?[12] Will You not rage against us till we are destroyed without remnant or survivor? [15] O Lord, God of Israel, You are benevolent, for we have survived as a remnant, as is now the case. We stand before You in all our guilt, for we cannot face You on this account."

[10:1] While Ezra was praying and making confession, weeping and prostrating himself before the House of God, a very great crowd of Israelites gathered about him, men, women, and children; the people were weeping bitterly. Then Shecaniah son of Jehiel of the family of Elam spoke up and said to Ezra, "We have trespassed against our God by bringing into our homes foreign women from the peoples of the land; but there is still hope for Israel despite this. Now then, let us make a covenant with our God to expel all these women and those who have been born to them, in accordance with the bidding of

---

* *Ezra* 9:1–7, 13–15; 10:1–12.
[10] *tore my garment ... sat desolate:* all signs of mourning.
[11] *remnant:* group of survivors.
[12] *such abhorrent practices:* the immoralities and idolatry of other peoples.

the Lord and of all who are concerned over the commandment of our God, and let the Teaching be obeyed. Take action, for the responsibility is yours and we are with you. Act with resolve!"

[5] So Ezra at once put the officers of the priests and the Levites and all Israel under oath to act accordingly, and they took the oath. Then Ezra rose from his place in front of the House of God and went into the chamber of Jehohanan son of Eliashib; there, he ate no bread and drank no water, for he was in mourning over the trespass of those who had returned from exile. Then a proclamation was issued in Judah and Jerusalem that all who had returned from the exile should assemble in Jerusalem, and that anyone who did not come in three days would, by decision of the officers and elders, have his property confiscated and himself excluded from the congregation of the returning exiles.

All the men of Judah and Benjamin assembled in Jerusalem in three days; it was the ninth month, the twentieth of the month. All the people sat in the square of the House of God, trembling on account of the event and because of the rains. [10] Then Ezra the priest got up and said to them, "You have trespassed by bringing home foreign women, thus aggravating the guilt of Israel. So now, make confession to the Lord, God of your fathers, and do His will, and separate yourselves from the peoples of the land and from the foreign women." The entire congregation responded in a loud voice, "We must surely do just as you say."

TEACHING

The Oneness of God*

These words of Moses explain the commandment "You shall have no other gods beside me." In Jewish tradition, the last paragraph of this selection is known as the **Shema** *[sheh-MAH], the Hebrew word meaning "hear," which opens this section. The last sentence has produced the use of the tefillin, small boxes with the* Shema *and three other passages inside that are bound by leather straps to the hand and forehead, and the mezuzah, a small box fastened to the doorpost that has the* Shema *and* Deuteronomy *11:13–21 inside. They are reminders of Jewishness and the duty to love and serve God alone.*

"And this is the Instruction—the laws and the rules—that the Lord your God has commanded to impart to you, to be observed in the land that you are about to cross into and occupy, so that you, your children, and your children's children may revere the Lord your God and follow, as long as you live, all His laws and commandments that I enjoin upon you, to the end that you may long endure. Obey, O Israel, willingly and faithfully, that it may go well with you and that you may increase greatly a land flowing with milk and honey, as the Lord, the God of your fathers, spoke to you.

"Hear, O Israel: The Lord is our God, the Lord alone. [5] You shall love the Lord your God with all your heart and with all your soul and with all your might. Take to heart these instructions with which I charge you this day. Impress them upon your children. Recite them when you stay at home and when you are away, when you lie down and when you get up. Bind them as a sign on your hand and let them serve as a symbol on your forehead; inscribe them on the doorposts of your house and on your gates."

---

*Deuteronomy 6:1–9.

God's Creation of the World*

Two narratives tell the story of God's creation of the world: one from Priestly traditions (1:1–2:3), the other from Old Epic traditions (2:4–25). They vary in content and style. In the first, God creates an orderly cosmos out of primeval chaos, with humankind as the capstone of creation. In the second, the creation of humanity is the central topic. Notice the different ways the two stories account for the creation of woman.

When God began to create heaven and earth—the earth being unformed and void, with darkness over the surface of the deep and a wind from God sweeping over the water—God said, "Let there be light"; and there was light. God saw that the light was good, and God separated the light from the darkness. [5] God called the light Day, and the darkness He called Night. And there was evening and there was morning, a first day.

God said, "Let there be an expanse in the midst of the water, that it may separate water from water." God made the expanse, and it separated the water which was below the expanse from the water which was above the expanse. And it was so. God called the expanse Sky. And there was evening and there was morning, a second day.

God said, "Let the water below the sky be gathered into one area, that the dry land may appear." And it was so. [10] God called the dry land Earth, and the gathering of waters He called Seas. And God saw that this was good. And God said, "Let the earth sprout vegetation: seed-bearing plants, fruit trees of every kind on earth that bear fruit with the seed in it." And it was so. The earth brought forth vegetation: seed-bearing plants of every kind, and trees of every kind bearing fruit with the seed in it. And God saw that this was good. And there was evening and there was morning, a third day.

God said, "Let there be lights in the expanse of the sky to separate day from night; they shall serve as signs for the set times—the days and the years; [15] and they shall serve as lights in the expanse of the sky to shine upon the earth." And it was so. God made the two great lights, the greater light to dominate the day and the lesser light to dominate the night, and the stars. And God set them in the expanse of the sky to shine upon the earth, to dominate the day and the night, and to separate light from darkness. And God saw that this was good. And there was evening and there was morning, a fourth day.

[20] God said, "Let the waters bring forth swarms of living creatures, and birds that fly above the earth across the expanse of the sky." God created the great sea monsters, and all the living creatures of every kind that creep, which the waters brought forth in swarms, and all the winged birds of every kind. And God saw that this was good. God blessed them, saying, "Be fertile and increase, fill the waters in the seas, and let the birds increase on the earth." And there was evening and there was morning, a fifth day.

God said, "Let the earth bring forth every kind of living creature: cattle, creeping things, and wild beasts of every kind." And it was so. [25] God made wild beasts of every kind and cattle of every kind, and all kinds of creeping things of the earth. And God saw that this was good. And God said, "Let us make man in our[13] image, after our likeness. They shall rule the fish of the sea, the birds of the sky, the cattle, the whole earth, and all the creeping things that creep on earth." And God created man in His image, in the image of God He created him; male and female He created them. God blessed them and God said to them, "Be fertile and increase, fill the earth and master it; and rule the fish of the sea, the birds of the sky, and all the living things that creep on earth."

---

*Genesis 1:1–31; 2:1–9, 15–25.
[13] *us, our:* God and the beings of the heavenly court. There is probably no idea of the plurality of God here.

God said, "See, I give you every seed-bearing plant that is upon all the earth, and every tree that has seed-bearing fruit; they shall be yours for food. [30] And to all the animals on land, to all the birds of the sky, and to everything that creeps on earth, in which there is the breath of life, all the green plants for food." And it was so. And God saw all that He had made, and found it very good. And there was evening and there was morning, the sixth day.

[2:1] The heaven and the earth were finished, and all their array. On the seventh day God finished the work that He had been doing, and He ceased on the seventh day from all the work that He had done. And God blessed the seventh day and declared it holy, because on it God ceased from all the work of creation that He had done.[14] Such is the story of heaven and earth when they were created.

[2:4, the second creation account] When the Lord God made earth and heaven—when no shrub of the field was yet on earth and no grasses of the field had yet sprouted, because the Lord God had not sent rain upon the earth and there was no man to till the soil, but a flow would well up from the ground and water the whole surface of the earth—the Lord God formed man from the dust of the earth. He blew into his nostrils the breath of life, and man became a living being.

The Lord God planted a garden in Eden, in the east, and placed there the man whom He had formed. And from the ground the Lord God caused to grow every tree that was pleasing to the sight and good for food, with the tree of life in the middle of the garden, and the tree of knowledge of good and bad. . . .

[2:15] The Lord God took the man and placed him in the garden of Eden, to till it and tend it. And the Lord God commanded the man, saying, "Of every tree of the garden you are free to eat; but as for the tree of knowledge of good and bad, you must not eat of it; for as soon as you eat of it, you shall die."

The Lord God said, "It is not good for man to be alone; I will make a fitting helper for him." And the Lord God formed out of the earth all the wild beasts and all the birds of the sky, and brought them to the man to see what he would call them; and whatever the man called each living creature, that would be its name. [20] And the man gave names to all the cattle and to the birds of the sky and to all the wild beasts; but for Adam no fitting helper was found. So the Lord God cast a deep sleep upon the man; and, while he slept, He took one of his ribs and closed up the flesh at that spot. And the Lord God fashioned the rib that He had taken from the man into a woman; and He brought her to the man. Then the man said,

"This one at last
Is bone of my bones
And flesh of my flesh.
This one shall be called Woman,
For from man was she taken."

Hence a man leaves his father and mother and clings to his wife, so that they become one flesh. [25] The two of them were naked, the man and his wife, yet they felt no shame.

---

[14] *God blessed the seventh day . . . done:* an allusion to the law of rest and renewal on the seventh day, the Sabbath.

The Revolt of Humanity*

Humans fall into sin by rebelling against God's command. Tempted by the serpent (in this story a wily creature, but in later Jewish and then Christian and Islamic tradition thought to be the devil in disguise), first the woman and then the man disobey God. God punishes all the guilty parties in various ways, but humanity's chief punishment is being driven out of the Garden. Orthodox Jews, like fundamentalist Christians and traditional Muslims, regard this as a fully historical event. Many Conservative and most

---

* Genesis 3:1–24.

Reform Jews, like more liberal Christians, see it as mythic—not historical but religiously true nonetheless.

Now the serpent was the shrewdest of all the wild beasts that the Lord God had made. He said to the woman, "Did God really say: 'You shall not eat of any tree of the garden'?" The woman replied to the serpent, "We may eat of the fruit of the other trees of the garden. It is only about fruit of the tree in the middle of the garden that God said: 'You shall not eat of it or touch it, lest you die.'" And the serpent said to the woman, "You are not going to die, [5] but God knows that as soon as you eat of it your eyes will be opened and you will be like divine beings who know good and bad." When the woman saw that the tree was good for eating and a delight to the eyes, and that the tree was desirable as a source of wisdom, she took of its fruit and ate. She also gave some to her husband, and he ate. Then the eyes of both of them were opened and they perceived that they were naked;[15] and they sewed together fig leaves and made themselves loincloths.

They heard the sound of the Lord God moving about in the garden at the breezy time of day; and the man and his wife hid from the Lord God among the trees of the garden. The Lord God called out to the man and said to him, "Where are you?" [10] He replied, "I heard the sound of You in the garden, and I was afraid because I was naked, so I hid." Then He asked, "Who told you that you were naked? Did you eat of the tree from which I had forbidden you to eat?" The man said, "The woman You put at my side—she gave me of the tree, and I ate." And the Lord God said to the woman, "What is this you have done?" The woman replied, "The serpent duped me, and I ate." Then the Lord God said to the serpent,

"Because you did this,
More cursed shall you be
Than all cattle
And all the wild beasts:
On your belly shall you crawl
And dirt shall you eat
All the days of your life.

[15] I will put enmity
Between you and the woman,
And between your offspring and hers;
They shall strike at your head,
And you shall strike at their heel."

And to the woman He said,
"I will make most severe
Your pangs in childbearing;
In pain shall you bear children.
Yet your urge shall be for your husband,
And he shall rule over you."[16]

To Adam He said, "Because you did as your wife said and ate of the tree about which I commanded you, 'You shall not eat of it,'
Cursed be the ground because of you;
By toil shall you eat of it
All the days of your life:
Thorns and thistles shall it sprout for you.
But your food shall be the grasses of the field;
By the sweat of your brow
Shall you get bread to eat,
Until you return to the ground—
For from it you were taken.
For dust you are,
And to dust you shall return."

[20] The man named his wife Eve, because she was the mother of all the living. And the Lord God made garments of skins for Adam and his wife, and clothed them.

And the Lord God said, "Now that the man has become like one of us, knowing good and bad, what if he should stretch out his hand and take also from the tree of life and eat, and live forever." So the Lord God banished him from the garden of Eden, to till the soil from which he was taken. He drove the man out, and stationed east of the garden of Eden the cherubim[17] and the fiery ever-turning sword, to guard the way to the tree of life.

---

[15] *naked:* Knowledge of their nakedness is a symbol of their loss of goodness and innocence.

[16] *he shall rule over you:* The original equality between man and woman is lost; the husband now has authority over the wife.

[17] *cherubim:* not "cherubs" but fearsome six-winged angels, half human and half lion.

Prayer for Divine Deliverance*

The Psalms show a strong personal relationship to God as well as a strong distinction between good and evil, both characteristic of Israelite religion. This psalm, a typical prayer for deliverance, first describes the difficulties of the believer and ends with expression of the believer's trust in God to deliver.

Give ear to my speech, O Lord; consider my utterance.
Heed the sound of my cry, my king and God, for I pray to You.
Hear my voice, O Lord, at daybreak; at daybreak I plead before You, and wait.
[5] For You are not a God who desires wickedness; evil cannot abide with You; wanton men cannot endure in Your sight.
You detest all evildoers; You doom those who speak lies; murderous, deceitful men the Lord abhors.
But I, through Your abundant love, enter Your house; I bow down in awe at Your holy temple.
O Lord, lead me along Your righteousness because of my watchful foes; make Your way straight before me.
[10] For there is no sincerity on their lips; their heart is malice; their throat is an open grave; their tongue slippery.
Condemn them, O God; let them fall by their own devices; cast them out for their many crimes, for they defy You.
But let all who take refuge in You rejoice, ever jubilant as You shelter them; and let those who love Your name exult in You.
For You surely bless the righteous man, O Lord, encompassing him with favor like a shield.

---
*Psalm 5.

The Messianic King**

This prophetic oracle promises a deliverer of Israel to come from among the descendants of King David. He will bring forth light, joy, peace, and justice. Orthodox Jews look forward to a literal fulfillment of this promise; others interpret it in the sense of progress toward justice in Judaism or in all of humanity.

But a shoot shall grow out of the stump of Jesse,
A twig shall sprout from his stock.
The spirit of the Lord shall alight upon him:
A spirit of wisdom and insight,
A spirit of counsel and valor,
A spirit of devotion and reverence for the Lord.
He shall sense the truth by his reverence for the Lord:
He shall not judge by what his eyes behold,
Nor decide by what his ears perceive.
Thus he shall judge the poor with equity
And decide with justice for the lowly of the land.
He shall strike down a land with the rod of his mouth
And slay the wicked with the breath of his lips.
[5] Justice shall be the girdle of his loins,
And faithfulness the girdle of his waist.
The wolf shall dwell with the lamb,
The leopard lie down with the kid;
The calf, the beast of prey, and the fatling together,
With a little boy to herd them.
The cow and the bear shall graze,
Their young shall lie down together;
And the lion, like the ox, shall eat straw.
A babe shall play

**Isaiah 11:1–9.

Over a viper's hole
And an infant pass his hand
Over an adder's den.
In all of My sacred mount
Nothing evil or vile shall be done;
For the land shall be filled with devotion to
   the Lord
As water covers the sea.

The Final Judgment of the World*

The apocalyptic view of the world and history can be richly symbolic, with dreams and visions featuring mixed-form animals, cosmic battles, and other fantastic events. In this passage, the winged lion represents the Babylonian empire, the bear is the Medes, the four-headed leopard is the Persians, and the dragon is the Greeks. The ten horns are the ten rulers succeeding Alexander in the Near East, and the "little horn" is the Syrian king Antiochus Epiphanes, whose brutal persecution of the Jews precipitated a Jewish revolt and whose destruction is foretold here. Although the rich symbolism of apocalyptic scripture did not carry over into later Judaism, an apocalyptic view of the main events at the end of time did: God will someday bring history to an end and judge all peoples and nations.

In the first year of King Belshazzar of Babylon, Daniel saw a dream and a vision of his mind in bed; afterward he wrote down the dream. Beginning the account, Daniel related the following: "In my vision at night, I saw the four winds of heaven stirring up the great sea. Four mighty beasts different from each other emerged from the sea. The first was like a lion but had eagles' wings. As I looked on, its wings were plucked off, and it was lifted off the ground and set on its feet like a man and given the mind of a man. [5] Then I saw a second, different beast, which was like a bear but raised on one side, and with three fangs in its mouth among its teeth; it was told, 'Arise, eat much meat.' After that, as I looked on, there was another one, like a leopard, and it had on its back four wings like those of a bird; the beast had four heads, and dominion was given to it. After that, as I looked on in the night vision, there was a fourth beast—fearsome, dreadful, and very powerful, with great iron teeth—that devoured and crushed, and stamped the remains with its feet. It was different from all the other beasts which had gone before it; and it had ten horns. While I was gazing upon these horns, a new little horn sprouted up among them; three of the older horns were uprooted to make room for it. There were eyes in this horn like those of a man, and a mouth that spoke arrogantly. As I looked on,

Thrones were set in place,
And the Ancient of Days[18] took His seat.
His garment was like white snow,
And the hair of His head was like lamb's wool.
His throne was tongues of flame;
Its wheels were blazing fire.
[10] A river of fire streamed forth before Him;
Thousands upon thousands served Him;
Myriads upon myriads attended Him;
The court sat and the books were opened.[19]

I looked on. Then, because of the arrogant words that the horn spoke, the beast was killed as I looked on; its body was destroyed and it was consigned to the flames. The dominion of the other beasts was taken away, but an extension of life was given to them for a time and season. As I looked on, in the night vision,

One like a human being[20]

---

*Daniel 7:1–14.
[18] *the Ancient of Days:* God, the Eternal One.
[19] *books were opened:* books in which the deeds of all people or their eternal destiny are written.
[20] *One like a human being:* This human figure represents the faithful Jews; traditionally this figure is identified as the Messiah.

Came with the clouds of heaven;
He reached the Ancient of Days
And was presented to Him.
Dominion, glory, and kingship were given to him;
All peoples and nations of every language must serve him.
His dominion is an everlasting dominion that shall not pass away,
And his kingship, one that shall not be destroyed."

Resurrection of the Dead*

One prominent element of apocalyptic scripture is the resurrection of the dead, God's summoning them out of their graves with new, eternal bodies to face a judgment that determines their eternal fate. Although this short passage says that "many" will arise, soon the idea is established in Judaism that all will arise. This belief is held firmly by the Orthodox; other Jews interpret it metaphorically or discard it. Here, God speaks to Daniel.

"At that time, the great prince, Michael, who stands beside the sons of your people,[21] will appear. It will be a time of trouble, the like of which has never been since the nation came into being. At that time, your people will be rescued, all who are found inscribed in the book. Many of those that sleep in the dust of the earth will awake, some to eternal life, others to reproaches, to everlasting abhorrence. And the knowledgeable will be radiant like the bright expanse of sky, and those who lead the many to righteousness will be like the stars forever and ever."

---

*Daniel 12:1–3.
[21] *Michael:* the guardian angel of Israel.

ETHICS

The Ten Commandments**

This is the first section of the law given by God to Israel at Mount Sinai after the Exodus from Egypt. The first group of commandments, up through false swearing, deals with humanity's duty to God; the last group deals with person-to-person obligations. Of all the ancient law codes, the Ten Commandments *(or the* **Decalogue***) is probably the most influential in Western religion and culture. The numbering of the commands varies among Jews and Christians, but all agree on the total of ten.*

God spoke all these words, saying:

I the Lord am your God who brought you out of the land of Egypt, the house of bondage: You shall have no other gods beside Me.

You shall not make for yourself a sculptured image, or any likeness of what is in the heavens above, or on the earth below, or in the waters under the earth. [5] You shall not bow down to them or serve them. For I the Lord your God am an impassioned God, visiting the guilt of the parents upon the children, upon the third and upon the fourth generations of those who reject Me, but showing kindness to the thousandth generation of those who love Me and keep My commandments.

**Exodus 20:1–14.

You shall not swear falsely by the name of the Lord your God; for the Lord will not clear one who swears falsely by His name.

Remember the sabbath day and keep it holy. Six days you shall labor and do all your work, [10] but the seventh day is a sabbath of the Lord your God: you shall not do any work—you, your son or daughter, your male or female slave, or your cattle, or the stranger who is within your settlements. For in six days the Lord made heaven and earth and sea, and all that is in them, and He rested on the seventh day; therefore the Lord blessed the sabbath day and hallowed it.

Honor your father and your mother, that you may long endure on the land that the Lord your God is assigning to you.

You shall not murder.

You shall not commit adultery.

You shall not steal.

You shall not bear false witness against your neighbor.

You shall not covet your neighbor's house: you shall not covet your neighbor's wife, or his male or female slave, or his ox or his ass, or anything that is your neighbor's.

Laws on Slaves, Violence, and Property*

Following the Ten Commandments *is a section of laws also traditionally traced to God's giving of the law to Moses. The laws on slavery reflect the humanitarian concern of Israel in the midst of a slave-owning and patriarchal culture. Although both male and female Hebrew slaves are given some protections, the male has more. The time limits on slavery imply that it is not the proper condition of humankind, or at least of Israelites. In the laws on violence, a distinction is made between intentional and unintentional acts. The law of retribution, "an eye for an eye," is often seen today as a crude and violent method of justice, but it is a humane limitation on the continual violence of blood feuds and private revenge. This selection closes with laws that protect the more vulnerable and helpless members of society.*

These are the rules that you shall set before them:

When you acquire a Hebrew slave, he shall serve six years; in the seventh year he shall go free, without payment. If he came single, he shall leave single; if he had a wife, his wife shall leave with him. If his master gave him a wife, and she has borne him children, the wife and her children shall belong to the master, and he shall leave alone. [5] But if the slave declares, "I love my master, and my wife and children: I do not wish to go free," his master shall take him before God.[22] He shall be brought to the door or the doorpost, and his master shall pierce his ear with an awl; and he shall then remain his slave for life.

When a man sells his daughter as a slave, she shall not be freed as male slaves are. If she proves to be displeasing to her master, who designated her for himself, he must let her be redeemed;[23] he shall not have the right to sell her to outsiders, since he broke faith with her. And if he designated her for his son, he shall deal with her as is the practice with free maidens. [10] If he marries another, he must not withhold from this one her food, her clothing, or her conjugal rights. If he fails her in these three ways, she shall go free, without payment.

He who fatally strikes a man shall be put to death. If he did not do it by design, but it came about by an act of God, I will assign you a place to which he can flee.[24]

Exodus 21:1–36; 22:15–26.

[22] *take him before God:* that is, at the sacred doorpost of the house.

[23] *redeemed:* bought from slavery by a relative or other interested party.

[24] *a place to . . . flee:* a place of safety in which to take refuge, often at an altar of God; hence our word "sanctuary" in the sense of "safe refuge."

When a man schemes against another and kills him treacherously, you shall take him from My very altar to be put to death.

[15] He who strikes his father or his mother shall be put to death.

He who kidnaps a man—whether he has sold him or is still holding him—shall be put to death.

He who insults his father or mother shall be put to death.

When men quarrel and one strikes the other with stone or fist, and he does not die but has to take to his bed—if he then gets up and walks outdoors upon his staff, the assailant shall go unpunished, except that he must pay for his idleness and his cure.

[20] When a man strikes his slave, male or female, with a rod, and he dies there and then, he must be avenged. But if he survives a day or two, he is not to be avenged, since he is the other's property.

When men fight, and one of them pushes a pregnant woman and a miscarriage results, but no other damage ensues, the one responsible shall be fined according as the woman's husband may exact from him, the payment to be based on reckoning. But if other damage ensues, the penalty shall be life for life, eye for eye, tooth for tooth, hand for hand, foot for foot, [25] burn for burn, wound for wound, bruise for bruise.

When a man strikes the eye of his slave, male or female, and destroys it, he shall let him go free on account of his eye. If he knocks out the tooth of his slave, male or female, he shall let him go free on account of his tooth.

When an ox gores a man or a woman to death, the ox shall be stoned and its flesh shall not be eaten, but the owner of the ox is not to be punished. If, however, that ox has been in the habit of goring, and its owner, though warned, has failed to guard it, and it kills a man or a woman—the ox shall be stoned and its owner, too, shall be put to death. [30] If ransom is laid upon him, he must pay whatever is laid upon him to redeem his life. So, too, if it gores a minor, male or female, the owner shall be dealt with according to the same rule. But if the ox gores a slave, male or female, he shall pay thirty shekels of silver to the master, and the ox shall be stoned.

When a man opens a pit, or digs a pit and does not cover it, and an ox or an ass falls into it, the one responsible for the pit must make restitution; he shall pay the price to the owner, but shall keep the dead animal.

[35] When a man's ox injures his neighbor's ox and it dies, they shall sell the live ox and divide its price; they shall also divide the dead animal. If, however, it is known that the ox was in the habit of goring, and its owner has failed to guard it, he must restore ox for ox, but shall keep the dead animal. . . .

[22:15[25]] If a man seduces a virgin for whom the bride-price[26] has not been paid, and lies with her, he must make her his wife by payment of a bride-price. If her father refuses to give her to him, he must still weigh out silver in accordance with the bride-price for virgins.

You shall not tolerate a sorceress.

Whoever lies with a beast shall be put to death.

Whoever sacrifices to a god other than the Lord alone shall be proscribed.[27]

[20] You shall not wrong a stranger or oppress him, for you were strangers in the land of Egypt.

You shall not ill-treat any widow or orphan. If you do mistreat them, I will heed their outcry as soon as they cry out to Me, and My anger shall blaze forth and I will put you to the sword, and your own wives shall become widows and your children orphans.

If you lend money to My people, to the poor among you, do not act toward them as a creditor: exact no interest from them. [25] If you take your neighbor's garment in pledge, you must return it to him before the sun sets; it is his only clothing, the sole covering for his skin. In what else shall he sleep? Therefore, if he cries out to Me, I will pay heed, for I am compassionate.

---

[25] The verse numbers differ by one between this translation and the Christian translations of this passage.
[26] *bride-price:* the husband's payment to the family of the bride.
[27] *proscribed:* put to death.

Justice for All*

Israel's strong sense of equal justice and correct judicial procedure is shown in this selection.

You must not carry false rumors; you shall not join hands with the guilty to act as a malicious witness. You shall neither side with the mighty to do wrong—you shall not give perverse testimony in a dispute so as to pervert it in favor of the mighty—nor shall you show deference to a poor man in his dispute.

When you encounter your enemy's ox or ass wandering, you must take it back to him. When you see the ass of your enemy lying under its burden and would refrain from raising it, you must nevertheless raise it with him.

You shall not subvert the rights of your needy in their disputes. Keep far from a false charge; do not bring death on those who are innocent and in the right, for I will not acquit the wrongdoer. Do not take bribes, for bribes blind the clear-sighted and upset the pleas of those who are in the right.

You shall not oppress a stranger,[28] for you know the feelings of the stranger, having yourselves been strangers in the land of Egypt.

Exodus 23:1–9.
[28] *stranger:* resident alien in the land.

Holy War**

In holy war, God fights with and for the people against their enemies during the conquest of the Promised Land. The Jewish Bible limits holy war to this conquest. The people and cities of Canaan are to be sacrificed to God by utter destruction. Notice that verses 10 through 14 specify a more humane method of warfare against non-Canaanite opponents. The last section sets limits on the destruction of the natural environment during warfare.

When you take the field against your enemies, and see horses and chariots—forces larger than yours—have no fear of them, for the Lord your God, who brought you from the land of Egypt, is with you. Before you join battle, the priest shall come forward and address the troops. He shall say to them, "Hear, O Israel: You are about to join battle with your enemy. Let not your courage falter. Do not be in fear, or in panic, or in dread of them. For it is the Lord your God who marches with you to do battle for you against your enemy, to bring you victory."

[5] Then the officials shall address the troops, as follows: "Is there anyone who has built a new house but has not dedicated it? Let him go back to his home, lest he die in battle and another dedicate it. Is there anyone who has planted a vineyard but has never harvested it? Let him go back to his home, lest he die in battle and another harvest it. Is there anyone who has paid the bride-price for a wife, but who has not yet married her? Let him go back to his home, lest he die in battle and another marry her." The officials shall go on addressing the troops and say, "Is there anyone afraid and disheartened? Let him go back to his home, lest the courage of his comrades flag like his." When the officials have finished addressing the troops, army commanders shall assume command of the troops.

[10] When you approach a town to attack it, you shall offer it terms of peace. If it responds

---

***Deuteronomy* 20:1–20.

peaceably and lets you in, all the people present there shall serve you at forced labor. If it does not surrender to you, but would join battle with you, you shall lay siege to it; and when the Lord your God delivers it into your hand, you shall put all its males to the sword. You may, however, take as your booty the women, the children, the livestock, and everything in the town—all its spoil—and enjoy the use of the spoil of your enemy, which the Lord your God gives you.

[15] Thus you shall deal with all towns that lie very far from you, towns that do not belong to nations hereabout. In the towns of the latter peoples, however, which the Lord your God is giving you as a heritage, you shall not let a soul remain alive. No, you must proscribe them—the Hittites and the Amorites, the Canaanites and the Perizzites, the Hivites and the Jebusites—as the Lord your God has commanded you, lest they lead you into doing all the abhorrent things that they have done for their gods and you stand guilty before the Lord your God.

When in your war against a city you have to besiege it a long time in order to capture it, you must not destroy its trees, wielding the ax against them. You may eat of them, but you must not cut them down. Are trees of the field human to withdraw before you into the besieged city? [20] Only trees that you know do not yield food may be destroyed; you may cut them down for constructing siegeworks against the city that is waging war on you, until it has been reduced.

Sexual Love*

The finest literary testimony to sexual love in the Bible *is the* Song of Songs, *which is modeled after Egyptian love poetry. Its poems are a dialogue between a man, traditionally thought to be Solomon, and a woman who take full delight in the emotional and physical dimensions of love. Later Judaism, as well as Christianity, made this book symbolic of the love of God for people. (The notes in brackets are not in scripture text but are explanations by the editors of the* Tanakh *translation.)*

[The woman speaks:] Oh, give me of the kisses
    of your mouth,
For your love is more delightful than wine.
Your ointments yield a sweet fragrance,
Your name is like finest oil—
Therefore do maidens love you.
Draw me after you, let us run
The king has brought me to his chambers.
Let us delight and rejoice in your love,
Savoring it more than wine—
Like new wine they love you!

[5] I am dark, but comely,[29]
O daughters of Jerusalem—
Like the tents of Kedar,
Like the pavilions of Solomon.
Don't stare at me because I am swarthy,
Because the sun has gazed upon me.
My mother's sons quarreled with me,
They made me guard the vineyards;
My own vineyard I did not guard.

Tell me, you whom I love so well;
Where do you pasture your sheep?
Where do you rest them at noon?
Let me not be as one who strays
Beside the flocks of your fellows.
If you do not know, O fairest of women,
Go follow the tracks of the sheep,
And graze your kids
By the tents of the shepherds.

[The man speaks:] I have likened you, my
    darling,
To a mare in Pharaoh's chariots:
[10] Your cheeks are comely with plaited
    wreaths,

Song of Songs 1:1–2:17.
[29] The *New Revised Standard Version* of the *Bible* translates this, "I am black and beautiful."

Your neck with strings of jewels.
We will add wreaths of gold
To your spangles of silver.

[The woman speaks:] While the king was on his couch,
My nard gave forth its fragrance.
My beloved to me is a bag of myrrh
Lodged between my breasts.
My beloved to me is a spray of henna blooms
From the vineyards of En-gedi.

[15, The man and woman exchange short compliments:] Ah, you are fair, my darling,
Ah, you are fair,
With your dove-like eyes.
And you, my beloved, are handsome,
Beautiful indeed
Our couch is in a bower;
Cedars are the beams of our house,
Cypresses the rafters.
[2:1] I am a rose of Sharon,
A lily of the valleys.

[The woman speaks:] Like a lily among thorns,
So is my darling among the maidens.
Like an apple tree among trees of the forest,
So is my beloved among the youths.
I delight to sit in his shade,
And his fruit is sweet to my mouth.
He brought me to the banquet room
And his banner of love was over me.
[5] "Sustain me with raisin cakes,
Refresh me with apples,
For I am faint with love."
His left hand was under my head,
His right arm embraced me.
I adjure you, O maidens of Jerusalem,
By gazelles or by hinds of the field:
Do not wake or rouse
Love until it please!

Hark, My beloved!
There he comes,
Leaping over mountains,
Bounding over hills.
My beloved is like a gazelle
Or like a young stag.
There he stands behind our wall,
Gazing through the window,
Peering through the lattice.
[10] My beloved spoke thus to me,
"Arise, my darling;
My fair one, come away!
For now the winter is past,
The rains are over and gone.
The blossoms have appeared in the land,
The time of pruning has come;
The song of the turtledove
Is heard in our land.
The green figs form on the fig tree,
The vines in blossom give off fragrance.
Arise, my darling;
My fair one, come away!"

[The man speaks:]
"O my dove, in the cranny of the rocks,
Hidden by the cliff,
Let me see your face,
Let me hear your voice;
For your voice is sweet
And your face is comely."
[15] Catch us the foxes,
The little foxes
That ruin the vineyards—
For our vineyard is in blossom.

[The woman speaks:] My beloved is mine
And I am his
Who browses among the lilies.
When the day blows gently
And the shadows flee,
Set out, my beloved,
Swift as a gazelle
Or a young stag,
For the hills of spices!

God's Call to an Unfaithful People*

In this oracle, Amos pronounces God's judgment on the unfaithful people of Israel. They enjoy worship and sacrifice to God but have neglected the basic commands of the law: justice and mercy. They have ignored God's chastisements, listed here. Now God promises a severe final punishment, indicated by the ominous words "Prepare to meet your God."

Hear this word, you cows of Bashan
On the hill of Samaria—
Who defraud the poor,
Who rob the needy;
Who say to your husbands,
"Bring, and let's carouse!"
My Lord God swears by His holiness:
Behold, days are coming upon you
When you will be carried off in baskets,
And, to the last one, in fish baskets,
And taken out—
Each one through a breach straight
  ahead—
And flung on the refuse heap[30]
—declares the Lord.

Come to Bethel and transgress;
To Gilgal, and transgress even more:[31]
Present your sacrifices the next
  morning
And your tithes on the third day;
[5] And burn a thank offering of leavened
  bread;
And proclaim freewill offerings loudly.
For you love that sort of thing,
  O Israelites
—declares my Lord God.

I, on My part, have given you
Cleanness of teeth in all your towns,
And lack of food in all your
  settlements.
Yet you did not turn back to Me
—declares the Lord.

I therefore withheld the rain from you
Three months before harvest time:
I would make it rain on one town
And not on another;
One field would be rained upon
While another on which it did not rain
Would wither.
So two or three towns would wander
To a single town to drink water,
But their thirst would not be slaked.
Yet you did not turn back to Me
—declares the Lord.

I scourged you with blight and
  mildew;
Repeatedly your gardens and
  vineyards,
Your fig trees and olive trees
Were devoured by locusts.
Yet you did not turn back to Me
—declares the Lord.

[10] I sent against you pestilence
In the manner of Egypt;
I slew your young men with the sword,
Together with your captured horses,
And I made the stench of your armies
Rise in your very nostrils.
Yet you did not turn back to Me
—declares the Lord.

I have wrought destruction among you
As when God destroyed Sodom and
  Gomorrah;[32]
You have become like a brand plucked from
  burning.
Yet you have not turned back to Me
—declares the Lord.

---

*Amos 4:1–13.
[30] These predictions look forward to the destruction of the northern kingdom of Israel by Assyria in 721 B.C.E.
[31] *Bethel, Gilgal:* Israelite cities with sanctuaries. Notice the biting sarcasm of this section.
[32] *Sodom and Gomorrah:* cities destroyed for their wickedness; see *Genesis* 19:1–29.

Assuredly,
Because I am doing that to you,
Even so will I act toward you,
   O Israel—
Prepare to meet your God, O Israel!
Behold,

He who formed the mountains,
And created the wind,
And has told man what His wish is,
Who turns blackness into daybreak,
And treads upon the high places of the earth—
His name is the Lord, the God of Hosts.

Two Views of Wisdom*

Of all the main types of literature in the Hebrew scriptures, the most international in form and content is the wisdom literature. In the first passage, from the beginning of Proverbs, *the first nine verses describe what wisdom can do for its followers—lead to knowledge, mental power, and moral strength. Notice in verse 20 and following verses the personification of wisdom as a woman. The second passage, from* Ecclesiastes, *gives a more pessimistic outlook on wisdom. Here it cannot answer life's riddles.* Proverbs *and* Ecclesiastes *are attributed to King Solomon, who had an ancient reputation as a sage.*

[*Proverbs* 1:1] The proverbs of Solomon, son of David, king of Israel:

For learning wisdom and discipline;
For understanding words of discernment;
For acquiring the discipline for success,
Righteousness, justice, and equity;
For endowing the simple with shrewdness,
The young with knowledge and foresight.
[5]—The wise man, hearing them, will gain more wisdom;
The discerning man will learn to be adroit;
For understanding proverb and epigram,
The words of the wise and their riddles.
The fear of the Lord is the beginning of knowledge;
Fools despise wisdom and discipline.
My son, heed the discipline of your father,
And do not forsake the instruction of your mother;
For they are a graceful wreath upon your head,
A necklace about your throat. . . .

[20] Wisdom cries aloud in the streets,
Raises her voice in the squares.
At the head of the busy streets she calls;
At the entrance of the gates, in the city, she speaks out:
"How long will you simple ones love simplicity,
You scoffers be eager to scoff,
You dullards hate knowledge?
You are indifferent to my rebuke;
I will now speak my mind to you,
And let you know my thoughts.
Since you refused me when I called,
And paid no heed when I extended my hand,
[25] You spurned all my advice,
And would not hear my rebuke,
I will laugh at your calamity,
And mock when terror comes upon you,
When terror comes like a disaster,
And calamity arrives like a whirlwind,
When trouble and distress come upon you.
Then they shall call me but I will not answer;
They shall seek me but not find me.
Because they hated knowledge,
And did not choose fear of the Lord,
[30] They refused my advice,
And disdained all my rebukes,
They shall eat the fruit of their ways,
And have their fill of their own counsels.

---

*Proverbs 1:1–9, 20–33; Ecclesiastes 1:1–9.

The tranquillity of the simple will kill them,
And the complacency of dullards will destroy them.
But he who listens to me will dwell in safety,
Untroubled by the terror of misfortune."

[*Ecclesiastes* 1:1] The words of Koheleth son of David, king in Jerusalem:

Utter futility!—said Koheleth—
Utter futility! All is futile!
What real value is there for a man
In all the gains he makes beneath the sun?

One generation goes, another comes,
But the earth remains the same forever.
[5] The sun rises, and the sun sets—
And glides back to where it rises.
Southward blowing,
Turning northward,
Ever turning blows the wind;
On its rounds the wind returns.
All streams flow into the sea,
Yet the sea is never full;
To the place [from] which they flow
The streams flow back again.
All such things are wearisome:
No man can ever state them;
The eye never has enough of seeing,
Nor the ear enough of hearing.
Only that shall happen
Which has happened,
Only that occur
Which has occurred;
There is nothing new
Beneath the sun!

The Virtuous Wife*

Given the context of a patriarchal society, the ideal wife depicted here is remarkably independent, appreciated for her abilities and relationships rather than for her beauty or her ability to bear children. The somewhat disjointed style of this poem is the result of its unique composition: In Hebrew, each line begins with a successive letter of the Hebrew alphabet.

What a rare find is a capable wife!
Her worth is far beyond that of rubies.
Her husband puts his confidence in her,
And lacks no good thing.
She is good to him, never bad,
All the days of her life.
She looks for wool and flax,
And sets her hand to them with a will.
She is like a merchant fleet,
Bringing her food from afar.
[15] She rises while it is still night,
And supplies provisions for her household,
The daily fare of her maids.
She sets her mind on an estate and acquires it;
She plants a vineyard by her own labors.
She girds herself with strength,
And performs her tasks with vigor.
She sees that her business thrives;
Her lamp never goes out at night.
She sets her hand to the distaff;
Her fingers work the spindle.
[20] She gives generously to the poor;
Her hands are stretched out to the needy.
She is not worried for her household because of snow,
For her whole household is dressed in crimson.
She makes covers for herself;
Her clothing is linen and purple.
Her husband is prominent in the gates,
As he sits among the elders of the land.
She makes cloth and sells it,
And offers a girdle to the merchant.
[25] She is clothed with strength and splendor;

---

*Proverbs 31:10–31.

She looks to the future cheerfully.
Her mouth is full of wisdom,
Her tongue with kindly teaching.
She oversees the activities of her
　　household
And never eats the bread of idleness.
Her children declare her happy;
Her husband praises her,

"Many women have done well,
But you surpass them all."
[30] Grace is deceptive,
Beauty is illusory;
It is for her fear of the Lord
That a woman is to be praised.
Extol her for the fruit of her hand,
And let her works praise her in the gates.

ORGANIZATION

The Ordination of Priests*

This passage outlines the sacrificial ceremony by which priests are ordained—that is, consecrated to the service of God. The ceremony here indicates the role of priests in Israel as intermediaries between God and the people. God here speaks to Moses ("you").

This is what you shall do to them in consecrating them to serve Me as priests: Take a young bull of the herd and two rams without blemish; also unleavened bread, unleavened cakes with oil mixed in, and unleavened wafers spread with oil—make these of choice wheat flour. Place these in one basket and present them in the basket, along with the bull and the two rams. Lead Aaron and his sons up to the entrance of the Tent of Meeting, and wash them with water. [5] Then take the vestments, and clothe Aaron with the tunic, the robe of the ephod [the main priestly garment], the ephod, and the breastpiece, and gird him with the decorated band of the ephod. Put the headdress on his head, and place the holy diadem upon the headdress. Take the anointing oil and pour it on his head and anoint him. Then bring his sons forward; clothe them with tunics and wind turbans upon them. And gird both Aaron and his sons with sashes. And so they shall have priesthood as their right for all time.

You shall then ordain Aaron and his sons. [10] Lead the bull up to the front of the Tent of Meeting, and let Aaron and his sons lay their hands upon the head of the bull. Slaughter the bull before the Lord, at the entrance of the Tent of Meeting, and take some of the bull's blood and put it on the horns of the altar with your finger; then pour out the rest of the blood at the base of the altar. Take all the fat that covers the entrails, the protuberance on the liver, and the two kidneys with the fat on them, and turn them into smoke upon the altar. The rest of the flesh of the bull, its hide, and its dung shall be put to the fire outside the camp; it is a sin offering.

[15] Next take the one ram, and let Aaron and his sons lay their hands upon the ram's head. Slaughter the ram, and take its blood and dash it against all sides of the altar. Cut up the ram into sections, wash its entrails and legs, and put them with its quarters and its head. Turn all of the ram into smoke upon the altar. It is a burnt offering to the Lord, a pleasing odor, an offering by fire to the Lord.

Then take the other ram, and let Aaron and his sons lay their hands upon the ram's head. [20] Slaughter the ram, and take some of its blood and put it on the ridge of Aaron's right ear and on the ridges of his sons' right ears, and on the thumbs of their right hands, and on the big toes of their

---

Exodus 29:1–37.

right feet; and dash the rest of the blood against every side of the altar round about. Take some of the blood that is on the altar and some of the anointing oil and sprinkle upon Aaron and his vestments, and also upon his sons and his sons' vestments. Thus shall he and his vestments be holy, as well as his sons and his sons' vestments.

You shall take from the ram the fat parts—the broad tail, the fat that covers the entrails, the protuberance on the liver, the two kidneys with the fat on them—and the right thigh; for this is a ram of ordination. Add one flat loaf of bread, one cake of oil bread, and one wafer, from the basket of unleavened bread that is before the Lord. Place all these on the palms of Aaron and his sons, and offer them as an elevation offering[33] before the Lord. [25] Take them from their hands and turn them into smoke upon the altar with the burnt offering, as a pleasing odor before the Lord; it is an offering by fire to the Lord. . . . The sacral vestments of Aaron shall pass on to his sons after him, for them to be anointed and ordained in. [30] He among his sons who becomes priest in his stead, who enters the Tent of Meeting to officiate within the sanctuary, shall wear them seven days. . . .

[35] Thus you shall do to Aaron and his sons, just as I have commanded you. You shall ordain them through seven days, and each day you shall prepare a bull as a sin offering for expiation; you shall purge the altar by performing purification upon it, and you shall anoint it to consecrate it. Seven days you shall perform purification for the altar to consecrate it, and the altar shall become most holy; whatever touches the altar shall become consecrated.

---

[33] *elevation offering:* a sacrifice of a vegetable product, moved back and forth, and up and down, before the altar.

A Call to Be a Prophet*

This passage from the ninth century B.C.E. is the fullest prophetic call vision in the Hebrew scriptures and certainly the most dramatic. Though highly negative in tone—Isaiah's job as a prophet will not be a happy one—the end of the passage (probably added later) promises some hope.

In the year that King Uzziah died, I beheld my Lord seated on a high and lofty throne; and the skirts of His robe filled the Temple. Seraphs stood in attendance on Him. Each of them had six wings: with two he covered his face, with two he covered his legs, and with two he would fly.

And one would call to the other,
"Holy, holy, holy!
The Lord of Hosts!
His presence fills all the earth!"

The doorposts would shake at the sound of the one who called, and the House kept filling with smoke. [5] I cried,

"Woe is me; I am lost!
For I am a man of unclean lips
And I live among a people
Of unclean lips;
Yet my own eyes have beheld
The King Lord of Hosts."

Then one of the seraphs flew over to me with a live coal, which he had taken from the altar with a pair of tongs. He touched it to my lips and declared,

"Now that this has touched your lips,
Your guilt shall depart
And your sin be purged away."

Then I heard the voice of my Lord saying, "Whom shall I send? Who will go for us?" And I said, "Here am I; send me." And He said, "Go, say to that people:

---

*Isaiah 6:1–13.

'Hear, indeed, but do not understand;
See, indeed, but do not grasp.'
[10] Dull that people's mind,
Stop its ears,
And seal its eyes—
Lest, seeing with its eyes
And hearing with its ears,
It also grasps with its mind,
And repents and saves itself."

I asked, "How long, my Lord?" And He replied:

"Till towns lie waste without inhabitants
And houses without people,
And the ground lies waste and desolate—
For the Lord will banish the population—
And deserted sites are many
In the midst of the land.

"But while a tenth part yet remains in it, it shall repent. It shall be ravaged like the terebinth and the oak, of which stumps are left even when they are felled: its stump shall be a holy seed."

Women as Judges and Prophets*

The leadership of Israel was predominantly male, but occasionally women rose to prominent positions. In the first selection, Deborah the "judge" (national leader) delivers her nation from a military threat. In the second selection, Huldah the prophet speaks the word of God to the king of Judah at a critical time of repentance and reform.

[*Judges* 4:4] Deborah, wife of Lappidoth, was a prophetess; she led Israel at that time. [5] She used to sit under the Palm of Deborah, between Ramah and Bethel in the hill country of Ephraim, and the Israelites would come to her for decisions.

She summoned Barak son of Abinoam, of Kedesh in Naphtali, and said to him, "The Lord, the God of Israel, has commanded: Go, march up to Mount Tabor, and take with you ten thousand men of Naphtali and Zebulun. And I will draw Sisera, Jabin's army commander, with his chariots and his troops, toward you up to the Wadi Kishon; and I will deliver him into your hands." But Barak said to her, "If you will go with me, I will go; if not, I will not go." "Very well, I will go with you," she answered. "However, there will be no glory for you in the course you are taking, for then the Lord will deliver Sisera into the hands of a woman." So Deborah went with Barak to Kedesh. [10] Barak then mustered Zebulun and Naphtali at Kedesh; ten thousand men marched up after him; and Deborah also went up with him. . . .

Sisera was informed that Barak son of Abinoam had gone up to Mount Tabor. So Sisera ordered all his chariots—nine hundred iron chariots—and all the troops he had to move from Harosheth-goiim to the Wadi Kishon. Then Deborah said to Barak, "Up! This is the day on which the Lord will deliver Sisera into your hands: the Lord is marching before you." Barak charged down Mount Tabor, followed by the ten thousand men, [15] and the Lord threw Sisera and all his chariots and army into a panic before the onslaught of Barak. Sisera leaped from his chariot and fled on foot as Barak pursued the chariots and the soldiers as far as Harosheth-goiim. All of Sisera's soldiers fell by the sword; not a man was left. [Verses 17 through 24 recount how Jael, a Kenite woman allied with Israel, killed Sisera while he was sleeping in her tent by hammering a nail into his head.]

[*II Kings* 22:11] When the king [Josiah] heard the words of the scroll of the Teaching,[34] he tore his clothes.[35] And the king gave orders

---

* *Judges* 4:4–10, 12–16; *II Kings* 22:11–20.
[34] *scroll of the Teaching:* probably an early form of the biblical book of *Deuteronomy*.
[35] *tore his clothes:* Ritually tearing the clothing one is wearing is a sign of mourning and repentance.

to the priest Hilkiah, and to Ahikam son of Shaphan, Achbor son of Michaiah, the scribe Shaphan, and Asaiah the king's minister: "Go, inquire of the Lord on my behalf, and on behalf of the people, and on behalf of all Judah, concerning the words of this scroll that has been found. For great indeed must be the wrath of the Lord that has been kindled against us, because our fathers did not obey the words of this scroll to do all that has been prescribed for us."

So the priest Hilkiah, and Ahikam, Achbor, Shaphan, and Asaiah went to the prophetess Huldah—the wife of Shallum son of Tikvah son of Harhas, the keeper of the wardrobe—who was living in Jerusalem in the Mishneh, and they spoke to her. [15] She responded: "Thus said the Lord, the God of Israel: Say to the man who sent you to me: Thus said the Lord: I am going to bring disaster upon this place and its inhabitants, in accordance with all the words of the scroll which the king of Judah has read. Because they have forsaken Me and have made offerings to other gods and vexed Me with all their deeds, My wrath is kindled against this place and it shall not be quenched. But say this to the king of Judah, who sent you to inquire of the Lord: Thus said the Lord, the God of Israel: As for the words which you have heard—because your heart was softened and you humbled yourself before the Lord when you heard what I decreed against this place and its inhabitants—that it will become a desolation and a curse—and because you tore your clothes and wept before Me, I for My part have listened—declares the Lord. [20] Assuredly, I will gather you to your fathers and you will be laid in your tomb in peace. Your eyes shall not see all the disaster which I will bring upon this place." So they brought back the reply to the king.

RITUAL

The Establishment of Circumcision*

Circumcision is the sign of the covenant and membership in the people of Israel. As such, it is the primary ritual in Judaism. It is performed on males only. Here its origins are traced to Abraham.

God further said to Abraham, "As for you, you and your offspring to come throughout the ages shall keep My covenant. [10] Such shall be the covenant between Me and you and your offspring to follow which you shall keep: every male among you shall be circumcised. You shall circumcise the flesh of your foreskin, and that shall be the sign of the covenant between Me and you. And throughout the generations, every male among you shall be circumcised at the age of eight days. As for the homeborn slave and the one bought from an outsider who is not of your offspring, they must be circumcised, homeborn and purchased alike. Thus shall My covenant be marked in your flesh as an everlasting pact. And if any male who is uncircumcised fails to circumcise the flesh of his foreskin, that person shall be cut off from his kin; he has broken My covenant...."

[23] Then Abraham took his son Ishmael, and all his homeborn slaves and all those he had bought, every male in Abraham's household, and he circumcised the flesh of their foreskins on that very day, as God had spoken to him. Abraham was ninety-nine years old when he circumcised the flesh of his foreskin, [25] and his son Ishmael was thirteen years old when he was circumcised in the flesh of his foreskin. Thus Abraham and his son Ishmael were circumcised on that very day; and all his household, his homeborn slaves and those that had been bought from outsiders, were circumcised with him.

---

*Genesis 17:9–14, 23–27.

The Establishment of the Passover*

In the first two paragraphs of this selection, the ingredients of the meal itself and the meaning of the Passover are given. In the third and fourth paragraphs, the Feast of Unleavened Bread (matzo) is treated; originally it was a harvest festival, but now it is incorporated into the Passover.

The Lord said to Moses and Aaron in the land of Egypt: This month shall mark for you the beginning of the months; it shall be the first of the months[36] of the year for you. Speak to the whole community of Israel and say that on the tenth of this month each of them shall take a lamb to a family, a lamb to a household. But if the household is too small for a lamb, let him share one with a neighbor who dwells nearby, in proportion to the number of persons; you shall contribute for the lamb according to what each household will eat. [5] Your lamb shall be without blemish, a yearling male; you may take it from the sheep or from the goats. You shall keep watch over it until the fourteenth day of this month; and all the assembled congregation of the Israelites shall slaughter it at twilight. They shall take some of the blood and put it on the two doorposts and the lintel of the houses in which they are to eat it. They shall eat the flesh that same night; they shall eat it roasted over the fire, with unleavened bread and with bitter herbs. Do not eat any of it raw, or cooked in any way with water, but roasted—head, legs, and entrails—over the fire. [10] You shall not leave any of it over until morning; if any of it is left until morning, you shall burn it.

This is how you shall eat it: your loins girded, your sandals on your feet, and your staff in your hand; and you shall eat it hurriedly: it is a Passover offering to the Lord. For that night I will go through the land of Egypt and strike down every first-born in the land of Egypt, both man and beast; and I will mete out punishments to all the gods of Egypt, I the Lord. And the blood on the houses where you are staying shall be a sign for you: when I see the blood I will pass over you, so that no plague will destroy you when I strike the land of Egypt.

This day shall be to you one of remembrance: you shall celebrate it as a festival to the Lord throughout the ages; you shall celebrate it as an institution for all time. [15] Seven days you shall eat unleavened bread; on the very first day you shall remove leaven from your houses, for whoever eats leavened bread from the first day to the seventh day, that person shall be cut off from Israel. You shall celebrate a sacred occasion on the first day, and a sacred occasion on the seventh day; no work at all shall be done on them; only what every person is to eat, that alone may be prepared for you. You shall observe the [Feast of] Unleavened Bread, for on this very day I brought your ranks out of the land of Egypt; you shall observe this day throughout the ages as an institution for all time. In the first month, from the fourteenth day of the month at evening, you shall eat unleavened bread until the twenty-first day of the month at evening. No leaven shall be found in your houses for seven days. For whoever eats what is leavened, that person shall be cut off from the community of Israel, whether he is a stranger or a citizen of the country. . . .

[24] You shall observe this [Passover] as an institution for all time, for you and for your descendants. And when you enter the land that the Lord will give you, as He has promised, you shall observe this rite. And when your children ask you, "What do you mean by this rite?" you shall say, "It is the Passover sacrifice to the Lord, because He passed over the houses of the Israelites in Egypt when He smote the Egyptians, but saved our houses."

**Exodus* 12:1–19, 24–27.
[36] *first of the months:* Nisan, a spring month that is the first month in the Jewish calendar.

The Observance of the Sabbath*

Throughout Jewish history, keeping the Sabbath, or seventh day of the week, has been an important sign of Judaism. In this passage, which expands on the Sabbath command in the Decalogue, *the penalty for breaking it, like the penalty for breaking the other commandments of the* Decalogue, *is death.*

The Lord said to Moses: Speak to the Israelite people and say: Nevertheless, you must keep My sabbaths, for this is a sign between Me and you throughout the ages, that you may know that I the Lord have consecrated you. You shall keep the sabbath, for it is holy for you. He who profanes it shall be put to death: whoever does work on it, that person shall be cut off from among his kin. [15] Six days may work be done, but on the seventh day there shall be a sabbath of complete rest, holy to the Lord; whoever does work on the sabbath day shall be put to death. The Israelite people shall keep the sabbath, observing the sabbath throughout the ages as a covenant for all time: it shall be a sign for all time between Me and the people of Israel. For in six days the Lord made heaven and earth, and on the seventh day He ceased from work and was refreshed.

---

*Exodus 31:12–17.

Offerings for the Forgiveness of Sin**

The sin offering is a sacrifice of repentance for unintentional sin. It restores the offender to God and secures the well-being of his community. The sections before this passage deal with offerings prescribed for the high priest, for the nation of Israel as a whole, and for the ruler. This passage deals with offerings prescribed for a common citizen. The ceremonies described here and in the next passage are reflective of later temple procedure, although the next passage speaks of the Tent of Meeting that was used immediately after the Exodus.

If any person from among the populace unwittingly incurs guilt by doing any of the things which by the Lord's commandments ought not to be done, and he realizes his guilt—or the sin of which he is guilty is brought to his knowledge—he shall bring a female goat without blemish as his offering for the sin of which he is guilty. He shall lay his hand upon the head of the sin offering, and the sin offering shall be slaughtered at the place of the burnt offering. [30] The priest shall take with his finger some of its blood and put it on the horns of the altar of burnt offering; and all the rest of its blood he shall pour out at the base of the altar. He shall remove all its fat, just as the fat is removed from the sacrifice of well-being; and the priest shall turn it into smoke on the altar, for a pleasing odor to the Lord. Thus the priest shall make expiation for him, and he shall be forgiven.

If the offering he brings as a sin offering is a sheep, he shall bring a female without blemish. He shall lay his hand upon the head of the sin offering, and it shall be slaughtered as a sin offering at the spot where the burnt offering is slaughtered. The priest shall take with his finger some of the blood of the sin offering and put it on the horns of the altar of burnt offering, and all the rest of its blood he shall pour out at the base of the altar. [35] And all its fat he shall remove just as the fat of the sheep of the sacrifice of well-being is removed; and this the priest shall turn into smoke on the altar, over the Lord's offerings by fire. Thus the priest shall

---

**Leviticus 4:27–5:7.

make expiation on his behalf for the sin of which he is guilty, and he shall be forgiven.

[5:1] If a person incurs guilt: When he has heard a public imprecation and—although able to testify as one who has either seen or learned of the matter—he does not give information, so that he is subject to punishment; or when a person touches any unclean thing—be it the carcass of an unclean beast or the carcass of unclean cattle or the carcass of an unclean creeping thing—and the fact has escaped him, and then, being unclean, he realizes his guilt; or when he touches human uncleanness—any such uncleanness whereby one becomes unclean—and, though he has known it, the fact has escaped him, but later he realizes his guilt; or when a person utters an oath to bad or good purpose—whatever a man may utter in an oath—and, though he has known it, the fact has escaped him, but later he realizes his guilt in any of these matters—[5] when he realizes his guilt in any of these matters, he shall confess that wherein he has sinned. And he shall bring as his penalty to the Lord, for the sin of which he is guilty, a female from the flock, sheep or goat, as a sin offering; and the priest shall make expiation on his behalf for his sin.

But if his means do not suffice for a sheep, he shall bring to the Lord, as his penalty for that of which he is guilty, two turtledoves or two pigeons, one for a sin offering and the other for a burnt offering.

The Day of Atonement*

This selection presents the sacrificial ceremonies of the Day of Atonement (Yom Kippur), tracing it to the time of Moses. Since the destruction of the Second Temple in 70 C.E., Jews have practiced the spiritual heart of the holy day as it is developed at the end of the passage: a day of rest, self-denial, confession, and making amends. Although the Jewish Bible presents all holy days as equal, in modern Jewish practice the Day of Atonement and New Year's Day (Rosh Hashanah) have become the most important.

The Lord spoke to Moses after the death of the two sons of Aaron who died when they drew too close to the presence of the Lord. The Lord said to Moses:

Tell your brother Aaron that he is not to come at will into the Shrine behind the curtain, in front of the cover that is upon the ark, lest he die; for I appear in the cloud over the cover. Thus only shall Aaron enter the Shrine: with a bull of the herd for a sin offering and a ram for a burnt offering. He shall be dressed in a sacral linen tunic, with linen breeches next to his flesh, and be girt with a linen sash, and he shall wear a linen turban. They are sacral vestments; he shall bathe his body in water and then put them on. And from the Israelite community he shall take two he-goats for a sin offering and a ram for a burnt offering. . . .

[11] Aaron shall then offer his bull of sin offering, to make expiation for himself and his household. He shall slaughter his bull of sin offering, and he shall take a panful of glowing coals scooped from the altar before the Lord, and two handfuls of finely ground aromatic incense, and bring this behind the curtain. He shall put the incense on the fire before the Lord, so that the cloud from the incense screens the cover that is over [the Ark of] the Pact, lest he die. He shall take some of the blood of the bull and sprinkle it with his finger over the cover on the east side; and in front of the cover he shall sprinkle some of the blood with his finger seven times. [15] He shall then slaughter the people's goat of sin offering, bring its blood behind the curtain, and do with its blood as he has done with the blood of the bull: he shall sprinkle it over the cover and in front of the cover.

---

*Leviticus 16:1–5, 11–19, 29–34.

Thus he shall purge the Shrine of the uncleanness and transgression of the Israelites, whatever their sins; and he shall do the same for the Tent of Meeting, which abides with them in the midst of their uncleanness. When he goes in to make expiation in the Shrine, nobody else shall be in the Tent of Meeting until he comes out.

When he has made expiation for himself and his household, and for the whole congregation of Israel, he shall go out to the altar that is before the Lord and purge it: he shall take some of the blood of the bull and of the goat and apply it to each of the horns of the altar; and the rest of the blood he shall sprinkle on it with his finger seven times. Thus he shall cleanse it of the uncleanness of the Israelites and consecrate it. . . .

[29] And this shall be to you a law for all time: In the seventh month, on the tenth day of the month, you shall practice self-denial; and you shall do no manner of work, neither the citizen nor the alien who resides among you. For on this day atonement shall be made for you to cleanse you of all your sins; you shall be clean before the Lord. It shall be a sabbath of complete rest for you, and you shall practice self-denial; it is a law for all time. The priest who has been anointed and ordained to serve as priest in place of his father shall make expiation. He shall put on the linen vestments, the sacral vestments. He shall purge the innermost Shrine; he shall purge the Tent of Meeting and the altar; and he shall make expiation for the priests and for all the people of the congregation. This shall be to you a law for all time: to make atonement for the Israelites for all their sins once a year. And Moses did as the Lord had commanded him.

Kosher and Nonkosher Foods*

This passage on dietary law gives a list of clean and unclean foods. The types of unclean animals specified here are (1) four-footed animals that do not chew the cud and have a split hoof, (2) carnivorous birds, (3) winged insects, (4) water animals lacking fins and scales, and (5) small creeping ("swarming") animals. In order to be kosher, acceptable animals must be butchered in a humane way, and all food must be served according to kosher regulations (for example, no mixing of dairy products and meat). These regulations form the basis of kosher inspection and certification today, and many food production businesses owned by non-Jews seek this certification for wider sales opportunities.

The Lord spoke to Moses and Aaron, saying to them: Speak to the Israelite people thus:

These are the creatures that you may eat from among all the land animals: any animal that has true hoofs, with clefts through the hoofs, and that chews the cud—such you may eat. The following, however, of those that either chew the cud or have true hoofs, you shall not eat: the camel—although it chews the cud, it has no true hoofs: it is unclean for you; [5] the daman [a type of sheep]—although it chews the cud, it has no true hoofs: it is unclean for you; the hare—although it chews the cud, it has no true hoofs: it is unclean for you; and the swine—although it has true hoofs, with the hoofs cleft through, it does not chew the cud: it is unclean for you. You shall not eat of their flesh or touch their carcasses; they are unclean for you.

These you may eat of all that live in water: anything in water, whether in the seas or in the streams, that has fins and scales—these you may eat. [10] But anything in the seas or in the streams that has no fins and scales, among all the swarming things of the water and among all the other living creatures that are in the water—they are an abomination for you and an abomination for you they shall remain: you shall not eat of their flesh and you shall abominate their carcasses. Everything in water

---

*Leviticus 11:1–31, 41–45.

that has no fins and scales shall be an abomination for you.

The following you shall abominate among the birds—they shall not be eaten, they are an abomination: the eagle, the vulture, and the black vulture; the kite, falcons of every variety; [15] all varieties of raven; the ostrich, the nighthawk, the sea gull; hawks of every variety; the little owl, the cormorant, and the great owl; the white owl, the pelican, and the bustard; the stork; herons of every variety; the hoopoe, and the bat.

[20] All winged swarming things that walk on fours shall be an abomination for you. But these you may eat among all the winged swarming things that walk on fours: all that have, above their feet, jointed legs to leap with on the ground—of these you may eat the following: locusts of every variety; all varieties of bald locust; crickets of every variety; and all varieties of grasshopper. But all other winged swarming things that have four legs shall be an abomination for you.

And the following shall make you unclean—whoever touches their carcasses shall be unclean until evening, [25] and whoever carries the carcasses of any of them shall wash his clothes and be unclean until evening—every animal that has true hoofs but without clefts through the hoofs, or that does not chew the cud. They are unclean for you; whoever touches them shall be unclean. Also all animals that walk on paws, among those that walk on fours, are unclean for you; whoever touches their carcasses shall be unclean until evening. And anyone who carries their carcasses shall wash his clothes and remain unclean until evening. They are unclean for you.

The following shall be unclean for you from among the things that swarm on the earth: the mole, the mouse, and great lizards of every variety; [30] the gecko, the land crocodile, the lizard, the sand lizard, and the chameleon. Those are for you the unclean among all the swarming things; whoever touches them when they are dead shall be unclean until evening. . . .

[41] All the things that swarm upon the earth are an abomination; they shall not be eaten. You shall not eat, among all things that swarm upon the earth, anything that crawls on its belly, or anything that walks on fours, or anything that has many legs; for they are an abomination. You shall not draw abomination upon yourselves through anything that swarms; you shall not make yourselves unclean therewith and thus become unclean. For I the Lord am your God: you shall sanctify yourselves and be holy, for I am holy. You shall not make yourselves unclean through any swarming thing that moves upon the earth. [45] For I the Lord am He who brought you up from the land of Egypt to be your God: you shall be holy, for I am holy.

LATER DEVELOPMENTS OF SCRIPTURAL THEMES

Jews have traditionally held the *Talmud* as an authoritative book. They often understood the *Bible,* and applied it to all the affairs of daily life, through the *Talmud*. Here are three passages from this important writing. In the first, taken entirely from the *Mishnah,* the rabbis explain the chain of transmission of the oral Torah from Moses to the writing of the *Mishnah*. In the second, the *Talmud* deals with the question of how Israel can continue without the Temple of Jerusalem, answering that study of the *Torah* suffices as a replacement of animal sacrifice. In the third, the biblical duty to have children is discussed in the *Talmud* and given here as an example of rabbinic interpretation and debate at work.

The Chain of Rabbinic Tradition: "The Sayings of the Fathers"*

This famous passage from the Mishnah, *which was incorporated with all the* Mishnah *into the* Talmud, *is concerned to trace the transmission of the oral Torah from Moses to the second century C.E., when the* Mishnah *was compiled. Throughout this selection the word* Torah *refers especially to the oral Torah, a "fence around the [written] law," the body of legal opinions developed by the rabbis and codified in the* Mishnah. *Notice the characteristic use of three sayings to sum up the teachings of leading figures in this chain of transmission.*[37]

Moses received the Torah from Sinai and delivered it to Joshua, Joshua delivered it to the elders, the elders to the prophets, and the prophets to the men of the great synagogue. They said three things: "Be deliberate in judgment, raise up many disciples, and make a fence around the law."

Simon the Just was one of the last men of the great synagogue. He used to say that the world stood on three things: on the law, the [temple] service, and the acts of the pious.

Antigonus of Soco received [the Torah] from Simon the Just. He used to say, "Do not be like servants who serve their master for the sake of receiving a reward; be like servants who serve their master without the intent of receiving a reward; and let the fear of heaven be upon you."

Jose, son of Joezer of Zeredah, and Jose, son of Jochanan of Jerusalem, received [the Torah] from him. Jose, son of Joezer of Zeredah, said, "Let your house be a house of assembly for the wise, dust yourself with the dust of their feet, and drink their words in thirstiness."

[5] Jose, son of Jochanan of Jerusalem, said, "Let your house be wide open, and let the poor be your children. Do not talk much with women, not even with your wife, much less with your neighbor's wife." Hence the wise men say, "Whoever converses much with women brings evil on himself, neglects the study of the law, and at last will go to hell."

Joshua, son of Perechiah, and Natai the Arbelite received the oral law from them. Joshua, son of Perechiah, said, "Get yourself a master, and obtain a companion [in learning], and judge all people with favor."

Natai the Arbelite said, "Withdraw from an evil neighbor, do not associate with the wicked, and do not flatter yourself to escape punishment."

Judah, son of Tabai, and Simon, son of Shetach, received it from them. Judah, son of Tabai said, "Do not consider yourself as the arranger of the law, and when the parties are before you in judgment, consider them as guilty; but when they are departed from you, consider them as innocent, when they have acquiesced in the sentence."

Simon, son of Shetach, said, "Be extremely careful in the examination of witnesses, and be cautious in your words, lest they [the witnesses] should learn to tell lies."

[10] Shemaiah and Abtalyon received it from them. Shemaiah said, "Love your business, hate power, and keep clear of the government."

Abtalyon said, "You Sages, be cautious of your words, lest you be doomed to captivity, and carried captive to a place of bad waters, and the disciples who follow you should drink of them, by which means the name of God may be profaned."

Hillel and Shammai received it from them. Hillel said, "Be like the disciples of Aaron, who loved peace and pursued peace, so that you love mankind, and allure them to the study of the law."

He used to say, "Whoever aggrandizes his name, destroys his name; he who does not increase his knowledge in the law shall be cut off; he who does not study the law is deserving of death, and he who serves himself with the crown of the law will perish."

Mishnah, Aboth 1.1–18.
[37] Taken, with editing, from Joseph Barclay, trans., *Hebrew Literature,* rev. ed. (New York: Colonial Press, 1901).

He also said, "If I do not perform good works myself, who can do them for me?" and "When I consider myself, what am I?" and "If not now, when?"

[15] Shammai said, "Let your study of the law be fixed, say little and do much, and receive all men with an open, pleasant face."

Rabbi Gamaliel said, "Get yourself an instructor, that you may not be in doubt, and do not accustom yourself to give [too many] tithes by conjecture."

Simon, his son, said, "All my life I have been brought up among wise men, and never found anything so good for the body as silence; neither is the study of the law the principal thing, but its practice; whoever multiplies words causes sin."

Rabbi Simon, son of Gamaliel, said the duration of the world depends on three things, justice, truth, and peace, as is said, "Judge truth, justice, and peace in your gates."[38]

---

[38] *Judge truth . . . gates:* a quotation from *Zechariah* 8:16.

The Replacement of Sacrifice by Study*

The Jewish people faced a problem in the first century C.E. and later: The Temple and its sacrifices, commanded by God in the scriptures as an essential part of Jewish religion, no longer existed after their destruction by Rome. After this catastrophe, how were they to interpret these commands in the Bible? *The rabbis found a solution that helped to consolidate their movement and promote the continued vitality of Judaism: The study of the* Torah *takes the place of sacrifice in the eyes of God.*[39]

"In every place incense is offered to my name, and a pure sacrifice; for my name is great in the nations, says the Lord of hosts" [*Malachi* 1:11]. What does the phrase "in every place" mean? Rabbi Samuel ben Nahmai said in the name of Rabbi Jonathan that this refers to the students of the (rabbinic) sages who study the Torah in every place. God accounts it to them as though they burned offerings and presented them to his name. The phrase "and a pure sacrifice" refers to one who studies the Torah in purity, that is, one who marries a wife and then studies the Torah.

"Come, bless the Lord, all you servants of the Lord, who stand in the house of the Lord in the night" [*Psalm* 134:1]. What is the meaning of the phrase "in the night"? Rabbi Johanan said that this refers to the students of the sages who devote themselves to the study of the Torah at night. The Torah speaks as though they were devoted to Temple rituals.

"Behold, I will build a house for the name of the Lord my God, and dedicate it to him for the burning to him of incense made from sweet spices. It shall have a continual offering of the showbread, and for burnt offerings morning and evening. . . . This is an ordinance forever for Israel" [*II Chronicles* 2:3]. Rabbi Giddal said in the name of Rabbi Judah the Prince this refers to the altar built in heaven, where Michael, the great Prince, stands and makes an offering. Rabbi Johanan said that this verse refers to the students of the sages who are devoted to the laws of the Temple ritual. Scripture credits them as though the Temple were standing in their days.

Rabbi Lakish put forth another verse and asked how it should be understood: "This is the law for the burnt offering, for the grain offering, for the transgression offering, and for the guilt offering" [*Leviticus* 7:37]. It teaches, he said, that when anyone devotes himself to the study

---

Babylonian Talmud, Minahot 110a.
[39] This passage and the following are translated by the editor.

of the Torah, it is as though he were making a burnt offering, a grain offering, a transgression offering, and a guilt offering. Rabbi Judah the Prince asked, "Then why does the verse say, 'for the burnt offering, for the grain offering'? It should have said, 'a burnt offering, a grain offering'!" Rather, it means that whoever occupies himself with the study of the Torah does not need burnt offerings, grain offerings, transgression offerings, or guilt offerings.

The Duty to Marry and Have Children*

In Jewish reckoning, the first commandment in the Torah is God's command to the human race, "Be fruitful and multiply." This passage discusses the implications of this command. Like all Talmudic passages, this one relies heavily on the interpretation of scripture, some of it straightforward and some highly creative.

A man must not abstain from carrying out the obligation to "be fruitful and multiply" [*Genesis* 1:28] unless he already has two children. The School of Shammai ruled that this means two sons, and the School of Hillel ruled that it means a son and a daughter, because it is written, "Male and female He created them" [*Genesis* 1:28; 5:2]. The duty of procreation applies to a man but not to a woman. Rabbi Yohanan the son of Seroka said that it applies to both [man and woman], for "God blessed them and said to them, 'Be fruitful and multiply'" [*Genesis* 1:28].[40]

This [*Mishnah*] passage means that if a man has children he may abstain from the duty of procreation, but he may not abstain from living with his wife. This supports the view of Rabbi Nahman, who reported a ruling in the name of Samuel that even though a man have many children, he may not remain without a wife, for it is written: "It is not good for a man to be alone" [*Genesis* 2:18].

Others held the opinion that if a man had children, he may abstain from the duty of procreation, and he may also abstain from the duty of living with a wife. Does this contradict what was reported by Rabbi Nahman in the name of Samuel? No. If he has no children, he is to marry a woman capable of having a child, but if he already has children, he may marry a woman who is incapable of having children.

Other rabbis taught that Rabbi Nathan said that according to the School of Shammai, a person satisfies the obligation to "be fruitful and multiply" if he has a son and a daughter, and according to the School of Hillel if he has either a son or a daughter. Rabbi [Judah the Prince] said, "Why this view of the School of Hillel? It is written, 'God created it not to be a waste, and he formed it to be inhabited' [*Isaiah* 45:18], and he has already contributed to making it a place of habitation [by having a child]."

What if a person had children while he was a pagan, and was later converted? Rabbi Yohanan said that he has already fulfilled the duty of procreation. However, Rabbi Lakish said that he has not fulfilled it, because at conversion one is like a born-again child.

The *Mishnah* disagrees with the view of Rabbi Joshua. Joshua stated that if a person married in his youth he is also to marry in his old age; and if he had children in his youth, he is also to have children in his old age. For it is written: "Sow your seed in the morning and do not withdraw your hand in the evening, for you do not know which will prosper, this or that, or whether both alike will be good" [*Ecclesiastes* 11:6].

Rabbi Tanhum said in the name of Rabbi Hanilai that a man who is without a wife has no joy, no blessing, and no good. He has no joy, for

---

*Babylonian Talmud, *Yebamoth* 61b–63.
[40] This paragraph is from *Mishnah* 6:6; the rest of the passage is the *Gemara* discussion of it.

it is written: "You shall rejoice, you and your household" [*Deuteronomy* 14:26]. He has no blessing, for it is written: "That a blessing may rest on your house [*Ezekiel* 44:30]. He has no good, for it is written: "It is not good for a man to be alone" [*Genesis* 2:18].

Rabbi Joshua the son of Levi said that a man who knows his wife to be a God-fearing woman and does not have sexual relations with her is a sinner, for it is written: "And you shall visit your habitation and you will not sin" [*Job* 5:24].

The rabbis taught that when a man loves his wife as himself, and honors her more than himself, and trains his sons and daughters in the right path, and arranges for their marriage at a young age—about this man the verse says, "And you shall know that your tent is at peace" [*Job* 5:24].

Rabbi Eleazar said that a man without a wife is not a complete man, for it is written: "Male and female created He them, and He called their name *adam*, 'man.'" [*Genesis* 1:27].

Avert your eyes from the charms of another man's wife, or you may be trapped in her snare. Do not become friends with her husband and drink wine and strong drink with him. Many men have been destroyed by the appearance of a beautiful woman, and she has killed a vast number.

Why Judaism Survives under Persecution*

Moses Maimonides (1135–1204) has been the most influential Jewish leader since antiquity. A rabbi and a philosopher, he has given spiritual and intellectual strength to generations of Jews from the twelfth century through modern times and the Holocaust. In this reading, taken from one of his most important letters, he explains the origin of the persecution of the Jews, which was experienced sporadically all the way back to the Exodus. He urges the Jewish people to stay true to their faith despite the pressures of persecution.[41]

The hostility of the nations toward us is due to our unique position as a people of faith. This is why their rulers oppress us, to visit upon us hatred and hostility. But the Creator endowed us with confidence, so that whenever persecution or fury against Israel arises, it will surely be endured. The power of the rulers oppresses us, and they exercise a hard rule against us. They persecute and torment us with oppressive decrees, but they cannot destroy us or wipe out our name.

Do you know, brothers, that in the time of the wicked Nebuchadnezzar, Israel was forced to worship foreign gods, and only Daniel, Hanaiah, Misael, and Azariah were rescued? In the end, this king and his authority were destroyed, and the truth was restored [*Daniel* 1–6]. The same thing happened in the time of the Second Temple, when the wicked dynasty of Seleucus came to power and persecuted Israel, trying to destroy our religion.[42] These Syrians forced Israel to desecrate the Sabbath and the covenant of circumcision, even to renounce publicly their belief in God. This oppression lasted fifty-two years, and then God annihilated both the government and the religion of the enemy.

God promised us through his prophets that we will never perish and that we shall never cease to be a people of faith. Our life is connected with the existence of the Lord. As it is said, "For I the Lord do not change; therefore you, sons of Jacob, have not perished" [*Malachi* 3:6]. And Moses, our teacher, said in the Torah, "Even after all that (sin), when they are in the land of their enemies, I will not reject them, neither will I abhor them, to destroy them and

---

*Maimonides, *Letter to Yemen*.
[41] Translated by the editor from *Iggeret Teman* (Letter to Yemen) (Vienna: Holub, 1873), p. 47.
[42] This refers to the Maccabean struggle in the second century B.C.E.

to break my covenant with them; for I am the Lord their God" [*Leviticus* 26:44].

Therefore, brothers, be strong and of good courage. If persecutions arise, let them not disconcert you. Let not the mighty hand of the enemy and the weakness of our nation frighten you. These events are but trial and proof of your faith and your love. By holding firm to the law of truth in times like these, you prove that you belong to those of Jacob's seed who fear God and who are called "the remnant whom the Lord has called."

Brothers of Israel, who are scattered over the whole earth, it is your duty to strengthen one another. The older should encourage the younger, and the prominent should encourage the common people. The nation should be united in the name of truth, which does not change. Raise your voice in strong faith, proclaiming to all that God is One, that Moses is his prophet and the greatest of all the prophets, that the Torah is the word of the Creator. Always keep in mind what happened on Mount Sinai.

My brothers, rear your children to understand that great event; explain its significance to every [Jewish] group and community. The event on Mount Sinai is the pivot on which our faith turns, the foundation of our truth. Understand, brothers, the meaning of that covenant: The nation as a whole witnessed the word of God and his presence. This even should strengthen our faith and enable us to resist the strain of persecutions and intolerance in times like these. It is said: "God has come to test you, that you may hold him in awe and not sin" [*Exodus* 20:20]. This means that experience should give you the power to withstand all trials to which we may be subjected in times to come. Therefore, brothers, hold fast to the covenant and be firm in your faith.

GLOSSARY

ark a special closet or recess in the synagogue wall on the side nearest Jerusalem in which *Bible* scrolls used for public worship are stored.

Bible the "Book" of Jewish scripture, numbering twenty-four books by Jewish count. In the Christian framework, it includes thirty-nine books of Jewish scripture and twenty-seven *New Testament* books.

covenant an agreement between God and the people of Israel setting forth obligations and privileges for each party.

Decalogue "Ten Words"; also known as the *Ten Commandments* (found in *Exodus* 20:1–17, restated in *Deuteronomy* 5:6–21).

Kethuvim [KETH-u-veem] "Writings"; the third division of the Jewish *Bible*.

lectionary a list of scripture readings for divine worship.

mezuzah [meh-ZOO-zah] a small box containing *Bible* verses that is attached to the doorpost of a Jewish house.

Nevi'im [NEH-vih-eem] "Prophets"; the second division of the Jewish *Bible*.

psalm [sahlm] a sacred song, in the style found in the biblical book of *Psalms,* used for divine worship.

revelation the communication of the divine person or truth to humanity.

Shema [sheh-MAH] Judaism's most basic statement of faith, found in *Deuteronomy* 6:4–9 and in two shorter passages. The word means "hear."

Talmud [TALL-mood] the Jewish law code, a compilation of the "oral Torah."

Tanakh [TAH-nahk] acronymic name for the Jewish *Bible,* formed from the first letters of *Torah, Nevi'im,* and *Kethuvim.*

tefillin [teh-FILL-in] small boxes containing *Bible* verses on tiny scrolls, bound by leather straps on the forehead and weaker arm of the Orthodox Jew during prayers.

Torah [TOH-rah] "Teaching" or "Law"; the first five books of the Jewish *Bible;* more broadly, God's teaching and revelation.

QUESTIONS FOR STUDY AND DISCUSSION

1. In what ways did the Jewish people link their history to their system of morality? Consider two focal points of the *Bible:* (a) the relationship of the Exodus and law; (b) the restoration of the Jews to their land after the exile and concerns for purity.

2. The Jewish scripture's three main sections are arranged in order of importance. What has it meant for Judaism that the *Torah* is first, *Prophets* second, and *Writings* third?

3. Discuss the tension in the *Bible* between Israel's call to be a light to the other nations and the demand to be a separate, holy people.

4. How has Judaism adapted its worship and rituals to a time when it has no Temple? Which rituals described in the passages in this chapter could be continued essentially as is, which had to be altered greatly, and which had to be discontinued?

5. How could the ancient Israelite ideal of equal justice be seen as an antecedent of modern European and North American ideals of justice?

6. Explain the standing of women in the Jewish *Bible*. To what degree did the Hebrew scriptures ameliorate the condition of women, and to what degree did they reinforce a patriarchal society?

7. Trace the theme of the chosen/covenant people through the Hebrew scriptures.

8. Explain the statement, "Judaism is a religion of the book."

SCRIPTURES IN FILM

Hollywood has not made films based directly on the Hebrew *Bible/Old Testament* for almost fifty years, despite the grand narratives of the *Bible* that are seemingly tailor-made for film. The Holocaust has so shaped recent Jewish life that it and other contemporary Jewish events have received the lion's share of attention in film (*Schindler's List, Sophie's Choice, A Beautiful Life,* and the rest). Students may want to view 1956's *The Ten Commandments,* directed by Cecil B. DeMille in the grandiose style of old-time Hollywood "biblical epics." A more recent treatment of a difficult contemporary topic is *Trembling before G-d,* directed by Simcha Dubowski (2001). This prize-winning film deals with Jews from Orthodox backgrounds who are dealing with their own same-sex orientation and with the traditional biblical reaction to it by other Orthodox Jews.

SUGGESTIONS FOR FURTHER READING

Primary Readings

The New Revised Standard Version of the Bible. New York: Oxford University Press, 1991. The best one-volume translation of the Jewish and Christian scriptures. The Hebrew scripture section is widely recognized for its accuracy.

A. Berlin and M. Z. Brettler, eds., *The Jewish Study Bible*. New York: Oxford University Press, 2003. Features the Jewish Publication Society's *Tanakh* translation first published in 1985 and provides excellent resources for understanding Jewish interpretation and use.

L. H. Schiffman, ed., *Texts and Traditions: A Source Reader for the Study of Second Temple and Rabbinic Judaism*. New York: KTAV, 1998. A comprehensive collection of primary sources for this formative period, especially *Bible* and *Talmud* selections.

Secondary Readings

R. Alter, *The Art of Biblical Narrative*. New York: Basic Books, 1981. An excellent introduction to the Jewish *Bible* as literature.

B. Anderson, *Understanding the Old Testament*, 4th ed. Englewood Cliffs, NJ: Prentice-Hall, 1986. The standard introductory study.

E. Fackenheim, *The Jewish Bible after the Holocaust—A Rereading*. Indianapolis: Indiana University Press, 1991. A prominent Jewish philosopher contends that the Jewish *Bible* is still the great spiritual resource of the Western religious traditions.

F. Greenspahn, "Does Judaism Have a Bible?" In L. J. Greenspoon and B. F. LeBeau, eds., *Sacred Text, Secular Times: The Hebrew Bible in the Modern World*. Omaha: Creighton University Press, 2000, pp. 1–12. An up-to-date critical discussion of the Hebrew canon in the life of Judaism.

J. Rosenbaum, "Judaism: Torah and Tradition." In F. M. Denny and R. L. Taylor, eds., *The Holy Book in Comparative Perspective*. Columbia: University of South Carolina Press, 1985, pp. 10–35. Examines the interplay of the *Bible* and other sacred literature of Judaism, especially the *Talmud*.

P. Trible, *Texts of Terror*. Philadelphia: Fortress, 1984. A powerful examination of some biblical passages from a religious and feminist perspective.

B. Visotzky, *Reading the Book: Making the Bible a Timeless Text*. New York: Anchor/Doubleday, 1991. Designed to provide an "introduction to the meaningful reading of Scripture," this book takes account of both rabbinic and modern methods of interpretation.

Ethiopian Orthodox Priests Read Scripture at a Festival in Addis Ababa
Ethiopian Orthodox priests in their satin robes stand under sequined velvet umbrellas as the *Bible* is read during the annual "Timket" celebrations in Addis Ababa, Ethiopia. Timket, the greatest Ethiopian festival of the year, commemorates Jesus Christ's baptism in the Jordan River by John the Baptist. *Credit:* © Wolfgang Rattay/Reuters/Corbis.

CHAPTER FOUR

Christianity

- In a congregation of the Church of Scotland, the bell tolls and the congregation stands out of respect for the Word as a layperson walks solemnly down the center aisle carrying a large Christian *Bible*. When the book is placed on the pulpit, the service begins.

- In a village of New Guinea, North American and European missionaries trained in linguistics work to decipher a tribal language, commit it to writing, and educate the tribespeople to read it. The purpose of their work is to translate the *New Testament* into the tribal language for use in training new believers in the faith and as a tool for converting other members of the tribe.

- In Rome, the Congregation for Divine Worship, the Vatican department responsible for guiding Roman Catholic religious services, presents to Pope John Paul II a report entitled "Authentic Liturgy" on inclusive language in the Bible and religious services. It states that scripture translations are to avoid many of the features of "inclusive language" because they obscure the meaning of the text. For example, where the original language of scripture says "brothers," "brothers and sisters" may not be used. This document stirs up some controversy in the Western churches, and it points up how issues of inclusive/exclusive language have become important in the contemporary churches, both Roman Catholic and Protestant.

INTRODUCTION

Christianity teaches salvation from sin and the gift of eternal life through the life, death, and resurrection of Jesus, the Son of God. A missionary religion from its beginning, it has become the world's most widespread faith. The *New Testament* has had paramount importance in the history of Christianity from the time of its writing in the century after the death of Jesus in 30 C.E. It has shaped the church's teaching, ethics, ritual, organization, and mission in the world. Although Christians differ in language, culture, organization, and the fine points of religious teaching, all believers have the books of the *New Testament* in common. Indeed, it has often been remarked that the *New Testament* is the *only* thing that all Christians have in common! This scripture has played such a prominent role in world events past and present that to know the *New Testament* and its patterns of use is to have a key to the understanding of Western culture as well as Christianity itself.

Names

The common name in Christianity for its scriptures is the **Bible,** composed of both the **Old Testament** (the Hebrew scriptures) and the **New Testament.** As in the Jewish *Bible,* **testament** or its synonym *covenant* refers to the relationship God has established with people. "New" signifies the early Christian belief that in Jesus God has acted in a new way for salvation. This is seen as a fulfillment of the promises made by God to the Jewish people. In *II Corinthians* 3:6–15, the early Christian missionary Paul calls Christian believers members of the "new covenant" and the books of Moses (the Jewish *Bible*) the "old covenant." The first term echoes *Jeremiah* 31:31, in which God promises, "I will make a new covenant with the house of Israel and the house of Judah." The expression "new covenant" was also used in the early Christian celebration of the ritual of Holy Communion, as its earliest recorded form attests: "In the same way [Jesus] took the cup also, after supper, saying, "'This cup is the new covenant in my blood'" (*I Corinthians* 11:25). In sum, "new covenant/testament" was a common term in early Christianity, and it did not take long to be formally attached to the body of Christian scripture.

The advantage of "New Testament" as a label is that it suggests the complexity of the early Christian attitude to Christianity's relationship with Judaism and the Jewish *Bible*. This relationship has both continuity with Judaism, as expressed by "covenant" or "testament," and discontinuity, as expressed by the qualifier "new." A disadvantage is that it leads to an all-too-easy misunderstanding of the role of the Jewish *Bible* in Christianity—namely that "old" means outmoded and completely replaced by the *New Testament*. This misconception ignores the fact that the Jewish *Bible* itself is part of the Christian scriptures and that the earliest scripture of Christianity—before its own writings were canonized—was the Jewish *Bible*. (For a chart showing the differences between the Protestant and Roman Catholic *Old Testaments*—the former identical with the Jewish *Bible*, the latter identical with the Greek translation of the Jewish Bible—see Table 3.2.)

In recent years there has been a growing tendency to counter this disadvantage by labeling the twenty-seven books of the *New Testament* with a different name. Some use "Christian scriptures." But this is even more disadvantageous than "New Testament" because it implies that the Jewish *Bible* is not part of the Christian scriptures. A few scholars call these books the "Second Testament" and the Jewish *Bible* the "First Testament," but this distinction is vague. Overall, *New Testament* seems the best choice. Despite its disadvantages, it is the commonly accepted label within the Christian church and in the academic community, and we use it here.

Overview of Structure

The *New Testament* is organized into two main sections: books about Jesus called gospels and letters of the apostles to early churches. The **gospels** are "good news" of the story of Jesus. The *Gospel of Matthew* tells the story of Jesus the Savior as the promised Messiah of Israel, going from his conception by the Holy Spirit in the womb of the Virgin Mary through his appearances after his resurrection from the dead. The *Gospel of Mark* tells the story of Jesus from baptism through the resurrection, presenting

Jesus as the Savior of the Gentiles (non-Jews). The *Gospel of Luke* also presents Jesus as the Savior of the Gentiles, with a secondary theme of God's concern for the poor, women, and outcasts. These three gospels are known as **synoptic,** or "seen in one view," because of their parallel structure and content in recounting the story of Jesus. The *Gospel of John* is the story of Jesus as the eternal, divine Son of God who came to earth to show God's glory in his life, death, and resurrection from the dead.

The gospels are followed by the *Acts of the Apostles,* the only book of the *New Testament* devoted to a historical account of the early church and its growth through its first approximately thirty-five years. *Luke* and *Acts* were written as a two-volume work by the same author; unfortunately, *John* now stands between them in the canonical order. The names of all these books were attached in the second century C.E.; when first written, the texts probably featured no authors' names.

Most of the rest of the *New Testament* consists of **letters,** or "epistles," of instruction and correction written by church leaders to various churches. Some scholars dispute the names on these letters, arguing that the texts are **pseudonymous,** written by someone other than the given author, usually by one of his followers or coworkers after his death. Letters that scholars think are genuinely written by the stated person are called **authentic.**

The first letters are those of the **apostle** ("one sent out" with the message of salvation) Paul and his coworkers, arranged mostly by length from longest to shortest and named according to their destination. *Romans* presents Paul's understanding of Christian teaching in a fairly systematic way to a church that he did not establish but was soon to visit. In *I Corinthians* Paul discusses various issues related to Christian doctrine, morality, and worship. In *II Corinthians*—a later letter that is probably, as it now stands, a composite of two or three letters Paul wrote to the church at Corinth after *I Corinthians*—Paul's main concern is to keep this Gentile-Christian church from straying to Jewish Christianity. *Galatians* has much this same theme—namely, that Christians from non-Jewish backgrounds need not be Jewish as well as Christian. *Ephesians,* probably written by a fellow worker of Paul's after his death, presents Jesus Christ as the cosmic savior who unifies races and nations. *Philippians,* a genuine Pauline letter, urges Christians to find joy in Christ. *Colossians,* probably written under Paul's name by a coworker, seeks like *Ephesians* to correct error by presenting Jesus Christ as the all-sufficient savior of the universe, not only of the church. *I Thessalonians* answers questions about what happens when the Lord Jesus returns in glory to judge the world at the end of time. *II Thessalonians,* probably pseudonymously written after the death of Paul, instructs Christians about how to wait for Jesus' return. The next three letters, *I* and *II Timothy* and *Titus,* are called the "Pastoral" letters because they are instructions under Paul's name about pastoral offices and church life at the end of the first century C.E. Finally, *Philemon* is Paul's attempt to reconcile a Christian slave owner to his runaway Christian slave who now seeks to return to that master.

The next section of the *New Testament* is traditionally known as the "General" or "Catholic" Letters (or Epistles). This name was given to them because church authorities supposed that they were written to the church as a whole, but today scholars view them as having just as specific an audience as the Pauline letters. Like the Pauline letters, these also seem to be arranged by length. This section begins with *Hebrews,* an anonymous letter written to encourage Christians not to turn to Judaism. The book of *James* exhorts its audience to live wise, righteous, and socially responsible lives. *I Peter* offers guidelines on Christian behavior, especially to those undergoing persecution for the faith. *II Peter* urges readers to stay true to traditional Christian teaching and reject false forms of the faith. The three letters of *John* combat false teachers while promoting love and hospitality among Christians. *Jude* is very similar in content and purpose to *II Peter*—defending the faith against falsehoods. Finally, the apocalyptic book, *Revelation*, offers visions of God's triumph at the end of the world, delivering believers from persecution by establishing the kingdom of heaven on earth.

For the order, authors (those probably pseudonymous are noted as "disputed"), approximate dates, genres, and size (in number of chapters) of the *New Testament* literature, see Table 4.1.

Table 4.1
The Books of the *New Testament*

Book	Traditional or Given Author	Date (C.E)	Genre	Chapters
Matthew	Matthew (disputed)	80s	gospel	28
Mark	Mark (disputed)	70	gospel	16
Luke	Luke (disputed)	80s	gospel	24
John	John (disputed)	90	gospel	21
Acts of the Apostles	Luke (disputed)	80s	history	28
Romans	Paul	55	letter	16
I Corinthians	Paul	53	letter	16
II Corinthians	Paul	55	letter	13
Galatians	Paul	55	letter	6
Ephesians	Paul (disputed)	90	letter	6
Philippians	Paul	61	letter	4
Colossians	Paul (disputed)	80s	letter	4
I Thessalonians	Paul	51	letter	5
II Thessalonians	Paul (disputed)	80s	letter	3
I Timothy	Paul (disputed)	90s	letter	6
II Timothy	Paul (disputed)	90s	letter	4
Titus	Paul (disputed)	90s	letter	3
Philemon	Paul	50s	letter	1
Hebrews	Anonymous	80s	letter-sermon	13
James	James (disputed)	90	letter-sermon	5
I Peter	Peter (disputed)	80	letter	5

(continued)

Table 4.1
The Books of the *New Testament* (continued)

Book	Traditional or Given Author	Date (C.E)	Genre	Chapters
II Peter	Peter (disputed)	120	letter	3
I John	John "the Elder"	95	essay	5
II John	John "the Elder"	96	letter	1
III John	John "the Elder"	97	letter	1
Jude	Jude (disputed)	100	letter	1
Revelation	John "the Prophet"	90s	apocalypse	22

Use

Because Christianity came from a Judaism with well-formed patterns of scripture usage, the use of the *New Testament* in the church strongly reflects the ways in which the Jewish *Bible* is used in Judaism. The first scripture of the church was the Jewish *Bible* in its Greek form, the *Septuagint*. The entire Jewish *Bible* had a strong influence in early Christianity, but certain sections were especially important. Some of these are mentioned in Chapter 3 on Judaism because they are important for both Judaism and Christianity. For reasons of space, the important Jewish *Bible* selections cannot be repeated or given here. So the reader should be familiar with the Exodus traditions, including the Passover feast (*Exodus* 12:1–27; 14:1–31); the rising Messianic hope (*Isaiah* 11:1–9; 42:1–7); expectations for the end of time (*Daniel* 7:1–14; 12:1–3); and the passages that the early church used to interpret the person and work of Jesus (e.g., *Psalm* 110; *Isaiah* 52:13–54:12).

As in Judaism, the primary use of the *Bible* in Christianity has always been in the service of divine worship. Most of the words and phrases used in worship come from the *Bible*. One of the high points of the service in all Catholic and many Protestant churches is the reading of a selection from the *Old Testament* and two selections from the *New Testament*, the last always a gospel reading. This lectionary system arose in the early Greek church, probably as an inheritance from Judaism. It quickly passed into Western Catholic Christianity. In the twentieth century, especially in its last quarter, many Protestant and Roman Catholic churches in Europe and North America adopted basically the same lectionary system. As a result, on any given Sunday most American Christians hear the same scripture readings and sermons based more or less on them. (Independent Protestants, such as fundamentalists and Pentecostalists, do not follow this system.)

The *Bible* itself occupies a privileged place in the physical arrangement of the typical Christian church. In churches of a "higher," more elaborate form of worship, it is often placed on a special ornate lectern. In more formal services, the book of the gospels is often brought before the altar, "incensed," and kissed by the priest as a sign of its holiness before it is read. In both Catholic and Eastern Orthodox traditions, the scripture books are often richly bound and decorated with gold, jewels, and icons. But even in Protestant churches with less formal worship the *Bible* is also revered. In such churches it is often placed on the main pulpit from which the minister conducts the entire service. In churches of the Baptist wing of Protestantism it is not unusual to see the preacher carrying the *Bible* in one hand and referring to it constantly during the sermon.

Many Christians supplement this formal use of the *Bible* with private devotional reading. Since the Reformation in the sixteenth century, Protestant churches have insisted on the right and duty of every Christian to read the *Bible* individually. This reading includes prayerful meditation on the meaning of the words and on the implication of this meaning for the life of the reader. Reading is also often done aloud by families as a part of the main meal of the day. Such private and familial use of scripture has formed a large part of Protestant spirituality. In the twentieth century, especially after the reforms of the Second Vatican Council in the 1960s, Roman Catholics also acknowledged the importance of private study and historical study of the Bible. Despite this emphasis on private usage of scripture, however, Christians throughout the world still come into contact with their *Bible* mostly during church services.

Alongside this devotional use of the *Bible* is academic study by means of the historical-critical method. This method seeks to understand the various parts of the *Bible* in their original historical context and tries to determine what the writings meant to their original readers. It tends to disregard the teachings of the various churches about the content of scripture. Because this approach puts the *Bible* in the same analytical framework as any other book from the ancient world, fundamentalists, both Protestant and Catholic alike, strongly reject it. An indication of the rapid advance that historical-critical study made in the Roman Catholic Church during the twentieth century is that probably the most influential *New Testament* scholar of the second half of the twentieth century, the late Raymond E. Brown, was a Catholic priest.

Origin and Development

At first glance, it would seem that the *New Testament* was written perhaps only one or two generations after the death and resurrection of Jesus and the beginnings of the church. Yet modern biblical scholarship has discovered that its writing was not completed until perhaps ninety years after Jesus' death. (The process of forming the canon was even longer.)

The pace of writing was retarded by several factors. First, the early church, which began as a group within Judaism, already had a complete body of scripture—the Jewish *Bible*. At first it found this scripture sufficient for its life, especially when it could interpret and use the Jewish *Bible* in its own way to bolster its claim that Jesus was the Messiah, the promised deliverer of Israel. Second, the early Christians quite comfortably used the words and deeds of Jesus in primarily oral form. They did not remember Jesus as a writer, and there was no urgency to write down his words. Indeed, they probably looked on the spoken words of Jesus as more immediate and potent than words about him written in a book. Third, many early Christians believed that the end of the world was very near, and with this expectation the lengthy process of writing, copying (by hand), and distributing books was not to be expected.

How, then, did the process of writing what was to become the *New Testament* begin? The genuine Pauline letters came first. Paul wrote letters to keep in contact with the churches he founded as he traveled around the northeastern Mediterranean provinces of the Roman Empire on his missionary travels. He used letters to instruct and exhort his churches and as a substitute for his own personal presence. These letters gained more importance after Paul's death (probably ca. 65 C.E.), and after his death his coworkers continued to write letters in his name to perpetuate and adapt his teachings for a new generation. Of course, at this stage there was probably no thought by Paul and his followers that these letters would become part of a new body of Christian scripture.

The gospels began to be written down around 70 C.E. The word *gospel* in English is derived from the Anglo-Saxon *godspel*. The Greek word (all the *New Testament* was written in Greek, the common language of the Mediterranean world) is *euangelion*, "good news," from which we get the word *evangelical*. The characteristic structure of the gospel book seems to have been invented by Mark: Jesus' ministry in Galilee, his journey to Jerusalem, teaching in Jerusalem, arrest, trial, death, and resurrection. This structure is evident in two other gospels, *Matthew* and *Luke*, which (the vast majority of scholars conclude) use *Mark* as a source. *John* does not use *Mark* as a source, so it differs from this basic outline.

Those two parts of the *New Testament*, commonly called "the gospel and the apostle," were the basic building blocks of the canon. In the second century C.E., Christians began sorting out true Christian writings from ones they considered false and heretical. The details of this process are hazy, but the main features seem clear. First, a canonical writing had to have a claim to apostolic authorship or authority. It had to be seen as being written either by an apostle, one "sent forth" with the Christian message (such as Matthew, John, Paul, and Peter), or by someone under apostolic authority (Mark, Luke). It had to give the appearance of going back to ancient times. Second, the content of the writings was weighed. In the fight with heresy in the second century, doctrinal content was important because writings that the church deemed heretical also claimed to be written by the apostles, and the only way to differentiate them from false teaching was to compare the content of their teaching to books held to be genuinely apostolic in content. In his *Church History*, for example, Eusebius tells the story of Serapion, the bishop of Antioch in Syria (about 190 C.E.), who heard a reading in church of the *Gospel of Peter*, a work he did not know. At first Serapion accepted it as apostolic. But when he learned that people whom he considered heretics were using its account of the death of Jesus to bolster their claim that Jesus did not die on the cross but returned to heaven before the crucifixion, Serapion forbade any further reading of the *Gospel of Peter* in the churches under his authority.

The third main factor in the process of canonization was the actual use of scripture by prominent Christian churches. The church at Antioch promoted *Matthew*, the province of Asia Minor (modern western Turkey) used *John* and *Luke*, and Rome used *Mark*. The support of these large and influential centers of early Christianity was crucial in the formation of the canon. The final factor was the competing canons of groups that the mainstream church considered heretical. Marcion, an early Christian leader who came to Rome about 145 C.E., argued that the God revealed by Jesus was not the creator God revealed in the Jewish *Bible*. As a result, Marcion totally rejected the Jewish *Bible* as canonical and made a special canon of Christian books out of the *Gospel of Luke* only and ten Pauline letters, rejecting everything else. This selection probably spurred the early church to insist on a wider canon: four gospels, all the Pauline letters that looked genuinely apostolic in content, and other letters from the twelve apostles of Jesus to their churches.

Thus, a consensus grew during the third and fourth centuries around the main books of the emerging canon of the *New Testament*. Seven books remained in doubt during this time, accepted by some churches but not by all: *Hebrews, James, II* and *III John, Jude, II Peter,* and *Revelation*. But as the widely scattered churches grew closer together in the third and fourth centuries, they began accepting these disputed books from each other. By 367 C.E., the twenty-seven-book canon was widely accepted, as the *Festal Letter* of Bishop Athanasius of Alexandria testifies. The catholic (which means "universal") church had a catholic *New Testament*.

HISTORY

The Birth of Jesus the Messiah*

The Gospel of Matthew *and the* Gospel of Luke *present Jesus as conceived by the action of the Spirit of God in the Virgin Mary. This miraculous conception signifies the divine Sonship of Jesus. This passage also focuses on the name* Jesus, *which in the Aramaic language of Palestine means "he will save."*[1]

Now the birth of Jesus Christ happened this way. While his mother Mary was engaged to Joseph, but before they came together, she was found to be pregnant through the Holy Spirit. Because Joseph, her husband to be, was a righteous man, and because he did not want to disgrace her, he intended to divorce her privately. [20] When he had contemplated this, an angel of the Lord appeared to him in a dream and said, "Joseph, son of David, do not be afraid to take Mary as your wife, because the child conceived in her is from the Holy Spirit. She will give birth to a son and you will name him Jesus, because he will save his people from their sins." This all happened so that what was spoken by the Lord through the prophet would be fulfilled: "Look! The virgin will conceive and bear a son, and they will call him Emmanuel," which means "God with us." When Joseph awoke from sleep he did what the angel of the Lord told him. He took his wife, [25] but did not have marital relations with her until she gave birth to a son,[2] whom he named Jesus.

---

*Matthew 1:18–25.

[1] All New Testament scripture quoted by permission from the NET Bible®™. Copyright © 2003 by Biblical Studies Press, L.L.C. www.netbible.com. All rights reserved.

[2] *until she gave birth to a son:* Roman Catholics and the Eastern Orthodox, who confess the lifelong virginity of Mary, do not interpret this verse to mean that Mary and Joseph did have sexual relations after Jesus' birth.

Jesus' Miracles*

In the gospels, as in the Hebrew scriptures, miracles signify the inbreaking of God into human life. They are seen not as "violations of natural law" but as acts of divine power for salvation. This selection has two types of miracles characteristic of the ministry of Jesus: exorcism of demons, showing the power of Jesus over supernatural evil; and healing of the sick, showing Jesus' ultimate victory over physical evil and death, which is central to early Christianity.

So they sailed over to the region of the Gerasenes, which is opposite Galilee. As Jesus stepped ashore, a certain man from the town met him who was possessed by demons. For a long time this man had worn no clothes and had not lived in a house but among the tombs. When he saw Jesus, he cried out, fell down before him, and shouted with a loud voice, "Leave me alone, Jesus, Son of the Most High God! I beg you, do not torment me!" For Jesus had commanded the evil spirit to come out of the man. (For many times it had seized him. So he was bound with chains and shackles and kept under guard, but he broke the bonds and was driven by the demon into deserted places.) [30] Jesus then asked him, "What is your name?" He said, "Legion," because many demons had entered him. And they began to beg him not to order them to depart into the abyss.[3] Now a large herd of pigs was feeding there on the hillside, and the demons begged Jesus to let them go into them. He gave them permission. So the demons came out of the man and went into the pigs, and the herd of pigs rushed down the steep slope into the lake and drowned. When the herdsmen saw what had happened, they ran off and spread the news in the town and countryside. [35] So the people went out to see what had happened, and they came to Jesus. They found the man from whom the demons had gone out, sitting at Jesus' feet, clothed and in his right mind, and they were afraid. Those who had seen it told them how the man who had been demon-possessed had been healed. Then all the people of the Gerasenes and the surrounding region asked Jesus to leave them alone, for they were seized with great fear; so he got into the boat and left. The man from whom the demons had gone out begged to go with him, but Jesus sent him away, saying, "Return to your home, and declare what God has done for you." So he went away, proclaiming throughout the whole town what Jesus had done for him.

[40] Now when Jesus returned, the crowd welcomed him, for they were all waiting for him. Then a man named Jairus, who was a ruler of the synagogue, came up. Falling at Jesus' feet, he pleaded with him to come to his house, because he had an only daughter, about twelve years old, and she was dying.

As Jesus was on his way, the crowds pressed around him. Now a woman was there who had been suffering from a hemorrhage for twelve years but could not be healed by anyone. She came up behind Jesus and touched the edge of his cloak, and at once the bleeding stopped. [45] Then Jesus asked, "Who was it who touched me?" When they all denied it, Peter said, "Master, the crowds are surrounding you and pressing against you!" But Jesus said, "Someone touched me, for I know that power has gone out from me." When the woman saw that she could not escape notice, she came trembling and fell down before him. In the presence of all the people, she explained why she had touched him and how she had been immediately healed. Then he said to her, "Daughter, your faith has made you well. Go in peace."

---

*Luke 8:26–56.
[3] *abyss:* a section of hell in which demons are confined to await final destruction.

While he was still speaking, someone from the synagogue ruler's house came and said, "Your daughter is dead; do not trouble the teacher any longer." [50] But when Jesus heard this, he told him, "Do not be afraid; just believe, and she will be healed." Now when he came to the house, Jesus did not let anyone go in with him except Peter, John, and James, and the child's father and mother. Now they were all wailing and mourning for her, but he said, "Stop your weeping; she is not dead but asleep." And they began making fun of him, because they knew that she was dead. But Jesus gently took her by the hand and said, "Child, get up." [55] Her spirit returned, and she got up immediately. Then he told them to give her something to eat. Her parents were astonished, but he ordered them to tell no one what had happened.[4]

---

[4] *tell no one what had happened:* probably connected with the "messianic secret"; see *Matthew* 16:20 (page 113 in the present book).

The Arrest, Trial, and Death of Jesus*

The sufferings of Jesus at the end of his life include betrayal by his disciple Judas, denial by Peter, a trial before the Jews on religious charges, a trial before the Roman governor Pontius Pilate on civil charges, and condemnation to be crucified. Throughout their narration of these sufferings, Mark and the other gospel writers portray Jesus gently accepting his suffering as the will of God and his death as a sacrifice for the sin of the world.

Right away, while Jesus was still speaking, Judas, one of the twelve, arrived. With him came a crowd armed with swords and clubs, and sent by the chief priests and experts in the law and elders. (Now the betrayer had given them a sign, saying, "The one I kiss is the man. Arrest him and lead him away under guard.") [45] When Judas came, he went to Jesus immediately and said, "Rabbi!" and kissed him. Then they took hold of him and arrested him. One of the bystanders drew his sword and struck the high priest's slave, cutting off his ear. Jesus said to them, "Have you come with swords and clubs to arrest me like you would an outlaw? Day after day I was with you, teaching in the temple courts, yet you did not arrest me. But this has happened so that the scriptures would be fulfilled." [50] Then all the disciples left him and fled. . . .

Then they led Jesus to the high priest, and all the chief priests and elders and experts in the law came together. And Peter had followed him from a distance, up to the courtyard of the high priest. He was sitting with the guards and warming himself by the fire. [55] The chief priests and the whole Sanhedrin were looking for evidence against Jesus so that they could put him to death, but they did not find anything. Many gave false testimony against him, but their testimony did not agree. Some stood up and gave this false testimony against him: "We heard him say, 'I will destroy this temple made with hands and in three days build another not made with hands.'" Yet even on this point their testimony did not agree.

[60] Then the high priest stood up before them and asked Jesus, "Have you no answer? What is this that they are testifying against you?" But he was silent and did not answer. Again the high priest questioned him, "Are you the Christ, the Son of the Blessed One?" "I am," said Jesus,

---

*Mark 14:43–50, 53–65; 15:1–41.

"and you will see the Son of Man sitting at the right hand of the Power and coming with the clouds of heaven."[5] Then the high priest tore his clothes and said, "Why do we still need witnesses? You have heard the blasphemy! What is your verdict?" They all condemned him as deserving death. [65] Then some began to spit on him, and to blindfold him, and strike him with their fists, saying, "Prophesy!" The guards also took him and beat him.

[15:1] Early in the morning, after forming a plan, the chief priests with the elders and the experts in the law and the whole Sanhedrin tied Jesus up, led him away, and handed him over to Pilate. So Pilate asked him, "Are you the king of the Jews?" He replied, "You say so." Then the chief priests began to accuse him repeatedly. So Pilate asked him again, "Have you nothing to say? See how many charges they are bringing against you!" [5] But Jesus made no further reply, so that Pilate was amazed.

During the feast it was customary to release one prisoner to the people, whomever they requested. A man named Barabbas was imprisoned with rebels who had committed murder during an insurrection. Then the crowd came up and began to ask Pilate to release a prisoner for them, as was his custom. So Pilate asked them, "Do you want me to release the king of the Jews for you?" [10] (For he knew that the chief priests had handed him over because of envy.) But the chief priests stirred up the crowd to have him release Barabbas instead. So Pilate spoke to them again, "Then what do you want me to do with the one you call king of the Jews?" They shouted back, "Crucify him!" Pilate asked them, "Why? What has he done wrong?" But they shouted more insistently, "Crucify him!" [15] Because he wanted to satisfy the crowd, Pilate released Barabbas for them. Then after he had Jesus flogged he handed him over to be crucified.

So the soldiers led him into the palace (that is, the governor's residence) and called together the whole cohort. They put a purple cloak on him and after braiding a crown of thorns, they put it on him. They began to salute him: "Hail, king of the Jews!" Again and again they struck him on the head with a staff and spit on him. Then they knelt down and paid homage to him. [20] When they had finished mocking him, they stripped him of the purple cloak and put his own clothes back on him. Then they led him away to crucify him.

The soldiers drafted a passer-by to carry his cross, a man coming from the country, Simon of Cyrene, the father of Alexander and Rufus.[6] They brought Jesus to a place called Golgotha (which is translated, "Place of the Skull"). They offered him wine mixed with myrrh, but he did not take it. Then they crucified him and divided his clothes, throwing dice for them, to decide what each would take. [25] It was nine o'clock in the morning when they crucified him. The inscription of the charge against him read, "The king of the Jews." And they crucified two outlaws with him, one on his right and one on his left. Those who passed by defamed him, shaking their heads and saying, "Aha! You who can destroy the temple and rebuild it in three days, [30] save yourself and come down from the cross!" In the same way even the chief priests—together with the experts in the law—were mocking him among themselves: "He saved others, but he cannot save himself! Let the Christ, the king of Israel, come down from the cross now, that we may see and believe!" Those who were crucified with him also spoke abusively to him.

Now when it was noon, darkness came over the whole land until three in the afternoon. Around three o'clock Jesus cried out with a loud voice, "Eloi, Eloi, lema sabachthani?" which means, "My God, my God, why have you

---

[5] Quoted from *Daniel* 7:13 in the Jewish scriptures, with an allusion to *Psalm* 110.
[6] *Simon, Alexander, Rufus:* That these names are given likely indicates that these men were known to the readers of *Mark*.

forsaken me?" [35] When some of the bystanders heard it they said, "Listen, he is calling for Elijah!" Then someone ran, filled a sponge with sour wine, put it on a stick, and gave it to him to drink, saying, "Leave him alone! Let's see if Elijah will come to take him down!"[7] But Jesus cried out with a loud voice and breathed his last. And the temple curtain was torn in two, from top to bottom. Now when the centurion, who stood in front of him, saw how he died, he said, "Truly this man was God's Son!" [40] There were also women, watching from a distance. Among them were Mary Magdalene, and Mary the mother of James the younger and of Joses, and Salome. When he was in Galilee, they had followed him and given him support. Many other women who had come up with him to Jerusalem were there too.

---

[7] *Elijah:* a fairly widespread Jewish belief at this time was that Elijah, an ancient Israelite prophet, would return at the end of time. Compare the contemporary Jewish practice of leaving an empty seat at the Passover Seder for Elijah.

The Resurrection of Jesus*

After Joseph of Arimathea buried the body of Jesus, three women from among his followers came on Sunday morning to finish the tasks of the funeral. They become the first witnesses of Jesus' resurrection. In this passage, the "young man" is an angel, and his message is that God has raised Jesus from the dead. The resurrection of Jesus and the life it brings became the center of early Christian belief.

When the Sabbath was over, Mary Magdalene, Mary the mother of James, and Salome bought aromatic spices so that they might go and anoint him. And very early on the first day of the week, at sunrise, they went to the tomb. They had been asking each other, "Who will roll away the stone for us from the entrance to the tomb?"[8] But when they looked up, they saw that the stone, which was very large, had been rolled back. [5] Then as they went into the tomb, they saw a young man dressed in a white robe sitting on the right side; and they were alarmed. But he said to them, "Do not be alarmed. You are looking for Jesus the Nazarene, who was crucified. He has been raised! He is not here. Look, there is the place where they laid him. But go, tell his disciples, even Peter, that he is going ahead of you into Galilee. You will see him there, just as he told you." Then they went out and ran from the tomb, for terror and bewilderment had seized them. And they said nothing to anyone, because they were afraid.

---

*Mark 16:1–8.
[8] *roll away the stone:* A massive disk-shaped stone had been rolled over the entrance of the tomb.

The Ascension of Jesus**

In Luke and Acts, which are written by the same author, Jesus ascends to heaven forty days after his resurrection. This selection draws a connection between the completion of the earthly ministry of Jesus and the consummation of history: The end is not yet; but in the interim between the present and the end, the church is to witness to Jesus throughout the world. This missionary commission began to be carried out in the first century C.E. and has motivated Christianity for several periods of its subsequent history.

**Acts 1:6–11.

So when they had gathered together, they began to ask him, "Lord, is this the time when you are restoring the kingdom to Israel?" He told them, "You are not permitted to know the times or periods that the Father has set by his own authority. But you will receive power when the Holy Spirit has come upon you, and you will be my witnesses in Jerusalem, and in all Judea and Samaria, and to the farthest parts of the earth."

After he had said this, while they were watching, he was lifted up and a cloud hid him from their sight. [10] As they were still staring into the sky while he was going, suddenly two men in white clothing stood near them and said, "Men of Galilee, why do you stand here looking up into the sky? This same Jesus who has been taken up from you into heaven will come back in the same way you saw him go into heaven."

The Coming of the Holy Spirit*

In dealing with the "speaking in tongues" that occurs on Pentecost, a Jewish holiday that comes fifty days after Passover, Acts works with two traditions: that the apostles are speaking an actual foreign language and that they speak in a language not human but interpreted by the listeners as their own. (Modern Pentecostalism picks up on the second tradition.) Peter's speech on this occasion explains the meaning of the Holy Spirit's coming as the fulfillment of scripture and the divine plan, bringing the presence and power of God to all in the church regardless of gender or social standing.

Now when the day of Pentecost had come, they were all together in one place. Suddenly a sound like a violent wind blowing came from heaven and filled the entire house where they were sitting. And tongues spreading out like a fire appeared to them and came to rest on each one of them. All of them were filled with the Holy Spirit, and they began to speak in other languages as the Spirit enabled them.

[5] Now there were devout Jews from every nation under heaven residing in Jerusalem. When this sound occurred, a crowd gathered and was in confusion, because each one heard them speaking in his own language. Completely baffled, they said, "Aren't all these who are speaking Galileans? And how is it that each one of us hears them in our own native language? Parthians, Medes, Elamites, and residents of Mesopotamia, Judea and Cappadocia, Pontus and Asia, [10] Phrygia and Pamphylia, Egypt and the parts of Libya near Cyrene, and visitors from Rome, both Jews and proselytes,[9] Cretans and Arabs—we hear them speaking in our own languages about the great deeds God has done!" All were astounded and greatly confused, saying to one another, "What does this mean?" But others jeered at the believers, saying, "They are drunk on new wine!"

But Peter stood up with the eleven, raised his voice, and addressed them: "You Jewish men and all you who live in Jerusalem, let this be known to you and listen carefully to what I say. [15] In spite of what you think, these men are not drunk, for it is only nine o'clock in the morning. But this is what was spoken about through the prophet Joel:

> 'And in the last days it will be,' God says, 'that
> I will pour out my Spirit on all people, and
> your sons and your daughters will prophesy,
> and your young men will see visions, and
> your old men will dream dreams.

---

*Acts 2:1–21.

[9] *Jews and proselytes:* born Jews and Gentiles converted to Judaism, respectively. All the nations listed in this "Table of Nations" had Jews then living in Jerusalem.

> Even on my slaves, both men and women,
>   I will pour out my Spirit in those days, and
>   they will prophesy.
> And I will perform wonders in the sky above
>   and miraculous signs on the earth below,
>   blood and fire and clouds of smoke.
> [20] The sun will be changed to darkness and the moon to blood before the great and glorious day of the Lord comes.
>
> And then everyone who calls on the name of the Lord will be saved.'"

Persecution of the Apostles*

The early Christian church met opposition from the same forces that acted to do away with Jesus. The apostles' calm and confident attitude to their persecutions is underscored here, and this attitude would remain important in the next few centuries as Roman persecution of the church grew stronger. Verse 29 sounds a theme that echoes through the history of the church: When the laws of this world and the law of God collide, "We must obey God rather than men."

When they had brought them, they stood them before the council, and the high priest questioned them, saying, "We gave you strict orders not to teach in this name. Look, you have filled Jerusalem with your teaching, and you intend to bring this man's blood on us!" But Peter and the apostles replied, "We must obey God rather than men. [30] The God of our forefathers raised up Jesus, whom you seized and killed by hanging him on a tree. God exalted him to his right hand as Leader and Savior, to give repentance to Israel and forgiveness of sins. And we are witnesses of these events, and so is the Holy Spirit whom God has given to those who obey him."

Now when they heard this, they became furious and wanted to execute them. But a Pharisee whose name was Gamaliel, a teacher of the law who was respected by all the people, stood up in the council and ordered the men to be put outside for a short time. [35] Then he said to the council, "Israelite men, pay close attention to what you are about to do to these men. For some time ago Theudas rose up, claiming to be somebody, and about four hundred men joined him. He was killed, and all who followed him were dispersed and nothing came of it. After him Judas the Galilean arose in the days of the census, and incited people to follow him in revolt.[10] He too was killed, and all who followed him were scattered. So in this case I say to you, stay away from these men and leave them alone, because if this plan or this undertaking originates with men, it will come to nothing, but if it is from God, you will not be able to stop them, or you may even be found fighting against God."

He convinced them, [40] and they summoned the apostles and had them beaten. Then they ordered them not to speak in the name of Jesus and released them. So they left the council rejoicing because they had been considered worthy to suffer dishonor for the sake of the name. And every day both in the temple courts and from house to house, they did not stop teaching and proclaiming the good news that Jesus was the Christ.

---

*Acts 5:27–42.
[10] *Theudas . . . Judas the Galilean:* messianic pretenders whose movements collapsed after they died.

The Council at Jerusalem*

The issue at this council was whether Gentile converts to Christianity should be required to be circumcised and keep at least some of the laws of Moses. Paul and Peter argued no; some conservative Jewish Christians, converts from the Pharisees, said yes. James, kinsman of Jesus and leader of the Jerusalem church at this time, gave the compromise ruling: No circumcision would be required of Gentile converts, but certain minimal laws of purity would be imposed. The result of this decision was that Christianity began to separate from its roots in Judaism, becoming a different religion.

Now some men came down from Judea and began to teach the brothers, "Unless you are circumcised according to the custom of Moses, you cannot be saved." When Paul and Barnabas had a major argument and debate with them, the church appointed Paul and Barnabas and some others from among them to go up to meet with the apostles and elders in Jerusalem about this point of disagreement. So they were sent on their way by the church, and as they passed through both Phoenicia and Samaria, they were relating at length the conversion of the Gentiles and bringing great joy to all the brothers. When they arrived in Jerusalem, they were received by the church and the apostles and the elders, and they reported all the things God had done with them. [5] But some from the religious party of the Pharisees who had believed stood up and said, "It is necessary to circumcise the Gentiles and to order them to observe the law of Moses."

Both the apostles and the elders met together to deliberate about this matter. After there had been much debate, Peter stood up and said to them, "Brothers, you know that some time ago God chose that from my mouth the Gentiles should hear the message of the gospel and believe. And God, who knows the heart, has testified to them by giving them the Holy Spirit just as he did to us, and he made no distinction between them and us, cleansing their hearts by faith. [10] So now why are you putting God to the test by placing on the neck of the disciples a yoke that neither our ancestors nor we have been able to bear? On the contrary, we believe that we are saved through the grace of the Lord Jesus, in the same way as they are."

The whole group kept quiet and listened to Barnabas and Paul while they explained all the miraculous signs and wonders God had done among the Gentiles through them. After they stopped speaking, James replied, "Brothers, listen to me. Simeon has explained how God first concerned himself to select from among the Gentiles a people for his name. [15] The words of the prophets agree with this, as it is written,

'After this I will return,
and I will rebuild the fallen tent of David;
I will rebuild its ruins and restore it,
so that the rest of humanity may seek the Lord,
namely, all the Gentiles I have called to be my own,'

says the Lord, who makes these things known from long ago.

"Therefore I conclude that we should not cause extra difficulty for those among the Gentiles who are turning to God, [20] but that we should write them a letter telling them to abstain from things defiled by idols and from sexual immorality and from what has been strangled and from blood. For Moses has had those who proclaim him in every town from ancient times, because he is read aloud in the synagogues every Sabbath."

---

*Acts 15:1–21.

TEACHING

The Parables of Jesus*

The parables were Jesus' distinctive form of teaching. Parables are stories that compare an experience in everyday life with some aspect of religious life, especially life in the Kingdom of God. Here is a collection of parables gathered by Mark or transmitted to him in the oral tradition. Many scholars view the interpretation of the parable of the sower, found in the third paragraph, as deriving not directly from Jesus but from the early church.

Again he began to teach by the lake. And such a large crowd gathered around him that he got into a boat on the lake and sat there while the whole crowd was on the shore by the lake. He taught them many things in parables, and in his teaching said to them: "Listen! A sower went out to sow. And as he sowed, some seed fell along the path, and the birds came and devoured it. [5] Other seed fell on rocky ground where it did not have much soil. It sprang up at once because the soil was not deep. When the sun came up it was scorched, and because it did not have a root, it withered. Other seed fell among the thorns, and they grew up and choked it, and it did not produce grain. But other seed fell on good soil and produced grain, sprouting and growing; some bore thirty times as much, some sixty, and some a hundred times." And he said, "Whoever has ears to hear had better listen!"

[10] When he was alone, those around him with the twelve asked him about the parables. He said to them, "The secret of the kingdom of God has been given to you. But to those outside, everything is in parables,

> so that although they look they may look but not see,
> and although they hear they may hear but not understand,
> so they may not repent and be forgiven."

He said to them, "Don't you understand this parable? Then how will you understand any parable? The sower sows the word. [15] These are the ones on the path where the word is sown: Whenever they hear, immediately Satan comes and snatches the word that was sown in them. These are the ones sown on rocky ground: As soon as they hear the word, they receive it with joy. But they have no root in themselves and do not endure. Then, when trouble or persecution comes because of the word, immediately they fall away. Others are the ones sown among thorns: They are those who hear the word, but worldly cares, wealthy pleasures, and the desire for other things come in and choke the word, and it produces nothing. [20] But these are the ones sown on good soil: They hear the word and receive it and bear fruit, one thirty times as much, one sixty, and one a hundred."

He also said to them, "A lamp isn't brought to be put under a basket or under a bed, is it? Isn't it to be placed on a lampstand? For nothing is hidden except to be revealed, and nothing concealed except to be brought to light. If anyone has ears to hear, he had better listen!" And he said to them, "Take care about what you hear. The measure you use will be the measure you receive, and more will be added to you. [25] For whoever has will be given more, but whoever does not have, even what he has will be taken from him."

He also said, "The kingdom of God is like someone who spreads seed on the ground. He goes to sleep and gets up, night and day, and the seed sprouts and grows, though he does not know how. By itself the soil produces a crop, first the stalk, then the head, then the full grain

---

*Mark 4:1–34.

in the head. And when the grain is ripe, he sends in the sickle because the harvest has come."

[30] He also asked, "To what can we compare the kingdom of God, or what parable can we use to present it? It is like a mustard seed, that when placed on the ground is the smallest of all the seeds scattered on the ground. But when it takes root, it grows up and becomes the greatest of all garden plants, and grows large branches so that the birds of the sky can nest in its shade."

So with many parables like these, he spoke the word to them, as they were able to hear. He did not speak to them without a parable. But privately he explained everything to his own disciples.

The Divine Word Became Human*

This hymn to Christ as the divine Word made human is perhaps the New Testament's *most exalted view of the Savior. Largely on the strength of John's gospel among early Christians, with help from some other writers (especially Paul), the early church came to see the divine nature of Jesus as the divine Son from all eternity. This main theme alternates here with a secondary theme: that John the Baptist is not the Messiah.*

In the beginning was the Word, and the Word was with God, and the Word was fully God. The Word was with God in the beginning. All things were created by him, and apart from him not one thing was created that has been created. In him was life, and the life was the light of mankind. [5] And the light shines on in the darkness, but the darkness has not mastered it.

A man came, sent from God, whose name was John. He came as a witness to testify about the light so that everyone may believe through him. He himself was not the light, but he came to testify about the light. The true light, who gives light to everyone, was coming into the world.

[10] He was in the world, and the world was created by him, but the world did not recognize him. He came to what was his own, but his own people did not receive him. But to all who have received him—those who believe in his name—he has given the right to become God's children—children not born by human parents or by human desire or a husband's decision, but by God.

Now the Word became flesh and took up residence among us. We saw his glory—the glory of the one and only, full of grace and truth, who came from the Father. [15] John testified about him and cried out, "This one was the one about whom I said, 'He who comes after me is greater than I am, because he existed before me.'" For we have all received from his fullness one gracious gift after another. For the law was given through Moses, but grace and truth came about through Jesus Christ. No one has ever seen God. The only one, himself God, who is in the presence of the Father, has made God known.

---

*John 1:1–18.

Nicodemus Visits Jesus**

This selection presents one early Christian view of salvation: as a "rebirth" by the power of the Holy Spirit that makes a person the child of God. In modern times, a part of evangelical Protestantism has fastened upon this passage, interpreting the "born-again" concept as an emotionally powerful

---

**John 3:1–21.

conversion experience. Christians of other Protestant, Roman Catholic, and Orthodox traditions hold that simply to believe in Jesus as Savior and be baptized is to be "born again."

Now a certain man, a Pharisee named Nicodemus who was a member of the Jewish ruling council, came to Jesus at night and said to him, "Rabbi, we know that you are a teacher who has come from God. For no one could perform the miraculous signs that you do unless God is with him." Jesus replied, "I tell you the solemn truth, unless a person is born from above,[11] he cannot see the kingdom of God." Nicodemus said to him, "How can a man be born when he is old? He cannot enter his mother's womb and be born a second time, can he?"

[5] Jesus answered, "I tell you the solemn truth, unless a person is born of water and spirit, he cannot enter the kingdom of God. What is born of the flesh is flesh, and what is born of the Spirit is spirit. Do not be amazed that I said to you, 'You must all be born from above.' The wind blows wherever it will, and you hear the sound it makes but do not know where it comes from and where it is going. So it is with everyone who is born of the Spirit."

Nicodemus replied, "How can these things be?" [10] Jesus answered, "Are you a teacher of Israel and yet you don't understand these things? I tell you the solemn truth, we speak about what we know and testify about what we have seen, but you people do not accept our testimony. If I have told you people about earthly things and you don't believe, how will you believe if I tell you about heavenly things? No one has ascended into heaven except the one who descended from heaven—the Son of Man. Just as Moses lifted up the serpent in the wilderness, so must the Son of Man be lifted up, [15] so that everyone who believes in him may have eternal life.

"For this is the way God loved the world: He gave his one and only Son that everyone who believes in him should not perish but have eternal life. For God did not send his Son into the world to condemn the world, but that the world should be saved through him. The one who believes in him is not condemned. The one who does not believe has been condemned already, because he has not believed in the name of the one and only Son of God. Now this is the basis for judging: that the light has come into the world and people loved the darkness rather than the light, because their deeds were evil. [20] For everyone who does evil deeds hates the light and does not come to the light, so that their deeds will not be exposed. But the one who practices the truth comes to the light, so that it may be plainly evident that his deeds have been done in God."

---

[11] *born from above:* From the Greek original of the *New Testament* it is possible to translate *from above* as "again." This was done in older translations and comes into evangelical Christianity's expression "born again."

A Sinful Woman Forgiven*

In this passage Jesus answers a Pharisee's criticism with a parable on the meaning of forgiveness. Jesus teaches the radical nature of God's love and its transforming power. The woman in this parable was, in post–New Testament times, identified as Mary Magdalene. This identification has been reinforced recently by The Da Vinci Code, *a novel by Dan Brown and the upcoming film based on it, but scholars almost unanimously reject it.*

Now one of the Pharisees asked Jesus to have dinner with him, so he went into the Pharisee's

---

*Luke 7:36–50.

house and took his place at the table. Then when a woman of that town, who was a sinner, learned that Jesus was dining at the Pharisee's house, she brought an alabaster jar of perfumed oil. As she stood behind him at his feet, weeping, she began to wet his feet with her tears. She wiped them with her hair, kissed them, and anointed them with the perfumed oil. Now when the Pharisee who had invited him saw this, he said to himself, "If this man were a prophet, he would know who and what kind of woman this is who is touching him, that she is a sinner."[12] [40] So Jesus answered him, "Simon, I have something to say to you." He replied, "Say it, Teacher."

"A certain creditor had two debtors; one owed him five hundred silver coins, and the other fifty.[13] When they could not pay, he canceled the debts of both. Now which of them will love him more?" Simon answered, "I suppose the one who had the bigger debt canceled." Jesus said to him, "You have judged rightly." Then, turning toward the woman, he said to Simon, "Do you see this woman? I entered your house, you gave me no water for my feet, but she has wet my feet with her tears and wiped them with her hair. [45] You gave me no kiss of greeting, but from the time I entered she has not stopped kissing my feet. You did not anoint my head with oil, but she has anointed my feet with perfumed oil. Therefore I tell you, her sins, which were many, are forgiven, thus she loved much; but the one who is forgiven little loves little." Then Jesus said to her, "Your sins are forgiven."

But those who were at the table with him began to say among themselves, "Who is this, who even forgives sins?" [50] He said to the woman, "Your faith has saved you; go in peace."

---

[12] *a sinner:* a notorious sinner, perhaps one who made her living by an occupation considered sinful by the law of Moses.

[13] *silver coins:* One silver coin, in Greek, *denarius,* was a day's pay for a common laborer.

Results of Justification*

Justification is God's act of making believers righteous through faith in the crucified and resurrected Jesus. In this justification, believers are reconciled to God. Protestant churches have used this and similar passages to support their leading doctrines of justification by faith alone rather than through human obedience to religious law. In the last ten years, Roman Catholic and Protestant churches have made great strides toward a common understanding of justification by faith.

Therefore, since we have been declared righteous by faith, we have peace with God through our Lord Jesus Christ, through whom we have also obtained access by faith into this grace in which we stand, and we rejoice in the hope of God's glory. Not only this, but we also rejoice in sufferings, knowing that suffering produces endurance, and endurance, character, and character, hope. [5] And hope does not disappoint, because the love of God has been poured out in our hearts through the Holy Spirit who was given to us.

For while we were still helpless, at the right time Christ died for the ungodly. (For rarely will anyone die for a righteous person, though for a good person perhaps someone might possibly dare to die.) But God demonstrates his own love for us, in that while we were still sinners,

---

*Romans 5:1–11.

Christ died for us. Much more then, because we have now been declared righteous by his blood, we will be saved through him from God's wrath. [10] For if while we were enemies we were reconciled to God through the death of his son, how much more, since we have been reconciled, will we be saved by his life?[14] Not only this, but we also rejoice in God through our Lord Jesus Christ, through whom we have now received this reconciliation.

---

[14] *his life:* Jesus' eternal life after his resurrection, which secures the believer's eternal life.

The End of Time*

Many New Testament *teachings about the end of time are taken from Judaism and adapted to Christianity. In the first passage,* Matthew *relates the teaching of Jesus about his role as the judge at the final judgment, after the resurrection of all the dead. In the second, the author of* Revelation *presents in striking apocalyptic style dreams and visions about the end.*

[*Matthew* 25:31] "When the Son of Man comes in his glory and all the angels with him, then he will sit on his glorious throne. All the nations will be assembled before him, and he will separate people one from another like a shepherd separates the sheep from the goats. He will put the sheep on his right and the goats on his left. Then the king will say to those on his right, 'Come, you who are blessed by my Father, inherit the kingdom prepared for you from the foundation of the world. [35] For I was hungry and you gave me food, I was thirsty and you gave me something to drink, I was a stranger and you invited me in, I was naked and you gave me clothing, I was sick and you took care of me, I was in prison and you visited me.' Then the righteous will answer him, 'Lord, when did we see you hungry and feed you, or thirsty and give you something to drink? When did we see you a stranger and invite you in, or naked and clothe you? When did we see you sick or in prison and visit you?' [40] And the king will answer them, 'I tell you the truth, just as you did it for one of the least of these brothers of mine, you did it for me.'

"Then he will say to those on his left, 'Depart from me, you accursed, into the eternal fire that has been prepared for the devil and his angels! For I was hungry and you gave me nothing to eat, I was thirsty and you gave me nothing to drink. I was a stranger and you did not receive me as a guest, naked and you did not clothe me, sick and in prison and you did not visit me.' Then they too will answer, 'Lord, when did we see you hungry or thirsty or a stranger or naked or sick or in prison, and did not give you whatever you needed?' [45] Then he will answer them, 'I tell you the truth, just as you did not do it for one of the least of these, you did not do it for me.' And these will depart into eternal punishment, but the righteous into eternal life."

[*Revelation* 20:1] Then I saw an angel descending from heaven, holding in his hand the key to the abyss and a huge chain. He seized the dragon—the ancient serpent, who is the devil and Satan—and tied him up for a thousand years. The angel then threw him into the abyss and locked and sealed it so that he could not deceive the nations until the one thousand years were finished. (After these things he must be released for a brief period of time.)

---

*Matthew 25:31–46; *Revelation* 20:1–21:4.

Then I saw thrones and seated on them were those who had been given authority to judge. I also saw the souls of those who had been beheaded because of the testimony about Jesus and because of the word of God. These had not worshiped the beast or his image and had refused to receive his mark on their forehead or hand. They came to life and reigned with Christ for a thousand years. [5] (The rest of the dead did not come to life until the thousand years were finished.) This is the first resurrection. Blessed and holy is the one who takes part in the first resurrection. The second death has no power over them, but they will be priests of God and of Christ, and they will reign with him for a thousand years.

Now when the thousand years are finished, Satan will be released from his prison and will go out to deceive the nations at the four corners of the earth, Gog and Magog,[15] to bring them together for the battle. They are as numerous as the grains of sand in the sea. They went up on the broad plain of the earth and encircled the camp of the saints and the beloved city, but fire came down from heaven and devoured them completely. [10] And the devil who deceived them was thrown into the lake of fire and sulfur, where the beast and the false prophet are too, and they will be tormented there day and night forever and ever.

Then I saw a large white throne and the one who was seated on it; the earth and the heaven fled from his presence, and no place was found for them. And I saw the dead, the great and the small, standing before the throne. Then books were opened, and another book was opened—the book of life. So the dead were judged by what was written in the books, according to their deeds. The sea gave up the dead that were in it, and Death and Hades gave up the dead that were in them, and each one was judged according to his deeds. Then Death and Hades were thrown into the lake of fire. This is the second death—the lake of fire. [5] If anyone's name was not found written in the book of life, that person was thrown into the lake of fire.

Then I saw a new heaven and a new earth, for the first heaven and earth had ceased to exist, and the sea existed no more. And I saw the holy city—the new Jerusalem—descending out of heaven from God, made ready like a bride adorned for her husband. And I heard a loud voice from the throne saying: "Look! The residence of God is among men and women. He will live among them, and they will be his people, and God himself will be with them as their God. He will wipe away every tear from their eyes, and death will not exist any more—or mourning, or crying, or pain; the former things have ceased to exist."

---

[15] *Gog and Magog:* nations allied with Satan to oppose the coming of God's kingdom. In *Ezekiel* 38–39 these are probably code words for Babylon, which in the book of *Revelation* is code in turn for Rome.

ETHICS

The Sermon on the Mount*

The Sermon on the Mount is the gospels' longest collection of the moral teachings of Jesus. It is largely a collection by the gospel writer, probably drawing on an early collection of Jesus' sayings called by modern scholars the Quelle, *"source." The sermon contains his understanding of Jesus' teaching on what it is to follow Jesus. The themes are many and varied: blessings on obedience, the law of Moses, the practice of piety, use of possessions, and following Jesus' words.*

---

*Matthew 5–7.

When he saw the crowds, he went up the mountain. After he sat down his disciples came to him. Then he began to teach them by saying:

"Blessed are the poor in spirit, for the kingdom of heaven belongs to them.
"Blessed are those who mourn, for they will be comforted.
"Blessed are the meek,[16] for they will inherit the earth.
"Blessed are those who hunger and thirst for righteousness, for they will be satisfied.
"Blessed are the merciful, for they will be shown mercy.
"Blessed are the pure in heart, for they will see God.
"Blessed are the peacemakers, for they will be called the children of God.
[10] "Blessed are those who are persecuted for righteousness, for the kingdom of heaven belongs to them.

"Blessed are you when people insult you and persecute you and say all kinds of evil things about you falsely on account of me. Rejoice and be glad because your reward is great in heaven, for they persecuted the prophets before you in the same way.

"You are the salt of the earth. But if salt loses its flavor, how can it be made salty again? It is no longer good for anything except to be thrown out and trampled on by people. You are the light of the world. A city located on a hill cannot be hidden. [15] People do not light a lamp and put it under a basket but on a lampstand, and it gives light to all in the house. In the same way, let your light shine before people, so that they can see your good deeds and give honor to your Father in heaven.

"Do not think that I have come to abolish the law or the prophets. I have not come to abolish but to fulfill. I tell you the truth, until heaven and earth pass away not the smallest letter or stroke of a letter will pass from the law until everything takes place. So anyone who breaks one of the least of these commands and teaches others to do this will be called least in the kingdom of heaven, but whoever does them and teaches others to do so will be called great in the kingdom of heaven. [20] For I tell you, unless your righteousness goes beyond that of the experts in the law and the Pharisees, you will never enter the kingdom of heaven.

"You have heard that it was said to an older generation, 'Do not murder,' and 'whoever murders will be subjected to judgment.' But I say to you that anyone who is angry with a brother will be subjected to judgment. And whoever insults a brother will be brought before the council, and whoever says 'Fool' will be sent to fiery hell. So then, if you bring your gift to the altar and there remember that your brother has something against you, leave your gift there in front of the altar. First go and be reconciled to your brother and then come and present your gift. [25] Reach agreement quickly with your accuser while on the way to court, or he may hand you over to the judge, and the judge hand you over to the warden, and you will be thrown into prison. I tell you the truth, you will not at all get out until you have paid the last penny.

"You have heard that it was said, 'Do not commit adultery.' But I say to you that whoever looks at a woman to desire her has already committed adultery with her in his heart. If your right eye causes you to sin, tear it out and throw it away.[17] It is better to lose one of your members than to have your whole body thrown into hell. If your right hand causes you to sin, cut it off and throw it away. It is better to lose one of your members than to have your whole body go into hell.

"It was said, 'Whoever divorces his wife must give her a legal document.' But I say to you that everyone who divorces his wife, except for immorality, makes her commit adultery, and whoever marries a divorced woman commits adultery.

---

[16] *meek:* humble.
[17] *tear it out and throw it away:* This is hyperbole, not to be taken literally. The meaning is that Jesus' followers are to take all necessary measures to avoid sin, even if they may seem extreme.

"Again, you have heard that it was said to an older generation, 'Do not break an oath, but fulfill your vows to the Lord.' But I say to you, do not take oaths at all—not by heaven, because it is the throne of God, [35] not by earth, because it is his footstool, and not by Jerusalem, because it is the city of the great King. Do not take an oath by your head, because you are not able to make one hair white or black. Let your word be 'Yes, yes' or 'No, no.' More than this is from the evil one.

"You have heard that it was said, 'An eye for an eye and a tooth for a tooth.' But I say to you, do not resist the evildoer. But whoever strikes you on the right cheek, turn the other to him as well. [40] And if someone wants to sue you and to take your tunic, also give him your coat. And if anyone forces you to go one mile, go with him two. Give to the one who asks you, and do not reject the one who wants to borrow from you.

"You have heard that it was said, 'Love your neighbor' and 'hate your enemy.' But I say to you, love your enemy and pray for those who persecute you, [45] so that you may be like your Father in heaven, since he causes the sun to rise on the evil and the good, and sends rain on the righteous and the unrighteous. For if you love those who love you, what reward do you have? Even the tax collectors do the same, don't they? And if you only greet your brothers, what more do you do? Even the Gentiles do the same, don't they? So then, be perfect, as your heavenly Father is perfect.[18]

[6:1] "Be careful about not living righteously merely to be seen by people. Otherwise you have no reward with your Father in heaven. Thus whenever you do charitable giving, do not blow a trumpet before you, as the hypocrites do in synagogues and on streets so that people will praise them. I tell you the truth, they have their reward. But when you do your giving, do not let your left hand know what your right hand is doing, so that your gift may be in secret. And your Father, who sees in secret, will reward you.

[5] "Whenever you pray, do not be like the hypocrites, because they love to pray while standing in synagogues and on street corners so that people can see them. Truly I say to you, they have their reward. But whenever you pray, go into your room, close the door, and pray to your Father in secret. And your Father, who sees in secret, will reward you. When you pray, do not babble repetitiously like the Gentiles, because they think that by their many words they will be heard. Do not be like them, for your Father knows what you need before you ask him. So pray this way:[19]

Our Father in heaven, may your name be honored,
[10] may your kingdom come,
may your will be done on earth as it is in heaven.
Give us today our daily bread,
and forgive us our debts, as we ourselves have forgiven our debtors.
And do not lead us into temptation, but deliver us from the evil one.

"For if you forgive others their sins, your heavenly Father will also forgive you. [15] But if you do not forgive others, your Father will not forgive you your sins.

"When you fast, do not look sullen like the hypocrites, for they make their faces unattractive so that people will see them fasting. I tell you the truth, they have their reward. When you fast put oil on your head and wash your face so that it will not be obvious to others when you are fasting, but only to your Father who is in secret. And your Father, who sees in secret, will reward you.

"Do not accumulate for yourselves treasures on earth, where moth and rust destroy and where thieves break in and steal. [20] But accumulate for yourselves treasures in heaven, where moth and rust do not destroy, and thieves do

---

[18] *perfect:* not sinless but mature and complete.
[19] *pray this way:* Jesus gives this prayer as a model, especially of brevity. That some English-speaking Christians say "debts" and others "trespasses" comes from different English translations of the *Bible*.

not break in and steal. For where your treasure is, there your heart will be also.

"The eye[20] is the lamp of the body. If then your eye is healthy, your whole body will be full of light. But if your eye is diseased, your whole body will be full of darkness. If then the light in you is darkness, how great is the darkness!

"No one can serve two masters, for either he will hate the one and love the other, or he will be devoted to the one and despise the other. You cannot serve God and money.

[25] "Therefore I tell you, do not worry about your life, what you will eat or drink, or about your body, what you will wear. Isn't there more to life than food and more to the body than clothing? Look at the birds of the sky: They do not sow, or reap, or gather into barns, yet your heavenly Father feeds them. Aren't you more valuable than they are? And which of you by worrying can add even one hour to his life? Why do you worry about clothing? Think about how the flowers of the field grow; they do not work or spin. Yet I tell you that not even Solomon in all his glory was clothed like one of these! [30] And if this is how God clothes the wild grass, which is here today and tomorrow is tossed into the fire to heat the oven, won't he clothe you even more, you people of little faith? So then, don't worry saying, 'What will we eat?' or 'What will we drink?' or 'What will we wear?' For the [Gentiles] pursue these things, and your heavenly Father knows that you need them. But above all pursue his kingdom and righteousness, and all these things will be given to you as well. So then, do not worry about tomorrow, for tomorrow will worry about itself. Today has enough trouble of its own.

[7:1] "Do not judge so that you will not be judged. For by the standard you judge you will be judged, and the measure you use will be the measure you receive. Why do you see the speck in your brother's eye, but fail to see the beam of wood in your own? Or how can you say to your brother, 'Let me remove the speck from your eye,' while there is a beam in your own? [5] You hypocrite! First remove the beam from your own eye, and then you can see clearly to remove the speck from your brother's eye. Do not give what is holy to dogs or throw your pearls before pigs; otherwise they will trample them under their feet and turn around and tear you to pieces.

"Ask and it will be given to you; seek and you will find; knock and the door will be opened for you. For everyone who asks receives, and the one who seeks finds, and to the one who knocks the door will be opened. Is there anyone among you who, if his son asks for bread, will give him a stone? [10] Or if he asks for a fish, will give him a snake? If you then, although you are evil, know how to give good gifts to your children, how much more will your Father in heaven give good gifts to those who ask him! In everything, treat others as you would want them to treat you, for this fulfills the law and the prophets.

"Enter through the narrow gate, because the gate is wide and the way is spacious that leads to destruction, and there are many who enter through it. But the gate is narrow and the way is difficult that leads to life, and there are few who find it.

[15] "Watch out for false prophets, who come to you in sheep's clothing but inwardly are voracious wolves. You will recognize them by their fruit. Grapes are not gathered from thorns or figs from thistles, are they? In the same way, every good tree bears good fruit, but the bad tree bears bad fruit. A good tree is not able to bear bad fruit, nor a bad tree to bear good fruit. Every tree that does not bear good fruit is cut down and thrown into the fire. [20] So then, you will recognize them by their fruit.

"Not everyone who says to me, 'Lord, Lord,' will enter into the kingdom of heaven, only the one who does the will of my Father in heaven. On that day, many will say to me, 'Lord, Lord, didn't we prophesy in your name, and in your name cast out demons and do many powerful deeds?' Then I will declare to them, 'I never knew you. Go away from me, you lawbreakers!'

---

[20] *eye:* probably the heart as the seat of emotion and thought; perhaps the conscience.

"Everyone who hears these words of mine and does them is like a wise man who built his house on rock. [25] The rain fell, the flood came, and the winds beat against that house, but it did not collapse because it had been founded on rock. Everyone who hears these words of mine and does not do them is like a foolish man who built his house on sand. The rain fell, the flood came, and the winds beat against that house, and it collapsed; it was utterly destroyed!"

When Jesus finished saying these things, the crowds were amazed by his teaching, because he taught them like one who had authority, not like their experts in the law.[21]

---

[21] *not like their experts in the law:* Jewish scribes taught on the authority of other scribal experts and made constant reference to them; Jesus teaches on his own authority.

Directions concerning Marriage*

Paul here gives detailed directions about marriage. His basic perspective, based mostly on his expectation of the imminent return of Jesus, is that marriage is good but to remain single is better. In this passage and the next, the quotations are slogans prominent in the church of Corinth to which Paul is responding. Notice Paul's careful distinction between the commands of Jesus and his own preferences. These ideas became influential in the ancient church and continue in churches that practice clerical celibacy.

Now with regard to the issues you wrote about: "It is good for a man not to have sexual relations with a woman." But because of immoralities, each man should have his own wife and each woman her own husband. A husband should give to his wife her sexual rights, and likewise a wife to her husband. It is not the wife who has the rights to her own body, but the husband. In the same way, it is not the husband who has the rights to his own body, but the wife. [5] Do not deprive each other, except by agreement for a definite time, so that you may devote yourselves to prayer. Then resume your relationship, so that Satan may not tempt you because of your lack of self-control. I say this as a concession, not as a command. I wish that everyone was as I am. But each has his own gift from God, one this way, another that.

To the unmarried and widows I say that it is best for them to remain as I am. But if they do not have self-control, let them get married. For it is better to marry than to burn with sexual desire. To the married I give this command—not I, but the Lord—a wife should not divorce a husband (but if she does, let her remain unmarried, or be reconciled to her husband), and a husband should not divorce his wife.

To the rest I say—I, not the Lord—if a brother has a wife who is not a believer and she is happy to live with him, he should not divorce her. And if a woman has a husband who is not a believer and he is happy to live with her, she should not divorce him. For the unbelieving husband is sanctified because of the wife, and the unbelieving wife because of her husband. Otherwise your children are unclean, but now they are holy. [15] But if the unbeliever wants a divorce, let it take place. In these circumstances the brother or sister is not bound. God has called you in peace. For how do you know, wife, whether you will bring your husband to salvation? Or how do you know, husband, whether you will bring your wife to salvation? . . .

[25] With regard to the question about people who have never married, I have no

---

*I Corinthians 7:1–16, 25–40.

command from the Lord, but I give my opinion as one shown mercy by the Lord to be trustworthy. Because of the impending crisis I think it best for you to remain as you are. The one bound to a wife should not seek divorce. The one released from a wife should not seek marriage. But if you marry, you have not sinned. And if a virgin marries, she has not sinned. But those who marry will face difficult circumstances, and I am trying to spare you. And I say this, brothers and sisters: The time is short. So then those who have wives should be as those who have none, [30] those with tears like those not weeping, those who rejoice like those not rejoicing, those who buy like those without possessions, those who use the world as though they were not using it to the full. For the present shape of this world is passing away.

And I want you to be free from concern. The unmarried man is concerned about the things of the Lord, how to please the Lord. But the married man is concerned about the things of the world, how to please his wife, and he is divided. An unmarried woman and virgin is concerned about the things of the Lord, to be holy both in body and spirit. But the married woman is concerned about the things of the world, how to please her husband. [35] I am saying this for your benefit, not to place a limitation on you, but so that without distraction you may give notable and constant service to the Lord.

If anyone thinks he is acting inappropriately toward his virgin, if she is past the bloom of youth and it seems necessary, he should do what he wishes; he does not sin. Let them marry. But the man who is firm in his commitment, and is under no necessity but has control over his will, and has decided in his own mind to keep his own virgin, does well. So then, the one who marries his own virgin does well, but the one who does not, does better.

A wife is bound as long as her husband is living. But if her husband dies, she is free to marry anyone she wishes (only someone in the Lord).[22] [40] But in my opinion, she will be happier if she remains as she is—and I think that I too have the Spirit of God!

---

[22] *only someone in the Lord:* a fellow Christian.

Love*

This "Hymn to Love," perhaps written by Paul or adapted by him for use in this letter, extols love as the greatest spiritual gift. It has three distinct themes in these three paragraphs: First, it contrasts love with other spiritual gifts; second, it describes love; third, it extols the persistence of love. This chapter in I Corinthians *is heard most often at marriage ceremonies, but the scope of love Paul covers here goes far beyond marriage.*

If I speak in the tongues of men and of angels, but I do not have love, I am a noisy gong or a clanging cymbal. And if I have prophecy, and know all mysteries and all knowledge, and if I have all faith so that I can remove mountains, but do not have love, I am nothing. If I give away everything I own, and if I give over my body in order to boast, but do not have love, I receive no benefit.

Love is patient, love is kind, it is not envious. Love does not brag, it is not puffed up. [5] It is not rude, it is not self-serving, it is not easily angered, or resentful. It is not glad about injustice, but rejoices in the truth. It bears all things, believes all things, hopes all things, endures all things.

---

*I Corinthians 13:1–13.

Love never ends. But if there are prophecies, they will be set aside; if there are tongues, they will cease; if there is knowledge, it will be set aside. For we know in part, and we prophesy in part, [10] but when what is perfect comes, the partial will be set aside. When I was a child, I talked like a child, I thought like a child, I reasoned like a child. But when I became an adult, I set aside childish ways. For now we see in a mirror indirectly, but then we will see face to face. Now I know in part, then I will know fully, just as I have been fully known. And now these three remain: faith, hope, and love. But the greatest of these is love.

Ethics in the Christian Household*

This discussion of ethics in the Christian household contains instructions for wives, husbands, children, parents, slaves, and masters. It presupposes the legitimacy of the household structure of the times but seeks to transform it with the Christian ethic.

Submit to one another out of reverence for Christ.

Wives, submit to your husbands as to the Lord, because the husband is the head of the wife as also Christ is the head of the church—he himself being the savior of the body. But as the church submits to Christ, so also wives should submit to their husbands in everything. [25] Husbands, love your wives[23] just as Christ loved the church and gave himself for her to sanctify her by cleansing her with the washing of the water by the word, so that he may present the church to himself as glorious—not having a stain or wrinkle, or any such blemish, but holy and blameless. In the same way husbands ought to love their wives as their own bodies. He who loves his wife loves himself. For no one has ever hated his own body but he feeds it and takes care of it, just as Christ also does the church, [30] for we are members of his body. "For this reason a man will leave his father and mother and will be joined to his wife, and the two will become one flesh." This mystery is great—but I am actually speaking with reference to Christ and the church. Nevertheless, each one of you must also love his own wife as he loves himself, and the wife must respect her husband.

[6:1] Children, obey your parents in the Lord for this is right. "Honor your father and mother" which is the first commandment accompanied by a promise, namely, "that it may go well with you and that you will live on the earth for a long time." Fathers, do not provoke your children to anger, but raise them up in the discipline and instruction of the Lord.

[5] Slaves, obey your human masters with fear and trembling, in the sincerity of your heart as to Christ, not like those who do their work only when someone is watching—as people-pleasers—but as slaves of Christ doing the will of God from the heart. Obey with enthusiasm, as though serving the Lord and not people because you know that each person, whether slave or free, if he does something good, this will be rewarded by the Lord. Masters, treat your slaves the same way, giving up the use of threats, because you know that both you and they have the same master in heaven, and there is no favoritism with him.

**Ephesians* 5:21–6:9.
[23] *Husbands, love your wives:* In the ancient Mediterranean world, as in most societies today where marriage is not based on romantic love, this command would not be seen as essential to marriage.

Being Subject to Authorities*

Romans 13 is the most important treatment in the New Testament of the relationship of the believer and the government, and the most influential through the history of the church. It couples specific and positive instructions about being subject to governing authorities with more general instructions about social ethics.

Let every person be subject to the governing authorities. For there is no authority except by God's appointment, and the authorities that exist have been instituted by God. So the person who resists such authority resists the ordinance of God, and those who resist will incur judgment (for rulers cause no fear for good conduct but for bad). Do you desire not to fear authority? Do good and you will receive its commendation, for it is God's servant for your good. But if you do wrong, be in fear, for it does not bear the sword in vain. It is God's servant to administer retribution on the wrongdoer. [5] Therefore it is necessary to be in subjection, not only because of the wrath of the authorities but also because of your conscience. For this reason you also pay taxes, for the authorities are God's servants devoted to governing. Pay everyone what is owed: taxes to whom taxes are due, revenue to whom revenue is due, respect to whom respect is due, honor to whom honor is due.

Owe no one anything, except to love one another, for the one who loves his neighbor has fulfilled the law. For the commandments "Do not commit adultery, do not murder, do not steal, do not covet" (and if there is any other commandment), are summed up in this, "Love your neighbor as yourself." [10] Love does no wrong to a neighbor. Therefore love is the fulfillment of the law.

---

*Romans 13:1–10.

The Fall of Rome**

This is the flip side of the positive view of civil government presented in Romans 13:1–7. The city of Rome is depicted symbolically as a "great prostitute;" the scarlet beast she rides is the Roman Empire. This selection concludes with a funeral song sung over the fallen Rome. This approach encourages quiet opposition to idolatrous and persecuting government, longing for its downfall at the coming of God's kingdom.

Then one of the seven angels who had the seven bowls came and spoke to me. "Come," he said, "I will show you the condemnation and punishment of the great prostitute who sits on many waters, with whom the kings of the earth committed sexual immorality and the earth's inhabitants got drunk with the wine of her immorality." So he carried me away in the Spirit to a wilderness, and there I saw a woman sitting on a scarlet beast that was full of blasphemous names and had seven heads and ten horns. Now the woman was dressed in purple and scarlet clothing, and adorned with gold, precious stones, and pearls. She held in her hand a golden cup filled with detestable things and unclean things from her sexual immorality. [5] On her forehead was written a name, a mystery: "Babylon the Great,[24] the Mother of prostitutes and of the detestable things of the earth."

**Revelation 17:1–18:5.
[24] *Babylon the great:* a code name for Rome, taken from the name of a great oppressing city-empire in the Jewish *Bible*.

I saw that the woman was drunk with the blood of the saints and the blood of those who testified to Jesus. I was greatly astounded when I saw her. But the angel said to me, "Why are you astounded? I will interpret for you the mystery of the woman and of the beast with the seven heads and ten horns that carries her. The beast you saw was, and is not, but is about to come up from the abyss and then go to destruction. The inhabitants of the earth—all those whose names have not been written in the book of life since the foundation of the world—will be astounded when they see that the beast was, and is not, but is to come. (This requires a mind that has wisdom.) The seven heads are seven mountains the woman sits on. They are also seven kings: [10] five have fallen; one is, and the other has not yet come, but whenever he does come, he must remain for only a brief time. The beast that was, and is not, is himself an eighth king and yet is one of the seven, and is going to destruction. The ten horns that you saw are ten kings who have not yet received a kingdom, but will receive ruling authority as kings with the beast for one hour. These kings have a single intent, and they will give their power and authority to the beast. They will make war with the Lamb,[25] but the Lamb will conquer them, because he is Lord of lords and King of kings, and those accompanying the Lamb are the called, chosen, and faithful."

[15] Then the angel said to me, "The waters you saw (where the prostitute is seated) are peoples, multitudes, nations, and languages. The ten horns that you saw, and the beast—these will hate the prostitute and make her desolate and naked. They will consume her flesh and burn her up with fire. For God has put into their minds to carry out his purpose by making a decision to give their royal power to the beast until the words of God are fulfilled. As for the woman you saw, she is the great city that has sovereignty over the kings of the earth."

[18:1] After these things I saw another angel, who possessed great authority, coming down out of heaven, and the earth was lit up by his radiance. He shouted with a powerful voice:

"Fallen, fallen, is Babylon the great!
She has become a lair for demons,
a haunt for every unclean spirit,
a haunt for every unclean bird,
a haunt for every unclean and detested beast.
For all the nations have fallen from the wine of
    her immoral passion,
and the kings of the earth have committed
    sexual immorality with her,
and the merchants of the earth have gotten rich
    from the power of her sensual behavior."

Then I heard another voice from heaven saying, "Come out of her, my people, so you will not take part in her sins and so you will not receive her plagues, [5] because her sins have piled up all the way to heaven and God has remembered her crimes."

---

[25] *Lamb:* a symbol of Jesus Christ.

ORGANIZATION

The Twelve Apostles and Their Mission*

The apostles, twelve in number to suggest the twelve tribes of ancient Israel, are named and commissioned here. Both the situation of Jesus (the restriction of his mission to the Jews) and the later church (itinerant prophets and evangelists) are reflected. This type of mission was important in the early spread of Christianity through Palestine and Syria.

---

*Matthew 10:1–15.

Jesus called his twelve disciples and gave them authority over unclean spirits so they could cast them out and heal every kind of disease and sickness. Now these are the names of the twelve apostles: First, Simon (called Peter), and Andrew his brother; James son of Zebedee and John his brother; Philip and Bartholomew; Thomas and Matthew the tax collector; James, the son of Alphaeus, and Thaddaeus; Simon the Zealot and Judas Iscariot, who betrayed him.

[5] Jesus sent out these twelve, instructing them as follows: "Do not go to Gentile regions and do not enter any Samaritan town. Go instead to the lost sheep of the house of Israel. As you go, preach this message: 'The kingdom of heaven is near.' Heal the sick, raise the dead, cleanse lepers, cast out demons. Freely you received, freely give. Do not take gold, silver or copper in your belts, [10] no bag for the journey, or an extra tunic, or sandals or staff, for the worker deserves his provisions. Whenever you enter a town or village, find out who is worthy there and stay with them until you leave. As you enter the house, give it greetings. And if the house is worthy, let your peace come on it, but if it is not worthy, let your peace return to you. And if anyone will not welcome you or listen to your message, shake the dust off your feet as you leave that house or that town. [15] I tell you the truth, it will be more bearable for the land of Sodom and Gomorrah in the day of judgment than for that town!"

Matthew's Church Order*

Matthew is the only gospel with comprehensive instructions for church life. This passage begins with sayings on humility and forgiveness and ends with procedures for dealing with persistent sin among church members.

At that time the disciples came to Jesus saying, "Who is the greatest in the kingdom of heaven?" He called a child, had him stand among them, and said, "I tell you the truth, unless you turn around and become like little children, you will never enter the kingdom of heaven! Whoever then humbles himself like this little child is the greatest in the kingdom of heaven. [5] And whoever welcomes a child like this in my name welcomes me.

"But if anyone causes one of these little ones who believe in me to sin, it would be better for him to have a huge millstone hung around his neck and to be drowned in the depth of the sea. Woe to the world because of stumbling blocks! It is necessary that stumbling blocks come, but woe to the person through whom they come. If your hand or your foot causes you to sin, cut it off and throw it away. It is better for you to enter life crippled or lame than to have two hands or two feet and be thrown into eternal fire. And if your eye causes you to sin, tear it out and throw it away. It is better for you to enter into life with one eye than to have two eyes and be thrown into fiery hell. . . .

[15] "If your brother sins, go and show him his fault when the two of you are alone. If he listens to you, you have regained your brother. But if he does not listen, take one or two others with you, that at the testimony of two or three witnesses every matter may be established. If he refuses to listen to them, tell it to the church. If he refuses to listen to the church, treat him like a Gentile or tax collector.

"I tell you the truth, whatever you bind on earth will have been bound in heaven, and whatever you release on earth will have been released

---

**Matthew* 18:1–10, 15–22.

in heaven. Again, I tell you the truth, if two of you on earth agree about whatever they ask, my Father in heaven will do it for them. [20] For where two or three are assembled in my name, I am there among them."

Then Peter came to him and said, "Lord, how many times must I forgive my brother who sins against me? As many as seven times?" Jesus said to him, "Not seven times, I tell you, but seventy-seven times."

Peter as the Rock*

Jesus here renames Simon as Peter, the rock on which the church is founded. Greek Petros *(Peter) is similar to* petra *(rock). Jesus gives Peter "the keys of the kingdom of heaven." Catholics see this gift as establishing the papacy, for the bishops of Rome, who are the successors of Peter, hold universal power over the church because of these "keys." Protestants and members of Eastern Orthodox churches dispute this understanding of* Matthew 16:13–20.

When Jesus came to the area of Caesarea Philippi, he asked his disciples, "Who do people say that the Son of Man is?" They answered, "Some say John the Baptist, others Elijah, and others Jeremiah or one of the prophets." [15] He said to them, "But who do you say that I am?"

Simon Peter answered, "You are the Christ, the Son of the living God." And Jesus answered him, "You are blessed, Simon son of Jonah, because flesh and blood did not reveal this to you, but my Father in heaven! And I tell you that you are Peter, and on this rock I will build my church, and the gates of Hades will not overpower it. I will give you the keys of the kingdom of heaven. Whatever you bind on the earth will have been bound in heaven, and whatever you release on earth will have been released in heaven." [20] Then he instructed his disciples not to tell anyone that he was the Christ.

---

*Matthew 16:13–20.

Qualifications of Bishops and Deacons**

Here we see the beginning of the threefold office in the church: bishop or overseer, presbyter (an elder or priest), and deacon. The threefold office has been the most common pattern of church organization among most Christians even when these particular names are not used. The duties of these offices are not given, but we can infer their duties from the lists of qualifications. The emphasis on skill in family relationships comes in part from the setting of early Christian congregations, which met in believers' homes. These offices are largely restricted to men, but scholars debate whether verse 11 may apply to women deacons.

This saying is trustworthy: "If someone aspires to the office of overseer, he desires a good work." The overseer then must be above reproach, the husband of one wife, temperate, self-controlled, respectable, hospitable, an apt teacher, not a drunkard, not violent, but gentle, not contentious, free from the love of money. He must manage his own household well and keep his children in control without losing his dignity. [5] But if someone does not know how

---

**I Timothy 3:1–13.

to manage his own household, how will he care for the church of God? He must not be a recent convert or he may become arrogant and fall into the punishment that the devil will exact. And he must be well thought of by those outside the faith, so that he may not fall into disgrace and be caught by the devil's trap.

Deacons likewise must be dignified, not two-faced, not given to excessive drinking, not greedy for gain, holding to the mystery of the faith with a clear conscience. [10] And these also must be tested first and then let them serve as deacons if they are found blameless. Likewise also their wives[26] must be dignified, not slanderous, temperate, faithful in every respect. Deacons must be husbands of one wife and good managers of their children and their own households. For those who have served well as deacons gain a good standing for themselves and great boldness in the faith that is in Christ Jesus.

---

[26] *their wives:* can also be translated "the women."

Women in the Early Church*

Christianity's traditional attitude toward women, which argues for some degree of equality and subjection at the same time, has its roots in the New Testament. *In the first passage, Jesus shows that women should participate with men in hearing his teaching, although this requirement might conflict with women's traditional roles. In the second reading, Paul expresses a much more restrictive view of the roles of women in the church. The third reading has been influential in the Christian movement for equality. The last passage features the most patriarchal statement of the place of women in the church and has been influential in the history of Christianity.*

[*Luke* 10:38] Now as they went on their way, Jesus entered a certain village where a woman named Martha welcomed him as a guest. She had a sister named Mary, who sat at the Lord's feet and listened to what he said. [40] But Martha was distracted with all the preparations she had to make, so she came up to him and said, "Lord, don't you care that my sister has left me to do all the work alone? Tell her to help me." But the Lord answered her, "Martha, Martha, you are worried and troubled about many things, but one thing is needed. Mary has chosen the best part; it will not be taken away from her."

[*I Corinthians* 11:2] I praise you because you remember me in everything and maintain the traditions just as I passed them on to you. But I want you to know that Christ is the head of every man, and the man is the head of a woman, and God is the head of Christ. Any man who prays or prophesies with his head covered disgraces his head. [5] But any woman who prays or prophesies with her head uncovered disgraces her head, for it is one and the same thing as having a shaved head. For if a woman will not cover her head, she should cut off her hair. But if it is disgraceful for a woman to have her hair cut off or be shaved, she should cover her head. For a man should not have his head covered, since he is the image and glory of God. But the woman is the glory of the man. For man did not come from woman, but woman from man. Neither was man created for the sake of woman, but woman for man. [10] For this reason a woman should have a symbol of authority on her head, because of the angels. In any case, in the Lord woman is not independent of man, nor is man independent of woman. For just as woman came from man, so man comes through woman. But all things come from God. Judge for yourselves: Is it proper for a woman to pray to

---

**Luke* 10:38–42; *I Corinthians* 11:2–16; *Galatians* 3:25–28; *I Timothy* 2:8–15.

God with her head uncovered? Does not nature itself teach you that if a man has long hair, it is a disgrace for him, [15] but if a woman has long hair, it is her glory? For her hair is given to her for a covering. If anyone intends to quarrel about this, we have no other practice, nor do the churches of God.

[*Galatians* 3:25] But now that faith has come, we are no longer under a guardian. For in Christ Jesus you are all sons of God through faith. For all of you who were baptized into Christ have clothed yourselves with Christ. There is neither Jew nor Greek, there is neither slave nor free, there is neither male nor female—for all of you are one in Christ Jesus.

[*I Timothy* 2:8] So I want the men to pray in every place, lifting up holy hands without anger or dispute. Likewise the women are to dress in suitable apparel, with modesty and self-control. Their adornment must not be with braided hair and gold or pearls or expensive clothing, [10] but with good deeds, as is proper for women who profess reverence for God. A woman must learn quietly with all submissiveness. But I do not allow a woman to teach or have authority over a man. She must remain quiet. For Adam was formed first and then Eve. And Adam was not deceived, but the woman, because she was fully deceived, fell into transgression. [15] But she will be delivered through childbearing, if she continues in faith and love and holiness with self-control.

RITUAL

Baptism*

At the conclusion of Matthew, *Jesus commands that the triadic divine name—Father, Son, and Holy Spirit—be used in baptism of people from all the nations of the earth. In* Romans 6, *Paul explains that when Christians are baptized they die with Christ to sin and begin to live holy lives for God.* **Baptism,** *a washing or immersion in water for forgiveness and new spiritual life, became the foundation for the Christian vision of the moral life.*

[*Matthew* 28:16] So the eleven disciples went to Galilee to the mountain Jesus had designated. When they saw him, they worshiped him, but some doubted. Then Jesus came up and said to them, "All authority in heaven and on earth has been given to me. Therefore go and make disciples of all nations, baptizing them in the name of the Father and the Son and the Holy Spirit, [20] teaching them to obey everything I have commanded you. And remember, I am with you always, to the end of the age."

[*Romans* 6:1] What shall we say then? Are we to remain in sin so that grace may increase? Absolutely not! How can we who died to sin still live in it? Or do you not know that as many as were baptized into Christ were baptized into his death? Therefore we have been buried with him through baptism into death, in order that just as Christ was raised from the dead through the glory of the Father, we too may walk in new life.

[5] For if we have become united with him in the likeness of his death, we will certainly also be united in the likeness of his resurrection. We know that our old man[27] was crucified with him so that the body of sin would no longer dominate us, so that we would no longer be enslaved to sin. (For someone who has died has been freed from sin.)

Now if we died with Christ, we believe that we will also live with him. We know that since

---

**Matthew* 28:16–20; *Romans* 6:1–14.
[27] *old man:* the old human nature, characterized by sin.

Christ has been raised from the dead, he is never going to die again; death no longer has mastery over him. [10] For the death he died, he died to sin once for all, but the life he lives, he lives to God. So you too consider yourselves dead to sin, but alive to God in Christ Jesus.

Therefore do not let sin reign in your mortal body so that you obey its desires, and do not present your members to sin as instruments to be used for unrighteousness, but present yourselves to God as those who are alive from the dead and your members to God as instruments to be used for righteousness. For sin will have no mastery over you, because you are not under law but under grace.

The Eucharist*

The Eucharist ("Thanksgiving [to God]") also goes by the names "Lord's Supper" and "Holy Communion." The first passage relates its institution during Jesus' last Passover meal, when Jesus identified the bread and wine of the Passover with his own body and blood, soon to be shed on the cross for the establishment of a "new covenant" of forgiveness and life. In the second passage, Jesus makes this identification in a symbolic way that has had a strong influence on how Christians view the Eucharist: His body and blood nourish one to eternal life.

[*Matthew* 26:17] Now on the first day of the feast of Unleavened Bread the disciples came to Jesus and said, "Where do you want us to prepare for you to eat the Passover?" He said, "Go into the city to a certain man and tell him, 'The Teacher says, "My time is near. I will observe the Passover with my disciples at your house."'" So the disciples did as Jesus had instructed them, and they prepared the Passover. . . . [26] While they were eating, Jesus took bread, and after giving thanks he broke it, gave it to his disciples, and said, "Take, eat, this is my body." And after taking the cup and giving thanks, he gave it to them, saying, "Drink from it, all of you, for this is my blood, the blood of the covenant, that is poured out for many for the forgiveness of sins. I tell you, from now on I will not drink of this fruit of the vine until that day when I drink it new with you in my Father's kingdom."

[*John* 6:25] When they found him on the other side of the lake, they said to him, "Rabbi, when did you get here?" Jesus replied, "I tell you the solemn truth, you are looking for me not because you saw miraculous signs, but because you ate all the loaves of bread you wanted. Do not work for the food that disappears, but for the food that remains to eternal life—the food that the Son of Man will give to you. For God the Father has put his seal of approval on him."

So then they said to him, "What must we do to accomplish the deeds God requires?" Jesus replied, "This is the deed God requires—to believe in the one whom he sent." [30] So they said to him, "Then what miraculous sign will you perform, so that we may see it and believe you? What will you do? Our ancestors ate the manna in the wilderness, just as it is written, 'He gave them bread from heaven to eat.'"

Then Jesus told them, "I tell you the solemn truth, it is not Moses who has given you the bread from heaven, but my Father is giving you the true bread from heaven. For the bread of God is the one who comes down from heaven and gives life to the world." So they said to him, "Sir, give us this bread all the time!"

[35] Jesus said to them, "I am the bread of life. The one who comes to me will never go hungry, and

---

*Matthew 26:17–19, 26–29; *John* 6:25–40, 52–59.

the one who believes in me will never be thirsty. But I told you that you have seen me and still do not believe. Everyone whom the Father gives me will come to me, and the one who comes to me I will never send away. For I have come down from heaven not to do my own will but the will of the one who sent me. Now this is the will of the one who sent me—that I should not lose one person of every one he has given me, but raise them all up at the last day. [40] For this is the will of my Father—for every one who looks on the Son and believes in him to have eternal life, and I will raise him up at the last day.". . .

[52] Then the Jews who were hostile to Jesus began to argue with one another, "How can this man give us his flesh to eat?" Jesus said to them, "I tell you the solemn truth, unless you eat the flesh of the Son of Man and drink his blood, you have no life in yourselves. The one who eats my flesh and drinks my blood has eternal life, and I will raise him up on the last day. [55] For my flesh is true food, and my blood is true drink. The one who eats my flesh and drinks my blood resides in me, and I in him. Just as the living Father sent me, and I live because of the Father, so the one who consumes me will live because of me. This is the bread that came down from heaven; it is not like the bread your ancestors ate, but then later died. The one who eats this bread will live forever."

Confession and Anointing*

The churches—Roman Catholic, Orthodox, and some Protestant—that practice the "anointing of the sick" appeal to this passage frequently. In the Roman Catholic Church, it is one of the seven sacraments, formerly called extreme unction or (more popularly) last rites. The anointing or ritual application with holy oil is connected here with confession of sin, prayer, and the use of the divine name.

Is anyone among you suffering? He should pray. Is anyone in good spirits? He should sing praises. Is anyone among you ill? He should summon the elders of the church, and they should pray for him and anoint him with oil in the name of the Lord. [15] And the prayer of faith will save the one who is sick and the Lord will raise him up—and if he has committed sins, he will be forgiven. So confess your sins to one another and pray for one another so that you may be healed. The prayer of a righteous person has great effectiveness. Elijah was a human being like us, and he prayed earnestly that it would not rain and there was no rain on the land for three years and six months! Then he prayed again, and the sky gave rain and the land sprouted with a harvest.

---

*James 5:13–18.

LATER DEVELOPMENT OF SCRIPTURAL THEMES

The Scripture Canon in Formation**

Marcion was one of the most influential Christian leaders of the second century. His rival church spread throughout the Roman Empire before it broke apart and was absorbed into other controversial groups. Marcion rejected the religion of the Old Testament as true for Christians. He accepted only the Gospel of Luke and ten of

---

**Irenaeus, *Against Heresies* 1.27.2; *Muratorian Canon*.

Paul's Letters *as authoritative and scriptural, editing out of them all traces of the God of the* Old Testament. *His was probably the first Christian canon, and it impelled other Christians to justify a larger* New Testament *canon and the continuing significance of the* Old Testament. *None of Marcion's writings have survived; the first selection is Irenaeus' quite hostile description of it.*[28] *Irenaeus (died ca. 200) was the orthodox bishop of Lyon. The second selection, the* Muratorian Canon, *was written in Rome, perhaps around 200. Originally in Greek, it was translated into such crude Latin that some of the text is difficult to interpret, and this translation into English preserves much of the barbarousness of the Latin. The beginning (which probably spoke about the* Gospel of Matthew*) and the ending are lost. This text is important for its indication of the motives and process of canonization.*[29]

[Irenaeus, *Against Heresies*] Marcion of Pontus succeeded [Cerdon, an early Gnostic], and developed his school, advancing the most daring blasphemy against the God of the law and the prophets. He declared him to be the author of evil, a lover of war, inconsistent in judging, and inconsistent in himself. Jesus was derived from that Father who is above the God that made the world. . . . He abolished the prophets and the law, and all the works of that God who made the world, whom also he calls "Ruler of the World." Beside all this, Marcion mutilates the Gospel according to Luke, removing all that is written about the birth of the Lord, and setting aside a great deal of his teachings in which the Lord is recorded as clearly confessing that the Maker of this universe is his Father. He likewise persuaded his disciples that he himself was more worthy of belief that those apostles who have handed down the gospel to us; he gave his disciples only a fragment of the Gospel. In a similar manner he also dismembered the epistles of Paul, removing all that is said by the apostle about that God who made the world. . . . He also removed those passages from the prophetic writings[30] which the apostle quotes to teach us that the prophets announced beforehand the coming of the Lord.

[*Muratorian Canon*] The third Gospel book is that according to Luke. This physician Luke after Christ's ascension, since Paul had taken him with him as a legal expert, composed it in his own name according to (his) thinking. Yet he himself did not see the Lord in the flesh; and therefore, as he was able to ascertain it, he begins to tell the story from the birth of John. The fourth of the Gospels, that of John of the Decapolis, one of the disciples. When his fellow-disciples and bishops urged him, he said: Fast with me from today for three days, and what will be revealed to each one let us relate to one another. In the same night it was revealed to Andrew, one of the apostles, that, while all were to go over (it), John in his own name should write everything down. And therefore, though various rudiments are taught in the several Gospel books, yet that matters nothing for the faith of believers, since by the one and guiding Spirit everything is declared in all. . . .

Luke, writing to the "most excellent Theophilus," summarizes the several things that in his own presence have come to pass, as also by the omission of the suffering of Peter he makes quite clear, and equally by [the omission] of the journey of Paul, who from the city [Rome] proceeded to Spain.

The letters of Paul themselves make clear to those who wish to know it which were written by him, from what place and for what reason. First of all to the Corinthians [to whom he forbids] the heresy of schism, then to the Galatians [to whom he forbids] circumcision, and then to the Romans, he explains that Christ is the rule of the Scriptures and moreover their

---

[28] Taken, with editing, from A. Roberts and J. Donaldson, *The Ante-Nicene Fathers,* vol. 1 (New York: Scribner, 1905), p. 352.
[29] E. S. Buchanon, "The Codex Muratorianus," *Journal of Theological Studies* 8 (1907), pp. 540–543.
[30] *prophetic writings:* from the *Old Testament.*

principle, he has written at considerable length. We must deal with these serially, since the blessed apostle Paul himself, following the rule of his predecessor John, writes by name only to seven churches in the following order: to the Corinthians the first (epistle), to the Ephesians the second, to the Philippians the third, to the Colossians the fourth, to the Galatians the fifth, to the Thessalonians the sixth, to the Romans the seventh. Although he wrote to the Corinthians and to the Thessalonians once more for their reproof, it is yet clearly recognizable that over the whole earth one church is spread. For John also in the Revelation writes indeed to seven churches, yet speaks to all. But to Philemon one, and to Titus one, and to Timothy two, [letters written] out of goodwill and love, are yet held sacred to the glory of the catholic Church for the ordering of ecclesiastical discipline. There is current also (an epistle) to the Laodiceans, another to the Alexandrians, forged in Paul's name for the sect of Marcion, and several others, which cannot be received in the catholic Church, as it is not fitting that honey should be mixed with gall.

The letter of Jude and two under the name of John are accepted as sound in the catholic Church, and the Wisdom written by friends of Solomon[31] in his honor. Also of the revelations we accept only those of John and Peter, which some of our people do not want to have read in the Church. But Hermas wrote the Shepherd quite lately in our time in the city of Rome, when on the throne of the church of the city of Rome the bishop Pius, his brother, was seated. And therefore it ought indeed to be read, but it cannot be read publicly in the Church to the people either among the prophets, whose number is settled, or among the apostles to the end of time.

---

[31] *Wisdom . . . of Solomon:* a book of the *Old Testament* canon of many Christian churches, but not in the Jewish *Bible.*

Early Noncanonical Jesus Tradition*

The Gospel of Thomas, *written sometime around 100–125* C.E., *is a rich collection of sayings, many of which may go back to early stages of Christianity. Many scholars see an independent stream of tradition in these sayings. At least a handful of sayings not found in the* New Testament *may go back to Jesus himself. Thomas never entered the canon of the mainstream ancient church but was likely among the scriptures of various Gnostic-Christian groups in the second and third centuries.*[32]

These are the secret words which the living Jesus spoke, and Didymos Judas Thomas wrote down.

[1] And he said, "He who finds the meaning of these words will not taste death."

[2] Jesus said, "Let him who seeks not cease seeking until he finds, and when he finds, he shall be troubled, and when he is troubled, he will marvel, and he will rule over the All."

[13] Jesus said to his disciples, "Make a comparison and tell me whom I am like." Simon Peter said to him, "You are like a righteous angel." Matthew said to him, "You are like a wise man." Thomas said to him, "Master, my mouth will not be able to say what you are like."

Gospel of Thomas 1–2, 13–14, 18, 22, 29, 42, 49–50, 53, 83–84, 99, 101, 104.

[32] From *Documents for the Study of the Gospels,* ed. David R. Cartlidge and David L. Dungan. Copyright © 1994 Augsburg Fortress Press. Used by permission.

Jesus said, "I am not your master. Because you drank, you are drunk from the bubbling spring which I measured out." And he took him; he went aside. He spoke to him three words. When Thomas returned to his companions, they asked him, "What did Jesus say to you?" Thomas said to them, "If I tell you one of the words which he said to me, you will pick up stones; you will throw them at me. And fire will come out of the stones and consume you."

[14] Jesus said to them, "If you fast, you will bring sin upon yourselves and, if you pray, you will be condemned and, if you give alms, you will do evil to your spirits. And if you enter any land and wander through regions, if they receive you, whatever they set before you, eat it. Heal the sick among them. For that which goes into your mouth will not defile you, but that which comes out of your mouth is what will defile you."

[18] The disciples said to Jesus, "Tell us how end will occur." Jesus said, "Have you found the beginning that you search for the end? In the place of the beginning, the end will be. Blessed is he who will stand at the beginning, and he will know the end, and he will not taste death."

[22] Jesus saw babies being suckled. He said to his disciples, "These babies who are being suckled are like those who enter the Kingdom." They said to him, "We are children, shall we enter the kingdom?" Jesus said to them, "When you make the two one, and when you make the inner as the outer and the outer as the inner and the upper as the lower, so that you will make the male and the female into a single one, so that the male will not be the male and the female [not] be female, when you make eyes in place of an eye, and a hand in place of a hand, and a foot in the place of a foot, (and) an image in place of an image, then shall you enter [the kingdom]."

[29] Jesus said, "If the flesh exists because of spirit, it is a miracle, but if spirit (exists) because of the body, it is a miracle of miracles. But I marvel at how this great wealth [of spirit] established itself in this poverty [of the body]."

[42] Jesus said, "Be wanderers."

[49] Jesus said, "Blessed are the solitary and the chosen, because you will find the Kingdom; because you come from it, you will again go there."

[50] Jesus said, "If they say to you, 'Where did you come from?' say to them, 'We come from the light, where the light came into being through itself. It stood and reveals itself in their image.' If they say to you, '[Who] are you?' say to them, 'We are his sons and we are chosen of the living Father.' If they ask you, 'What is the sign of your Father who is in you?' say to them, 'It is movement and repose.'"

[53] His disciples said to him, "Is circumcision profitable or not?" He said to them, "If it were profitable, their father would beget them circumcised from their mother. But the true circumcision in the Spirit has found complete usefulness."

[83] Jesus said, "The images are manifest to man, and the light in them is hidden in the image of the light of the Father. He will not reveal himself, and his image will be hidden by his light."

[84] Jesus said, "When you see your likeness, you rejoice. But when you see your images which came into being before you, which do not die or manifest, how much will you will bear!"

[99] The disciples said to him, "Your brothers and your mother are standing outside." He said to them, "Those here who do the will of my Father are my brothers and mother; they will enter the Kingdom of my Father."

[101] He who does not hate his [father] and his mother in my way will not be able to be my [disciple], and he who does [not] love his father and his mother in my way, will not be able to be my [disciple], . . . but [my] true [mother] gave me life.

[104] They said (to him), "Come, let us pray today, and let us fast." Jesus said, "Why? What sin have I committed, or by what have I been conquered? But after the bridegroom has left the Bridal Chamber, then let them fast and pray."

Gnostic Christianity and Orthodox Christianity in Conflict*

The Gospel of Truth, *from the* Nag Hammadi Codex, *was known to Irenaeus, the orthodox bishop of Lyon and the leading Christian opponent of Christian Gnosticism. Some historians argue that the early Christian Gnostic Valentinus was the author of this gospel; at the least it reflects Valentinianism. It begins with a discussion of the* pleroma *("fullness"), which many Gnostics believed to be the supreme God who includes the many emanations responsible for creation and salvation.*[33] *In the second selection Irenaeus gives a defense of orthodox Christianity against Valentinianism and then provides a succinct description of Valentinianism's main teaching.*[34]

[*Gospel of Truth*] This is the word of the gospel of the discovery of the pleroma, for those who await the salvation which is coming from on high. While their hope which they are waiting for is waiting—they whose image is light with no shadow in it—then at that time the pleroma is about to come. The deficiency of matter has not arisen through the limitlessness of the Father, who is about to bring the time of the deficiency, although no one could say that the incorruptible one will come in this way. But the depth of the Father was multiplied and the thought of error did not exist with him. It is a thing that falls, it is a thing that easily stands upright again in the discovery of him who has come to him whom he shall bring back. For the bringing back is called repentance.

For this reason incorruptibility breathed forth; it pursued the one who had sinned in order that he might rest. For forgiveness is what remains for the light in the deficiency, the word of the pleroma....

That is why Christ was spoken of in their midst, so that those who were disturbed might receive a bringing back, and he might anoint them with the ointment. The ointment is the mercy of the Father who will have mercy on them. But those whom he has anointed are the ones who have become perfect. For full jars are the ones that are usually anointed. But when the anointing of one jar is dissolved, it is emptied, and the reason for there being a deficiency is the thing through which its ointment goes. For at that time a breath draws it, one by the power of the one with it. But from him who has no deficiency no seal is removed, nor is anything emptied. But what he lacks the perfect Father fills again. He is good. He knows his plantings because it is he who planted them in his paradise. Now his paradise is his place of rest. . . .

When therefore it pleased him that his name which is uttered should be his Son, and he gave the name to him, that is, him who came forth from the depth, he spoke about his secret things, knowing that the Father is a being without evil. For that very reason he brought him forth in order to speak about the place and his resting-place from which he had come forth, and to glorify the pleroma, the greatness of his name and the gentleness of the Father. About the place each one came from he will speak, and to the region where he received his essential being he will hasten to return again, and to be taken from that place—the place where he stood—receiving a taste from that place and receiving nourishment, receiving growth. And his own resting-place is his pleroma.

Therefore all the emanations of the Father are pleromas, and the root of all his emanations is in the one who made them all grow up in himself.

Gospel of Truth 34–43; Irenaeus, *Against Heresies,* Preface 1.1–2, 7.1–5.

[33] From J. M. Robinson, ed., *The Nag Hammadi Library in English* (New York: Harper & Row, 1977), pp. 45–49. Used by permission.

[34] Taken, with editing, from A. Roberts and J. Donaldson, *The Ante-Nicene Fathers,* vol. 1 (New York: Scribner, 1905), pp. 315–316, 325–326.

He assigned them their destinies. Each one of them is apparent in order of their own thought. . . . For the place to which they send their thought, that place is their root, which takes them up in all the heights to the Father. They possess his head which is rest for them and they hold on close to him, as though to say that they have participated in his face by means of kisses. But they do not appear in this way, for they did not surpass themselves nor lack the glory of the Father nor think of him as small nor that he is harsh nor that he is wrathful, but a being without evil, imperturbable, gentle, knowing all spaces before they have come into existence, and having no need to be instructed.

This is the manner of those who possess something from above of the immeasurable greatness, as they stretch out after the one alone and the perfect one, the one who is there for them. And they do not go down to Hades nor have they envy nor groaning nor death within them, but they rest in him who is at rest, not striving nor being involved in the search for truth. But they themselves are the truth; and the Father is within them and they are in the Father, being perfect, being undivided in the truly good one, being in no way deficient in anything, but they are set at rest, refreshed in the Spirit. And they will heed their root. They will be concerned with those things in which he will find his root and not suffer loss to his soul. This is the place of the blessed; this is their place.

[Irenaeus, *Against Heresies*] Certain men have set the truth aside, and bring in lying words and vain genealogies, which, as the apostle says, "minister disputes rather than godly edifying which is in faith." By means of their craftily-constructed plausibilities, they draw away the minds of the inexperienced and take them captive. Therefore I have felt constrained, my dear friend, to compose the following treatise in order to expose and counteract their machinations.

These men falsify the words of God, and prove themselves evil interpreters of the good word of revelation. They also overthrow the faith of many by drawing them away, under a pretense of [superior] knowledge,[35] from Him who founded and adorned the universe, as if they had something more excellent and sublime to reveal than that God who created the heaven and the earth and all things that are in them. By means of specious and plausible words, they cunningly allure the simple-minded to inquire into their system. But they nevertheless clumsily destroy them, while they initiate them into their blasphemous and impious opinions about the Demiurge.[36] These simple ones are unable, even in such a matter, to distinguish falsehood from truth.

Error is never set forth in its naked deformity, lest it should be detected at once. But it is craftily decked out in an attractive dress, so as, by its outward form, to make it appear to the inexperienced truer than the truth itself, ridiculous as that may seem. . . . Therefore, some are to be carried off, even as sheep are by wolves, because they do not perceive the true character of these men. Outwardly they are covered with sheep's clothing (against whom the Lord has enjoined us to be on our guard), and because their language resembles ours, while their sentiments are very different. Thus I have deemed it my duty (after reading some of the *Commentaries*, as they call them, of the disciples of Valentinus, and after making myself acquainted with their tenets through personal dealings with some of them) to unfold to you, my friend, these portentous and profound mysteries, which do not fall within the range of every intellect, because all have not sufficiently purged their brains. I do this in order that you, obtaining an acquaintance with these things, may in turn explain them to all those with whom you are connected. Exhort them to avoid such an abyss of madness and of blasphemy against Christ. . . .

---

[35] *knowledge:* the Greek original is *gnosis*, from which "Gnostic" is derived.

[36] *Demiurge:* the evil Aeon who made the world.

[7.1] When all the seed shall have come to perfection, they state that then their mother Achamoth shall pass from the intermediate place, and enter in within the Pleroma, and shall receive as her spouse the Savior, who sprang from all the Aeons, that thus a conjunction may be formed between the Savior and Sophia, that is, Achamoth. These, then, are the bridegroom and bride, while the nuptial chamber is the full extent of the Pleroma. The spiritual seed, again, being divested of their animal souls, and becoming intelligent spirits, shall in an irresistible and invisible manner enter in within the Pleroma, and be bestowed as brides on those angels who wait upon the Savior. The Demiurge himself will pass into the place of his mother Sophia; that is, the intermediate habitation. In this intermediate place, also, shall the souls of the righteous repose; but nothing of an animal nature shall find admittance to the Pleroma. When these things have taken place as described, then shall that fire which lies hidden in the world blaze forth and burn; and while destroying all matter, shall also be extinguished along with it, and have no further existence. They affirm that the Demiurge was acquainted with none of these things before the advent of the Savior.

There are also some who maintain that he also produced Christ as his own proper son, but of an animal nature, and that mention was made of him by the prophets. This Christ passed through Mary just as water flows through a tube. A dove, that Savior who belonged to the Pleroma, descended upon him at the time of his baptism. In him there existed also that spiritual seed which proceeded from Achamoth. They hold, accordingly, that our Lord, while preserving the type of the first-begotten and primary tetrad, was compounded of these four substances—of the spiritual, in so far as He was from Achamoth; of the animal, as being from the Demiurge by a special dispensation; of the bodily, formed with unspeakable skill; and of the Savior, as respects that dove which descended upon Him. He also continued free from all suffering, since indeed it was not possible that He should suffer who was at once incomprehensible and invisible. And for this reason the Spirit of Christ, who had been placed within Him, was taken away when He was brought before Pilate.

They maintain, further, that not even the seed which He had received from the mother [Achamoth] was subject to suffering. It, too, was impassible,[37] because it was spiritual, and invisible even to the Demiurge himself. It follows, then, according to them, that the animal Christ, and that which had been formed mysteriously by a special dispensation, underwent suffering, that the mother might exhibit through him a type of the Christ above, namely, of him who extended himself through Stauros,[38] and imparted to Achamoth shape, so far as substance was concerned. For they declare that all these transactions were counterparts of what took place above.

---

[37] *impassible:* not capable of suffering.
[38] *Stauros:* the Greek word for "cross."

Women and Gnosticism*

In this Christian-Gnostic book from the second century, Mary Magdalene encourages the disciples of Jesus to carry out the task of preaching he has given them, and she relates to them some of the teaching Jesus had given privately to her, including a vision of the ascending soul being questioned by the heavenly powers. This text shows that women

---

*Gospel of Mary 7:8–18.

often had a higher place in Gnostic Christianity than in orthodox Christianity, but even in Gnosticism their position was challenged.[39]

When the blessed one had said this he greeted them all, saying, "Peace be with you. Receive my peace to yourselves. Beware that no one lead you astray, saying, 'Lo here!' or 'Lo there!' For the Son of Man is within you. Follow after him! Those who seek him will find him. Go then and preach the gospel of the kingdom. Do not lay down any rules beyond what I appointed for you, and do not give a law like the lawgiver[40] lest you be constrained by it." When he had said this, he departed.

But they were grieved. They wept greatly, saying, "How shall we go to the Gentiles and preach the gospel of the kingdom of the Son of Man? If they did not spare him, how will they spare us?"

Then Mary stood up, greeted them all, and said to her brethren, "Do not weep and do not grieve or be irresolute, for his grace will be entirely with you and will protect you. But rather let us praise his greatness, for he has prepared us (and) made us into men."[41] When Mary said this, she turned their hearts to the Good, and they began to discuss the words of the [Savior].

[10] Peter said to Mary, "Sister, we know that the Savior loved you more than the rest of women. Tell us the words of the Savior which you remember—which you know (but) we do not, nor have we heard them."

Mary answered and said, "What is hidden from you I will proclaim to you." And she began to speak to them these words: "I," she said, "I saw the Lord in a vision and I said to him, 'Lord, I saw you today in a vision.' He answered and said to me, 'Blessed are you, that you did not waver at the sight of me. For where the mind is, there is the treasure.' I said to him, 'Lord, now does he who sees the vision see through the soul or through the spirit?' The Savior answered and said, 'He does not see through the soul or through the spirit, but the mind which [is] between the two—that is [what] sees the vision and it is . . .'[42] [15] And desire said, 'I did not see you descending, but now I see you ascending. Why do you lie, since you belong to me?' The soul answered and said, 'I saw you. You did not see me or recognize me. I served you as a garment, and you did not know me.' When it had said this, it went away rejoicing greatly. . . .'"

When Mary had said this, she fell silent, since it was to this point that the Savior had spoken with her. But Andrew answered and said to the brethren, "Say what you (wish to) say about what she has said. I at least do not believe that the Savior said this. For certainly these teachings are strange ideas." Peter answered and spoke concerning these same things. He questioned them about the Savior: "Did he really speak privately with a woman (and) not openly to us? Are we to turn about and all listen to her? Did he prefer her to us?"

Then Mary wept and said to Peter, "My brother Peter, what do you think? Do you think that I thought this up myself in my heart, or that I am lying about the Savior?" Levi answered and said to Peter, "Peter, you have always been hot-tempered. Now I see you contending against the woman like the adversaries. But if the Savior made her worthy, who are you indeed to reject her? Surely the Savior knows her very well. That is why he loved her more than us. Rather let us be ashamed and put on the perfect man, and separate as he commanded us and preach the gospel, not laying down any other rule or other law beyond what the Savior said."

---

[39] From J. M. Robinson, ed., *The Nag Hammadi Library in English* (San Francisco: Harper & Row, 1977), pp. 472–473. Used by permission.
[40] *lawgiver:* Moses.
[41] *made us into men:* the Gnostic-Christian *Gospel of Thomas* ends with this same teaching of "making women male." Scholars disagree about its meaning.
[42] Pages 11–14 of the manuscript are missing at this point.

Papal Primacy Derived from Petrine Primacy*

Pope Leo I, called "Leo the Great," bishop of Rome from about 440 to 461, was a staunch promoter of papal power. This passage is the classic early statement on the origin and nature of papal power. Leo uses an interpretation of several New Testament passages to claim that the bishop of Rome is the successor of Peter. This argument was influential on Emperor Valentinus III, who in 445 decreed that the bishop of Rome is head of the entire church.[43]

It is profitable and worthy to raise the mind's eye to the contemplation of the glory of the most blessed apostle Peter, and to celebrate this day[44] in honor of him. He was watered with so many large streams from the very fountain of all graces that he received many special privileges of his own, while no privilege has passed to others except through him. . . .

"You are Peter, and on this rock I will build my Church, and the gates of hell shall not prevail against it."[45] On this strength, he says, I will build an eternal temple, and the loftiness of my Church, reaching to heaven, shall rise upon the firmness of this faith. . . . "I will give you the keys of the kingdom of heaven; whatever you bind on earth shall be bound in heaven, and whatever you loose on earth shall be loosed in heaven."[46] The right of this power did indeed pass on to the other apostles, and the order of this decree passed on to all the leaders of the Church. But this power that was imparted to all was first entrusted to one person. Therefore this power is granted to Peter separately, because all the rulers of the Church are invested with the figure of Peter. Peter's privilege remains wherever judgment is passed from him. . . .

Again as his passion came near, which was to shake the firmness of the disciples, the Lord says, "Simon, behold Satan has desired to have you that he may sift you as wheat. But I have prayed for you that your faith may not fail, and when you have returned, strengthen your brothers, that you may not enter temptation."[47] The danger from the temptation was common to all apostles, and they all needed the help of divine protection, since the devil wanted to harass and shatter them all. Yet the Lord takes special care of Peter, because the state of the others would be more certain if the mind of their leader were not overcome. So then in Peter the strength of all is fortified, and the help of divine grace is given so that the stability that Christ gave to Peter is conveyed through Peter to the apostles.

Beloved, since we see such protection divinely granted to us, we justly rejoice in the merits and dignity of our leader [Peter]. We render thanks to the eternal King, our Redeemer, the Lord Jesus Christ, for having given so great a power to him whom he made chief of the whole Church. If anything, even in our time, is rightly done and rightly ordered, we must ascribe it to Peter's working and his guidance, to whom Christ said, "And when you have returned, strengthen your brethren." The Lord after his resurrection, in answer to the triple profession of eternal love, said three times to Peter, with mystical intent, "Feed my sheep."[48] Beyond a doubt, the pious shepherd does this even now, and fulfills the charge of his Lord. He confirms us with his exhortations, and does not cease to pray for us, so that we may not be overcome by temptation. If, as we must believe, he extends this care of his piety to all God's people everywhere, how much more will he condescend to grant his help to us his children.

---

*Pope Leo I, *Sermons* 4.2–4.
[43] Taken, with editing, from T. W. Allies, *The See of Peter* (London, 1850).
[44] *this day:* the anniversary day of Pope Leo, as mentioned at the end of this selection.
[45] *on this rock . . . it:* a quotation of Jesus in *Matthew* 16:18.
[46] *Matthew* 16:19.
[47] *Luke* 22:31–32.
[48] *John* 21:15–19.

GLOSSARY

apostle "one sent out" with the message of salvation, especially the twelve main disciples of Jesus.

authentic writings that most modern biblical scholars commonly accept as actually written by the persons whose names they bear.

baptism a washing with, or immersion in, water for forgiveness and new spiritual life.

Bible the scriptures of Christianity, the thirty-nine books of the *Old Testament* and the twenty-seven books of the *New Testament*.

gospel "good news"; at first, the oral message of "good news" about salvation in Jesus; later, the name given to the books that tell the story of the life, death, and resurrection of Jesus.

letters occasional writings of instruction addressed to churches, so called because they share many or all the features of the common Greco-Roman letter; also called *epistles*.

New Testament the collection of twenty-seven books, mostly gospels and letters, written within the first hundred years of Christianity and constituting the unique, Christian portion of the Christian *Bible*.

Old Testament the name that early Christianity gave to the books of the Jewish *Bible*, which it incorporated into the Christian *Bible*.

pseudonymous writings that most modern biblical scholars do not commonly accept as authentic.

synoptic gospel books that can be "seen in one view" (*synopsis*) because of their parallel structure and content: *Matthew, Mark,* and *Luke*.

testament the relationship that God established with his people; also called *covenant*. Christians saw a "new covenant" established in Jesus, leading them to call their new scriptures the *New Testament*.

QUESTIONS FOR STUDY AND DISCUSSION

1. In what ways do the four gospels center on the suffering, death, and resurrection of Jesus?

2. Summarize in your own words the main points of the teaching of Jesus. How does the teaching of Jesus relate to Jesus' life, death, and resurrection as portrayed in the gospels?

3. In what ways do the acts and teaching of Jesus, the *Acts of the Apostles,* and Paul's letters show Christianity to be a "missionary religion"?

4. What degree of continuity and discontinuity can be discerned in these readings from the teaching of Jesus to the teaching of Paul?

5. Why is Jesus so harsh toward hypocrisy in the *Sermon on the Mount*? In what ways could hypocrisy have been a problem in early Christianity?

6. In what ways does the *New Testament* better the condition of women, and in what ways does it not? Discuss both the first century C.E. and today.

7. How does the *New Testament* promote love as the chief virtue in the religious life?

8. To what extent, if any, do the organization of the church and church offices reflect the distinctive teachings of the *New Testament*?

SCRIPTURES IN FILM

Of all major world religions, Christianity is the most fully, if not always the most artistically, represented in feature films. *The Gospel according to St. Matthew* (1964, unrated), directed by Pier Paolo Pasolini, is the most cinematically artistic. *The Passion of the Christ* (2004, rated R), directed by Mel Gibson, is a controversial, thought-provoking depiction of the death of Jesus. *The Gospel of John* (2003, rated PG-13) uses the English text of an entire gospel to tell the story of Jesus' ministry, death, and resurrection. For a taste of apocalyptic style in the *New Testament* and in modern film, see *The Seventh Seal* (1958, unrated), directed by Ingmar Bergman, one of the classics of world cinema, and (interesting but with much less cinematic excellence) *The Seventh Sign* (1989, rated R), directed by Carl Schultz and starring Demi Moore.

SUGGESTIONS FOR FURTHER READING

Primary Readings

B. M. Metzger and R. E. Murphy, eds., *The New Oxford Annotated Bible*. New York: Oxford University Press, 1991. The standard translation of the *Bible* in an edition with excellent introductions and notes.

The New English Bible. New York: Oxford and Cambridge University Presses, 1970. A translation known for its literary beauty.

D. Senior et al., eds., *The Catholic Study Bible*. New York: Oxford University Press, 1990. An excellent study *Bible* for both Catholics and others who wish to know more about the contemporary Catholic understanding of the *Bible*. Contains the text of the *New American Bible*, which is similar to that of the *New Revised Standard Version*.

Secondary Readings

R. E. Brown, *An Introduction to the New Testament*. New York: Doubleday, 1997. The most recent and best survey of scholarship.

E. P. Sanders, *The Historical Figure of Jesus*. London: Penguin, 1993. Arguably one of the best recent introductions to the "historical Jesus."

E. Schüssler Fiorenza, *In Memory of Her*, rev. ed. Philadelphia: Fortress, 1995. An updating of a classic study of the status and role of women in the *New Testament* from a strongly feminist perspective.

B. Witherington, *Women in the New Testament*. Cambridge: Cambridge University Press, 1985. A thorough and readable study of the status and role of women in the ministry of Jesus and in the early church from a moderate feminist perspective.

***Private Reading of the* Qur'an**
Muhammed Mukti, a teacher of the *Qur'an,* reads the holy book in the Karanganyar City Mosque in Central Java, Indonesia, the nation of the world with the most Muslims. His *Qur'an* rests on a stand to keep it off the ground and thus treat it respectfully. *Credit:* Joanna Pinneo, Foreign Missions Board, SBC.

CHAPTER FIVE

Islam

- In a city in Saudi Arabia, a boy who is auspiciously four years, four months, and four days old celebrates a special event. He goes to the *Qur'an* school to recite formally his first verse of the *Qur'an*. The verse is written in honey on a small slate. When the boy finishes practicing the verse, he recites it formally and the honey is dissolved in water. The boy then drinks the water, which has been sweetened by the holy words of the *Qur'an*. The words he has spoken become a part of him, and he returns home with his family to a celebration.

- In a village near Khartoum, Sudan, a large crowd of Muslims has gathered to hear perhaps the most famous healer in Africa, Sheik Abdel Azziz ibn Ali. This Sudanese cleric soon emerges to stand on a platform and sing the *Qur'an*. As his chant grows in intensity, the crowd responds in various emotional ways, and some people loudly report that they have now been cured of chronic diseases. The sheik defends himself against occasional charges of charlatanism by saying, "All I do is recite the *Qur'an*."

- In Philadelphia, Pennsylvania, a recently converted Muslim woman studies the *Qur'an* as she rides the bus to her job. She looks first at the mostly unfamiliar Arabic original on the right-hand pages, then reads carefully the English interpretation of it on the left-hand pages, and finally looks back at the Arabic. When she leaves the bus, she feels inspired and directed to serve God during that day.

INTRODUCTION

Islam confesses that "there is no God but God" and that "Muhammad is God's prophet" who has come to teach and spread the way of submission and obedience to the one God. Muslims believe that the angel Gabriel revealed the *Qur'an* to Muhammad over an approximately twenty-year period, from his call to be a prophet until his death in 632 C.E. The words of the *Qur'an* were *given to* Muhammad, not *written by* him. Its only author is God, and every word comes from God. The *Qur'an* is the basic authority for Islamic religious life, Islam's continuing guide during fourteen hundred years of history. As W. C. Smith observed, the *Qur'an* "has fired the imagination, and inspired the poetry, and formulated the inhibitions, and guided the ecstasies, and teased the intellects, and ordered the family relations and the legal chicaneries, and nurtured the piety, of hundreds of millions of people in widely diverse climes and over a series of radically divergent centuries."[1] Therefore, one who understands the *Qur'an* and its use has been well introduced to Islam.

---

[1] W. C. Smith, "The Study of Religion and the Study of the Bible," in M. Levering, ed., *Rethinking Scripture: Essays from a Comparative Perspective* (Albany: State University of New York Press, 1989), p. 21.

Name

Qur'an is Arabic for "recitation, reading." These two meanings suggest the twin aspects of oral and written revelation, both of them important in understanding the *Qur'an* and its place in Islam. (The two meanings are closer than we might imagine, because the "reading" is typically out loud.) God gave the message to Muhammad, and Muhammad spoke it to his followers. Indeed, the oral meaning predominates in the *Qur'an* itself, where the word *Qur'an* refers primarily to oral revelations, not to the written book of human history that we know as the *Qur'an*. But the oral revelations in turn were based on the heavenly written *Qur'an*, the "well-preserved tablet" and the "mother of the Book." They began to be recorded in writing during Muhammad's lifetime and were collected into a book, the *Qur'an*, soon after his death. So the movement of revelation, as Muslims would explain it, goes from the eternal, heavenly *Qur'an*, to Gabriel's oral revelation of this *Qur'an* to Muhammad, then orally from Muhammad to his followers, and finally from his followers to the written *Qur'an*. In each stage, the *Qur'an* has a strong oral dimension in its formal recitation called **tilawa** [tee-LAH-wuh], and in always vocalized informal reading. The circle of revelation is complete and perfect: The heavenly *Qur'an* and the *Qur'an* on earth are identical.

The usual English spelling of the Muslim scripture is *Qur'an*. Often the older spelling "Koran" is found, especially in journalism, but more recent scholarship prefers the newer spelling as closer to the Arabic pronunciation. *Qur'an* is pronounced "kuhr-AHN." Between the two syllables is a glottal stop that is stronger in Arabic than the similar sound that speakers of English naturally make when they pronounce the beginning of the second syllable. The apostrophe between the syllables reminds us of this glottal stop.

Use

Even before its existence as a text, the *Qur'an* enjoyed standing as the ultimate authority in Islam. Still, from the first generations of Islam arose a second body of authority, first in oral form and then written. This second authority is the **hadith** [hah-DEETH], narrative "traditions" about Muhammad and the first generation of Muslims. These traditions were meant to form a historical context by which the *Qur'an* could be interpreted, and they deal especially with the life of Muhammad in a way that the *Qur'an* does not.

It was almost inevitable that these *hadith* should arise. The *Qur'an*, with its almost complete lack of any historical framework, needs such a framework by which its difficulties, seeming inconsistencies, and other interpretive issues can be ironed out. Qur'anic interpretation has been, from the very first, an effort to understand and apply to Muslim life the teachings given through Muhammad (the *Qur'an*) in the context of the traditions (the *hadith*). The principle arose quickly that every interpretation of the *Qur'an* must have a tradition to back it up. The collection and preservation of these traditions became a major task of religious scholarship in Islam.

The Sunni and Shi'a branches of Islam have the same *Qur'an* but differ in their approach to the *hadith*. Shi'ites believe that the split between these two groups goes back to the period shortly after the death of Muhammad, when a few of the faithful accepted Ali, Muhammad's cousin, as his successor, but most went with his general

Abu Bakr, then with Umar and Uthman. Most Shi'ites believe that the *hadith* passed on through the correct followers of Ali are much more trustworthy than the other *hadith*, some of which are rejected. This rejection has led to some of the differences between Sunni and Shi'ite legal practices, such as temporary marriages contracted for a few days or months, which are accepted by most Shi'ites.

In the Middle Ages (soon after the birth of Islam in the seventh century), commentary became the lens through which the *Qur'an* was viewed. This commentary, called **tafsir** [TAHF-sear] became an important branch of Muslim theology. Tafsir combined analysis of both the *Qur'an* and the relevant *hadith* to produce a detailed and often massive body of literature. In this period of interpretation, which lasted until the nineteenth century, all higher study of the *Qur'an* was indirect—the scripture was read only through the commentaries, and the commentaries specified its meaning. Only in the mosques and among the common people was the *Qur'an* allowed to speak more or less for itself.

In recent times, a period of modernism challenged the monopoly of the commentaries. A movement arose to revive the most ancient forms of Islam and reform it by ending the authority of the medieval commentators. Some methods new to Islam but well known in Europe were introduced to attempt to recover the original meaning of the *Qur'an*. The Indian Muslim scholar M. Azad, for example, argued that it is necessary to study the life and language of Arabia at the time of Muhammad to understand what the *Qur'an* meant to its original hearers and readers. D. Rahbar, in his *The God of Justice* (1960), argued that it is more important to compare Qur'anic passages against each other in determining their meaning than to rely on *hadith* and later commentators. This liberalizing movement was generally confined to the more Westernized upper classes. Since about 1980, a tide of conservatism in the Muslim world, led by the increasingly influential Shi'ite branch of Islam, has effectively limited the movement to modernize the interpretation of the *Qur'an*.

Among ordinary Muslims during most of Islamic history, the esteem and reverence that is shown to the *Qur'an* is evidenced in everyday actions. To use the Muslim scripture in any way, one must first ritually wash. Although Muslims often sit on the floor to study the *Qur'an*, especially in a mosque, the *Qur'an* itself is never allowed to touch the floor but rests on a low bookstand. A person who carries several books must always place the *Qur'an* on top. Pious Muslims read portions of it every day, and they read the entire *Qur'an* during Ramadan, guided by special division marks in the Arabic text. Large portions of it are committed to memory, and it is considered a mark of special piety to memorize the entire *Qur'an*.

The *Qur'an* is also used for purposes of magic, especially to ward off evil curses by humans and **jinn,** spirits who inhabit the world and who can have a supernatural influence, most often evil, on people. Its last two chapters are plainly countermagical, designed to keep away evil supernatural powers. Verses from other chapters are also copied out and used as amulets to bring blessing and ward off evil.

Overview of Structure

The *Qur'an,* which is approximately the length of the *New Testament,* is divided into 114 chapters called **surahs** [SOO-rahs]. The first surah, ***Fatihah*** [fah-TEE-huh] (Opening), is a preface to the book. Beginning with Surah 2, the chapters are organized by approximate length, from longest to shortest. This means that a new reader of the *Qur'an* first encounters long chapters ranging over many unrelated topics. The *Qur'an* generally reverses the order in which Muhammad revealed the surahs to his followers. The long, more prosaic surahs that begin the *Qur'an* typically come from the last part of Muhammad's prophetic career, and the shorter, more poetic surahs come from the first part. To Muslims, this sequence is of no importance because the sacredness and authority of the text derive from its origin, not from its order. To non-Muslim readers, however, it presents a challenge that often leads them to lay aside the *Qur'an* out of sheer puzzlement. Some English translations try to make the *Qur'an* more intelligible to non-Muslim readers by rearranging the chapters into an order that more or less follows Muhammad's life.

The internal structure of each surah is as follows (see Table 5.1).

- A title heads the chapter. Most titles are short, and some are drawn from the opening words of the chapter. More typically, the title is taken from one isolated and sometimes metaphoric word in the chapter, such as "The Cave" (18) or "Light" (24). A few surahs are titled after the Arabic letter or letters with which they begin, as is Surah 50. Only occasionally does the title of a surah indicate its main topic, so a new reader of the *Qur'an* cannot depend on chapter titles as a guide to content.

- A number follows the title. It serves to identify the chapter more fully.

- The *Qur'an* then indicates whether the chapter was given to Muhammad while he was in Mecca or Medina. The Meccan chapters tend to be found in the second half of the *Qur'an,* the Medinan chapters in the first half. Many passages are of mixed origin, containing material from both stages of the Prophet's career. This is recognized by modern non-Muslim scholars and by Muslim traditionalists.

- Next comes the **Bismillah** [biss-MILL-uh], which in full runs *Bismillah al-Rahman, al-Rahim*. It is usually translated "In the name of God, the Compassionate, the Merciful." The translation by Abdel Haleem that we use in this chapter renders the *Bismillah* in a way that preserves the close relationship of *al-Rahman* and *al-Rahim*: "the Lord of Mercy, the Giver of Mercy." This resonant

Table 5.1
Structure of a Typical Surah

THE SAND DUNES	Title
46:1–11	Number
(Mecca)	Origin
In the Name of God, the Compassionate, the Merciful	*Bismillah*
Ha-min. This Book is reveled by God, the Mighty One, the Wise One.	
It was to manifest the Truth that We created the heavens and the earth and all that lies between them; We created them to last for an appointed term;	Ayah1
Yet the unbelievers give no heed to our warning.	Ayah2

Arabic formula, both an invocation of God and a blessing of God, is always spoken before reading a passage as well as at many other times in a Muslim's life. It likely goes back to the time of Muhammad, but whether it was actually used in his time to mark the head of a chapter is less certain.

- Each chapter is further divided into **ayahs** [EYE-yuhs], numbered verses. These divisions were added after Muhammad's death for ease in locating passages, especially in the longer chapters. The verses vary greatly in length; one ayah can be as long as several sentences or as short as a few words. *Ayah* literally means "sign," and this word is found many times in the *Qur'an* to denote the signs of nature and history that point to the reality and power of the one God.

- The body of the chapters usually has one or more topics. Generally, the longer a chapter is, the more numerous and varied are the topics. The wording of the chapters presents the speech of God. God speaks in a majestic "We/Us/Our," capitalized in translations. "You" in the singular refers to Muhammad; at other times, in the plural, "you" refers to Muhammad's audience. Many utterances begin with "Say," and what follows this word is presented as God's revelation to Muhammad's audience. Passages that narrate biblical incidents are briefly recounted, with the emphasis on their teaching, not on the story itself.

- Just as they have a variety of topics, the chapters also have a variety of endings. Often there is a plea to Muhammad to persist in his calling, or a summons for Muslims to persevere, or a promise of reward or punishment in the next life.

Origin and Development

The first stage of the *Qur'an* was its reception as revelation by Muhammad. A few times he heard the audible voice of the angel Gabriel, but usually he received the revelation while in a trance or asleep. Muslims believe that whatever the mode of revelation, Muhammad received the *Qur'an* from God and that God is its only author. European scholars in the nineteenth century searched for literary sources of the *Qur'an* on the assumption that Muhammad drew on other sources and wrote the *Qur'an* himself. But more recent non-Muslim scholarship recognizes that beyond the question of sources, the *Qur'an* has its main origin in the internal experience of Muhammad. The question of whether his experience has a divine origin is one that historians and scholars of religion cannot answer.

The next stage in the development of the *Qur'an* was its oral transmission in prophetic utterances to Muhammad's followers. Muhammad spoke to them the words that Gabriel commanded him to speak, which are often introduced in the *Qur'an* by the imperative "Say." His disciples committed his sayings to memory and spoke them to others, and these early "reciters" of the *Qur'an* played an important part in its survival and transmission. But, as a *hadith* narrates, Muhammad's followers also wrote the sayings down at his command on "pieces of paper, stones, palm-leaves, shoulder-blade bones and ribs, and bits of leather"—in other words, on any material at hand.

The *Qur'an* in its final form bears witness to some difficulties in composition: substitution of verses, new revelations that cancel out older ones, and long periods between revelations. A *hadith* even speaks of "Satanic verses" in which Muhammad initially was led by Satan to give a revelation that favored some form of polytheism (the "daughters of Allah"). He later rejected them in favor of the strict monotheism that is the essential element of Islam.

After Muhammad's death in 632 and the Battle of Yamamah in 633, it was feared that knowledge of the *Qur'an* (still mostly recited orally) might die out. The process of recording all of it in writing began under the first caliph, Umar. But different versions arose, with consequent disputes over which *Qur'an* was better. To end these troubles, Caliph Uthman (r. 644–656) commissioned respected and learned men to produce a single recognized version using the best manuscripts and the memories of those with recognized knowledge of the *Qur'an*. This version, believed to be a true copy of the "Mother of the Book," became the only authorized text recognized by the Muslim community. Other texts were systematically collected and destroyed. Today almost all Muslims view the Uthmanic edition as identical to the *Qur'an* of Muhammad. No attempt to go behind this authorized version has been made, for it would be considered blasphemy to suggest that this is not the exact *Qur'an* that God gave originally to Muhammad.

The Arabic language in which the *Qur'an* is written is an important part of its origin and continuing appeal. It is often emphasized that Muhammad gave his followers an "Arabic *Qur'an*." Just as Jews and Christians had scriptures in their own languages, Arabs have an Arabic book. Muslims view the Arabic style of the *Qur'an*, especially its poetry, as matchless. Indeed, it is a sin to imitate its style or content in any way. Moreover, the *Qur'an* itself is not considered translatable into other languages. Although Muslims and non-Muslims alike have translated the *Qur'an* into many languages, which are typically put interlinearly or on facing pages with the Arabic text, the faithful commonly argue that these translations are only an approximation of the *Qur'an*, a rough indication of its content. They are not the scripture itself, which can exist only in Arabic. Even believers who do not learn Arabic memorize formulas and passages from the *Qur'an* in Arabic. Arabic is thus in at least a basic way the common language of Muslims throughout the world, and the *Qur'an* contributes to the unity of the Muslim community.

HISTORY

The Call of Muhammad*

In traditional Muslim understanding, Surah 96, "The Clinging Form," is the story of Muhammad's call vision. A hadith relates that while Muhammad was meditating in a cave, an angel appeared to him and commanded him to recite (iqra', the imperative form of Qur'an). *Muhammad at first refused, but the angel choked and threatened him into submission. This story is told in the first five verses; the rest are said to come from a later time. Most modern scholars identify "The Star," Surah 53, as Muhammad's call vision. It is related as a*

---

*Qur'an 96; 53:1–18.

challenge to those who "question what he sees." Muhammad's vision is inspired and authoritative because it is "received from one who is powerful and mighty." Surah 53 tells of two visions, and Islamic tradition (hadith) *says that these are the only two times when Muhammad actually saw Gabriel.*[2]

THE CLINGING FORM
Surah 96
(Mecca)

In the Name of God, the Lord of Mercy, the Giver of Mercy

Read![3] In the name of your Lord who created: He created man from a clinging form.[4] Read! Your Lord is the Most Bountiful One who taught by [means of] the pen,[5] [5] who taught man what he did not know.

But man exceeds all bounds when he thinks he is self-sufficient. All will return to your Lord. Have you seen the man who forbids [10] Our servant to pray? Have you seen whether he is rightly guided, or encourages true piety? Have you seen whether he denies the truth and turns away from it? Does he not realize that God sees all? [15] No! If he does not stop, We shall drag him by his forehead—his lying, sinful forehead. Let him summon his comrades; We shall summon the guards of Hell. No! Do not obey him. [Prophet:] bow down in worship and draw close.

THE STAR
Surah 53:1–18
(Mecca)

In the name of God, the Lord of Mercy, the Giver of Mercy

By the setting star! Your companion[6] has not strayed; he is not deluded; he does not speak from his own desire. The *Qur'an* is nothing less than a revelation that is sent to him. [5] It was taught to him by [an angel] with mighty powers and great strength, who stood on the highest horizon and then approached—coming down until he was two bow-lengths away or even closer—[10] and revealed to God's servant what he revealed.

[The Prophet's[7]] own heart did not distort what he saw. Are you going to dispute with him what he saw with his own eyes? A second time he saw him: by the lote tree beyond which none may pass [15] near the Garden of Return,[8] when the tree was covered in nameless splendor. His sight never wavered, nor was it too bold, and he saw some of the greatest signs of his Lord.

---

[2] Unless otherwise noted, all *Qur'an* passages are taken from M. A. S. Abdel Haleem, *The Qur'an* (Oxford: Oxford University Press, 2004). Copyright © 2004 M. A. S. Abdel Haleem. Used by permission of Oxford University Press.

[3] *Read:* out loud, therefore "recite."

[4] *a clinging form:* a beginning stage in the development of a human being in the womb. It emphasizes the dependency of humans, in contrast to the attitude shown in verse 7.

[5] *by [means of] the pen:* the coming of revelation from the heavenly *Qur'an* and its writing down into what was to become the earthly *Qur'an*.

[6] *Your companion:* Muhammad, who was living among his tribe, the Quraysh, at the time of this surah.

[7] *[The Prophet's]:* the bracketed words throughout are by the translator, Abdel Haleem, to make plain who is being addressed or (less often) who is being referred to.

[8] *lote tree, Garden of Return:* The lote tree is at the border of the highest heaven; the Garden of Return lies in the presence of God. This second vision is of heaven, which explains why Muhammad saw there "some of the greatest signs of his Lord."

The Mission of Muhammad*

Surah 11, "Hud," describes the tasks of Muhammad as God's prophet. It is named after the prophet Hud, sent before Muhammad to warn an Arab tribe to turn to the one God. He is a messenger who is to proclaim, "Serve none but God." Submission (islam) to God is the only way to serve him faithfully. Muhammad also warns of the terrors of hell that await those who refuse his message and promises rich rewards to those who obey. Muhammad brings no signs, treasures, or angels; his message itself is the miracle. In the face of opposition, Muhammad received the encouragement recorded in Surah 93, "Daylight." It offers a glimpse into his personal experience: He was an orphan, in error, and poor, from which conditions God delivered him. The surah ends with a call for Muhammad to be faithful to his mission.

HUD
Surah 11:1–16
(Mecca)

In the Name of God, the Lord of Mercy, the Giver of Mercy

Alif Lam Ra. [This is] a Scripture whose verses are perfected, then set out clearly, from One who is all wise, all aware. [Say, Prophet,] "Worship no one but God. I am sent to you from Him to warn and to give good news. Ask your Lord for forgiveness, then turn back to Him. He will grant you wholesome enjoyment until an appointed time, and give His grace to everyone who has merit. But if you turn away, I fear for you that you will suffer on a terrible Day: it is to God that you will all return, and He has power over everything."

[5] See how they [the disbelievers] wrap themselves up, to hide their feelings from Him. But even when they cover themselves with their clothes, He knows what they conceal and what they reveal. He knows well the innermost secrets of the heart. There is not a creature that moves on earth whose provision is not His concern. He knows where it lives and its [final] resting place; it is all [there] in a clear record. It is He who created the heavens and the earth in six Days—His rule extends over the waters too—so as to test which of you does best.

Yet [Prophet], if you say to them, "You will be resurrected after death," the disbelievers will answer, "This is clearly nothing but sorcery." If We defer their punishment for a determined time, they are sure to say, "What is holding it back?" But on the Day it comes upon them, nothing will divert it from them; what they mocked will be all around them. How desperate and ungrateful man becomes when We let him taste Our mercy and then withhold it! [10] And if We let him taste mercy after some harm has touched him, he is sure to say, "Misfortune has gone away from me." He becomes exultant and boastful! Not so those who are steadfast and do good deeds: they will have forgiveness and a great reward.

So [Prophet] are you going to abandon some part of what is revealed to you, and let your heart be oppressed by it, because they say, "Why is no treasure sent down to him, why has no angel come with him?" You are only there to warn; it is God who is in charge of everything. If they say, "He has invented it himself," say, "Then produce ten invented surahs like it,[9] and call in whoever you can beside God, if you are truthful." If they do not answer you, then you will all know that it is sent down containing knowledge from God, and that there is no god but Him. Then will you submit[10] to Him?

[15] If any desire [only] the life of this world with all its finery, We shall repay them in full in this life for their deeds—they will be given no less—but such people will have nothing in the

---

*Qur'an 11:1–16; 93.

[9] *produce ten . . . like it:* This response by Muhammad to his opponents, often found in the *Qur'an*, is called the **challenge verses.**

[10] *submit:* the verb related to *islam*, "submission."

Hereafter but the Fire; their work here will be fruitless and their deeds futile.

DAYLIGHT
Surah 93
(Mecca)

In the name of God, the Lord of Mercy, the Giver of Mercy

By the morning brightness and by the night when it grows still, your Lord has not forsaken you [Prophet], nor does He hate you, and the future will be better for you than the past; [5] your Lord is sure to give you so much that you will be well satisfied. Did He not find you an orphan and shelter you? Did He not find you lost and guide you? Did He not find you in need and make you self-sufficient?

So do not be harsh with the orphan [10] and do not chide the one who asks for help; talk about the blessings of your Lord.

Opposition to Muhammad*

Muhammad experienced strong opposition to his ministry, especially in the Meccan phase. The first selection, from Surah 52, catalogs many of the charges of Muhammad's Meccan opponents, who are referred to as "they." The second selection, Surah 63, deals with another type of opposition to Muhammad, from "hypocrites" who seemingly acknowledged Muhammad and accepted Islam but only for their own advantage. Verses 7 and 8 of Surah 63 relate how some opponents tried to stifle Islam by forbidding people from giving charity to followers of Muhammad. These hypocrites are residents of Medina, where Muhammad was widely followed as a religious and political leader.

[Surah 52:29b] By the grace of your Lord [Prophet], you are neither an oracle nor a madman. [30] If they say, "He is only a poet: we shall await his fate," say, "Wait if you wish; I too am waiting." Does their reason really tell them to do this, or are they simply insolent people? If they say, "He has made it up himself"—they certainly do not believe—let them produce one like it, if what they say is true.

[35] Were they created without any agent? Were they the creators? Did they create the heavens and the earth? No! They do not have faith. Do they possess your Lord's treasures or have control over them? Do they have a ladder to climb, in order to eavesdrop [on Heaven's secrets]? Let their eavesdropper produce clear proof. Does God have daughters while you have sons?[11]

[40] Do you [Prophet] demand a payment from them that would burden them with debt? Do they have [access to] the unseen? Could they write it down? Do they think they can ensnare you? It is the disbelievers who have been ensnared. Do they really have another god beside God? God is far above anything they set alongside Him.

Even if they saw a piece of heaven falling down on them, they would say, "Just a heap of clouds," [45] so leave them, Prophet, until they face the day when they will be thunderstruck, the Day when their snares will be of no use to them, when they will get no help. Another punishment awaits the evildoers, though most of them do not realize it. Wait patiently [Prophet] for your Lord's judgment: you are under Our watchful eye. Celebrate the praise of your Lord when you rise. Glorify Him at night and at the fading of the stars.

---

*Qur'an 52:29b–49; 63.
[11] *daughters . . . sons:* The "daughters of God" were the female deities in the pre-Islamic religions of the Arabs. This charge rests on the higher value that Arabs put on sons than on daughters.

THE HYPOCRITES
Surah 63
Medina

In the name of God, the Lord of Mercy, the Giver of Mercy

When the hypocrites come to you [Prophet], they say, "We bear witness that you are the Messenger of God." God knows that you truly are His Messenger and He bears witness that the hypocrites are liars—they use their oaths as a cover and so bar others from God's way. What they have been doing is truly evil, because they professed faith and then rejected it. So their hearts have been sealed and they do not understand.

When you see them [Prophet], their outward appearance pleases you; when they speak, you listen to what they say. But they are like propped-up timbers—they think every cry they hear is against them—and they are the enemy. Beware of them. May God confound them! How devious they are!

[5] They turn their heads away in disdain when they are told, "Come, so that the Messenger of God may ask forgiveness for you," and you see them walking away arrogantly. It makes no difference whether you ask forgiveness for them or not, God will not forgive them. God does not guide such treacherous people. They are the ones who say, "Give nothing to those who follow God's Messenger, until they abandon him," but to God belong the treasures of the heavens and earth, though the hypocrites do not understand this. They say, "Once we return to Medina the powerful will drive out the weak," but power belongs to God, to His Messenger, and to the believers, though the hypocrites do not understand this.

Believers, do not let your wealth and your children distract you from remembering God: those who do so will be the ones who lose. [10] Give out of what We have provided for you, before death comes to one of you and he says, "My Lord, if You would only reprieve me for a little while, I would give in charity and become one of the righteous." God does not reprieve a soul when its turn comes. God is fully aware of what you do.

The Night Journey*

Surah 17 is entitled "The Night Journey," although only the first two verses deal with this topic. This chapter is also called "The Children of Israel" for one of its later themes. The angel Gabriel took Muhammad to Jerusalem (called by Muslims Al-Quds), and most Muslim interpreters and ordinary believers hold that he ascended there to heaven for a brief time. Muhammad's journey to Jerusalem is an important reason for later Islam's viewing it as the third holiest city in the world, after Mecca and Medina.

THE NIGHT JOURNEY
Surah 17:1–3
(Mecca)

In the Name of God, the Lord of Mercy, the Giver of Mercy

---

*Qur'an 17:1–2.

Glory to Him who made His servant travel by night from the sacred place of worship to the furthest place of worship,[12] whose surroundings We have blessed, to show him some of Our signs. He alone is the All Hearing, the All Seeing. We also gave Moses the Scripture, and made it a guide for the Children of Israel. Entrust yourselves to no one but Me, you descendants of those We carried with Noah; he was truly a thankful servant.

---

[12] *the sacred place of worship:* the main mosque in Mecca. The *furthest place of worship* is the holy mosque of Jerusalem on the site of the ancient Jewish temple. Both uses of "place of worship" are the translation of *masjid*, "place of prayer," or in English "mosque."

The Flight to Medina*

When he was driven out of Mecca by his opponents, Muhammad hid in a cave for three days with his lone companion, Abu Bakr. God's deliverance of the Prophet from this threat to his life made a deep impression on him, giving him a sense of confidence that would transform his life. This verse is addressed to the citizens of Mecca.

Even if you do not help the Prophet, God helped him when the disbelievers drove him out: when the two of them were in the cave, he [Muhammad] said to his companion, "Do not worry, God is with us." God sent His calm down to him, aided him with forces invisible to you, and brought down the disbelievers' plan. God's plan is higher: God is almighty and wise.

---

*Qur'an 9:40.

The Wives of Muhammad**

The most extensive view of the personal life of Muhammad that the Qur'an *offers is of his marriages during the Medinan period. Earlier, in Mecca, the Prophet was married only to Kadijah, of whom the* Qur'an *does not speak. In Medina, Muhammad had many wives and concubines, which became controversial.*

Prophet, say to your wives, "If your desire is for the present life and its finery, then come, I will make provision for you and release you with kindness. But if you desire God, His Messenger, and the Final Home, then remember that God has prepared great rewards for those of you who do good." [30] Wives of the Prophet, if any of you does something clearly outrageous, she will be doubly punished—that is easy for God—but if any of you is obedient to God and His Messenger and does good deeds, know that We shall give her a double reward and have prepared a generous provision for her.

Wives of the Prophet, you are not like any other woman. If you truly fear God, do not speak too softly in case the sick at heart should lust after you, but speak in an appropriate manner; stay at home, and do not flaunt your attractions as they used to in the pagan past; keep up the prayer, give the prescribed alms, and obey God and His Messenger. God wishes to keep uncleanness away from you, people of the [Prophet's] House, and make you completely pure. Remember what is recited in your houses of God's revelations and wisdom, for God is all subtle, all aware.

**Qur'an 33:28–40, 50.

[35] For men and women who are devoted to God—believing men and women, obedient men and women, truthful men and women, steadfast men and women, humble men and women, charitable men and women, fasting men and women, chaste men and women, men and women who remember God often—God has prepared forgiveness and a rich reward.

When God and His Messenger have decided on a matter that concerns them, it is not fitting for any believing man or woman to claim freedom of choice in that matter: whoever disobeys God and His Messenger is far astray. When you [Prophet] said to the man[13] who had been favored by God and by you, "Keep your wife and be mindful of God," you hid in your heart what God would later reveal. You were afraid of people, but it is more fitting that you fear God. After Zayd divorced her, We gave her to you in marriage so that there might be no fault in believers marrying the wives of their adopted sons after they had divorced them. God's command must be carried out: the Prophet is not at fault for what God has ordained for him. This was God's practice with those who went before—God's command must be fulfilled—[and with all] those who deliver God's messages and fear only Him and no other: God's reckoning is enough.

[40] Muhammad is not the father of any one of you men;[14] he is God's Messenger and the seal of the prophets: God knows everything. . . .

[50] Prophet, We have made lawful for you the wives whose dowries you have paid, and any slaves God has assigned to you through war, and the daughters of your uncles and aunts on your father's and mother's sides, who migrated with you. Also any believing woman who offers herself [without dowry] to the Prophet and whom the Prophet desires to wed. This only applies to you [Prophet] and not the rest of the believers. We know exactly what we have made obligatory for them concerning their wives and slave-girls—so that you should not be blamed.

---

[13] *the man:* Zayd, an adopted son of Muhammad, was unhappily married to Zainab. He wanted to divorce her, but Muhammad advised him not to. God wished otherwise and here tells Muhammad to allow the divorce and marry Zainab himself. This provides justification in Islam for marriage to divorced wives of adopted sons.

[14] *Muhammad is not the father . . . men:* The Prophet had many wives but no male heirs, implied here to be God's will.

The Death of Muhammad*

The Qur'an *does not narrate the death of Muhammad but raises it as an issue. Muhammad is indeed mortal, as mortal as any other man. This Medinan passage serves to reinforce the* Qur'an*'s view of Muhammad as a purely human prophet.*

We have not granted everlasting life to any other human being before you either [Muhammad]— if you die, will [the disbelievers] live for ever?

[35] Every soul is certain to taste death. We test you all through the bad and the good, and to Us you will all return. When the disbelievers see you, they laugh at you: "Is this the one who talks about your gods?" They reject any talk of the Lord of Mercy.

---

*Qur'an 21:34–36.

TEACHING

God's Absolute Oneness*

One of the main themes of the Qur'an *is the absolute oneness of God. The first passage is given against jinn (spirits) being considered divine, and against the notion of God having sons and daughters. The wording of Surah 112, entitled "Oneness," seems to suggest that it is specifically anti-Christian, against the Christian belief that God the Father begot the Son and that the two are equal in being and power. Traditional Muslim interpretation holds it to be both anti-Christian and anti-Arab polytheism. An important* hadith *relates that this chapter is equal in value to two-thirds of the* Qur'an.

[6:100] Yet they made the jinn partners with God, though He created them, and without any true knowledge they attribute sons and daughters to Him. Glory be to Him! He is far higher than what they ascribe to Him, the Creator of the heavens and earth! How could He have children when He has no spouse, when He created all things, and has full knowledge of all things?

This is God, your Lord, there is no God but Him, the Creator of all things, so worship Him; He is in charge of everything. No vision can take Him in, but He takes in all vision. He is the All Subtle, the All Aware.

ONENESS
Surah 112
(Mecca)

In the name of God, the Lord of Mercy, the Giver of Mercy

Say, "He is God the One, God the eternal. He fathered no one nor was He fathered. No one is comparable to Him."

---

*Qur'an 6:100–103; 112.

God's Names**

"The best names belong to God," the Qur'an *affirms (59:24). Two of these names, "compassionate" and "merciful" (in this translation, "Lord of Mercy" and "Giver of Mercy"), occur in every* Bismillah *and dozens of times in the chapters proper. God has ninety-nine most gracious names in the* Qur'an, *as fixed by traditional interpretation (see the* hadith *"On God" on page 165). The first thirteen are listed here, from "Compassionate" to "Modeler." These names are used in Muslim devotion to express the greatness of God in a very poetic and rhythmic fashion.*

He is God: there is no other god but Him. It is He who knows what is hidden as well as what is in the open. He is the Lord of Mercy, the Giver of Mercy.

He is God: there is no other god but Him, the Controller, the Holy One, Source of Peace, Granter of Security, Guardian over all, the Almighty, the Compeller, to whom all greatness belongs; God is far above anything they consider to be His partner.

He is God: the Creator, the Originator, the Fashioner. The best names belong to Him. Everything in the heavens and earth glorifies Him. He is the Almighty, the Wise.

**Qur'an 59:22–24.

God's Power*

The first selection sings the praise of God the Creator. It ends, like many other teachings in the Qur'an, on a moral note: The creation shows God's truth and the straight (correct) path of life. Creation is here connected to revelation. The second selection ties the power of God in creation firmly to Muhammad's call for repentance and belief.

[24:41 (Medina)] [Prophet], do you not see that all those who are in the heavens and earth praise God, as do the birds with wings outstretched? Each knows its [own way] of prayer and glorification: God has full knowledge of what they do. Control of the heavens and earth belongs to God, and to God is the final return.

Do you not see that God drives the clouds, then gathers them together and piles them up until you see rain pour from their midst? He sends hail down from [such] mountains in the sky, pouring it on whomever He wishes and diverting it from whomever He wishes—the flash of its lightning almost snatches sight away. God alternates night and day—there truly is a lesson in this for those who have eyes to see— [45] and God created each animal out of [its own] fluid. Some of them crawl on their bellies, some walk on two legs, and some on four. God creates whatever He will; God has power over everything.

We have sent verses that clarify the right path: God guides whomever He will to a straight path.

[6:95 (Mecca)] It is God who splits open the seed and the fruit stone: He brings out the living from the dead and the dead from the living— that is God—so how can you turn away from the truth?

He makes the dawn break; He makes the night for rest; and He made the sun and the moon to a precise measure. That is the design of the Almighty, the All Knowing. It is He who made the stars, so that they can guide you when land and sea are dark: We have made the signs clear for those who have knowledge.

It is He who first produced you from a single soul, then gave you a place to stay [in life] and a resting place [after death]. We have made Our revelations clear to those who understand. It is He who sends down water from the sky. With it We produce the shoots of each plant, then bring greenery from it, and from that We bring out grains, one riding on the other in close-packed rows.

From the date palm come clusters of low-hanging dates, and there are gardens of vines, olives, and pomegranates, alike yet different— watch their fruits as they grow and ripen! In all this there are signs for those who would believe.

**Qur'an* 24:41–46; 6:95–99.

God's Predestination**

Predestination is God's eternal choice of his own people from among the fallen human race. In the first reading, God is said to predestine many religions for humanity but only Islam for the saved. The Qur'an affirms the sovereignty of God and human responsibility to live morally, but it puts the emphasis on the former. Predestination and fate play a large role in affairs both big and small in Muslim life. In Arab countries, perhaps the most frequently heard expression is Enshallah, *"if God wills," a word reflected at the beginning of the first passage. The second reading presents a statement typical of the* Qur'an *about the predestination of individuals. God's leading of people*

***Qur'an* 42:8–13; 7:177–182.

into error presents no moral problem, because these are the "heedless," who are and always will be immoral and disobedient. Both passages come from Medina.

[42:8] So We have revealed an Arabic *Qur'an* to you, in order that you may warn the capital city and all who live nearby. And warn [especially] about the Day of Gathering,[15] of which there is no doubt, when some shall be in the Garden and some in the blazing Flame. If God had so pleased, He could have made them a single community, but He admits to His mercy whoever He will; the evildoers will have no one to protect or help them.

How can they take protectors other than Him? God alone is the Protector; He gives life to the dead; He has power over all things. [10] Whatever You may differ about is for God to judge. [Say], "Such is God, my Lord. In Him I trust and to Him I turn, the creator of the heavens and earth." He made mates for you from among yourselves—and for the animals too—so that you may multiply. There is nothing like Him: He is the All Hearing, the All Seeing. The keys of the heavens and the earth are His; He provides abundantly or sparingly for whomever He will; He has full knowledge of all things.

In matters of faith, He has laid down for you [people] the same commandment that He gave Noah, which We have revealed to you [Muhammad] and which We enjoined on Abraham and Moses and Jesus: "Uphold the faith and do not divide into factions within it"—what you [Prophet] call upon the idolaters to do is hard for them; God chooses whoever He pleases for Himself and guides toward Himself those who turn to Him.

Had it been God's will, He could have made them all of one religion. But God brings whom He will into His mercy; the wrongdoers have none to befriend or help them.

Have they set up other guardians besides Him? Surely God alone is the Guardian. He resurrects the dead and has power over all things.

Whatever the subject of your disputes, the final word belongs to God. Such is God, my Lord. In Him I have put my trust, and to Him I turn in repentance.

[10] Creator of the heavens and the earth, He has given you wives from among yourselves, and cattle male and female; by this means He multiplies His creatures. Nothing can be compared with Him. He alone hears all and sees all. His are the keys of the heavens and the earth. He gives abundantly to whom He will and sparingly to whom He pleases. He has knowledge of all things.

He has ordained for you the faith which He enjoined on Noah, and which We have revealed to you; which We enjoined on Abraham, Moses, and Jesus, saying: "Observe the Faith and do not divide yourselves into factions." But hard for the pagans is that to which you call them. God chooses for it whom He will, and guides to it those that repent.

[7:177] How foul is the image of those who reject Our signs! It is themselves they wrong: whomever God guides is truly guided, and whomever God allows to stray is a loser. We have created many jinn and people who are destined for Hell, with hearts they do not use for comprehension, eyes they do not use for sight, ears they do not use for hearing. They are like cattle, no, even further astray—these are the ones who are entirely heedless.

[180] The Most Excellent Names belong to God: use them to call on Him and keep away from those who distort them—they will be requited for what they do. Among those We created are a group of people who guide with truth and act justly according to it, but We lead those who reject Our messages to ruin, step by step, without them realizing it.

---

[15] *Day of Gathering:* the day when all people will be gathered before God for judgment.

Jinn*

Like the angels and humanity, jinn are a mixed lot: Some are good and some evil. This passage presents the words of a band of formerly evil jinn who hear the message of God in the Qur'an *and repent, taking up Islam. They serve as a pattern and encouragement for the people to whom Muhammad testifies to do the same. Notice the oral nature of* Qur'an *here—it is the recitation of Gabriel's message to Muhammad.*

THE JINN
Surah 72:1–15
(Mecca)

In the Name of God, the Lord of Mercy, the Giver of Mercy

Say [Prophet], "It has been revealed to me that a group of jinn once listened in and said, 'We have heard a wondrous *Qur'an,* that gives guidance to the right path, and we have come to believe. We shall never set up partners with our Lord. He has neither spouse nor child—He is far above this in majesty! Outrageous things have been said about God by the foolish among us, [5] although we had thought that no man or jinn would [dare to] tell a lie about Him.

"'Men have sought refuge with [us] jinn in the past, but they only misguided them further. They thought, as you did, that God would never raise anyone from the dead. We tried to reach heaven but discovered it to be full of stern guards and shooting stars—we used to sit in places there, listening, but anyone trying to listen now will find a shooting star lying in wait for him—[10] [so now] we do not know whether those who live on earth are due for misfortune, nor whether their Lord intends to guide them.

"'Some of us are righteous and others less so; we follow different paths. We know we can never frustrate God on earth; we can never escape Him. We came to believe when we heard the guidance: whoever believes in his Lord need fear no loss or injustice. Some of us submit to Him[16] and others go the wrong way. Those who submit to God have found wise guidance, [15] but those who go wrong will be fuel for Hellfire.'"

---

* *Qur'an* 72:1–15.
[16] *Some of us submit to him:* can also be translated "Some of us are Muslims."

Creation**

The Qur'an *has several poetic recitals of creation. Surah 15 is one of the fullest. This passage also tells the origin of Satan (Iblis) as an evil angel and his temptation of humanity to sin. In the second reading, Surah 16, "The Bee," the focus is on the created world familiar to an Arab audience.*

[15:16] We have set constellations up in the sky and made it beautiful for all to see, and guarded it from every stoned satan[17]; any eavesdropper will be pursued by a clearly visible flame. As for the earth, We have spread it out, set firm mountains on it, and made everything grow there in due balance. [20] We have provided sustenance in it for you and for all those creatures for whom you do not provide. There is not a thing whose storehouses are not with Us. We send it down

---

** *Qur'an* 15:16–48; 16:1–17.
[17] *stoned satan:* the devil, who is rejected by true Muslims. This may allude to the practice of ritually stoning a pillar that represents Satan during the pilgrimage to Mecca.

only according to a well-defined measure: We send the winds to fertilize, and We bring down water from the sky for you to drink—you do not control its sources. It is We who give life and death; it is We who inherit [everything]. We know exactly those of you who come first and those who come later. [25] [Prophet], it is your Lord who will gather them all together: He is all wise, all knowing.

We created man out of dried clay formed from dark mud—the jinn We created before, from the fire of scorching wind. Your Lord said to the angels, "I will create a mortal out of dried clay, formed from dark mud. When I have fashioned him and breathed My spirit into him, bow down before him," [30] and the angels all did so. But not Iblis[18]: he refused to bow down like the others. God said, "Iblis, why did you not bow down like the others?"

He answered, "I will not bow to a mortal You created from dried clay, formed from dark mud."

"Get out of here!" said God. "You are an outcast, [35] rejected until the Day of Judgment."

Iblis said, "My Lord, give me respite until the Day when they are raised from the dead."

"You have respite," said God, "until the Day of the Appointed Time."

Iblis then said to God, "Because You have put me in the wrong, I will lure mankind on earth and put them in the wrong, [40] all except Your devoted servants."

God said, "[Devotion] is a straight path to me: you will have no power over My servants, only over the ones who go wrong and follow you. Hell is the promised place for all these, with seven gates, each gate having its allotted share of them. [45] But the righteous will be in Gardens with springs—'Enter them in peace and safety!'—and We shall remove any bitterness from their hearts: [they will be like] brothers, sitting on couches, face to face. No weariness will ever touch them there, nor will they ever be expelled."

THE BEE
Surah 16
(Mecca)

In the Name of God, the Lord of Mercy, the Giver of Mercy

God's Judgment is coming, so do not ask to bring it on sooner. Glory be to Him! He is far above anything they join with Him! He sends down angels with inspiration at His command to whichever of His servants He chooses: "Declare that there is no god but Me. Beware of Me." He created the heavens and earth for a true purpose, and He is far above whatever they join with Him! He created man from a drop of fluid, and yet man openly challenges Him.

[5] And livestock—He created them for you too. You derive warmth and other benefits from them: you eat some of them; you find beauty in them when you bring them home to rest and when you drive them out to pasture. They carry your loads to lands you yourselves could not reach without great hardship—truly your Lord is kind and merciful!—horses, mules, and donkeys for you to ride and use for show, and other things you know nothing about. God points out the right path, for some of them lead the wrong way; if He wished, He could guide you all.

[10] It is He who sends down water for you from the sky. Some of it you drink, and the shrubs that you feed to your animals come from it. With it He grows for you corn, olives, palms, vines, and all kinds of fruit. There truly is a sign in this for those who reflect. By His command He has made the night and day, the sun, moon, and stars all of benefit to you. There truly are signs in this for those who use their reason. He has made of benefit to you the

---

[18] *Iblis:* Satan, the devil. This personal name is probably derived from the Greek for "devil," *diabolos*.

many-colored things He has multiplied on the earth. There truly are signs in this for those who take heed.

It is He who made the sea of benefit to you: you eat fresh fish from it and bring out jewelry to wear; you see the ships cutting through its waves so that you may go in search of His bounty and give thanks. [15] He has made mountains stand firm on the earth, to prevent it shaking under you, and rivers and paths so that you may find your way, and landmarks and stars to guide people. Can He who creates be compared to one who cannot create? Why do you not take heed?

Adam, Eve, and the Fall*

Here the fall of humanity into sin and rebellion against God is strongly related to the fall of Satan into sin. Humanity is forgiven when it "receives the revelations of God" and follows them; this is the positive model for those who receive God's revelations through Muhammad and follow them. On the other hand, those who reject these revelations will receive Hell as their punishment.

[Prophet], when your Lord told the angels, "I am putting a successor on earth,"[19] they said, "How can You put someone there who will cause damage and bloodshed when we celebrate Your praise and proclaim Your holiness?" but He said, "I know things you do not."

He taught Adam the names of all things, then He showed them to the angels, and said, "Tell me the names of these if you truly [think you can]."

They said, "May You be glorified! We have knowledge only of what You have taught us. You are the All Knowing and All Wise."

Then He said, "Adam, tell them the names of these."

When Adam told them their names, God said, "Did I not tell you that I know what is hidden in the heavens and the earth, and that I know what you reveal and what you conceal?"

When We told the angels, "Bow down before Adam," they all bowed. But not Iblis, who refused and was arrogant: he was one of the disobedient. [35] We said, "Adam, live with your wife in this garden and both of you eat freely there as you will, but do not go near this tree, or you will both become wrongdoers," but Satan made them slip, and removed them from the state they were in.

We said, "Get out, all of you! You are each other's enemy. On earth you will have a place to stay and livelihood for a time." Then Adam received some words from his Lord and He accepted his repentance: He is the Ever Relenting, the Most Merciful.

---

*Qur'an 2:30–37.

[19] *I am putting a successor on earth:* God was about to make humankind.

The Holy *Qur'an***

The revelations to Muhammad, which later formed the Qur'an, *took several forms. The first passage refers to direct, audible speech and to the less direct inspiration that comes "from behind a veil." Whatever the form, Muslims believe that all revelations come from God by way of his angel Gabriel. The second passage recounts the qualities of the* Qur'an: *its origin as a revelation from God, its miraculous nature, its connection to the faith*

**Qur'an 42:50–53; 46:1–8; 2:87–91.

of Islam, and its Arabic character. A recurrent theme of this surah is the defense of the Qur'an *against the charge that it is false. In the third passage, the* Qur'an *claims to be the capstone of the prior scriptures of Judaism and Christianity. It confirms the* Bibles *of these faiths and shares much the same content, but the peoples of these latter books reject Islam.*

[42:50 (Mecca)] It is not granted to any mortal that God should speak to him except through revelation or from behind a veil, or by sending a messenger to reveal by His command what He will: He is exalted and wise. So We have revealed a spirit to you [Prophet] by Our command. You knew neither the Scripture nor the faith, but We made it a light, guiding with it whomever We will of Our servants. You give guidance to the straight path, the path of God, to whom belongs all that is in the heavens and earth: truly everything will return to God.

[46:1 (Mecca)] This Scripture is sent down from God, the Almighty, the Wise. It was for a true purpose and a specific term that We created heaven and earth and everything in between, yet those who deny the truth ignore the warning they have been given. Say [Prophet], "Consider those you pray to other than God: show me which part of the earth they created or which share of the heavens they own; bring me a previous scripture or some vestige of divine knowledge—if what you say is true." Who could be more wrong than a person who calls on those other than God, those who will not answer him till the Day of Resurrection, those who are unaware of his prayers, those who, when all mankind is gathered, will become his enemies and disown his worship?

When Our revelations are recited to them in all their clarity, the disbelievers say of the Truth that has reached them, "This is clearly sorcery," or they say, "He has invented it himself." Say [Prophet], "If I have really invented it, there is nothing you can do to save me from God. He knows best what you say amongst yourselves about it; He is sufficient as a witness between me and you; He is the Most Forgiving, the Most Merciful." Say, "I am not the first of God's messengers. I do not know what will be done with me or you; I only follow what is revealed to me; I only warn plainly." [10] Say, "Have you thought: what if this *Qur'an* really is from God and you reject it? What if one of the Children of Israel testifies to its similarity [to earlier scripture] and believes in it, and yet you are too proud to [do the same]? God certainly does not guide evildoers."

Those who disbelieve say of the believers, "If there were any good in this *Qur'an* they would not have believed in it before we did," and, since they refuse to be guided by it, they say, "This is an ancient fabrication."

[2:87 (Medina)] We gave Moses the Scripture and We sent messengers after him in succession. We gave Jesus, the Son of Mary, clear signs and strengthened him with the Holy Spirit. So how is it that, whenever a messenger brings you something you do not like, you become arrogant, calling some impostors and killing others?

They say, "Our hearts are impenetrably wrapped [against whatever you say]," but God has rejected them for their disbelief; they have little faith. When a Scripture came to them from God confirming what they already had, and when they had been praying for victory against the disbelievers, even when there came to them something they knew [to be true], they disbelieved it; God rejects those who disbelieve. . . .

[91] When it is said to them, "Believe in God's revelations," they reply, "We believe in what was revealed to us." But they do not believe in what came afterwards, though it is the truth confirming what they already have.

On Unbelievers, Jews, and Christians*

Surah 9, "Repentance," the first reading, outlines the Islamic approach to "unbelievers" and "idolaters" who follow the pre-Islamic religions of Arabia. This passage has no Bismillah; it was probably originally attached to Surah 8. A hadith traced to Caliph Uthman states that it was revealed by Muhammad shortly before his death, and he left no instructions on it. In the second reading, Jesus is presented as a righteous prophet who called his people to submit to the true God. He died, but not by crucifixion, and his death has no saving effect. This portrayal sought to undercut the Christian claim that salvation is produced by Jesus' death and resurrection. Nevertheless, Muslims tend to have a positive attitude toward Jesus as one of the leading prophets. The last passage indicates how Muhammad hoped to convert the Jews and Christians of Medina to his new faith, but this effort failed. He then turned overtly hostile to them. They are to convert to Islam or live as subject peoples under the authority of Muslim government.

REPENTANCE
Surah 9
(Medina)

A release by God and His Messenger from the treaty you [believers] made with the polytheists [is announced]. You [polytheists] may move freely about the land for four months, but you should bear in mind both that you will not escape God, and that God will disgrace those who ignore [Him]. On the Day of the Great Pilgrimage [there will be] a proclamation from God and His Messenger to all people: "God and His Messenger are released from [treaty] obligations to the polytheists. It will be better for you [polytheists] if you repent; know that you cannot escape God if you turn away." [Prophet], warn those who ignore [God] that they will have a painful punishment. As for those who have honored the treaty you made with them and who have not supported anyone against you: fulfill your agreement with them to the end of their term. God loves those who are mindful of Him.

[5] When the four forbidden months are over, wherever you find the polytheists, kill them, seize them, besiege them, ambush them. But if they turn [to God], maintain the prayer, and pay the prescribed alms, let them go on their way, for God is most forgiving and merciful. If any one of the polytheists should seek your protection [Prophet], grant it to him so that he may hear the word of God—then take him to a safe place—for they are people with no knowledge. What sort of treaty could these polytheists make with God and His Messenger? As for those with whom you made a treaty at the Sacred Mosque, so long as they remain true to you, be true to them; God loves those who are mindful of Him.... [13] How could you not fight a people who have broken their oaths, who tried to drive the Messenger out, who attacked you first? Do you fear them? It is God you should fear, if you are true believers. Fight them: God will punish them at your hand, He will disgrace them, He will help you conquer them, He will heal the believers' feelings.... [17] It is not right that the polytheists should tend God's places of worship while testifying to their own disbelief.... The only ones who should tend God's places are those who believe in God and the Last Day, who keep up the prayer, who pay the prescribed alms, and who fear no one but God.

[3:38] There and then Zachariah prayed to his Lord, saying, "Lord, from Your grace grant me virtuous offspring: You hear every prayer."

The angels called out to him, while he stood praying in the sanctuary, "God gives you news

---
*Qur'an 9:1–7; 3:38–50; 2:111–121, 132–136.

of John, confirming a Word from God. He will be noble and chaste, a prophet, one of the righteous."

[40] He said, "My Lord, how can I have a son when I am so old and my wife is barren?"

[An angel] said, "It will be so: God does whatever He will."

He said, "My Lord, give me a sign."

"Your sign," [the angel] said, "is that you will not communicate with anyone for three days, except gestures. Remember your Lord often; celebrate His glory in the evening and at dawn."

The angels said to Mary: "Mary, God has chosen you and made you pure: He has truly chosen you above all women. Mary, be devout to your Lord, prostrate yourself in worship, bow down with those who pray." This is an account of things beyond your knowledge that We reveal to you [Muhammad]: you were not present among them when they cast lots to see which of them should take charge of Mary; you were not present with them when they argued [about her].

[45] The angels said, "Mary, God gives you news of a Word from Him, whose name will be the Messiah, Jesus, son of Mary, who will be held in honor in this world and the next, who will be one of those brought near to God. He will speak to people in his infancy and in his adulthood. He will be one of the righteous."

She said, "My Lord, how can I have a son when no man has touched me?"

[The angel] said, "This is how God creates what He will: when He has ordained something, He only says, 'Be,' and it is. He will teach him the Scripture and wisdom, the Torah and the Gospel, He will send him as a messenger to the Children of Israel: 'I have come to you with a sign from your Lord: I will make a bird for you out of clay, then breathe into it and, with God's permission, it will become a real bird;[20] I will heal the blind and the leper, and bring the dead back to life with God's permission; I will tell you what you may eat and what you may store up in your houses. There truly is a sign for you in this, if you are believers. [50] I have come to confirm the truth of the Torah which preceded me, and to make some things lawful to you which used to be forbidden. I have come to you with a sign from your Lord. Be mindful of God, obey me.'"

They plotted,[21] and God plotted. God is the supreme Plotter. He said: "Jesus, I am about to cause you to die and lift you up to Me. I shall take you away from the unbelievers[22] and exalt your followers above them till the Day of Resurrection. Then to Me you shall all return and I shall judge your disputes. The unbelievers shall be sternly punished in this world and in the world to come; there shall be none to help them. [50] As for those that have faith and do good works, they shall be given their reward in full. God does not love the evil-doers."

[2:111] They also say, "No one will enter Paradise unless he is a Jew or a Christian." This is their own wishful thinking.

[Prophet], say, "Produce your evidence if you are telling the truth." In fact, any who direct themselves wholly to God and do good will have their reward with their Lord: no fear for them, nor will they grieve. The Jews say, "The Christians have no ground whatsoever to stand on," and the Christians say, "The Jews have no ground whatsoever to stand on," though they both read the Scripture, and those who have no knowledge say the same; God will judge between them on the Day of Resurrection concerning their differences. . . .

They have asserted, "God has a child." May He be exalted! No! Everything in the heavens and earth belongs to Him, everything devoutly

---

[20] This story is found in a post–New Testament, second-century Christian book, the *Apocryphon of James*. It probably came to Muhammad by oral tradition.

[21] *They plotted:* Jesus' opponents seek to bring him to death.

[22] *take you away:* Muslims believe that a look-alike was substituted for Jesus just before his death on the cross, so that he only seemed to die. Instead, he was taken up to God before his death. Western scholars commonly hold that this view reflects the views of a Christian group that the mainstream church regarded as heretical.

obeys His will. He is the Originator of the heavens and the earth, and when He decrees something, He says only, "Be," and it is.

Those who have no knowledge also say, "If only God would speak to us!" or, "If only a miraculous sign would come to us!" People before them said the same things: their hearts are all alike. We have made Our signs clear enough to those who have solid faith. We have sent you [Prophet] with the truth, bearing good news and warning. You will not be responsible for the inhabitants of the Blaze.

[120] The Jews and the Christians will never be pleased with you unless you follow their ways. Say, "God's guidance is the only true guidance." If you were to follow their desires after the knowledge that has come to you, you would find no one to protect you from God or help you. Those to whom We have given the Scripture, who follow it as it deserves, are the ones who truly believe in it. Those who deny its truth will be the losers. . . .

[132] Were you [Jews] there to see when death came upon Jacob? When he said to his sons, "What will you worship after I am gone?" they replied, "We shall worship your God and the God of your fathers, Abraham, Ishmael, and Isaac, one single God: we devote ourselves to Him." That community passed away. What they earned belongs to them, and what you earn belongs to you: you will not be answerable for their deeds.

[135] They say, "Become Jews or Christians, and you will be rightly guided." Say [Prophet], "No, [ours is] the religion of Abraham, the upright, who did not worship any god besides God." So [you believers], say, "We believe in God and in what was sent down to us and what was sent down to Abraham, Ishmael, Isaac, Jacob, and the Tribes, and what was given to Moses, Jesus, and all the prophets by their Lord. We make no distinction between any of them, and we devote ourselves to Him."

Resurrection and Judgment*

Like Judaism and Christianity, Islam foresees a literal resurrection of the body from death; soul and body are rejoined to face judgment. The Meccan origin of these passages is reflected in their lyrical style and power. The second passage, vivid in its emotional intensity, describes the last judgment that follows the resurrection on the last day. The use of "right" and "left" is reminiscent of the New Testament teaching that at the last judgment the righteous will stand at God's right and the unrighteous at the left.

THE RESURRECTION
Surah 75
(Mecca)

In the Name of God, the Lord of Mercy, the Giver of Mercy

---

*Qur'an 75:1–15; 69:14–35.

By the Day of Resurrection and by the self-reproaching soul![23] Does man think We shall not put his bones back together? In fact, We can reshape his very fingertips. [5] Yet man wants to deny what is ahead of him; he says, "So, when will this Day of Resurrection be?"

When eyes are dazzled and the moon eclipsed, when the sun and the moon are brought together, [10] on that Day man will say, "Where can I escape?" Truly, there is no refuge: they will all return to your Lord on that Day. On that Day, man will be told what he put first and what he put last. Truly, man is a clear witness against himself, [15] despite all the excuses he may put forward.

[69:14 (Mecca)] When the Trumpet is sounded a single time, when the earth and its mountains are raised high and then crushed with a single blow, [15] on that Day the Great Event will come to pass. The sky will be torn apart; on that Day it will be so frail. The angels will appear by its sides and, on that Day, eight of them will bear the throne of your Lord above them.

On that Day you will be brought to judgment and none of your secrets will remain hidden. He who is given his Record in his right hand will say, "Here is my Record, read it. [20] I knew I would meet my Reckoning," and so he will have a pleasant life in a lofty Garden, with clustered fruit within his reach. It will be said, "Eat and drink to your heart's content as a reward for what you have done in days gone by."

[25] But he who is given his Record in his left hand will say, "If only I had never been given any Record and knew nothing of my Reckoning. How I wish death had been the end of me. My wealth has been no use to me, and my power has vanished."

[30] "Take him, put a collar on him, lead him to burn in the blazing Fire, and [bind him] in a chain seventy meters long: he would not believe in Almighty God, he never encouraged feeding the hungry, [35] so today he has no real friend here, and the only food he has is the filth that only sinners eat."

---

[23] *By the day . . . soul:* two oaths to affirm the truth of the passage.

Heaven and Hell*

Surah 76, "Man," the first passage, is one of the fullest descriptions in the Qur'an *of the blessings of heaven. They are physical to the point of sensuousness, with little explicit development of the spiritual blessing or happiness of the residents of heaven. Surah 56, "That Which Is Coming," the second passage, deals with the two types of heavenly attendants that will be given to the faithful in heaven. "Immortal youths" will wait on them with food and drink, and the houris, beautiful dark-eyed women, will be wed to faithful men (the* Qur'an *never speaks explicitly about the rewards of women in heaven). In Surah 77, "Winds Sent Forth," the third passage, the punishments of the damned are described in vivid imagery. The purpose was to threaten and warn the Arabs against the godless way that leads to eternal destruction, and encourage them in the way of eternal life.*

MAN
Surah 76
(Mecca)

In the name of God, the Lord of Mercy, the Giver of Mercy

Was there not a period of time when man was nothing to speak of? We created man from a drop of mingled fluid to put him to the test; We

---

*Qur'an 76:1–22; 56:1–50; 77:1–39.

gave him hearing and sight; We guided him to the right path, whether he was grateful or not.

We have prepared chains, iron collars, and blazing Fire for the disbelievers, but [5] the righteous will have a drink mixed with *kafur*,[24] a spring for God's servants, which flows abundantly at their wish. They fulfill their vows; they fear a day of widespread woes; they give food to the poor, the orphan, and the captive, though they love it themselves, saying, "We feed you for the sake of God alone: We seek neither recompense nor thanks from you. [10] We fear the Day of our Lord—a woefully grim day." So God will save them from the woes of that Day, give them radiance and gladness, and reward them for their steadfastness, with a Garden and silken robes. They will sit on couches, feeling neither scorching heat nor biting cold, with shady [branches] spread above them and clusters of fruit hanging close at hand. [15] They will be served with silver plates and gleaming silver goblets according to their fancy, and they will be given a drink infused with ginger from a spring called Salsabil.[25] Everlasting youths will attend them—if you could see them, you would think they were scattered pearls, [20] and if you were to look around, you would see a vast, blissful kingdom—and they will wear garments of green silk and brocade. They will be adorned with silver bracelets. Their Lord will give them a pure drink. [It will be said], "This is your reward. Your endeavors are appreciated."

THAT WHICH IS COMING
Surah 56
(Mecca)

In the name of God, the Lord of Mercy, the Giver of Mercy

When that which is coming arrives, no one will be able to deny it has come, bringing low and raising high. When the earth is shaken violently [5] and the mountains are ground to powder and turn to scattered dust, then you be sorted into three classes.

Those on the Right—what people they are! Those on the Left—what people they are! [10] And those in front—ahead indeed![26] For these [in front] will be the ones brought nearest to God in Gardens of Bliss: many from the past and a few from later generations. [15] On couches of well-woven cloth they will sit facing each other; everlasting youths will go round among them with glasses, flagons, and a pure liquid that causes no headache or intoxication; [20] [there will be] any fruit they want; the meat of any bird they like; and beautiful companions like hidden pearls: a reward for what they used to do. [25] They will hear no idle or sinful talk there, only clean and wholesome speech.

Those on the Right, what people they are! They will dwell amid thornless lote trees and clustered acacia [30] with spreading shade, constantly flowing water, abundant fruits, unfailing, unforbidden, with incomparable companions [35] We have specially created—virginal, loving, of matching age—for those on the right, many from the past [40] and many from later generations.

WINDS SENT FORTH
Surah 77
(Mecca)

In the name of God, the Lord of Mercy, the Giver of Mercy

By the [winds] sent forth in swift succession, violently storming, scattering far and wide, carefully distinguishing [their targets], [5] delivering a message that excuses or warns, what you are promised will come to pass. When the stars are dimmed and the sky torn apart, [10] when the mountains are turned to dust and the

---

[24] *kafur*: a sweet-smelling herb.
[25] *Salsabil*: Arabic for "ginger."
[26] *those in front*: The righteous are divided into two groups, the blessed ("those on the right") and the more blessed ("those in front").

messengers given their appointed time—for what Day has all this been set? The Day of Decision. What will explain to you what the Day of Decision is? [15] Woe, on that Day, to those who denied the truth! Did We not destroy earlier generations? We shall make later generations follow them: this is how We deal with sinners. Woe, on that Day, to those who denied the truth!

[20] Did We not make you from a humble fluid which We housed in a safe lodging for a determined period?[27] We determine [it]: how excellently We determine! Woe, on that Day, to those who denied the truth! [25] Did We not make the earth a home for the living and the dead? Did We not place firm, lofty mountains on it and provide you with sweet water? Woe, on that Day, to those who denied the truth!

They will be told, "Go to that which you used to deny! [30] Go to a shadow of smoke!" It rises in three columns; no shade does it give, nor relief from the flame; it shoots out sparks as large as tree-trunks and as bright as copper. Woe, on that Day, to those who denied the truth! [35] On that Day they will be speechless, and they will be given no chance to offer any excuses. Woe, on that Day, to those who denied the truth! [They will be told], "This is the Day of Decision: We have gathered you and earlier generations. If you have any plots against Me, try them now."

---

[27] *humble fluid . . . safe lodging:* The fluid is semen, and the receptacle is the womb. One traditional Arab commentator says it is "unworthy" because man is ashamed of the process of procreation by which he comes into being.

ETHICS

The Conduct of Believers*

The ethical dimensions of the Islamic life are spread evenly throughout the Qur'an. *Occasional passages summarize the duty of the believer. This selection from Mecca deals comprehensively with the moral structure of Islam. Notice its relationship to the* Ten Commandments *of Judaism.*

Your Lord has commanded that you should worship none but Him, and that you be kind to your parents. If either or both of them reach old age with you, say no word that shows impatience with them, and do not be harsh with them, but speak to them respectfully and, out of mercy, lower your wing[28] in humility toward them and say, "Lord, have mercy on them, just as they cared for me when I was little." [25] Your Lord knows best what is in your heart. If you are good, He is most forgiving to those who return to Him. Give relatives their due, and the needy, and travelers—do not squander your wealth wastefully: those who squander are the brothers of Satan, and Satan is most ungrateful to his Lord—but if, while seeking some bounty that you expect from your Lord, you turn them down, then at least speak some word of comfort to them. Do not be tight-fisted, nor so open-handed that you end up blamed and overwhelmed with regret. [30] Your Lord gives abundantly to whoever He will, and sparingly to whoever He will: He knows and observes His servants thoroughly.

Do not kill your children for fear of poverty—We shall provide for them and for you—killing them is a great sin. And do not go anywhere near

---

*Qur'an 17:23–38.
[28] *lower your wing:* treat courteously.

adultery: it is an outrage, and an evil path. Do not take life—which God has made sacred—except by right. If anyone is killed wrongfully, We have given authority to the defender of his rights, but he should not be excessive in taking life, for he is already aided [by God].

Do not go near the orphan's property, except with the best intentions, until he reaches the age of maturity. Honor your pledges: you will be questioned about your pledge. [35] Give full measure when you measure, and weigh with accurate scales: that is better and fairer in the end. Do not follow blindly what you do not know to be true: ears, eyes, and heart, you will be questioned about all these. Do not strut arrogantly about the earth: you cannot break it open, nor match the mountains in height. The evil of all these is hateful to your Lord.

Women*

In the Semitic culture of ancient Arabia, society was strongly patriarchal; in Muslim cultures in the Middle East and elsewhere, it continues to be so today. This state of affairs is reflected in the first passage, on the general relations between the sexes, and in the second, on marriage, sexual relations, and divorce. Despite this patriarchal structure, women did have some rights, as the beginning of the first reading indicates. Both readings, like most legal material in the Qur'an, *come from the later, Medinan phase.*

[4:19] You who believe, it is not lawful for you to inherit women against their will, nor should you treat your wives harshly, hoping to take back some of the dowry you gave them, unless they are guilty of something clearly outrageous. Live with them in accordance with what is fair and kind: if you dislike them, it may well be that you dislike something in which God has put much good. [20] If you wish to replace one wife with another, do not take any of her dowry back, even if you have given her a great amount of gold. How could you take it when this is unjust and a blatant sin? How could you take it when you have lain with each other and they have taken a solemn pledge from you?

Do not marry women that your fathers married—with the exception of what is past—this is indeed a shameful thing to do, loathsome and leading to evil. . . .

[34] Husbands are in full charge of their wives, with [the bounties] God has given to some more than others and with what they spend out of their own money. Righteous wives are devout and guard what God would have them guard in their husbands' absence. If you fear high-handedness from your wives, [first] remind them [of the teachings of God], then ignore them when you go to bed, [and] then hit them. If they obey you, you have no right to act against them: God is most high and great.

If you [believers] fear that a couple may break up, appoint one arbiter from his family and one from hers. Then, if the couple wants to put things right, God will bring about reconciliation between them: He is all knowing, all aware.

Worship God; join nothing with Him. Be good to your parents, to relatives, to orphans, to the needy, to neighbors near and far, to travelers in need, and to your slaves. God does not like arrogant, boastful people, who are miserly and order other people to be the same, hiding the bounty God has given them. We have prepared a humiliating torment for such ungrateful people. [Nor does He like those] who spend their wealth to show off, who do not believe in Him or the Last Day. Whoever has Satan as his companion has an evil companion! What harm would it do them to believe in God

---

*Qur'an 4:19–22, 34–39; 2:220–223, 227–233.

and the Last Day, and give charitably from the sustenance God has given them? God knows them well.

[2:220] Do not marry idolatresses until they believe: a believing slave woman is certainly better than an idolatress, even though she may please you. And do not give your women in marriage to idolaters until they believe: a believing slave is certainly better than an idolater, even though he may please you. Such people call [you] to the Fire, while God calls [you] to the Garden and forgiveness by His leave. He makes His messages clear to people, so that they may bear them in mind.

They ask you [Prophet] about menstruation. Say, "Menstruation is a painful condition, so keep away from women during it. Do not approach them until they are cleansed; when they are cleansed, you may approach them as God has ordained. God loves those who turn to Him, and He loves those who keep themselves clean. Your women are your fields, so go into your fields whichever way you like, and send [something good] ahead for yourselves. . . ." [Prophet], give good news to the believers. . . .

[227] Divorced women must wait for three monthly periods before remarrying, and, if they really believe in God and the Last Day, it is not lawful for them to conceal what God has created in their wombs: their husbands are entitled to take them back during this period provided they wish to put things right. Wives have [rights] similar to their [obligations], according to what is recognized to be fair, and husbands have a degree [of right] over them: [both should remember that] God is almighty and wise.

Divorce can happen twice, and [each time] wives either be kept on in an acceptable manner or released in a good way. It is not lawful for you to take back anything that you have given [your wives] except where both fear that they cannot maintain [the marriage] within the bounds set by God: if you [arbiters] suspect that the couple may not be able to do this, then there will be no blame on either of them if the woman opts to give something for her release. These are the bounds set by God: do not overstep them. It is those that overstep God's bounds who are doing wrong. [230] If a husband re-divorces his wife after the second divorce, she will not be lawful for him until she has taken another husband; if that one divorces her, there will be no blame if she and the first husband return to one another, provided they feel that they can keep within the bounds set by God. These are God's bounds, which He makes clear for those who know.

When you divorce women and they have reached their set time, then either keep or release them in a fair manner. Do not hold on to them with intent to harm them and commit aggression: anyone who does this wrongs himself. Do not make a mockery of God's revelations; remember the favor He blessed you with, and the Scripture and wisdom He sent to teach you. Be mindful of God and know that He has full knowledge of everything. When you divorce women and they have reached their set time, do not prevent them from remarrying their husbands if they both agree to do so in a fair manner. Let those of you who believe in God and the Last Day take this to heart: that is more wholesome and purer for you. God knows and you do not.

Mothers suckle their children for two whole years, if they wish to complete the term, and clothing and maintenance must be borne by the father in a fair manner. No one should be burdened with more than they can bear: no mother shall be made to suffer harm on account of her child, nor any father on account of his. The same duty is incumbent on the father's heir. If, by mutual consent and consultation, the couple wish to wean [the child], they will not be blamed, nor will there be any blame if you wish to engage a wet nurse, provided you pay as agreed in a fair manner. Be mindful of God, knowing that He sees everything you do.

The Different Dimensions of Struggle (Jihad)*

The Qur'an *urges* jihad [jee-HAHD], *"struggle" or "striving" against unbelief of all sorts in order to spread the faith. Jihad is often called "struggle in the way of Allah." This struggle includes prayer, study, the "war" against evil in oneself, and military conflict to spread and defend the faith. In the first passage, God commends those who struggle/strive in his way. The second passage presents a problem that arose for Muhammad about what to do with those who refuse to fight in the military aspects of jihad. The answer came by revelation that those who will not fight should have no share in the war booty or in eternal life. In the third passage, Muhammad is preparing to sponsor a holy war against Mecca, from which he had fled for his life. In these instructions, the basic guidelines for all holy war in Islam arise: It is obligatory for all who can participate, and its aim is to spread the faith and crush opposition to Islam.*

[6:16] Did you suppose that you would be left in peace, that God does not know who among you struggles? God knows all that you do. . . . Do you count quenching a pilgrim's thirst and attending the Holy Sanctuary to be equal to believing in God and judgment on the last day, and struggling in the way of God? They are not equal in God's sight. God does not guide those who do evil. Those who truly believe, and have left their homes and struggle with their wealth and their lives in God's way are very precious in God's sight. They will be triumphant.

[48:11] The desert Arabs who stayed behind[29] will say to you, "We were busy with our property and our families: ask forgiveness for us," but they say with their tongues what is not in their hearts. Say, "Whether it is God's will to do you harm or good, who can intervene for you?" No! God is fully aware of everything you [people] do. No! You thought that the Messenger and the believers would never return to their families and this thought warmed your hearts. Your thoughts are evil, for you are corrupt people: We have prepared a blazing Fire for those who do not believe in God and His Messenger. Control of the heavens and earth belongs to God and He forgives whoever He will and punishes whoever He will: God is most forgiving and merciful.

[15] When you [believers] set off for somewhere that promises war gains, those who [previously] stayed behind will say, "Let us come with you." They want to change God's words, but tell them [Prophet], "You may not come with us: God has said this before." They will reply, "You begrudge us out of jealousy." How little they understand!

Tell the desert Arabs who stayed behind, "You will be called to face a people of great might in war and to fight them, unless they surrender: if you obey, God will reward you well, but if you turn away, as you have done before, He will punish you heavily—the blind, the lame, and the sick will not be blamed." God will admit anyone who obeys Him and His Messenger to Gardens graced with flowing streams; He will painfully punish anyone who turns away.

God was pleased with the believers when they swore allegiance to you [Prophet] under the tree: He knew what was in their hearts and so He sent tranquillity down to them and rewarded them with a speedy triumph and with many future gains—God is mighty and wise: [20] He has promised you [people] many future gains—He has hastened this gain for you: He has held back the hands of hostile people from you as a sign for

---

*Qur'an 6:16, 19–20; 48:11–21; 2:190–194, 216–218.

[29] *desert Arabs who stayed behind:* These are certain tribes who refused to participate in a military campaign led by Muhammad against unbelieving opponents.

the faithful—and He will guide you to a straight path. There are many other gains [to come], over which you have no power. God has full control over them: God has power over all things.

[2:190 (Medina)] Fight in God's cause against those who fight you, but do not overstep the limits. God does not love those who overstep the limits. Kill them wherever you encounter them, and drive them out from where they drove you out, for persecution is more serious than killing. Do not fight them at the Sacred Mosque unless they fight you there. If they do fight you, kill them—this is what such disbelievers deserve—but if they stop, then God is most forgiving and merciful. Fight them until there is no more persecution, and [your] worship is devoted to God. If they cease hostilities, there can be no [further] hostility, except toward aggressors. A sacred month for a sacred month: violation of sanctity [calls for] fair retribution. So if anyone commits aggression against you, attack him as he attacked you, but be mindful of God, and know that He is with those who are mindful of Him. . . .

[216] Fighting is ordained for you, though you dislike it. You may dislike something although it is good for you, or like something although it is bad for you: God knows and you do not. They ask you [Prophet] about fighting in the prohibited month. Say, "Fighting in that month is a great offense, but to bar others from God's path, to disbelieve in Him, prevent access to the Sacred Mosque, and expel its people, are still greater offenses in God's eyes: persecution is worse than killing." They will not stop fighting you [believers] until they make you revoke your faith, if they can. If any of you revoke your faith and die as disbelievers, your deeds will come to nothing in this world and the Hereafter, and you will be inhabitants of the Fire, there to remain. But those who have believed, migrated, and striven for God's cause, it is they who can look forward to God's mercy: God is most forgiving and merciful.

Law Codes*

The Qur'an has several developed law codes dealing with various topics of everyday life. As a sample, here is a passage on the treatment of orphans and women. That orphans are treated before women may be an indication that they were more of a problem at the time of Muhammad.

WOMEN
Surah 4:1–10
(Medina)

In the name of God, the Lord of Mercy, the Giver of Mercy

People, be mindful of your Lord, who created you from a single soul, and from it created its mate, and from the pair of them spread countless men and women far and wide. Be mindful of God, in whose name you make requests of one another. Beware of severing the ties of kinship: God is always watching over you. Give orphans their property, do not replace [their] good things with bad, and do not consume their property with your own—a serious crime. If you fear that you will not deal fairly with orphan girls, you may marry whichever [other] women seem good to you, two, three, or four. If you fear that you cannot be equitable [to them], then marry only one, or your slave(s): that is more likely to make you avoid bias. Give women their dowry as a gift upon marriage, though if they are happy to give up some of it for you, you may enjoy it with clear conscience.

[5] Do not entrust your property to the feeble-minded. God has made it a means of

---

*Qur'an 4:1–10.

support for you: make provision for them from it, clothe them, and address them kindly. Test orphans until they reach marriageable age; then, if you find they have sound judgment, hand over their property to them. Do not consume it wastefully before they come of age: if the guardian is well off he should abstain from the orphan's property, and if he is poor he should use only what is fair. When you give them their property, call witnesses in; God takes full account of everything you do.

Men shall have a share in what their parents and closest relatives leave, and women shall have a share in what their parents and closest relatives leave, whether the legacy be small or large: this is ordained by God. If other relatives, orphans, or needy people are present at the distribution, give them something too, and speak kindly to them. Let those who would fear for the future of their own helpless children, if they were to die, show the same concern [for orphans]; let them be mindful of God and speak out for justice. [10] Those who consume the property of orphans unjustly are actually swallowing fire into their own bellies: they will burn in the blazing Flame.

WORSHIP AND RITUAL

The Opening of the *Qur'an**

The first chapter in the Qur'an *is its* Fatihah, *"Opening," which stands as a devotional preface to the book. A beautiful poem of praise to God, the* Fatihah *[fah-TEE-huh] sums up the content of the* Qur'an: *praise to the one God, and submission to his way in the "straight path." This is by far the most recited chapter in the* Qur'an.

THE OPENING
Surah 1

In the name of God, the Lord of Mercy, the Giver of Mercy!

Praise belongs to God, Lord of the Worlds, the Lord of Mercy, the Giver of Mercy, Master of the Day of Judgment. [5] It is You we worship; it is You we ask for help. Guide us to the straight path: the path of those You have blessed, those who incur no anger and who have not gone astray.

**Qur'an* 1.

Confession of Faith*

The first pillar (main practice) of Islam is the confession of faith that states, "There is no God but God, and Muhammad is God's prophet." This formula does not occur in this developed and exact way in the Qur'an, *but the two parts of it do occur in early forms. The conclusion of the first selection, Surah 57, "Iron," "Have faith in God and in his apostle," links the two parts of the confession. In the second selection, the first half of the confession is found in an exact and formal use.*

**Qur'an* 57:1–7; 37:32–39.

IRON
Surah 57
(Mecca)

In the name of God, the Lord of Mercy, the Giver of Mercy

Everything in the heavens and earth glorifies God—He is the Almighty, the Wise. Control of the heavens and earth belongs to Him; He gives life and death; He has power over all things. He is the First and the Last; the Outer and the Inner; He has knowledge of all things.

It was He who created the heavens and earth in six days and then established Himself on the throne. He knows what enters the earth and what comes out of it; what descends from the sky and what ascends to it. He is with you wherever you are; He sees all that you do; [5] control of the heavens and earth belongs to Him. Everything is brought back to God. He makes night merge into day and day into night. He knows what is in every heart.

Believe in God and His Messenger, and give out of what He has given to you. Those of you who believe and give will have a great reward.

[37:32 (Mecca)] On that Day they will all share the torment: this is how We deal with the guilty. [35] Whenever it was said to them, "There is no deity but God," they became arrogant, and said, "Are we to forsake our gods for a mad poet?" No: he brought the truth and confirmed the earlier messengers. You will taste the painful torment, and be repaid only according to your deeds.

Prayer*

*At first Muhammad and his followers faced Jerusalem during prayer, as was the Jewish custom. Later, after relations with the Jews of Medina had soured, Muhammad changed the direction of prayer—**qiblah** [KIB-luh]—to the holy shrine at Mecca. The duty and direction of prayer are discussed in the* Qur'an, *but the content of prayer is not, perhaps because the* Qur'an *itself is rich with prayers and other devotional material.*

The foolish people will say, "What has turned them away from the prayer direction they used to face?" Say, "East and West belong to God. He guides whoever He will to the right way." We have made you [believers] into a just community, so that you may bear witness [to the truth] before others and so that the Messenger may bear witness [to it] before you. We [previously] made the direction the one you used to face in order [now] to distinguish those who follow the Messenger from those who turn on their heels: that test was hard, except for those God has guided. God would never let your faith go to waste [believers], for God is most compassionate and most merciful toward people.

Many a time We have seen you [Prophet] turn your face toward Heaven, so We are turning you toward a prayer direction that pleases you. Turn your face in the direction of the Sacred Mosque: wherever you [believers] may be, turn your faces to it. Those who were given the Scripture know with certainty that

---

*Qur'an 2:142–149.

this is the Truth from their Lord: God is not unaware of what they do. [145] Yet even if you brought every proof to those who were given the Scripture, they would not follow your prayer direction, nor will you follow theirs, nor indeed will any of them follow one another's direction.

If you [Prophet] were to follow their desires, after the knowledge brought to you, you would be doing wrong. Those We gave Scripture know it as well as they know their own sons, but some of them hide the truth that they know. The truth is from your Lord, so do not be one of those who doubt. Each community has its own direction to which it turns: race to do good deeds and wherever you are, God will bring you together. God has power to do everything.

[Prophet], wherever you may have started out, turn your face in the direction of the Sacred Mosque—this is the truth from your Lord: He is not unaware of what you do.

Alms*

In Islam, the giving of alms (zakat) is mandatory. Alms are more of a tax than an offering, but believers are urged to give fully and willingly. Surah 107, "Alms," the first passage, castigates those who evade the alms tax; the second passage deals especially with who may receive alms.

ALMS
Surah 107
(Mecca: 1–3; Medina: 4–7)

In the Name of God, the Lord of Mercy, the Giver of Mercy

[Prophet], have you considered the person who denies the Judgment? It is he who pushes aside the orphan and does not urge others to feed the needy. So woe to those who pray [5] but are heedless of their prayer; those who are all show and forbid common kindnesses.

[9:53 (Medina)] Say, "Whether you[30] give willingly or unwillingly, what you give will not be accepted, for you are disobedient people." The only thing that prevents what they give from being accepted is the fact that they disbelieve in God and His Messenger, perform the prayer lazily, and give grudgingly. [55] So [Prophet] do not let their possessions or their children impress you. Through these God intends to punish them in this world and for their souls to depart while they disbelieve. . . .

Some of them find fault with you [Prophet] regarding the distribution of alms: they are content if they are given a share, but angry if not. If only they would be content with what God and His Messenger have given them, and say, "God is enough for us—He will give us some of His bounty and so will His Messenger—to God alone we turn in hope." [60] Alms are meant only for the poor, the needy, those who administer them, those whose hearts need winning over, to free slaves and help those in debt, for God's cause and for travelers in need. This is ordained by God; God is all knowing and wise.

---

*Qur'an 107; 9:53–60.
[30] *You:* hypocrites among the Muslims.

The Fast*

As the beginning of this Medinan passage indicates, fasting was a pre-Islamic custom among the Arabs. Muhammad adapts it with his own regulations to Islam. Easily discernible here is the transition between pre-Islamic and Islamic fasting.

You who believe, fasting is prescribed for you, as it was prescribed for those before you, so that you may be mindful of God. Fast for a specific number of days, but if one of you is ill, or on a journey, he should fast on other days later. For those who can fast only with extreme difficulty, there is a way to compensate—feed a needy person. But if anyone does good of his own accord, it is better for him, and fasting is better for you, if only you knew.

[185] It was in the month of Ramadan that the *Qur'an* was revealed as guidance for mankind, clear messages giving guidance and distinguishing between right and wrong. So any one of you who is present[31] that month should fast, and anyone who is ill or on a journey should make up for the lost days by fasting on other days later. God wants ease for you, not hardship. He wants you to complete the prescribed period and to glorify Him for having guided you, so that you may be thankful. [Prophet], if My servants ask you about Me, I am near. I respond to those who call Me, so let them respond to Me, and believe in Me, so that they may be guided.

You [believers] are permitted to lie with your wives on the night of the fast; they are close as garments to you, as you are to them. God knew that you were deceiving yourselves,[32] so He turned to you in mercy and pardoned you. Therefore you may now lie with them and seek what God has ordained for you. Eat and drink until you can tell a white thread from a black one in the light of the coming dawn. Then resume the fast till nightfall and do not approach them, but stay at your prayers in the mosques.

---

* *Qur'an* 2:183–187.
[31] *any one of you who is present:* To judge from the context, "present at home" seems to be meant.
[32] *God knew that you were deceiving yourselves:* At first all sexual intercourse was forbidden during the month of Ramadan, but this regulation proved too difficult to carry out without hypocrisy, so now intercourse is allowed during the night only.

Pilgrimage**

The first selection explains that the Sacred Mosque of Mecca, which houses the Kaaba (the holy stone) and its shrine, was reclaimed by Muhammad from Arab polytheism with the argument that it was founded by Abraham and Ishmael, the first Muslims. According to Surah 106, "Quraysh," the second selection, the tribe of the Quraysh, Muhammad's own tribe, will receive God's protection in return for keeping the Holy Mosque. In the third selection, rules for the pilgrimage are given.

[2:125] We made the House[33] a resort and a sanctuary for people, saying, "Take the spot where Abraham stood as your place of prayer." We commanded Abraham and Ishmael: "Purify

---

** *Qur'an* 2:125–129; 106; 2:196–199.
[33] *the House:* the Sacred Mosque of Mecca, the holiest site in Islam. It is the house of the Kaaba and the house of worship for all Muslims.

My House for those who walk round it, those who stay there, and those who bow, and prostrate themselves in worship." Abraham said, "My Lord, make this land secure and provide with produce those of its people who believe in God and the Last Day." . . .

As Abraham and Ishmael built up the foundations of the House [they prayed], "Our Lord, accept [this] from us. You are the All Hearing, the All Knowing. Our Lord, make us devoted to you; make our descendants into a community devoted to You. Show us how to worship and accept our repentance, for You are the Ever Relenting, the Most Merciful. Our Lord, make a messenger of their own rise up from among them, to recite Your revelations to them, teach them the Scripture and wisdom, and purify them: You are the Mighty, the Wise."

QURAYSH
Surah 106
(Mecca)

In the name of God, the Lord of Mercy, the Giver of Mercy.

[He did this] to make the Quraysh feel secure, secure in their winter and summer journeys.[34] So let them worship the Lord of this House: who provides them with food to ward off hunger, safety to ward off fear.

[2:196 (Medina)] Complete the pilgrimages, major and minor, for the sake of God. If you are prevented [from doing so], then [send] whatever offering for sacrifice you can afford, and do not shave your heads until the offering has reached the place of sacrifice. If any of you is ill, or has an ailment of the scalp, he should compensate by fasting, or feeding the poor, or offering sacrifice. In times of peace, anyone wishing to take a break between the minor pilgrimage and the major one must make whatever offering he can afford. If he lacks the means, he should fast for three days during the pilgrimage, and seven days on his return, making ten days in all. This applies to those whose household is not near the Sacred Mosque. Always be mindful of God, and be aware that He is stern in His retribution.

The pilgrimage takes place during the prescribed months. There should be no indecent speech, misbehavior, or quarreling for anyone undertaking the pilgrimage—whatever good you do, God is well aware of it. Provide well for yourselves: the best provision is to be mindful of God—always be mindful of Me, you who have understanding—but it is no offense to seek some bounty from your Lord. When you surge down from Arafat remember God at the sacred place. Remember Him: He has guided you. Before that you were astray. Surge down where the rest of the people do, and ask forgiveness of God: He is most forgiving and merciful.

---

[34]*journeys:* trade caravans. The well-being of the Quraysh tribe of Mecca depended on the success of two main caravans.

The Mosque*

The word for mosque *in Arabic is* masjid, *"place of prostration." A mosque is a place of prayer, praise, and hope in the next world. The restrictions on attending mosques are given in the second reading. They are for Muslims only, and Muslims are urged to be faithful as they come to the mosque. These two passages are given from Medina.*

[24:36] God speaks in metaphors to men. God has knowledge of all things.

---

*Qur'an 24:36–38; 9:15–18.

His light is found in temples which God has sanctioned to be built for the remembrance of His name. In them, morning and evening, His praise is sung by men whom neither trade nor profit can divert from remembering Him, from offering prayers, or from giving alms; who dread the day when men's hearts and eyes shall writhe with anguish; who hope that God will requite them for their noblest deeds and lavish His grace upon them. God gives without measure to whom He will.

[9:15] It ill becomes the idolaters to visit the mosques of God, for they are self-confessed unbelievers. Vain shall be their works, and in the Fire they shall abide for ever.

None shall visit the mosques of God except those who believe in God and the Last Day, attend to their prayers and render the alms levy and fear none but God. These shall be rightly guided.

Do you pretend that he who gives a drink to the pilgrims and pays a visit to the Sacred Mosque is as worthy as the man who believes in God and the Last Day, and fights for God's cause? These are not held equal by God. God does not guide the wrongdoers.

Against Evil Magic*

Here are formulas to recite against evil magic. The last two chapters in the Qur'an *deal with this theme. The traditional explanation of these surahs in Muslim interpretation is that they are used to dispel doubt. Used by the ordinary Muslim, however, such formulas often take on a semimagical character. The power of these passages when recited will protect a believer from evil both human and supernatural.*

DAYBREAK
Surah 113
(Mecca)

Say [Prophet], "I seek refuge with the Lord of daybreak against the evil in what He has created, the evil in the night when darkness gathers, the evil in witches when they blow on knots, [5] the evil in the envier when he envies."

PEOPLE
Surah 114
(Mecca)

In the name of God, the Lord of Mercy, the Giver of Mercy

Say, "I seek refuge with the Lord of people, the controller of people, the God of people, against the evil of the slinking whisperer—[5] who whispers into the heart of people—whether they be jinn or people."

---

*Qur'an 113; 114.

LATER DEVELOPMENTS OF SCRIPTURAL THEMES

Selections from the *Hadith*

The hadith ("traditions") are sayings by Muhammad passed down in early Islam, sayings that did not find their way into the Qur'an. They are called the "unrecited revelation." This designation rests on the belief common to Muslims that Muhammad's words were divinely inspired, not only when he recited the Qur'an but in all of his utterances after his prophetic call. The Qur'an and the hadith form the basis of the religious law that has governed Islam since early times.

Muslim theologians divide each hadith in two parts. First is the **isnad** [EES-nahd], the authority on which the tradition stands. This is a list of the individuals who orally passed down the specific tradition, from the person who heard the saying of Muhammad and first framed the story to the last person to report it before it was written down two centuries after the Prophet's death. (The whole chain of transmission is not given in the selections here.) For a tradition to be considered authentic, it must show an unbroken chain of transmission, and each person in the chain must be reliable. The second part of a hadith is the **matn** [MAH-ten], the text of the saying itself. Sometimes it is a short saying, and other times it is framed by a story.[35]

The last four selections deal with jihad, "struggle/warfare" for the faith. "On the Martyr in Jihad" gives the privileges of death in combat for the faith, called martyrdom. "On Plunder in Jihad" defends the Islamic practice of taking captured people and property as booty against the ancient Israelite prohibition of plunder. In "On Women and Children in Jihad," a brief command is given forbidding the killing of women and children in jihad. In the last, "On the Steps for Jihad against Enemies," procedures are laid down for dealing with religious opponents who have come under Muslim control in jihad.

On Innovations: It is related from Irbad bin Sariyah that he said, "On a certain day the Apostle of God said prayers with us; then he drew near to us and gave us eloquent instruction that brought tears to our eyes and by which our hearts were affected.

"A man said, 'O Apostle of God, this is a farewell address, therefore give us a command.'

"He replied, 'I command you the fear of God, and giving ear and obedience even if he is an Abyssinian slave; for those of you who will live after me will see many schisms. Therefore it is your duty to follow my rule of faith and the rule of faith of the rightly guided caliphs. Seize it and hold it fast. Beware of new things, for all new things are an innovation, and all innovation is a going astray.'"

On Ritual Washings: It is related from Othman that he performed his ablutions and poured water on his hands three times, and then he washed his mouth, and then cleansed his nose. After that he washed his face three times, then he washed his right arm to his elbow three times, then he washed his left arm to his elbow three times. After that he wiped his hand over his head, then he washed his right foot three times, then the left three times. After that he said, "I saw the Apostle of God perform his ablutions like these ablutions of mine. Then he [the apostle of God] said, 'Whoever performs his ablutions like these ablutions of mine, and then prays two sets of prayers, while his mind speaks nothing the while, all his preceding sins will be forgiven him.'"

---

[35] The passages that follow are taken, with editing, from W. Goldsack, *Selections from Muhammadan Traditions* (Madras: Christian Literature Society for India, 1923).

On Prayer: It is related from Abdullah bin Omar that, "The Apostle of God said, 'The time for the midday prayer is when the sun declines, and a man's shadow becomes equal to his height, and the afternoon prayer has not arrived. The time for the afternoon prayer is so long as the sun has not become yellow; and the time for the evening prayer is so long as the ruddy light of twilight has not disappeared; and the time of the night prayer is to the first half of the night; and the time for the morning prayer is from the breaking of the dawn until the sun rises. When the sun rises, then withhold from the morning prayer, for truly it rises between the two horns of Satan.'"

It is related from Ubadah binus-Samit that, "The Apostle of God said, 'There can be no prayer for the one who does not recite the opening chapter of the Book.'"

On Alms: It is related from Abu Musaul-Ashari that, "The Apostle of God said, 'Alms are obligatory on every Muslim.'

"They said, 'And if he has nothing?' He replied, 'Then let him work with his hands, and gain something for himself, and give alms.'

"They said, 'And if he is not able to work, or has not done so?' He replied, 'Then let him assist those who are in need and in distress.'

"They said, 'And if he does not do that?' He replied, 'Then let him order people to do right.'

"They said, 'And if he does not do that?' He replied, 'Then let him withhold himself from evil; and truly that will be alms for him.'"

It is related from Abu Umamah that he said, "I heard the Apostle of God say, in his public address, in the year of the farewell pilgrimage,[36] 'Let not a woman spend anything in alms from the house of her husband, except with the permission of her husband.'

"It was said, 'O Apostle of God, not even food?'

"He replied, 'That is the best of our property.'"

On God: It is related from Ubai bin Kab that, "The Apostle of God said, 'O Abu Al Mandhar, do you know which verse from the Book of God most High which is with you is the greatest?'

"I said, 'God and His Apostle know best.'

"He said, 'O Abu Al Mandhar, do you know which verse from the Book of God which is with you is greatest?'

"I said, 'God, there is no God but He, the Living, the Self-subsisting.' Ubai said, 'And he struck me on my breast and said, "O Abu Al Mandhar, may knowledge be welcome to you."'"

It is related from Abu Hurairah that, "The Apostle of God said, 'Truly God Most High has ninety-nine names. Whoever counts them will enter paradise. He is Allah, beside whom there is no other God, the Merciful, the Compassionate, the King, the Holy, the Peace, the Faithful, the Protector, the Mighty, the Compeller, the Proud, the Creator, the Maker, the Fashioner, the Forgiver, the Dominant, the Bestower, the Provider, the Opener, the Knower, the Restrainer, the Speaker, the Abaser, the Exalter, the Honorer, the Destroyer, the Hearer, the Seer, the Ruler, the Just, the Subtle, the Aware, the Clement, the Grand, the Forgiving, the Grateful, the Exalted, the Great, the Guardian, the Strengthener, the Reckoner, the Majestic, the Generous, the Watcher, the Approver, the Comprehensive, the Wise, the Loving, the Glorious, the Raiser, the Witness, the Truth, the Advocate, the Strong, the Firm, the Patron, the Laudable, the Counter, the Beginner, the Restorer, the Quickener, the Killer, the Living, the Subsisting, the Finder, the Glorious, the One, the Eternal, the Powerful, the Prevailing, the Bringer-forward, the Deferrer, the First, the Last, the Evident, the Hidden, the Governor, the Exalted, the Righteous, the Accepter of Repentance, the Avenger, the Pardoner, the Kind,

---

[36] *farewell pilgrimage:* the Prophet's last pilgrimage to Mecca before his death.

the Ruler of the Kingdom, the Lord of Majesty and Liberality, the Equitable, the Collector, the Independent, the Enricher, the Giver, the Withholder, the Distresser, the Profiter, the Light, the Guide, the Incomparable, the Enduring, the Inheritor, the Director, the Patient.'"

On the Power of Reading the Qur'an: It is related from Abu Sa'idu'l-Khudri that Usaid bin Hudair said, "On a certain night when I was reading, and my horse was tethered near me, behold! the horse wheeled round. Then I became silent, and it also became steady. Then I read (again), and it wheeled round. Then I became silent, and it ceased wheeling round. I again read, and the horse wheeled round as before. Then I turned away, and my son Yahya was near it, and he feared that it would injure him. And when I moved the child away I raised his head to the heavens, and behold! something like a cloud and in it objects resembling lamps.

"And when the morning came I informed the Prophet. . . . 'I feared, O Apostle of God, that it would tread on Yahya who was near it, and I moved near to him, and raised my head to the heavens, and behold! something resembling a cloud, in which were objects like lamps, and I went out in order that I should not see them.'

"He replied, 'And do you know what that was?' He said, 'No.'

"He said, "Those were angels that came near at the sound of your voice. If you had continued to read, they would have remained until the morning, and men would have seen them. They would not have remained hidden.'"

On the Martyr in Jihad: It is related from Abu Miqdam bin Madikarib that the Apostle of God said, "The martyr has six privileges near God: he is forgiven his sins on (the shedding of) the first drop of blood; he is shown his resting-place in paradise; he is redeemed from the punishment of the grave[37]; he is made secure from the great fear (of hell); and a crown of glory is placed on his head, one ruby of which is better than the world and all that is in it; he will marry seventy-two wives from the company of the houris[38]; and his prayer will be accepted for seventy of his relatives."

On Plunder in Jihad: It is related from Abu Hurairah that the Prophet said, "One of the Prophets [Joshua] went out to fight; and he said to his people, 'Let no man follow me who has married a wife and wishes to take her to his house, but has not yet done so; nor the one who has built a house, but has not yet raised a roof over it; nor the man who has bought a sheep or camel and is expecting it to give birth.' Then he went forth to war.

"And he drew near a certain village at the time of evening prayer. Then he said to the sun, 'Truly you are under orders, and I am also under orders. O God, restrain it for us.' Then it was restrained (from setting) until God gave him the victory. After that he gathered together the plunder; and a fire came to devour it, but it did not consume it. And he said, 'Truly there is deceit among you with regard to the plunder. Therefore let a man from each tribe pledge his oath.'

"Then the hand of a certain man stuck to his hand. He said, 'The deceit concerning the plunder is among you.' Then they [the offenders] brought a golden head like the head of a cow. Then he set it down and the fire came and devoured it.'"

And the relater has added in another tradition, 'Plunder was not lawful for any one before us. Afterwards God made plunder lawful for us. He saw our weakness and impotence and made it lawful for us.'

On Women and Children in Jihad: It is related from Abdullah bin Omar, "The Apostle of God prohibited the killing of women and children."

---

[37] *punishment of the grave:* punishment of particularly sinful people begins before the resurrection and judgment.
[38] *houris:* beautiful dark-eyed virgins created for righteous men in heaven. See *Qur'an* 44:51–59.

On the Steps for Jihad against Enemies: It is related from Sulaiman bin Buraidah, from his father, that he said, "When the Apostle of God appointed a leader over any army or marauding band, he was in the habit of giving him orders regarding his special duties concerning the fear of God and good behavior toward those Muslims who were with him.

"After that the Apostle of God would say, 'Go forth to war in the name of God in his road. Fight with those who disbelieve in God. Go forth to war. Do not use deceit or break a covenant, or mutilate [anyone], or kill children. And when you meet your enemy the polytheists, then invite them to the rights and privileges of Islam or defeat. If they give an affirmative answer, accept it from them and withdraw from them. After that invite them to Islam; and if they give an affirmative answer to you, then accept it from them and withdraw from them. After that invite them to remove themselves from their homes to the homes of the refugees, and inform them that if they do that, then for them is what is given to the refugees; and their duties are the same as those of the refugees. But if they refuse to change from their homes, then inform them that they will remain as the desert Arabs who have embraced Islam. The commands of God will be obligatory upon them which are obligatory upon other believers; but they will get nothing of the plunder and spoils unless they go to fight along with the other Muslims. But if they refuse (to become Muslims) then demand from them the poll-tax.[39] If they answer you in the affirmative, then accept it from them, and withdraw from them. But if they refuse (to pay), then seek help from God and fight them.'"

---

[39] *poll-tax:* tax levied on each person; the term is usually associated in our usage with voting, but that is not the case here.

A Sunni Creed*

Abu Hasan al-Ash'ari was a prominent Sunni theologian in the early tenth century. He drew up what is probably the first creedal statement in Islam, and it has been influential in Sunni circles ever since. The creed occasionally names other Islamic groups, mostly Shi'ite, that deny the doctrines of the creed. The references in brackets are to the Qur'an;[40] *the numbers have been adjusted to match the* Qur'an *translation used above.*

Abu Hasan al-Ash'ari said: . . .

The essence of our belief is that we confess faith in Allah, His angels, His Books, His Messenger, the revelation of Allah, and what the trustworthy have handed down on the authority of Allah's Messenger, rejecting none of them.[41]

We confess that Allah is One—There is none worthy of worship but He—unique, eternal, possessing neither consort nor child; and that Muhammad is His servant and Messenger, whom He sent with the guidance and the real Religion.

We believe that Paradise is real and Hell is real; and that there is no doubt regarding the Coming Hour; and that Allah will raise up all those who are in the graves; and that Allah is established on His throne (as He has said, "The Merciful is established on the Throne" [20:5]); and that He has a face (as He has said, "but the Face of thy Lord shall abide resplendent with

---

* *Creed of Abu Hasan al-Ash'ari*
[40] Copyright © 2005 Salafi Publications. www.salafipublications.com. Used by permission.
[41] *rejecting none of them:* this is an affirmation of the Sunni approach to the *hadith*.

majesty and glory" [55:27]); And that He has two hands, (without asking how) (as He has said "I have created with my two hands," [38:75] and he has said, "nay! Outstretched are both His hands" [5:69]); and that He has an eye, without asking how (as He has said "under Our eyes it floated on" [54:14]).

[We believe] that anybody who thinks that the names of Allah are other than He is in error; and that Allah has Knowledge (as He has said, "In His knowledge He sent it down," [4:166]), and as He said, "And no female conceives and brings forth without His knowledge" [35:11]). We also assert that Allah has hearing and sight, and we do not deny it as the Mu'tazila,[42] the Jahmiyyah, and the Kharijites[43] deny it; And we assert that Allah has Prowess (as He has said, "saw they not that Allah Who created them was mightier than they in Prowess?" [41:15]).

We believe that the Word of Allah is uncreated, and that He has created nothing without first saying to it, "Be!" And it is as he has said, "Our word to a thing when we will it is but to say, 'Be!,' and it is" [16:40]), and that there is no good or evil on earth save what Allah wishes: and that things exist by Allah's wish; and that not a single person has the capacity to do anything until Allah causes him to act, and we are not independent of Allah, nor can we pass beyond the range of Allah's knowledge.

We believe that there is no creator save Allah, and the works of human beings are things created and decreed by Allah (as He has said, "Allah has created you and what you make" [37:96]); and that human beings have not the power to create anything, but are themselves created (as He has said, " Is there a creator other than Allah?" [35:3], and as He has said, "they create nothing, but are themselves created," [16:20] and as he said, "Shall He who creates be as he who does not create?," [16:17] and as He has said, "were they created by nothing or were they themselves the creators?," [52:35] for this is mentioned in Allah's Book frequently); and that Allah favors the Believers by granting them obedience to Him, is gracious to them, considers them, does what is salutary for them, guides them; whereas He causes the Disbelievers to stray, does not guide them, does not give them the grace to believe.

If He were gracious to deviators and rebels, and did what is salutary for them they would be sound; and if He guided them, they would be guided; as He has said, "He whom Allah guides is the rightly guided and they whom he misleads will be the lost" [7:178], and that Allah has power to do what is salutary for the infidels and be gracious to them, that they may become believers, nevertheless He wills that they be infidels, as He knows; and that He forsakes them and seals up their hearts; and that good and evil are dependent upon the general and the particular decrees of Allah, His sweet and His bitter; and we know that what passes us by was not to befall us, and what befalls us was not to pass us by; and that human beings do not control for themselves what is hurtful or what is helpful, except what Allah wishes; and that we ought to commit our affairs to Allah and assert our complete need of and dependence upon Him.

We believe, too, that the *Qur'an* is the uncreated word of Allah, and that he who believes that the *Qur'an* is created is an infidel.

We hold that Allah will be seen in the next world by sight (as the moon is seen on the night it is full, so shall the faithful see Him, as we are told in the traditions that come down on the authority of Allah's Messenger); and we believe

---

[42] *Mu'tazila:* This now-extinct group contemporaneous with al-Ash'ari explained Islam with Greek philosophical concepts and taught on many topics that this creed deals with: whether the *Qur'an* was created or eternal, whether evil was created by God, the issue of predestination versus free will, whether God's attributes in the *Qur'an* were to be interpreted allegorically or literally, and whether sinning believers would have eternal punishment in hell.

[43] *Kharijites:* a general term for a variety of Islamic sects that reject the caliphate of Ali. They first emerged in the late seventh century C.E., concentrated in today's southern Iraq, and are distinct from the Sunnis and Shi'ites.

that the infidels will be veiled from Him when the faithful see Him in Paradise (as Allah has said, "Yes, they shall be shut out as by a veil from their Lord on that day" [83:15], and that Moses asked Allah for the sight of Him in this world, and "Allah manifested Himself to the mountain" and "turned it to dust," [7:143], and taught Musa [Moses] by it that he should not see Him in this world.

It is our opinion that we ought not to declare a single one of the people of the Qiblah[44] an infidel for a sin of which he is guilty, such as fornication or theft or the drinking of wine, as the Kharijites hold, thinking that such people are infidels. But he who commits any of these mortal sins such as fornication or theft presumptuously, declaring it lawful and not acknowledging that is forbidden, is an infidel. . . .

We hold that Allah changes men's hearts, and that their hearts are between two of Allah's fingers, and that Allah will place the heavens on a finger and the earth on a finger, as we are told in the tradition that comes down on the authority of Allah's Messenger.

We hold that we ought not to relegate any of the Monotheists, or those who hold fast to the faith, to Paradise or to Hell, save him in whose favor the Messenger of Allah has borne witness concerning Paradise; and we hope that sinners will attain to Paradise, but we fear that they will be punished in Hell. . . .

We believe in the punishment of the grave, and the Pool, and hold that the Scales are real, and the Bridge is real, and the resurrection after death is real, and that Allah will line up human beings at the Station, and settle the account with the faithful.

We believe that faith consists of words and deeds, and is subject to increase and decrease; and we receive the authentic traditions regarding it related on the authority of the Messenger of Allah, which the trustworthy have transmitted, one just man from another, until the tradition goes back to the Messenger of Allah, we believe in affection toward our forebears in faith, whom Allah chose for the company of His Prophet, we praise them with the praise wherewith Allah praised them, and are attached to them all.

We believe that the excellent Imam,[45] after the Messenger of Allah, is Abu Bakr the Veracious, and that Allah strengthened the Religion by him and gave him success against the renegades, and the Muslims promoted him to the imamate just as the Messenger of Allah made him leader of prayer, and they all named him the caliph of Allah's Messenger; then after him came 'Umar; then Uthman (those who fought with him did so wrongfully and unrighteously); then 'Ali; therefore these are the Imams after the Messenger of Allah. . . . We hold that the four Imams are orthodox, divinely guided, excellent caliphs, unmatched by others in excellence.

We accept all the traditions for which the Sunnis vouch: the descent in to the lower heavens, and the Lord's saying, "Is there any who has a request? Is there any who asks forgiveness?," and the other things they relate and vouch for; dissenting from what the deviators and followers of error assert.

We rely, where we differ, upon our Lord's book, and the sunnah (tradition) of our Prophet, and the unanimous consent of the Muslims and what it signifies; and we do not introduce into Allah's religion innovations that Allah does not allow, nor we do we believe of Allah what we do not know.

We believe that Allah will come in the day of resurrection (as He has said, "and thy Lord shall come and the Angels rank on rank" [80:23]); and that Allah is near His servants, even as He wishes (as He has said, "We are nearer to him than his jugular vein," [50:16] and as He said, "then He came nearer and approached and was at the distance of two bows or even closer" [53:8, 9]).

It belongs to our religion to observe the Friday Assembly, and the feasts, and the remaining prayers and public devotions under the leadership

---

[44] *People of the Qiblah:* Muslims, who pray in the direction of Mecca.
[45] *Imam:* leader of the Muslim religion and community after Muhammad.

of every pious man or impious . . .; and we believe that the wiping of the sandals is a sunnah at home and in travel, contrarily to the belief of anybody who denies it; and we approve prayer for the welfare of the imams of the Muslims, and the confession of their imamate; and we regard it as error on anybody's part to "going out" against them when they have clearly abandoned rectitude; and we believe in abstinence from "going out" against them with the sword, and abstinence from fighting in civil commotions.

We confess the going forth of the false messiah (ad-Dajjal), as it is contained in the tradition related on the authority of Allah's Messenger. We believe in the punishment of the grave, and in Munkar and Nakir, and their interrogation of those who are buried in the graves. . . .

We approve alms on behalf of the Muslim dead, and prayer for their welfare; and we believe that Allah helps them by it.

We accept it as true that there are sorcerers and sorcery in the world, and that sorcery exists in the world.

We believe in praying for those of the people of the Qiblah who are dead, the pious and the impious, and in the lawfulness of being their heirs.

We confess that Paradise and Hell are created; and that he who dies or is slain [does so] at his appointed term; and that sustenance is from Allah who gives it to His creatures in the permitted and the forbidden; and that Satan whispers to man and causes him to doubt and infects him, contrarily to the belief of the Mu'tazilah and the Jahmiyyah (as Allah has said, "they who swallow down usury shall arise in the resurrection only as he arises whom Satan hath infected by his touch," [2:275] and as he has said, "against the mischief of the stealthily withdrawn whisperer, who whispers in man's breast—against jinn and men." [114:4–6]).

We believe that Allah can design particularly for the just the signs he manifests to them.

Our belief regarding the children of the polytheists is that Allah will kindle a fire for them in the next world, and then will say to them, "Rush into it!," as the tradition tells us concerning it.

We hold that Allah knows what human beings are doing, and what they are going to do, what has been, what is, and how what is not would have been if it had been.

We believe in obedience to the Imams and in the sincere counsel of the Muslims.

We approve separation from every innovative tendency, and the avoidance of people of impulses to stray [from the faith].

A Shi'ite Creed*

The most populous Shi'ite group by far is the "Twelver" sect, so called because it holds that there were twelve imams after Muhammad. The last imam, called the Mahdi, is "occluded"—that is, hidden until the end of the world comes. This "creed" is a statement of Shi'ite essentials. Notice that it is put in the mouth of Muhammad; only there is it authoritative.[46]

And the Prophet [Muhammad] said: "The Imams after me are twelve, the first of them is the Prince of Believers, 'Ali ibn Abi Talib, and the last of them is the Mahdi, the *Qa'im* (upholder of the true religion). Obedience to them is obedience to me and disobedience to them is disobedience to me; and he who denies one of them has verily denied me."

---

*Ibn Babawayh al-Qummi, *Risalatu'l I'tiqadat*.
[46] From A. A. Fyzee, ed., *A Shi'ite Creed* (London: Oxford University Press, 1932).

[Concerning the first eleven Imams] the Prince of Believers ['Ali ibn Abi Talib, the first Imam], on whom be peace, was murdered by 'Abdu'r Rahman ibn Muljam al-Muradi, may Allah curse him and he was buried in Ghari. And Hasan ibn 'ali [the second Imam], on both of whom be peace, he was poisoned by his wife Ja'da bint Ash'ath of Kinda, may Allah curse them both, and he died on account of that. And Husayn ibn 'Ali [the third Imam] was slain in Karbala. His murderer was Sinan ibn Anas an-Nakha'I, the curse of Allah on them both. And 'Ali' bin Husayn, the Sayyid Zaynu'l-Abidin [the fourth Imam], was poisoned by al-Walid ibn 'Abdu'l-Malik, Allah cursed him. And Muhammad al-Baqir ibn 'Ali [the fifth Imam] was poisoned by Ibrahim ibn al-Walid, may Allah curse him. And Ja'far as Sadiq [the sixth Imam] was poisoned by Abu Ja'far al'Mansur ad-Dawaniqi, may Allah curse him. And Musa al-Kazim ibn Ja'far [the seventh Imam] was poisoned by Harunu'r-Rashid, may Allah curse him. And 'Ali ar-Rida ibn Musa [the eighth Imam] was poisoned by Ma'mun, may Allah curse him. And Abu Ja'far Muhammad at-Taqi ibn 'Ali [the ninth Imam] was poisoned by al-Mu'tasim, may Allah curse him. And 'Ali an-Naqi ibn Muhammad [the tenth Imam] was poisoned by al-Mutawakkil, may Allah curse him. And Hasan al'Askari ibn 'Ali [the eleventh Imam] was poisoned by al'Mu'tamid, may Allah curse him.

And our belief is that these events actually occurred, and that there was no doubt in the minds of the people regarding the Imam's affairs, as some of those who exceed the bounds (of belief) allege.... And verily the Prophets and Imams, on whom be peace, had informed (people) that they would all be murdered.

[Concerning the twelfth Imam, Mahdi] we believe that the Proof of Allah in His earth and His caliph among His slaves in this age of ours is the Upholder *(al'Qa'im)*.... He it is concerning whose name and descent the Prophet was informed by Allah the Mighty and Glorious, and he it is who will fill the earth with justice and equity, just as now it is full of oppression and wrong. And he it is through whom Allah will make His faith manifest in order to supersede all religion, though the polytheists may have disliked (it). He it is whom Allah will make victorious over the whole world until from every place the call to prayer will be heard and all religion will belong entirely to Allah, Exalted is He above all. He it is who is Rightly Guided (the *Mahdi*), about whom the Prophet gave information that when he appears, Jesus, son of Mary, will descend upon the earth and pray behind him, and he who prays behind him is like one who prays behind the Prophet of Allah, because he is his caliph. And we believe that there can be no Qa'im other than him; he may live in the state of occultation (as long as he likes); and were he to live in the state of occultation for the space of the existence of this world, there would nevertheless be no Qa'im other than him. For, the Prophet and the Imams have indicated him by his name and descent; him they appointed as their successor, and of him they gave glad tiding—the Blessing of Allah on all of them.

Sufi Poetry on Love for God*

Shabistari's Secret Rose Garden *(1317) is considered the greatest mystical poetry of Sufism. Like much mystical religious poetry, it draws on the language of human love to express the believer's relationship with God. It treats such themes as the self and the one, the spiritual journey, time, and the ecstasy of "divine inebriation" —being intoxicated with God. Shabistari's poetry is one of the*

---

* *The Secret Rose Garden* 1.

clearest and most concise guides to the inner meaning of Sufism. In this first chapter, titled "The Perfect Face of the Beloved," Shabistari speaks of God's nature in terms of the parts of God's "face."[47]

THE EYE AND THE LIP

What is the nature of the eye and the lip? Let us consider.
Alluring and intoxicating glances shine from His eye.
The essence of existence issues from His ruby lip.
Hearts burn with desire because of His eye,
And are healed again by the smile of His lip.
Because of His eye hearts are aching and drunken.
His ruby lip gives soul-garments to men.
His eye does not perceive this visible world,
Yet often His lip quivers with compassion.
Sometimes He charms us with a touch of humanity,
And gives help to the despairing.
It is His smile that gives life to man's water and, clay;
It is His breath that opens heaven's gate for us.
A corn-baited snare is each glance of that eye,
And a wine-shop lurks in each corner.
When He frowns the wide world is laid waste,
But is restored every moment by His kiss.
Our blood is at fever point because of His eye,
Our souls demented because of His lip.
How He has despoiled our hearts by a frown!
How He has uplifted our souls by a smile!
If you ask of Him an embrace,
His eye will say "Yea," His lip "Nay."
He finished the creation of the world by a frown,
Now and then the soul is revived by a kiss.
We would give up our lives with despair at His frown,
But would rise from the dead at his kiss.
. . . When the world meditates on His eye and His lip,
It yields itself to the intoxication of wine.

THE CHEEK AND THE DOWN

The theatre of Divine beauty is the cheek,
And the down[48] is the entrance to His holy presence.
Beauty is erased by His cheek when he says,
"Without my presence you are non-existent."
In the unseen world the down is as green meadows
Leading to the mansion of Eternal Life.
The blackness of His curl turns day into night,
The down of His cheek holds the secret of life.
If only you can glimpse His face and its down,
You will understand the meaning of plurality and unity.
His curl will teach you the knowledge of this world;
His down will reveal hidden paths.
Imagine seven verses in which each letter
Contains oceans of mysteries;
Such is His cheek.
And imagine, hidden beneath each hair of His cheek,
Thousands of oceans of mysteries;
Such is His down.
As the heart is God's throne in the water,
So is the down the ornament of the soul.

---

[47] From *The Secret Rose Garden of Sa'd Ud Din Mahmud Shabistari*, trans. Florence Lederer (London: J. Murray, 1920), pp. 27–29, 32–33.
[48] *down:* the first, soft growth of a beard.

GLOSSARY

ayah [EYE-yuh] "sign"; a verse in the *Qur'an*.

Bismillah [biss-MILL-uh] the opening formula for surahs in the *Qur'an*: "In the name of God, the Compassionate, the Merciful."

challenge verses short passages of the *Qur'an* in which the Prophet calls on his opponents to produce anything like his revelation.

Fatihah [fah-TEE-huh] "Opening"; the first chapter of the *Qur'an*, used as a prayer in Islam.

hadith [hah-DEETH] "traditions"; a traditional report recording a saying or an action of Muhammad.

isnad [EES-nahd] the authority on which a section of *hadith* stands, usually given as a list of names in a chain of tradition.

jihad [jee-HAHD] "struggle," both personal, inner struggle through prayer and study and armed struggle through military conflict to promote and defend Islam.

jinn spirits, both good and evil, distinguishable from angelic beings and the deity.

matn [MAH-ten] the main text of a *hadith*.

qiblah [KIB-luh] the direction Muslims face during prayer.

Qur'an [kuhr-AHN] "recitation, reading"; the scripture of Islam.

surah [SOO-rah] a chapter of the *Qur'an*.

tafsir [TAHF-sear] the branch of Islamic scholarship that deals with commentary on the *Qur'an*.

tilawa [tee-LAH-wuh] ritual recitation of the *Qur'an*.

QUESTIONS FOR STUDY AND DISCUSSION

1. How does the *Qur'an* give both direct (explicit) and indirect (implicit) information about the career of Muhammad?

2. In what sense is Islam especially Arabic? What does it mean for a universal religion like Islam to have a scripture that cannot be translated and still fully remain God's word for all peoples?

3. Explain the statement "Islam is a religion of the book."

4. Describe the status of women in the *Qur'an* and in Islam in general. To what degree may it be possible to improve this status and still keep within the bounds of the *Qur'an*?

5. How does almsgiving function to promote compassion and social justice?

6. Relate the cognitive to the noncognitive uses of the *Qur'an*. Which do you see as primary, and why?

7. How does the *Qur'an*'s view of creation and the world add to the views presented in Jewish and Christian scripture?

8. Free will and predestination are problems that touch many religions. They even touch other areas of thought, especially philosophy and psychology, with debates between behaviorists and humanists. Explain your views on this topic, and relate them to the *Qur'an* and the creed of al-Ash'ari.

9. Compare the Sunni and Shi'ite statements of faith. What do they have in common, and on what points do they differ?

SCRIPTURES IN FILM

The traditional Muslim reluctance to picture the face of Muhammad has influenced films about Muslim origins. The best one can do is films that depict Muslim life today as it draws on the *Qur'an*. *Malcolm X* (1992, rated PG-13), directed by Spike Lee and starring Denzel Washington, shows the struggle of the Black Muslim movement to return to Muslim roots. Also significant but of lesser cinematic value is *The Message* (1976, rated PG), directed by Moustapha Akkad, the story of Muhammad (without depicting him directly) and early Islam.

SUGGESTIONS FOR FURTHER READING

Primary Readings

Alim: version 4.5. ISL Software, 1997. A multimedia CD-ROM featuring Arabic text, recitation, transliteration, translations, and some *hadith* passages.

A. J. Arberry, ed., *The Koran Interpreted.* New York: Macmillan, 1955. This translation probably does the best job of suggesting in English the literary quality of the original.

K. Cragg, *Readings in the Qur'an.* London: Collins, 1988. An abridgment of the *Qur'an* to two-thirds of its size, arranged by eight themes, with a comprehensive introduction.

N. J. Dawood, trans., *The Koran.* New York: Penguin, 1990. This reliable translation is probably the most widely read edition available.

M. A. S. Abdel Haleem, *The Qur'an.* Oxford: Oxford University Press, 2004. A new translation, highly acclaimed for its accuracy and readability.

T. B. Irving, *The Qur'an: The First American Translation.* Brattleboro, VT: Amana, 1985. This translation is in good idiomatic English; the notes are from a traditional Muslim perspective and help the reader understand the role of the *Qur'an* in Muslim life.

M. Sells, *Approaching the Qur'an: The Early Revelations.* Ashland, OR: White Cloud Press, 1999. Fresh, powerful translations of the earlier, more poetic surahs, with a compact disk recording Qur'anic recitations of several of these surahs.

al-Tabari, *The Commentary on the Qur'an,* vol. 1. Translation, introduction, and notes by J. Cooper. Oxford: Oxford University Press, 1989. The first of five projected volumes, this book provides clear insight on Qur'anic commentary as practiced by the *Qur'an*'s most influential commentator.

Secondary Readings

A. Barlas, *"Believing Women" in Islam: Unreading Patriarchal Interpretations of the Qur'an.* Austin: University of Texas Press, 2002. Develops a reading of the *Qur'an* arguing for its originally egalitarian and antipatriarchal nature.

R. Bonney, *Jihad: From Qur'an to Bin Laden.* New York: Palgrave Macmillan, 2005. A fresh, balanced examination of jihad from the *Qur'an* and the *hadith* to the present day.

F. M. Denny, "Islam: Qur'an and Hadith." In F. M. Denny and R. L. Taylor, eds., *The Holy Book in Comparative Perspective.* Charleston: University of South Carolina Press, 1985, pp. 84–108. An up-to-date discussion of the relationship of the *Qur'an* and the *hadith*.

W. A. Graham, "An Arabic Recital": *Qur'an* as a Spoken Book." In W. A. Graham, *Beyond the Written Word.* Cambridge: Cambridge University Press, 1987, pp. 79–115. An excellent treatment of the oral aspects of the *Qur'an*.

J. D. McAuliffe, *Qur'anic Christians: An Analysis of Classical and Modern Exegesis.* Cambridge: Cambridge University Press, 1991. An excellent study of the history of Islamic interpretation of the *Qur'an* by way of an important interreligious question: the meaning of those passages that make remarks about Christians.

F. Rahman, *The Leading Ideas of the Qur'an*. Minneapolis: Bibliotheca, 1980. A fine treatment of the most important themes of the *Qur'an* by a leading Muslim theologian.

J. I. Smith, "Islam." In A. Sharma, ed., *Women in World Religions*. Albany: State University of New York Press, 1987, pp. 235–250. A treatment of the place of women in Islam, with a fine discussion of what the *Qur'an* says about women and how it is and is not applied in contemporary Muslim societies.

B. Stowasser, *Women in the Qur'an, Traditions, and Commentaries*. New York: Oxford University Press, 1994. An excellent treatment of the status and role of women in scripture, *hadith,* and commentary.

W. M. Watt, *Bell's Introduction to the Qur'an*. Edinburgh: Edinburgh University Press, 1970. This is probably the best one-volume introduction to the *Qur'an*.

The Grandin Press, Palmyra, New York
The Book of Mormon was first published here in 1830. The size of the first printing—five thousand copies—was unusually large for the time and indicates the initial strength of the Church of Jesus Christ of Latter-day Saints. A distinguishing feature of most scriptures of the new religious movements is their immediate mass publication.
Credit: Copyright © 2000 Intellectual Reserve, Inc. Used by permission.

CHAPTER SIX

New Religious Movements

✤ A weary business traveler settles into her room in the Marriott Hotel in Chicago. Looking for a bit of inspiration at the end of her day, she opens the top drawer of the nightstand alongside the bed, expecting to find a Christian *Bible*. On top of the Bible, however, is a copy of the *Book of Mormon,* subtitled "Another Testament of Jesus Christ." She is puzzled for a moment, until she remembers that the Marriott family that owns this hotel chain is devoutly Mormon and, like all devout Mormons, eager to spread the scriptures of Mormonism.

✤ In Manhattan's Madison Square Garden, two thousand couples are waiting to be joined in marriage by the Reverend Sun Myung Moon and his wife Hak Ja Han Moon, the founders of the Unification Church. The Moons arranged these marriages, and many of the couples have only recently met. As a part of the ceremony, words from the Unification scripture, *Divine Principle,* are intoned over the assembled crowd. These words emphasize one of the key ideas in Unification teaching: Under the religious direction of the Moons, the True Parents, the world will be saved by its repopulation with true children of God, believing Unificationists.

✤ In Boston, a young woman gets up in a meeting to tell of her recent cure. A Christian Scientist, she has used her faith to regain her health after suffering from a form of cancer. Like Christian Scientists for more than a century before her, she attributes her health to the spiritual power she found while reading Mary Baker Eddy's book, *Science and Health with Key to the Scriptures.*

INTRODUCTION

New religious movements, a recent term in the field of religious studies, generally denotes religious groups that arose since the start of the nineteenth century and now have sufficient size, longevity, and cultural impact to merit academic study of them. Most recently published encyclopedias, handbooks, and textbooks on religion use this term and provide information about the groups to which it refers.[1] "New religious movements" is preferable in many ways to other recent terms such as "alternative religious movements" and "marginal religious movements," and it is clearly preferable to the older "cults" and "sects." Although those last two terms still have some validity—especially in the sociological study of religion, where scholars try to use them objectively—they have become so laden with value judgments that most scholars no longer use them to characterize the new religious movements.

---

[1] For an excellent concise treatment of new religious movements, see W. H. Swatus Jr., ed., *Encyclopedia of Religion and Society* (Walnut Creek, CA: AltaMira, 1998), pp. 328–333.

Hundreds of groups around the world today are in a sense new religious movements, and each year sees the birth of more. In this chapter we focus on four Western movements that have become significant worldwide, that make and use scriptures, and that are important for students of world religions to encounter: the Baha'i tradition, the Church of Jesus Christ of Latter-day Saints, the Christian Science Church, and the Unification Church.

The inclusion of these groups in this chapter is not intended to imply that they see themselves as new religious movements; often they do not. Neither do they see themselves as related to each other; indeed, they are not. Although scholars call these religious movements "new," we must note that all branch off from older religions. Baha'i arose in the nineteenth century from Shi'ite Islam and sees itself as the successor of Islam. The Church of Jesus Christ of Latter-day Saints, the Christian Science Church, and the Unification Church see themselves as Christian, and most experts in comparative religions view this labeling as basically correct. That all three accept the Christian *Bible* as their first canon is a good indication of their Christian roots. Moreover, outsiders to Christianity, such as Buddhists, would almost certainly recognize them as belonging to the stream of Christian tradition.

Some of these new religious movements are highly controversial in North America and in other parts of the world. However, many of the other faiths examined in this book were also controversial when they were new. Careful students of religion will want to form judgments about these four new movements that are based in some measure on what believers say about themselves in their own sacred writings.

Because each of the movements treated in this chapter is separate from the others, we examine each movement and its scripture in turn, in the order in which it first appeared. In the remainder of this introductory section, we consider briefly the names of the various scriptures, their use, their structures, and their origin and development.

Names

Most of the scriptures of the new religious movements (unlike those of the older, traditional faiths) were written and published by the founders in their lifetime. Thus, the founding authors themselves gave these scriptures the names by which they are known.

Baha'i calls its scriptures **Holy Writings.** This name may seem bland and unilluminating, but it does imply something important about Baha'i scriptures: their originally written character. The *Qur'an* (Recitation) originated orally as the transmission of God's words; in contrast, the *Holy Writings* are the "Pen of God," a phrase often repeated in the earliest Baha'i scriptures.

The Church of Jesus Christ of Latter-day Saints has a three-part scripture. The **Book of Mormon** is the leading part, and it is from this title that the followers of this movement came to be known as "Mormons." (This is the only instance among the major world religions of a faith being named, or in this case nicknamed, from the name of its scripture.) A second, shorter scripture is the **Pearl of Great Price,** a selection of inspired translations by Mormon founder Joseph Smith (1805–1844). The final scripture is **Doctrine and Covenants,** which contains the continuing revelation of God's word through Latter-day Saint prophets, especially Joseph Smith. The *Book of Mormon,* but not the other two texts, is also considered scriptural by the Community of Christ, formerly known as the Reorganized Church of Jesus Christ of Latter-day Saints, an early splinter group. In addition to this "second canon" of scripture, the Latter-day Saint church has a "first canon" of the Christian *Bible*—in particular the King James Version of 1611.

The founder of Christian Science, Mary Baker Eddy (1821–1910), was a prolific writer, like many founders of new religious movements. Although new religious movements sometimes consider everything their founders wrote to be scriptural, the Christian Science Church has carefully delineated only one book as scripture: ***Science and Health with Key to the Scriptures*** (first published in 1875). Mrs. Eddy herself guided this delineation. The title of the book accurately suggests its content: a "science" that uses prayer, Christian scripture (the King James Version), and Eddy's book itself to heal body, mind, and spirit.

The Unification Church's sole scripture, written by its founder Sun Myung Moon (b. 1920), is the ***Divine Principle.*** "Principle" here means teaching, and it refers to Moon's distinctive reinterpretation of Christianity (the "Divine" of the title) in combination with select Asian teachings such as yin and yang, with devotion to Korea, and with a virulent anticommunism to produce a new religious movement.

Use

The use of scripture in the new religious movements is typically more limited than its use in the more traditional religions. Believers within these new groups do not regularly use their scriptures in ritual; they pay them no veneration, and the books themselves are not ornately published or decorated. (The new religious movements that use the Christian *Bible* alongside their own scriptures often show the *Bible* some formal respect short of veneration.) Neither do they typically use their books to organize the structure of their religious communities. Instead, they use their scriptures in three key ways.

- ❖ Believers are expected to study the scriptures, in groups and privately. At times this use crosses over into meditation. For example, Christian Scientists believe that healing comes from proper study and use of Mary Baker Eddy's *Science and Health with Key to the Scriptures*. In the Baha'i faith, the wording of the early scriptures, based as it is on lyrical Qur'anic style, encourages a meditative approach.

- ❖ The scriptures are used to teach key doctrines. They were written in large measure to teach new religious truth in the context of an older traditional religion, and the continuation of this tradition is important. For example, Sun Myung Moon's teachings in the *Divine Principle* are known and carried out by Unification Church leaders at all levels.

- New religious movements typically use their scriptures in missionary activities to spread their faith. Two examples must suffice here. The Christian Science Church widely distributes *Science and Health with Key to the Scriptures* at a subsidized price. The *Book of Mormon* is strongly advertised on American television and in print ads inviting people to send for a free copy. Given its role in the missionizing goals of the Latter-day Saints church, the *Book of Mormon* has become one of the world's most important scriptures.

A telling indication that these groups view their own writings as scriptural is the physical appearance of the books themselves. Though not ornate, these books are typically designed to look like the books they supplement or replace. The *Holy Writings* of Baha'i resembles the *Qur'an*. The *Divine Principle* of the Unification Church is, like the traditional Christian *Bible*, published with a black cover and black end papers. The Latter-day Saint Church designs the *Book of Mormon* to resemble the format of the *Bible* that it publishes.

Overview of Structure

The scriptures of new religious movements tend to show much less variety in structure and genre than the scriptures of traditional religions. They are usually non-narrative prose and strongly oriented to teaching the new doctrines. Three reasons help to explain this internal sameness. First, because they are "second canon" works, following up on the *Qur'an* (Baha'i) or on the Christian *Bible*, they are more tightly focused than other scriptures. Second, the relatively short period of time in which they were written, compared to the centuries-long process of scriptural creation in most other traditions, gives them a sharper focus. (The *Book of Mormon*, however, does claim to have been written by multiple authors over a thousand-year period.) Third, they are mostly written by the first founders of the various religious movements, not by later leaders.

The *Holy Writings* of Baha'i are organized in four parts corresponding to their four authors. First are the writings of a man known as the Bab ("Gate" to God), born Sayyid Ali-Muhammad Shiraz (1819–1850). These writings form a sort of preface to Baha'i. Next are the writings of Baha'u'llah, born Mirza Husayn-Ali Nur (1817–1892), the main founder of the faith. In the Baha'i canon, these two groups of writings are considered directly revelatory from God and thus most authoritative. Next are the writings of Abdu'l-Baha (1843–1921), the third leader, and finally the writings of his grandson Shoghi Effendi (1897–1957), the final leader of Baha'i, whose death effectively closed the canon. These writings are a collection of letters, narratives, prayers, and laws.

The scriptures of the Church of Jesus Christ of Latter-day Saints are fairly complex. They record a story of ancient American peoples descended from ancient Hebrews who left Judah around 600 B.C.E., the appearance of the resurrected Jesus Christ to these Americans, and the rebirth of the true Christian church in the nineteenth century with Joseph Smith Jr. The *Book of Mormon* has fifteen main parts known, with one exception, as books. Like the *Bible*, these books are subdivided into chapters and verses. Mormons believe that these texts are based on writings appearing on four groups of metal plates: those of Nephi [NEE-fy], Mormon, and Ether, and brass plates that, according to founder Joseph Smith, people fleeing Jerusalem in 600 B.C.E. brought to the Americas. In 421 C.E., Moroni, the last of the Nephite prophets, is believed to have sealed the sacred plates and hidden them by divine instruction. Smith said that in 1823 this same Moroni visited him as a resurrected prophet and directed him to these sacred plates. Smith reported that he translated the writing on the plates into English. He published the text in 1830 as the *Book of Mormon*. The plates themselves, Mormons believe, were returned to Moroni and then hidden away for all time.

The second Latter-day Saint scripture, *Pearl of Great Price,* was first compiled in 1851 by Franklin Richards, then a member of the church's Council of the Twelve Apostles and in charge of the church's missions in Great Britain. Richards intended to increase circulation among Latter-day Saints of Joseph Smith's testimony and translations. The book quickly received wide acceptance, especially in mission fields, and became a scripture of the church by the action of its First Presidency (highest official body) in 1880. *Pearl of Great Price* contains five main sections: *Selections from the Book of Moses* is an excerpt from Joseph Smith's translation of *Genesis*. *The Book of Abraham* is a translation of writings by the patriarch Abraham on Egyptian papyri that Joseph Smith obtained in 1835. *Joseph Smith—Matthew* is an excerpt by Smith from the *New Testament*'s *Gospel of Matthew* as understood in the Mormon church; it is a commentary of sorts on Matthew. *Joseph Smith—History* is extracts of Joseph Smith's official testimony about his own life. *Articles of Faith of the Church of Jesus Christ of Latter-day Saints* is a statement by Joseph Smith.

The third Latter-day Saint scripture, *Doctrine and Covenants,* has 138 sections, plus two "official declarations." It contains revelations on doctrines and community life, some narrative, some theological, and some legal, from 1823 until 1978. Its "official declarations" deal with two controversial topics—the ending of polygamy and the admission of blacks to the priesthood.

The scripture of Christian Science is in two parts, as its title implies. The first part, "Science and Health," consists of a preface by the author and fourteen chapters on various topics: Christian doctrines, spiritualism and hypnotism, medicine, and Christian Science practices of prayer and healing. The second part, "Key to Scriptures," has three chapters, one each treating *Genesis* and the *Apocalypse* (*Revelation* in the *New Testament*), and a glossary. "Fruitage," a final section added later, is a collection of written testimonies to the healing power of Christian Science, and especially to the role of *Science and Health with Key to the Scriptures* in this healing. This book has not been revised since the edition of 1910—the last edition that Mary Baker Eddy published—and has kept in all subsequent printings the 1910 pagination and line numbers.

The *Divine Principle* of the Unification Church is heavily didactic in content and style, as its abstract title implies. Its organization is also complex. Thirteen chapters are divided into numerous sections and subsections. Topics treated include "Principle of Creation," "The Human Fall," "The Messiah," "Predestination," "Christology," "The Periods in Providential History and the Determination of their Lengths," "Preparation Period for the Second Advent of the Messiah," and "Second Advent." These chapter titles vaguely imply what the content of this book makes plain—namely that Jesus, the first Messiah, did not accomplish God's mission, and a second Messiah has now been born in Korea, God's new chosen nation. *Divine Principle* does not make it explicit, but in other places Moon has proclaimed himself to be this second Messiah.

Origin and Development

It is possible to make four general observations about the origin and development of scripture in the new religious movements, especially as contrasted with the scriptures of older religions.

- ❖ The scriptures of the new religious movements have little or no oral tradition behind them; instead they went straight into print. The *Holy Writings* of Baha'i, the *Book of Mormon, Science and Health with Key to the Scriptures,* and the *Divine Principle* of the Unification Church were all taken by their respective authors from composition to publication. They do not reflect a long tradition shaped by community use, but they do reflect the thinking of individual authors.

- ❖ The scriptures of the new religious movements are "instant scripture" in that they are immediately accepted and used as scripture by believers. In the traditional faiths, a good deal of time passes while writings are compiled, recognized as scriptural, and put into a canon. As soon as the founder of a new movement produces a book, the movement adopts the text as authoritative.

- ❖ The new religious movements tend to have a remarkably large amount of scriptural literature, compared to the older traditions. Everything each founder wrote—many of the founders were very prolific writers—is typically considered scriptural, but special emphasis is placed on certain works. For example, in the Latter-day Saint and Baha'i movements, the scriptural literature continued to grow even after the death of the founders. These movements tend to have a body of scripture as large as the body of scripture of the more traditional religions they seek to supplant.

- ❖ Despite their fixed, published form, most scriptures of the new religious movements are amenable to change. For example, the Latter-day Saint text *Doctrine and Covenants* is open-ended. An addition to it can change or amplify previous revelation, even previous revelation recorded in the *Book of Mormon*. The Unification Church's *Divine Principle* was revised in 1996, and a careful comparison of this and the previous edition shows a few significant changes in content.

We focus now on each of the new religious movements in turn. The Baha'i scriptures have a fourfold development that corresponds to their current structure as outlined earlier. Each step is built on those that precede it, to make a coherent written tradition and teaching for the faith. First are the writings of the Bab, next are the writings of Baha'u'llah, then the writings of Abdu'l-Baha, the third leader, and finally the writings of his grandson Shoghi Effendi.

The *Book of Mormon*, the main scripture of the Church of Jesus Christ of Latter-day Saints, serves as a basis for newer scriptures in the Mormon canon. Ironically, the

Book of Mormon tends to be more similar than later official church writings and teachings to the mainstream Protestant Christianity against which the movement arose, especially as regards the controversial doctrines that have tended to set the Latter-day Saints apart from other Christians. For example, the *Book of Mormon* promotes monogamy and discourages (but does not forbid) polygamy (see *Jacob* 2:27, 30), but *Doctrine and Covenants* preserves both the approval of polygamy (sections 132, 37–38, 52, 61–62) and the official disapproval of it ("Official Declaration 1"). Although opponents of the church point to more than three thousand alleged changes in the *Book of Mormon* since its initial publication, the majority of them are corrections and updates of spelling and grammar. In essence, this important book remains as Joseph Smith Jr. wrote it.

The development of Christian Science scripture began with the writing of "Science and Health." Then in "Key to the Scriptures" Mary Baker Eddy applied the ideas from "Science and Health" to parts of the Christian *Bible*. The concluding "Fruitage" was compiled on the basis of earlier editions of "Science and Health," especially testimonies about the healing power of its ideas. *Science and Health with Key to the Scriptures* grew in stages from its first publication in 1875 until it reached its final form in 1910.

The Unification Church's *Divine Principle* has gone through three English-language editions since its first publication in 1959. The last of these, in 1996, is a much more fluent translation than the first two. However, these three editions are not just new translations of the Korean original; a few entire sections have been added or deleted, especially from the second to third edition. Because the Unification movement has no other scripture, this text shifts as the religion changes.

THE SCRIPTURE OF BAHA'I

The Essence of Baha'i Teaching and a Sketch of the Life of Baha'u'llah*

Here the last leader of the Baha'i movement gives its definitive teaching. He stresses the oneness of humanity under the oneness of God. This powerful vision for world harmony, written in the middle of the twentieth century, has become the leading characteristic of the Baha'i movement.[2]

The fundamental principle enunciated by Baha'u'llah . . . is that religious truth is not absolute but relative, that Divine Revelation is a continuous and progressive process, that all the great religions of the world are divine in origin, that their basic principles are in complete harmony, that their aims and purposes are one and the same. Their teachings are but facets of one truth, their functions are complementary, and they differ only in the nonessential aspects

---

*Shoghi Effendi, *The Promised Day Is Come*, Preface.
[2] All Baha'i writings are from the website Bahai-library.org. Copyright ©1996 National Spiritual Assembly of the Baha'is in the United States. Used by permission.

of their doctrines. Their missions represent successive stages in the spiritual evolution of human society. . . .

His mission is to proclaim that the ages of the infancy and of the childhood of the human race are past. The convulsions associated with the present stage of its adolescence are slowly and painfully preparing it to attain the stage of manhood. They are heralding the approach of that Age of Ages when swords will be beaten into plowshares, when the Kingdom promised by Jesus Christ will have been established, and the peace of the planet definitely and permanently ensured. Baha'u'llah does not claim finality for his Revelation. Rather, he stipulates that he has been commissioned by the Almighty to vouchsafe to humanity a fuller measure of the truth, at so critical a juncture in its fortunes. It must be disclosed at future stages in the constant and limitless evolution of mankind.

The Baha'i Faith upholds the unity of God, recognizes the unity of God's prophets, and inculcates the principle of the oneness and wholeness of the entire human race. It proclaims the necessity and the inevitability of the unification of mankind, and asserts that it is gradually approaching. It claims that nothing short of the transmuting spirit of God, working through his chosen Mouthpiece in this day, can ultimately succeed in bringing it about. It enjoins upon its followers the primary duty of an unfettered search after truth, condemns all manner of prejudice and superstition, declares the purpose of religion to be the promotion of friendship and harmony, proclaims its essential harmony with science, and recognizes it as the foremost agency for the pacification and the orderly progress of human society. . . .

Mirza Husayn-'Ali, surnamed Baha'u'llah (the Glory of God), a native of Mazindaran, whose advent the Bab [Herald and Forerunner of Baha'u'llah] had foretold . . . was imprisoned in Teheran, Iran. He was banished in 1852 from his native land to Baghdad, and thence to Constantinople and Adrianople, and finally to the prison city of Akka, where he remained imprisoned for no less than twenty-four years, and in whose neighborhood he passed away in 1892. In the course of his banishment, and particularly in Adrianople and Akka, he formulated the laws and ordinances of his Dispensation and expounded, in over a hundred volumes, the principles of his Faith. He proclaimed his Message to the kings and rulers of both the East and the West, both Christian and Muslim, addressed the Pope, the Caliph of Islam, the Chief Magistrates of the Republics of the American continent, the entire Christian clergy, the leaders of Shi'ite and Sunni Islam, and the high priests of the Zoroastrian religion. In these writings he proclaimed his Revelation, summoned those whom he addressed to heed his call and espouse his Faith, warned them of the consequences of their refusal, and denounced, in some cases, their arrogance and tyranny. . . .

The Faith that this order serves, safeguards, and promotes is essentially supernatural, supranational, entirely nonpolitical, and nonpartisan. It is diametrically opposed to any policy or school of thought that seeks to exalt any particular race, class, or nation. It is free from any form of ecclesiasticism, has neither priesthood nor rituals, and is supported exclusively by voluntary contributions made by its avowed adherents. Though loyal to their respective governments, though imbued with the love of their own country, and anxious to promote at all times its best interests, the followers of the Baha'i Faith view mankind as one entity and are profoundly attached to its vital interests. They will not hesitate to subordinate every particular interest, be it personal, regional, or national, to the overriding interests of the generality of mankind, knowing full well that in a world of interdependent peoples and nations the advantage of the part is best to be reached by the advantage of the whole. No lasting result can be achieved by any of the component parts if the general interests of the entity itself are neglected.

Baha'i, Islam, and Christianity*

The Bab ("Gate" to God) saw himself as the "hidden Imam" (leader) promised in Shi'ite Islam. In this selection from his writings, addressed to the shah (king) of Iran, the precursor of the faith deals with Muslim and Christian opposition and asserts the superiority of his faith to theirs. Notice how the style of the Bab's writings is very similar to the style of the Qur'an; *the chapter-and-verse references to the* Qur'an *are in the original.*

[1] All praise be to God Who has, through the power of Truth, sent down this Book unto his servant, that it may serve as a shining light for all mankind.... Verily this is none other than the sovereign Truth; it is the Path which God has laid out for all that are in heaven and on earth. Let him then who will, take for himself the right path unto his Lord.... This is indeed the eternal Truth that God, the Ancient of Days, has revealed unto his omnipotent Word—He Who has been raised up from the midst of the Burning Bush. This is the Mystery which has been hidden from all that are in heaven and on earth, and in this wondrous Revelation it has, in very truth, been set forth in the Mother Book by the hand of God, the Exalted.... O concourse of kings and of the sons of kings! Lay aside, one and all, your dominion which belongs to God.... Let not your sovereignty deceive you, O Shah, for "every soul shall taste of death," (*Qur'an* 3:182) and this, in very truth, has been written down as a decree of God.

[61] Verily, those who ridicule the wondrous, divine Verses revealed through his Remembrance are but making themselves the objects of ridicule, and We, in truth, aid them to grow in their iniquity. Indeed God's knowledge transcends all created things.... The infidels, of a truth, seek to separate God from his Remembrance, but God has determined to perfect his Light through his Remembrance, and indeed He is potent over all things....

Verily, Christ is Our Word that We communicated unto Mary; and let no one say what the Christians term as "the third of three" (*Qur'an* 5:77); it slanders the Remembrance Who ... is invested with supreme authority. Indeed God is but one God, and far be it from his glory that there should be anyone else besides Him. All those who shall attain unto Him on the Day of Resurrection are but his servants, and God is, of a truth, a sufficient Protector. Verily I am none other but the servant of God and his Word, and none but the first one to bow down in supplication before God, the Most Exalted; and indeed God witnesses all things.

[62] O people of the *Qur'an*! You are as nothing unless you submit unto the Remembrance of God and unto this Book. If you follow the Cause of God, We will forgive your sins; but if you turn aside from our command, We will, in truth, condemn your souls in Our Book unto the Most Great Fire. We, verily, do not deal unjustly with men, even to the extent of a speck on a date-stone.

---

*The Bab, *Qayyumu'l-Asma* 1, 61–62.

Baha'i Laws**

Baha'u'llah's Kitab-I-Aqdas *(Most Holy Book) is the most influential statement of Baha'i laws. Reflecting the Muslim background of this new religious movement, great emphasis is placed on knowing and obeying God's laws. The sections given here include treatment of prayer (12–14), fasting (16), pilgrimage (32), criminals (45), marriage (65), scripture (149–150), and a single language for the world (189).*

**Baha'u'llah, *Kitab-I-Aqdas* 1–2, 12–14, 16, 30–34, 45, 63–65, 149–150, 189.

In the name of him who is the supreme ruler over all that has been and all that is to be! The first duty prescribed by God for his servants is the recognition of Him Who is the Dayspring of his Revelation and the Fountain of his laws, Who represents the Godhead in both the Kingdom of his Cause and the world of creation. Whoever achieves this duty has attained unto all good; and whoever is deprived thereof has gone astray, though he be the author of every righteous deed. Every one who reaches this most sublime station, this summit of transcendent glory, must observe every ordinance of him. . . .

[2] They whom God has endued with insight will readily recognize that the precepts laid down by God constitute the highest means for the maintenance of order in the world and the security of its peoples. He who turns away from them is accounted among the abject and foolish. We have commanded you to refuse the dictates of your evil passions and corrupt desires, and not to transgress the bounds that the Pen of the Most High has fixed, for these are the breath of life unto all created things. The seas of Divine wisdom and Divine utterance have risen under the breath of the breeze of the All-Merciful. Hasten to drink your fill, O men of understanding! They that have violated the Covenant of God by breaking his commandments, and have turned back on their heels, these have erred grievously in the sight of God, the All-Possessing, the Most High. . . .

[12] It has been ordained that obligatory prayer is to be performed by each of you individually. Except for the Prayer for the Dead, the practice of congregational prayer has been annulled. He is truly the Ordainer, the All-Wise. God has exempted women who are in their monthly courses from obligatory prayer and fasting. Let them, instead, after performance of their washings, give praise unto God, repeating ninety-five times between the noon of one day and the next, "Glorified be God, the Lord of Splendor and Beauty." Thus has it been decreed in the Book, if you are of them that comprehend. When traveling, if you should stop and rest in some safe spot, perform—men and women alike—a single prostration in place of each unsaid Obligatory Prayer. While prostrating say, "Glorified be God, the Lord of Might and Majesty, of Grace and Bounty." Whoever is unable to do this, let him say only "Glorified be God." . . . Thus the Lord makes plain the ways of truth and guidance, ways that lead to one way, which is this Straight Path. . . .

[16] O Pen of the Most High! Say: People of the world! We have enjoined upon you fasting during a brief period, and at its close have designated for you Naw-Rúz as a feast. . . . It befits the people of Baha'i, throughout these days [that precede the fast], to provide good cheer for themselves, their kindred and, beyond them, the poor and needy, and with joy and exultation to hail and glorify their Lord, to sing his praise and magnify his Name. When they end this, let them begin the fast. . . . The traveler, the ailing, those who are with child, are not bound by the Fast. They have been exempted by God as a token of his grace. . . .

[30] The Lord has ordained that in every city a House of Justice be established wherein shall gather counselors. . . . They should consider themselves as entering the Court of the presence of God, the Exalted, the Most High, and as beholding Him who is unseen. They should be the trusted ones of the Merciful among men, and regard themselves as the guardians appointed of God for all that dwell on earth. It is incumbent upon them to take counsel together and to have regard for the interests of the servants of God, for his sake, even as they regard their own interests, and to choose that which is fitting and proper. . . .

O people of the world! Build houses of worship throughout the lands in the name of him who is the Lord of all religions. Make them as perfect as is possible and adorn them with that which befits them, not with images and effigies. Then, with radiance and joy, celebrate in them the praise of your Lord, the Most Compassionate. Truly, by his remembrance the eye is cheered and the heart is filled with light.

The Lord has ordained that those of you who are able shall make pilgrimage to the sacred House, and from this he has exempted women as a mercy on his part. He is truly All-Bountiful, the Most Generous. . . .

Whoever lays claim to a Revelation direct from God, before the expiration of a full thousand years, such a man is assuredly a lying impostor. We pray God that he may graciously assist him to retract and repudiate such claim. Should he repent, God will, no doubt, forgive him. If, however, he persists in error, God will certainly send down one who will deal mercilessly with him. Terrible, indeed, is God in punishing! Whoever interprets this verse otherwise than its obvious meaning is deprived of the Spirit of God and of his mercy which encompasses all created things. Fear God, and follow not your idle fancies. Nay, rather, follow the bidding of your Lord, the Almighty, the All-Wise. Before long clamorous voices will be raised in most lands. Shun them, O My people, and follow not the iniquitous and evil-hearted. . . .

[45] Exile and imprisonment are decreed for the thief, and, on the third offense, place a mark upon his forehead so that, thus identified, he may not be accepted in the cities of God and His countries. Beware lest, through compassion, you neglect to carry out the statutes of the religion of God; do that which has been bidden you by God who is compassionate and merciful. We school you with the rod of wisdom and laws, like the father who educates his son, and this for naught but the protection of your own selves and the elevation of your stations. . . .

[63] God has prescribed marriage for you. Beware that you take not unto yourselves more wives than two.[3] When someone contents himself with a single partner from among the women who serve God, both he and she shall live in tranquillity. He who would take into his service a[nother] young woman may do so with propriety. Such is the ordinance which, in truth and justice, has been recorded by the Pen of Revelation. . . . Marriage is dependent upon the consent of both parties. Desiring to establish love, unity, and harmony among Our servants, We have conditioned it, once the couple's wish is known, upon the permission of their parents, lest enmity and rancor should arise among them. In this We have yet other purposes. Thus has Our commandment been ordained. . . .

[149] Recite the verses of God every morning and evening. Whoever fails to recite them has not been faithful to the Covenant of God and his Testament, and whoever turns away from these holy verses in this Day is of those who throughout eternity have turned away from God. Fear God, O My servants, one and all. Pride not yourselves on much reading of the verses or on a multitude of pious acts by night and day; for were a man to read a single verse with joy and radiance it would be better for him than to read with lassitude all the Holy Books of God, the Help in Peril, the Self-Subsisting. . . . Lay not upon your souls that which will weary them and weigh them down, but rather what will lighten and uplift them, so that they may soar on the wings of the Divine verses toward the Dawning-place of his manifest signs; this will draw you nearer to God. [150] Teach your children the verses revealed from the heaven of majesty and power, so that, in most melodious tones, they may recite the Tablets of the All Merciful. . . .

[189] O members of parliaments throughout the world! Select a single language for the use of all on earth, and adopt likewise a common script. . . . This will be the cause of unity, if you could only comprehend it, and the greatest instrument for promoting harmony and civilization. Would that you might understand!

---

[3] *more wives than two:* Islam permits three at most.

Baha'i Prayers*

The Short Obligatory (required) Prayer is for use at any time. The Medium Obligatory Prayer is to be recited three times a day—at morning, noon, and evening. Its italics indicate directions for prayer. The Prayer for America was written when Baha'i leaders visited the United States early in the twentieth century.

[Short Obligatory Prayer] I bear witness, O my God, that Thou hast created me to know Thee and to worship Thee. I testify, at this moment, to my powerlessness and to Thy might, to my poverty and to Thy wealth. There is none other God but Thee, the Help in Peril, the Self-Subsisting.

[Medium Obligatory Prayer] *Whoever wishes to pray, let him wash his hands, and while he washes, let him say:*

Strengthen my hand, O my God, that it may take hold of Thy Book with such steadfastness that the hosts of the world shall have no power over it. Guard it, then, from meddling with whatsoever doth not belong unto it. Thou art, verily, the Almighty, the Most Powerful. I have turned my face unto Thee, O my Lord! Illumine it with the light of Thy countenance. Protect it, then, from turning to anyone but Thee.

Then let him stand up, and facing the Qiblih [Point of Adoration], let him say:

God testifies that there is no other God but Him. His are the kingdoms of Revelation and of creation. He, in truth, has manifested Him Who is the Dayspring of Revelation, Who conversed on Sinai, through Whom the Supreme Horizon has been made to shine, and the [boundary] beyond which there is no passing has spoken, and through Whom the call has been proclaimed unto all who are in heaven and on earth: "Lo, the All-Possessing is come. Earth and heaven, glory and dominion are God's, the Lord of all men, and the Possessor of the Throne on high and of earth below!"

Let him, then, bend down, with hands resting on the knees, and say:

Exalted art Thou above my praise and the praise of anyone beside me, above my description and the description of all who are in heaven and all who are on earth!

Then, standing with open hands, palms upward toward the face, let him say:

Disappoint not, O my God, him that has, with beseeching fingers, clung to the hem of Thy mercy and Thy grace, O Thou Who of those who show mercy art the Most Merciful!

Let him, then, be seated and say:

I bear witness to Thy unity and Thy oneness, and that Thou art God, and that there is none other God beside Thee. Thou hast, verily, revealed thy Cause, fulfilled Thy Covenant, and opened wide the door of Thy grace to all that dwell in heaven and on earth. Blessing and peace, salutation and glory, rest upon Thy loved ones, whom the changes and chances of the world have not deterred from turning unto Thee, and who have given their all, in the hope of obtaining that which is with Thee. Thou art, in truth, the Ever-Forgiving, the All-Bountiful.

[Prayer for America] O Thou kind Lord! This gathering is turning to Thee. These hearts are radiant with Thy love. These minds and spirits are exhilarated by the message of Thy glad tidings. O God! Let this American democracy become glorious in spiritual degrees even as it has aspired to material degrees, and render this just government victorious. Confirm this revered nation to upraise the standard of the oneness of humanity, to promulgate the Most Great Peace, to become thereby most glorious and praiseworthy among all the nations of the world. O God! This American nation is worthy of Thy favors and is deserving of Thy mercy. Make it precious and near to Thee through Thy bounty and bestowal.

---

*Short Obligatory Prayer, Medium Obligatory Prayer, Prayer for America.

THE SCRIPTURE OF THE CHURCH OF JESUS CHRIST OF LATTER-DAY SAINTS

Joseph Smith's Story*

This autobiographical account tells of Joseph Smith's first vision and angelic visitation, discovery of the Book of Mormon, *and the founding of the church. As the first paragraph indicates, the experience of his vision and conversion was the most contentious point with his opponents, and it continues to be so today.*[4]

Owing to the many reports which have been put in circulation by evil-disposed and designing persons, in relation to the rise and progress of the Church of Jesus Christ of Latter-day Saints, all of which have been designed by the authors thereof to militate against its character as a Church and its progress in the world—I have been induced to write this history, to disabuse the public mind, and put all inquirers after truth in possession of the facts, as they have transpired, in relation both to myself and the Church, so far as I have such facts in my possession. In this history I shall present the various events in relation to this Church, in truth and righteousness, as they have transpired, or as they at present exist, being now [1838] the eighth year since the organization of the said Church.

I was born in the year of our Lord 1805, on the twenty-third day of December, in the town of Sharon, Windsor county, State of Vermont. . . . My father, Joseph Smith, Senior, left the State of Vermont, and moved to Palmyra, in the State of New York, when I was in my tenth year, or thereabouts. In about four years after my father's arrival in Palmyra, he moved with his family into Manchester in the same county of Ontario. . . . [5] Some time in the second year after our removal to Manchester, there was in the place where we lived an unusual excitement on the subject of religion. It commenced with the Methodists, but soon became general among all the sects in that region of country. Indeed, the whole district or county seemed affected by it, and great multitudes united themselves to the different religious parties, which created no small stir and division amongst the people, some crying, "Lo, here!" and others, "Lo, there!" Some were contending for the Methodist faith, some for the Presbyterian, and some for the Baptist. . . .

I was at this time in my fifteenth year. My father's family was proselyted to the Presbyterian faith, and four of them joined that church, namely, my mother, Lucy; my brothers Hyrum and Samuel Harrison; and my sister Sophronia. During this time of great excitement my mind was called up to serious reflection and great uneasiness; but though my feelings were deep and often poignant, still I kept myself aloof from all these parties, though I attended their several meetings as often as occasion would permit. In process of time my mind became somewhat partial to the Methodist sect, and I felt some desire to be united with them; but so great were the confusion and strife among the different denominations, that it was impossible for a person young as I was, and so unacquainted with men and things, to come to any certain conclusion who was right and who was wrong . . . . [10] In the midst of this war of words and tumult of opinions, I often said to myself: What is to be done? Who of all these parties are right; or, are they all wrong together? If any one of them be right, which is it, and how shall I know it? . . .

Pearl of Great Price, Joseph Smith—History 1, 1–22, 25–35, 40–47, 59–62, 67–74.

[4] All excerpts from Mormon scriptures are from "The Scriptures—Internet Edition" (http://www.scriptures.lds.org). Copyright © 2000 Intellectual Reserve, Inc. All rights reserved. Used by permission.

So, in accordance with this, my determination to ask of God, I retired to the woods to make the attempt. It was on the morning of a beautiful, clear day, early in the spring of eighteen hundred and twenty. It was the first time in my life that I had made such an attempt, for amidst all my anxieties I had never as yet made the attempt to pray vocally. [15] After I had retired to the place where I had previously designed to go, having looked around me, and finding myself alone, I kneeled down and began to offer up the desires of my heart to God. I had scarcely done so, when immediately I was seized upon by some power which entirely overcame me, and had such an astonishing influence over me as to bind my tongue so that I could not speak. Thick darkness gathered around me, and it seemed to me for a time as if I were doomed to sudden destruction. But, exerting all my powers to call upon God to deliver me out of the power of this enemy which had seized upon me, and at the very moment when I was ready to sink into despair and abandon myself to destruction . . . just at this moment of great alarm, I saw a pillar of light exactly over my head, above the brightness of the sun, which descended gradually until it fell upon me. It no sooner appeared than I found myself delivered from the enemy which held me bound. When the light rested upon me I saw two Personages, whose brightness and glory defy all description, standing above me in the air. One of them spake unto me, calling me by name and said, pointing to the other—"This is My Beloved Son. Hear Him!"

My object in going to inquire of the Lord was to know which of all the sects was right, that I might know which to join. No sooner, therefore, did I get possession of myself, so as to be able to speak, than I asked the Personages who stood above me in the light, which of all the sects was right (for at this time it had never entered into my heart that all were wrong)—and which I should join. I was answered that I must join none of them, for they were all wrong; and the Personage who addressed me said that all their creeds were an abomination in his sight; that those adherents were all corrupt; that: "they draw near to me with their lips, but their hearts are far from me, they teach for doctrines the commandments of men, having a form of godliness, but they deny the power thereof." [20] He again forbade me to join with any of them; and many other things did he say unto me, which I cannot write at this time. When I came to myself again, I found myself lying on my back, looking up into heaven. When the light had departed, I had no strength; but soon recovering in some degree, I went home. And as I leaned up to the fireplace, mother inquired what the matter was. I replied, "Never mind, all is well—I am well enough off." I then said to my mother, "I have learned for myself that Presbyterianism is not true."

It seems as though the adversary was aware, at a very early period of my life, that I was destined to prove a disturber and an annoyer of his kingdom; else why should the powers of darkness combine against me? . . . [25] [M]y telling the story had excited a great deal of prejudice against me among adherents of religion, and was the cause of great persecution, which continued to increase; and though I was an obscure boy, only between fourteen and fifteen years of age, and my circumstances in life such as to make a boy of no consequence in the world, yet men of high standing would take notice sufficient to excite the public mind against me, and create a bitter persecution; and this was common among all the sects—all united to persecute me. . . .

[O]n the evening of the twenty-first of September, after I had retired to my bed for the night, I betook myself to prayer and supplication to Almighty God for forgiveness of all my sins and follies, and also for a manifestation to me, that I might know of my state and standing before him. I had full confidence in obtaining a divine manifestation, as I previously had one. [30] While I was thus in the act of calling upon God, I discovered a light appearing in my room, which continued to increase until the room was lighter than at noonday, when immediately a personage appeared at my bedside, standing in the air, for his feet did not touch the floor. . . . When I first looked upon him, I was afraid; but the fear soon left me. He called me by name, and said unto me that he was a messenger sent from the presence of God to me, and that his name was Moroni; that God had a work for me to do; and that my name should be had for good and evil among all nations, kindreds, and tongues, or that it should be both good and evil spoken of among all people. He said there was a book deposited, written upon gold plates, giving an account of the former inhabitants of this continent, and the source from whence they sprang. He also said that the fullness of the everlasting Gospel was contained in it, as delivered by the Savior to the ancient inhabitants; [35] also, that there were two stones in silver bows—and these stones, fastened to a breastplate, constituted what is called the Urim and Thummim[5]—deposited with the plates; and the possession and use of these stones were what constituted "seers" in ancient or former times; and that God had prepared them for the purpose of translating the book. . . . [40] Again, he told me that when I got those plates of which he had spoken—for the time that they should be obtained was not yet fulfilled—I should not show them to any person; neither the breastplate with the Urim and Thummim; only to those to whom I should be commanded to show them; if I did I should be destroyed. While he was conversing with me about the plates, the vision was opened to my mind that I could see the place where the plates were deposited, and that so clearly and distinctly that I knew the place again when I visited it. . . .

[59] At length the time arrived for obtaining the plates, the Urim and Thummim, and the breastplate. On the twenty-second day of September, 1827, having gone as usual at the end of another year to the place where they were deposited, the same heavenly messenger delivered them up to me with this charge: that I should be responsible for them; that if I should let them go carelessly, or through any neglect of mine, I should be cut off; but that if I would use all my endeavors to preserve them, until he, the messenger, should call for them, they should be protected. [60] I soon found out the reason why I had received such strict charges to keep them safe, and why it was that the messenger had said that when I had done what was required at my hand, he would call for them. For no sooner was it known that I had them, than the most strenuous exertions were used to get them from me. Every stratagem that could be invented was resorted to for that purpose. The persecution became more bitter and severe than before, and multitudes were on the alert continually to get them from me if possible. But by the wisdom of God, they remained safe in my hands, until I had accomplished by them what was required at my hand. When, according to arrangements, the messenger called for them, I delivered them up to him; and he has them in his charge until this day, being the second day of May, 1838. . . .

[67] We still continued the work of translation, when, in the ensuing month (May, 1829), we on a certain day went into the woods to pray and inquire of the Lord respecting baptism for the remission of sins, that we found mentioned in the translation of the plates. While we were thus employed, praying and calling upon the Lord, a messenger from heaven descended in a cloud of light, and having laid his hands upon us, he ordained us, saying: "Upon you my fellow servants, in the name of Messiah, I confer the Priesthood of Aaron, which holds the keys of the ministering of angels, and of the gospel of repentance, and of baptism by immersion for the remission of sins; and this shall never be taken again from the earth until the sons of Levi do offer again an offering unto the Lord in

---

[5] *Urim and Thummim:* a device consulted by the chief priest of ancient Israel to determine God's response to a yes-or-no question. The Hebrew scriptures do not specify how the device is used; Joseph Smith here uses it as "seer stones" for translating the *Book of Mormon.*

righteousness." [70] He said this Aaronic Priesthood had not the power of laying on hands for the gift of the Holy Ghost, but that this should be conferred on us hereafter; and he commanded us to go and be baptized, and gave us directions that I should baptize Oliver Cowdery, and that afterwards he should baptize me. Accordingly we went and were baptized. I baptized him first, and afterwards he baptized me—after which I laid my hands upon his head and ordained him to the Aaronic Priesthood, and afterwards he laid his hands on me and ordained me to the same Priesthood—for so we were commanded. The messenger who visited us on this occasion and conferred this Priesthood upon us, said that his name was John, the same that is called John the Baptist in the New Testament, and that he acted under the direction of Peter, James, and John, who held the keys of the Priesthood of Melchizedek, which Priesthood, he said, would in due time be conferred on us, and that I should be called the first Elder of the Church, and he (Oliver Cowdery) the second. It was on the fifteenth day of May, 1829, that we were ordained under the hand of this messenger, and baptized. Immediately on our coming up out of the water after we had been baptized, we experienced great and glorious blessings from our Heavenly Father. . . .

Our minds being now enlightened, we began to have the scriptures laid open to our understandings, and the true meaning and intention of their more mysterious passages revealed unto us in a manner which we never could attain to previously, nor ever before had thought of. In the meantime we were forced to keep secret the circumstances of having received the Priesthood and our having been baptized, owing to a spirit of persecution which had already manifested itself in the neighborhood.

The First Description of the *Book of Mormon**

The original title page of the Book of Mormon *(1830) has been printed in every succeeding edition. Written by Joseph Smith Jr., the title page serves as an apt description of the* Book of Mormon's *content. The original punctuation, replete with dashes, and original capitalization are presented here.*

THE BOOK OF MORMON, AN ACCOUNT WRITTEN BY THE HAND OF MORMON UPON PLATES TAKEN FROM THE PLATES OF NEPHI

Wherefore, it is an abridgment of the record of the people of Nephi, and also of the Lamanites—Written to the Lamanites, who are a remnant of the house of Israel; and also to Jew and Gentile—Written by way of commandment, and also by the spirit of prophecy and of revelation—Written and sealed up, and hid up unto the Lord, that they might not be destroyed—To come forth by the gift and power of God unto the interpretation thereof—Sealed by the hand of Moroni, and hid up unto the Lord, to come forth in due time by way of the Gentile—The interpretation thereof by the gift of God.

An abridgment taken from the Book of Ether also, which is a record of the people of Jared, who were scattered at the time the Lord confounded the language of the people, when they were building a tower to get to heaven—Which is to show unto the remnant of the House of Israel what great things the Lord has done for their fathers; and that they may know the covenants of the Lord, that they are not cast off forever—And also to the convincing of the

---

**Book of Mormon,* original title page.

Jew and Gentile that JESUS is the CHRIST, the ETERNAL GOD, manifesting himself unto all nations—And now, if there are faults they are the mistakes of men; wherefore, condemn not the things of God, that you may be found spotless at the judgment-seat of Christ.

TRANSLATED BY JOSEPH SMITH, JUNIOR.

The Coming of Jesus Christ in 34 C.E. to the New World*

This reading tells the story of the appearance of Jesus Christ, after his resurrection, to Americans descended from Israelite settlers. In this account, Jesus uses this appearance to teach the rudiments of true faith.

And now it came to pass that there were a great multitude gathered together, of the people of Nephi, round about the temple which was in the land Bountiful; and they were marveling and wondering one with another, and were showing one to another the great and marvelous change which had taken place. And they were also conversing about this Jesus Christ, of whom the sign had been given concerning his death. And it came to pass that while they were thus conversing one with another, they heard a voice as if it came out of heaven; and they cast their eyes round about, for they understood not the voice which they heard; and it was not a harsh voice, neither was it a loud voice; nevertheless, and notwithstanding it being a small voice it did pierce them that did hear to the center, insomuch that there was no part of their frame that it did not cause to quake; yea, it did pierce them to the very soul, and did cause their hearts to burn. And it came to pass that again they heard the voice, and they understood it not.

[5] And again the third time they did hear the voice, and did open their ears to hear it; and their eyes were towards the sound thereof; and they did look steadfastly towards heaven, from whence the sound came. And behold, the third time they did understand the voice which they heard; and it said unto them: "Behold my Beloved Son, in whom I am well pleased, in whom I have glorified my name—hear him." And it came to pass, as they understood they cast their eyes up again towards heaven; and behold, they saw a Man descending out of heaven; and he was clothed in a white robe; and he came down and stood in the midst of them; and the eyes of the whole multitude were turned upon him, and they dared not open their mouths, even one to another, and knew not what it meant, for they thought it was an angel that had appeared unto them. And it came to pass that he stretched forth his hand and spake unto the people, saying: [10] "Behold, I am Jesus Christ, whom the prophets testified shall come into the world. And behold, I am the light and the life of the world; and I have drunk out of that bitter cup which the Father has given me, and have glorified the Father in taking upon me the sins of the world, in the which I have suffered the will of the Father in all things from the beginning." And it came to pass that when Jesus had spoken these words the whole multitude fell to the earth; for they remembered that it had been prophesied among them that Christ should show himself unto them after his ascension into heaven. . . .

[31] "Behold, verily, verily, I say unto you, I will declare unto you my doctrine. And this is my doctrine, and it is the doctrine which the Father has given unto me; and I bear record of

---

*Book of Mormon, 3 Nephi 11.1–41.

the Father, and the Father beareth record of me, and the Holy Ghost beareth record of the Father and me; and I bear record that the Father commandeth all men, everywhere, to repent and believe in me. And whoso believeth in me, and is baptized, the same shall be saved; and they are they who shall inherit the kingdom of God. And whoso believeth not in me, and is not baptized, shall be damned. [35] Verily, verily, I say unto you, that this is my doctrine, and I bear record of it from the Father; and whoso believeth in me believeth in the Father also; and unto him will the Father bear record of me, for he will visit him with fire and with the Holy Ghost. And thus will the Father bear record of me, and the Holy Ghost will bear record unto him of the Father and me; for the Father, and I, and the Holy Ghost are one. And again I say unto you, you must repent, and become as a little child, and be baptized in my name, or you can in nowise receive these things. . . . Therefore, go forth unto this people, and declare the words which I have spoken, unto the ends of the earth."

Destruction of the Nephites and Burial of the Golden Plates*

The Book of Mormon *relates how the tribe of Nephites was destroyed in warfare in 385* C.E. *by their enemies the Lamanites. Approximately twenty years later, the prophet Moroni, Mormon's son, buried the golden plates of scripture in the Hill Cumorah, outside of what is now Palmyra in upstate New York.*

Now I finish my record concerning the destruction of my people, the Nephites. And it came to pass that we did march forth before the Lamanites. And I, Mormon, wrote an epistle unto the king of the Lamanites, and desired of him that he would grant unto us that we might gather together our people unto the land of Cumorah, by a hill which was called Cumorah, and there we could give them battle. And it came to pass that the king of the Lamanites did grant unto me the thing which I desired. . . .

[6] And it came to pass that when we had gathered in all our people in one to the land of Cumorah, behold I, Mormon, began to be old. Knowing it to be the last struggle of my people, and having been commanded of the Lord that I should not suffer the records which had been handed down by our fathers, which were sacred, to fall into the hands of the Lamanites (for the Lamanites would destroy them), therefore I made this record out of the plates of Nephi, and hid up in the hill Cumorah all the records which had been entrusted to me by the hand of the Lord, save it were these few plates which I gave unto my son Moroni. And it came to pass that my people, with their wives and their children, did now behold the armies of the Lamanites marching towards them; and with that awful fear of death which fills the breasts of all the wicked, did they await to receive them.

And it came to pass that they came to battle against us, and every soul was filled with terror because of the greatness of their numbers. And it came to pass that they did fall upon my people with the sword, and with the bow, and with the arrow, and with the ax, and with all manner of weapons of war. [10] And it came to pass that my men were hewn down, yea, even my ten thousand who were with me, and I fell wounded in the midst; and they passed by me that they did not put an end to my life.

And when they had gone through and hewn down all my people save it were twenty and four of us, (among whom was my son Moroni) and we having survived the dead of our people, did behold on the morrow, when the Lamanites had returned unto their camps, from the top of

---

*Book of Mormon, Mormon 6:1–3, 6–11, 16–22.

the hill Cumorah, the ten thousand of my people who were hewn down, being led in the front by me. . . .

[16] And my soul was rent with anguish, because of the slaying of my people, and I cried: "O you fair ones, how could you have departed from the ways of the Lord! O you fair ones, how could you have rejected that Jesus, who stood with open arms to receive you! Behold, if you had not done this, you would not have fallen. But behold, you are fallen, and I mourn your loss. O you fair sons and daughters, you fathers and mothers, you husbands and wives, you fair ones, how is it that you could have fallen! [20] But behold, you are gone, and my sorrows cannot bring your return. And the day soon cometh that your mortal body must put on immortality, and these bodies which are now moldering in corruption must soon become incorruptible bodies; and then you must stand before the judgment-seat of Christ, to be judged according to your works; and if it so be that you are righteous, then are you blessed with your fathers who have gone before you. O that you had repented before this great destruction had come upon you. But behold, you are gone, and the Father, yea, the Eternal Father of heaven, knoweth your state; and he doeth with you according to his justice and mercy."

Preparations for the Trek to Utah*

The following account outlines some of the well-planned provisions, both physical and spiritual, for the Latter-day Saints' trek in 1847–1848 from Missouri to the Great Salt Lake basin of northern Utah. After years of persecution in New York, Ohio, Illinois, and Missouri, church leaders wanted to move to a location that was promising enough to support their growing community but not so promising as to attract non–Latter-day Saint settlers. The trek was planned and led by Brigham Young, who succeeded the martyred Joseph Smith.

The Word and Will of the Lord concerning the Camp of Israel in their journeys to the West: Let all the people of the Church of Jesus Christ of Latter-day Saints, and those who journey with them, be organized into companies, with a covenant and promise to keep all the commandments and statutes of the Lord our God. Let the companies be organized with captains of hundreds, captains of fifties, and captains of tens, with a president and his two counselors at their head, under the direction of the Twelve Apostles. And this shall be our covenant—that we will walk in all the ordinances of the Lord.

[5] Let each company provide themselves with all the teams, wagons, provisions, clothing, and other necessaries for the journey, that they can. When the companies are organized let them go to with their might, to prepare for those who are to tarry. Let each company, with their captains and presidents, decide how many can go next spring; then choose out a sufficient number of able-bodied and expert men, to take teams, seeds, and farming utensils, to go as pioneers to prepare for putting in spring crops. Let each company bear an equal proportion, according to the dividend of their property, in taking the poor, the widows, the fatherless, and the families of those who have gone into the army, that the cries of the widow and the fatherless come not up into the ears of the Lord against this people. Let each company prepare houses, and fields for raising grain, for those who are to remain behind this season; and this is the will of the Lord concerning his people.

[10] Let every man use all his influence and property to remove this people to the place

---

*Doctrine and Covenants 136.1–11, 17–24, 30–42.

where the Lord shall locate a stake of Zion. And if you do this with a pure heart, in all faithfulness, you shall be blessed; you shall be blessed in your flocks, and in your herds, and in your fields, and in your houses, and in your families. . . . [17] Go thy way and do as I have told you, and fear not thine enemies; for they shall not have power to stop my work. Zion shall be redeemed in mine own due time. And if any man shall seek to build up himself, and seeketh not my counsel, he shall have no power, and his folly shall be made manifest.

[20] Seek ye; and keep all your pledges one with another; and covet not that which is thy brother's. Keep yourselves from evil to take the name of the Lord in vain, for I am the Lord your God, even the God of your fathers, the God of Abraham and of Isaac and of Jacob. I am he who led the children of Israel out of the land of Egypt; and my arm is stretched out in the last days, to save my people Israel. Cease to contend one with another; cease to speak evil one of another. Cease drunkenness; and let your words tend to edifying one another. . . . [30] Fear not thine enemies, for they are in mine hands and I will do my pleasure with them. My people must be tried in all things, that they may be prepared to receive the glory that I have for them, even the glory of Zion; and he that will not bear chastisement is not worthy of my kingdom.

Let him that is ignorant learn wisdom by humbling himself and calling upon the Lord his God, that his eyes may be opened that he may see, and his ears opened that he may hear; for my Spirit is sent forth into the world to enlighten the humble and contrite, and to the condemnation of the ungodly. Thy brethren have rejected you and your testimony, even the nation that has driven you out. [35] And now cometh the day of their calamity, even the days of sorrow, like a woman that is taken in travail; and their sorrow shall be great unless they speedily repent, yea, very speedily. For they killed the prophets, and them that were sent unto them; and they have shed innocent blood, which crieth from the ground against them. Therefore, marvel not at these things, for you are not yet pure. You cannot yet bear my glory, but you shall behold it if you are faithful in keeping all my words that I have given you, from the days of Adam to Abraham, from Abraham to Moses, from Moses to Jesus and his apostles, and from Jesus and his apostles to Joseph Smith, whom I did call upon by mine angels, my ministering servants, and by mine own voice out of the heavens, to bring forth my work; which foundation he did lay, and was faithful; and I took him to myself. Many have marveled because of his death; but it was needful that he should seal his testimony with his blood, that he might be honored and the wicked might be condemned.

[40] Have I not delivered you from your enemies, only in that I have left a witness of my name? Now, therefore, hearken, O you people of my church; and you elders listen together; you have received my kingdom. Be diligent in keeping all my commandments, lest judgments come upon you, and your faith fail you, and your enemies triumph over you. So no more at present. Amen and Amen.

The Essence of Latter-day Saint Teaching*

This short statement, written and signed by Joseph Smith, shows in its main points how Latter-day Saint teaching both agrees with, and departs from, mainstream Christian teaching. Notice that point 11 asserts the right to practice the faith as believers see fit but point 12 asserts the duty to be obedient to political authorities.

---

*Pearl of Great Price, Articles of Faith 1–13.

1. We believe in God, the Eternal Father, and in His Son, Jesus Christ, and in the Holy Ghost.

2. We believe that men will be punished for their own sins, and not for Adam's transgression.

3. We believe that through the Atonement of Christ, all mankind may be saved, by obedience to the laws and ordinances of the Gospel.

4. We believe that the first principles and ordinances of the Gospel are: first, Faith in the Lord Jesus Christ; second, Repentance; third, Baptism by immersion for the remission of sins; fourth, Laying on of hands for the gift of the Holy Ghost.

5. We believe that a man must be called of God, by prophecy, and by the laying on of hands by those who are in authority, to preach the Gospel and administer in the ordinances thereof.

6. We believe in the same organization that existed in the Primitive Church, namely, apostles, prophets, pastors, teachers, evangelists, and so forth.

7. We believe in the gift of tongues, prophecy, revelation, visions, healing, interpretation of tongues, and so forth.

8. We believe the *Bible* to be the word of God as far as it is translated correctly; we also believe the *Book of Mormon* to be the word of God.

9. We believe all that God has revealed, all that He does now reveal, and we believe that He will yet reveal many great and important things pertaining to the Kingdom of God.

10. We believe in the literal gathering of Israel and in the restoration of the Ten Tribes; that Zion (the New Jerusalem) will be built upon the American continent; that Christ will reign personally upon the earth; and, that the earth will be renewed and receive its paradisiacal glory.

11. We claim the privilege of worshiping Almighty God according to the dictates of our own conscience, and allow all men the same privilege, let them worship how, where, or what they may.

12. We believe in being subject to kings, presidents, rulers, and magistrates, in obeying, honoring, and sustaining the law.

13. We believe in being honest, true, chaste, benevolent, virtuous, and in doing good to all men. . . . If there is anything virtuous, lovely, or of good report or praiseworthy, we seek after these things.

Church Pronouncements on Polygamy and Men of African Descent*

In the early years of the Latter-day Saint church, one of the most controversial practices was polygamy, which continues to this day among some splinter groups in Utah. In the middle of the twentieth century, especially as the church grew in the developing world, its prohibition on admitting Africans and men of African descent to the priesthood became controversial. The Official Declaration of 1890 reasserts the church's official disavowal of polygamy even as it admits that polygamy is still occurring to some degree; it is accompanied by an anguished letter on this change by the church's president, Wilford Woodruff. The Official Declaration of 1978 is an open letter to the church from Spencer Kimball, N. Eldon Tanner, and Marion G. Romney allowing all "worthy male members," including Africans and men of African descent, to be ordained as Mormon priests. These revisions of the teaching of the church are based on revelations to the church presidents of the time.

[Official Declaration of 1890] Press dispatches having been sent for political purposes, from Salt Lake City, which have been widely published, to the effect that the Utah Commission, in their

---

*Doctrine and Covenants, Official Declarations of 1890 and 1978.

recent report to the Secretary of the Interior, allege that plural marriages are still being solemnized and that forty or more such marriages have been contracted in Utah since last June or during the past year, also that in public discourses the leaders of the Church have taught, encouraged and urged the continuance of the practice of polygamy—

I, therefore, as President of the Church of Jesus Christ of Latter-day Saints, do hereby, in the most solemn manner, declare that these charges are false. We are not teaching polygamy or plural marriage, nor permitting any person to enter into its practice, and I deny that either forty or any other number of plural marriages have during that period been solemnized in our Temples or in any other place in the Territory. One case has been reported, in which the parties allege that the marriage was performed in the Endowment House, in Salt Lake City, in the Spring of 1889, but I have not been able to learn who performed the ceremony; whatever was done in this matter was without my knowledge. In consequence of this alleged occurrence the Endowment House was, by my instructions, taken down without delay.

Inasmuch as laws have been enacted by Congress forbidding plural marriages, which laws have been pronounced constitutional by the court of last resort, I hereby declare my intention to submit to those laws, and to use my influence with the members of the Church over which I preside to have them do likewise.

There is nothing in my teachings to the Church or in those of my associates, during the time specified, which can be reasonably construed to inculcate or encourage polygamy; and when any Elder of the Church has used language which appeared to convey any such teaching, he has been promptly reproved. And I now publicly declare that my advice to the Latter-day Saints is to refrain from contracting any marriage forbidden by the law of the land.

WILFORD WOODRUFF
President of the Church of Jesus Christ of Latter-day Saints

[Excerpts from a letter by President Wilford Woodruff regarding the Official Declaration of 1890] The question is this: Which is the wisest course for the Latter-day Saints to pursue—to continue to attempt to practice plural marriage, with the laws of the nation against it and the opposition of sixty millions of people, and at the cost of the confiscation and loss of all the Temples, and the stopping of all the ordinances therein, both for the living and the dead, and the imprisonment of the First Presidency and Twelve and the heads of families in the Church, and the confiscation of personal property of the people (all of which of themselves would stop the practice); or, after doing and suffering what we have through our adherence to this principle to cease the practice and submit to the law, and through doing so leave the Prophets, Apostles and fathers at home, so that they can instruct the people and attend to the duties of the Church, and also leave the Temples in the hands of the Saints, so that they can attend to the ordinances of the Gospel, both for the living and the dead?

The Lord showed me by vision and revelation exactly what would take place if we did not stop this practice. If we had not stopped it . . . all ordinances would be stopped. . . . Confusion would reign . . . , and many men would be made prisoners. This trouble would have come upon the whole Church, and we should have been compelled to stop the practice. Now, the question is, whether it should be stopped in this manner, or in the way the Lord has manifested to us, and leave our Prophets and Apostles and fathers free men, and the temples in the hands of the people, so that the dead may be redeemed. A large number has already been delivered from the prison house in the spirit world by this people,[6] and shall the work go on or stop? . . . I say to you that that is exactly the condition we as a people would have been in had we not taken the course we have. . . .

---

[6] *A large number . . . people:* a reference to baptism for the dead done by Latter-day Saints, allowing them entrance into heaven.

I saw exactly what would come to pass if there was not something done. I have had this spirit upon me for a long time. But I want to say this: I should have let all the temples go out of our hands; I should have gone to prison myself, and let every other man go there, had not the God of heaven commanded me to do what I did do; and when the hour came that I was commanded to do that, it was all clear to me. I went before the Lord, and I wrote what the Lord told me to write. . . . I leave this with you, for you to contemplate and consider. The Lord is at work with us.

[Official Declaration of June 8, 1978] To all general and local priesthood officers of the Church of Jesus Christ of Latter-day Saints throughout the world:

As we have witnessed the expansion of the work of the Lord over the earth, we have been grateful that people of many nations have responded to the message of the restored gospel, and have joined the Church in ever-increasing numbers. This, in turn, has inspired us with a desire to extend to every worthy member of the Church all of the privileges and blessings which the gospel affords.

Aware of the promises made by the prophets and presidents of the Church who have preceded us that at some time, in God's eternal plan, all of our brethren who are worthy may receive the priesthood, and witnessing the faithfulness of those from whom the priesthood has been withheld, we have pleaded long and earnestly in behalf of these, our faithful brethren, spending many hours in the Upper Room of the Temple supplicating the Lord for divine guidance.

He has heard our prayers, and by revelation has confirmed that the long-promised day has come when every faithful, worthy man in the Church may receive the holy priesthood, with power to exercise its divine authority, and enjoy with his loved ones every blessing that flows from it, including the blessings of the temple. Accordingly, all worthy male members of the Church may be ordained to the priesthood without regard for race or color. Priesthood leaders are instructed to follow the policy of carefully interviewing all candidates for ordination to either the Aaronic or the Melchizedek Priesthood to insure that they meet the established standards for worthiness.

We declare with soberness that the Lord has now made known his will for the blessing of all his children throughout the earth who will hearken to the voice of his authorized servants, and prepare themselves to receive every blessing of the gospel.

THE SCRIPTURE OF CHRISTIAN SCIENCE

Introduction to Christian Science Scripture and to the Work of Mary Baker Eddy*

This selection is Mary Baker Eddy's own autobiographical introduction to her main book. It also details the origin and development of this book, which shows a common feature of scriptures in the new religious movements: Their writing usually accompanies the religion's founding.[7]

To those leaning on the sustaining infinite, today is big with blessings. . . . The time for thinkers has come. Truth, independent of doctrines and time-honored systems, knocks at the portal of humanity. . . .

Since the author's discovery of the might of Truth in the treatment of disease as well as of sin,

---

Science and Health with Key to the Scriptures, Preface.
[7] All excerpts from *Science and Health with Key to the Scriptures* are taken from the 1917 edition (Boston: A.V. Stewart), which has the same wording and pagination as the edition currently in print.

her system has been fully tested and has not been found wanting; but to reach the heights of Christian Science, man must live in obedience to its divine Principle. To develop the full might of this Science, the discords of corporeal sense must yield to the harmony of spiritual sense, even as the science of music corrects false tones and gives sweet concord to sound. Theology and physics teach that both Spirit and matter are real and good, whereas the fact is that Spirit is good and real, and matter is Spirit's opposite. The question, What is Truth, is answered by demonstration, by healing both disease and sin; and this demonstration shows that Christian healing confers the most health and makes the best men. On this basis Christian Science will have a fair fight. Sickness has been combated for centuries by doctors using material remedies; but the question arises, Is there less sickness because of these practitioners? A vigorous "No" is the response. . . .

As early as 1862 [the author] began to write down and give to friends the results of her Scriptural study, for the Bible was her sole teacher; but these compositions were crude, the first steps of a child in the newly discovered world of Spirit. She also began to jot down her thoughts on the main subject, but these jottings were only infantile lispings of Truth. A child drinks in the outward world through the eyes and rejoices in the draught. He is as sure of the world's existence as he is of his own; yet he cannot describe the world. He finds a few words, and with these he stammeringly attempts to convey his feeling. Later, the tongue voices the more definite thought, though still imperfectly. So was it with the author. . . . Today, though rejoicing in some progress, she still finds herself a willing disciple at the heavenly gate, waiting for the Mind of Christ. . . .

Before writing this work, *Science and Health*, she made copious notes of Scriptural exposition, which have never been published. This was during the years 1867 and 1868. These efforts show her comparative ignorance of the stupendous life-problem up to that time, and the degrees by which she came at length to its solution. She values them as a parent may treasure the memorials of a child's growth, and she would not have them changed. The first edition of *Science and Health* was published in 1875. . . .

The divine Principle of healing is proved in the personal experience of any sincere seeker of Truth. Its purpose is good, and its practice is safer and more potent than that of any other sanitary method. The unbiased Christian thought is soonest touched by Truth, and convinced of it. . . . Many imagine that the phenomena of physical healing in Christian Science present only a phase of the action of the human mind, which action in some unexplained way results in the cure of disease. On the contrary, Christian Science rationally explains that all other pathological methods are the fruits of human faith in matter, faith in the workings, not of Spirit, but of the fleshly mind which must yield to Science. The physical healing of Christian Science results now, as in Jesus' time, from the operation of divine Principle, before which sin and disease lose their reality in human consciousness and disappear as naturally and as necessarily as darkness gives place to light and sin to reformation. Now, as then, these mighty works are not supernatural, but supremely natural. They are the sign of Immanuel, or "God with us," a divine influence ever present in human consciousness. . . .

When God called the author to proclaim His Gospel to this age, there came also the charge to plant and water His vineyard. The first school of Christian Science Mind-healing was started by the author with only one student in Lynn, Massachusetts, about the year 1867. In 1881, she opened the Massachusetts Metaphysical College in Boston, under the seal of the Commonwealth, a law relative to colleges having been passed, which enabled her to get this institution chartered for medical purposes. . . . During seven years over four thousand students were taught by the author in this College. Meanwhile she was pastor of the first established Church of Christ, Scientist; President of the first Christian Scientist Association, convening monthly; publisher of her own works; and (for a portion of this time) sole editor and publisher of the *Christian Science Journal,* the first periodical issued by Christian Scientists. She closed her College, October 29, 1889, in the height of its prosperity with a deeply-lying conviction that the next two years of her life should be given to the preparation of the revision of *Science and Health,* which was published in 1891. She retained her charter and, as its President, reopened the College in 1899 as auxiliary to her church. Until June 10, 1907, she had never read this book throughout consecutively in order to elucidate her idealism.

In the spirit of Christ's charity, as one who "hopeth all things, endureth all things," and is joyful to bear consolation to the sorrowing and healing to the sick, she commits these pages to honest seekers for Truth.

The Essence of Christian Science Teaching*

The "Recapitulation" (ending summary) of Science and Health with Key to the Scriptures *gives the main points of Christian Science teaching in very brief form. Notice how the main doctrines of mainstream Protestant Christianity at the end of the nineteenth century are recast in Christian Science.*

The following is a brief exposition of the important points, or religious tenets, of Christian Science:

1. As adherents of Truth, we take the inspired Word of the Bible as our sufficient guide to eternal Life.

2. We acknowledge and adore one supreme and infinite God. We acknowledge His Son, one Christ; the Holy Ghost or divine Comforter; and man in God's image and likeness.

3. We acknowledge God's forgiveness of sin in the destruction of sin and the spiritual understanding that casts out evil as unreal. But the belief in sin is punished so long as the belief lasts.

4. We acknowledge Jesus' atonement as the evidence of divine, efficacious Love, unfolding man's unity with God through Christ Jesus the Way-shower; and we acknowledge that man is saved through Christ, through Truth, Life, and Love as demonstrated by the Galilean Prophet in healing the sick and overcoming sin and death.

5. We acknowledge that the crucifixion of Jesus and his resurrection served to uplift faith to understand eternal Life, even the allness of Soul, Spirit, and the nothingness of matter.

6. And we solemnly promise to watch and pray for that Mind to be in us which was also in Christ Jesus; to do unto others as we would have them do unto us; and to be merciful, just, and pure.

---

*Science and Health with Key to the Scriptures, "Recapitulation."

Prayer and Its Role**

Prayer and meditation are the chief religious activity in Christian Science and its main method of healing sickness of body and mind. Here Mary Baker Eddy gives her interpretation of the Lord's Prayer *("Our Father") in accordance with Christian Science teachings.*

Our Master taught his disciples one brief prayer, which we name after him the Lord's Prayer. Our Master said, "After this manner therefore pray ye,"

**Science and Health with Key to the Scriptures, "Prayer."

and then he gave that prayer which covers all human needs. There is indeed some doubt among Bible scholars, whether the last line is not an addition to the prayer by a later copyist; but this does not affect the meaning of the prayer itself. In the phrase, "Deliver us from evil," the original properly reads, "Deliver us from the evil one." This reading strengthens our scientific apprehension of the petition, for Christian Science teaches us that "the evil one," or one evil, is but another name for the first lie and all liars. Only as we rise above all material sensuousness and sin, can we reach the heaven-born aspiration and spiritual consciousness, which is indicated in the Lord's Prayer and which instantaneously heals the sick. Here let me give what I understand to be the spiritual sense of the Lord's Prayer.

Our Father which art in heaven, *Our Father-Mother God, all-harmonious,* Hallowed be Thy name. *Adorable One.* Thy kingdom come. *Thy kingdom is come; Thou art ever-present.* Thy will be done in earth, as it is in heaven. *Enable us to know,—as in heaven, so on earth,—God is omnipotent, supreme.* Give us this day our daily bread; *Give us grace for to-day; feed the famished affections;* And forgive us our debts, as we forgive our debtors. *And Love is reflected in love;* And lead us not into temptation, but deliver us from evil; *And God leadeth us not into temptation, but delivereth us from sin, disease, and death.* For Thine is the kingdom, and the power, and the glory, forever. *For God is infinite, all power, all Life, Truth, Love, over all, and All.*

Healing Practices*

The healing practices of the church are based on prayer and meditation that recognize that only the spiritual is good and the material is evil and illusory. Such prayer and meditation lead to fullness of spiritual insight and goodness. The topics that open each paragraph are in the original.

Bodily presence: If we are sensibly with the body and regard omnipotence as a corporeal, material person, whose ear we would gain, we are not "absent from the body" and "present with the Lord" in the demonstration of Spirit. We cannot "serve two masters." To be present with the Lord is to have, not mere emotional ecstasy or faith, but the actual demonstration and understanding of Life as revealed in Christian Science. To be "with the Lord" is to be in obedience to the law of God, to be absolutely governed by divine Love—by Spirit, not by matter.

Spiritualized consciousness: Become conscious for a single moment that Life and intelligence are purely spiritual,—neither in nor of matter,— and the body will then utter no complaints. If suffering from a belief in sickness, you will find yourself suddenly well. Sorrow is turned into joy when the body is controlled by spiritual Life, Truth, and Love. . . . The Lord's Prayer is the prayer of Soul, not of material sense. Entirely separate from the belief and dream of material living, is the Life divine, revealing spiritual understanding and the consciousness of man's dominion over the whole earth. . . .

Spiritual sanctuary: The Father in secret is unseen to the physical senses, but He knows all things and rewards according to motives, not according to speech. To enter into the heart of prayer, the door of the erring senses must be closed. Lips must be mute and materialism silent, that man may have audience with Spirit, the divine Principle, Love, which destroys all error.

---

*Science and Health with Key to the Scriptures, "Christian Science Practice."

Effectual invocation: In order to pray aright, we must enter into the closet and shut the door. We must close the lips and silence the material senses. In the quiet sanctuary of earnest longings, we must deny sin and plead God's allness. We must resolve to take up the cross, and go forth with honest hearts to work and watch for wisdom, Truth, and Love. We must "pray without ceasing." Such prayer is answered, in so far as we put our desires into practice. The Master's injunction is, that we pray in secret and let our lives attest our sincerity.

Trustworthy beneficence: Christians rejoice in secret beauty and bounty, hidden from the world, but known to God. Self-forgetfulness, purity, and affection are constant prayers. Practice not profession, understanding not belief, gain the ear and right hand of omnipotence and they assuredly call down infinite blessings. Trustworthiness is the foundation of enlightened faith. Without a fitness for holiness, we cannot receive holiness.

Loftiest adoration: A great sacrifice of material things must precede this advanced spiritual understanding. The highest prayer is not one of faith merely; it is demonstration. Such prayer heals sickness, and must destroy sin and death.

Interpretation of *Genesis* 1*

Here Mary Baker Eddy teaches the ultimate unreality of matter, belief in which is the main cause of suffering. Gender is a mental construct, not a reality. Notice how she stresses the feminine aspects of God, most unusual for her time.

Genesis 1:1. In the beginning God created the heaven and the earth.

Ideas and identities: The infinite has no beginning. This word "beginning" is employed to signify "the only"—that is, the eternal verity and unity of God and man, including the universe. The creative Principle—Life, Truth, and Love—is God. The universe reflects God. There is but one creator and one creation. This creation consists of the unfolding of spiritual ideas and their identities, which are embraced in the infinite Mind and forever reflected. These ideas range from the infinitesimal to infinity, and the highest ideas are the sons and daughters of God.

Genesis 1:27. So God created man in His own image, in the image of God created He him; male and female created He them.

Ideal man and woman: To emphasize this momentous thought, it is repeated that God made man in His own image, to reflect the divine Spirit. It follows that man is a generic term. Masculine, feminine, and neuter genders are human concepts. In one of the ancient languages the word for "man" is used also as the synonym of "mind." This definition has been weakened by anthropomorphism, or a humanization of Deity. The word "anthropomorphic," in such a phrase as "an anthropomorphic God," is derived from two Greek words, signifying "man" and "form," and may be defined as a mortally mental attempt to reduce Deity to corporeality. The life-giving quality of Mind is Spirit, not matter. The ideal man corresponds to creation, to intelligence, and to Truth. The ideal woman corresponds to Life and to Love. In divine Science, we have not as much authority for considering God masculine, as we have for considering Him feminine, for Love imparts the clearest idea of Deity.

Divine personality: The world believes in many persons; but if God is personal, there is

---

*Science and Health with Key to the Scriptures, "Genesis."

but one person, because there is but one God. His personality can only be reflected, not transmitted. God has countless ideas, and they all have one Principle and parentage. The only proper symbol of God as person is Mind's infinite ideal. What is this ideal? Who shall behold it? This ideal is God's own image, spiritual and infinite. Even eternity can never reveal the whole of God, since there is no limit to infinitude or to its reflections.

Two Testimonials to Healing*

Testimonies to spiritual healing have been commonplace in Christian Science from the very beginning. These two testimonials, like all the others, relate healing directly to the reading and use of Eddy's Science and Health with Key to the Scriptures. *As the first paragraph implies, this section was added to the first editions of* Science and Health *to create the fuller book.*

Thousands of letters could be presented in testimony of the healing efficacy of Christian Science and particularly concerning the vast number of people who have been reformed and healed through the perusal or study of this book. For the assurance and encouragement of the reader, a few of these letters are here republished from *The Christian Science Journal* and *Christian Science Sentinel*. The originals are in the possession of the Editor, who can authenticate the testimonials which follow. . . .

Cancer and Consumption [tuberculosis] Healed: I was a great sufferer for many years from internal cancer and consumption. I was treated by the best of physicians in New York, Minneapolis, and Duluth, and was finally given up as incurable, when I heard of Christian Science. A neighbor who had been healed of consumption, kindly loaned me *Science and Health* by Mrs. Eddy, which I read and became interested in. In three months' time, I was healed, the truth conveyed to me by this book being the healer, and not only of these diseases, but I was made whole mentally as well. I have not been in bed one day since, or rather in eleven years. I have had many good demonstrations during this time, have passed through many a "fiery trial," but this blessed truth has caused me to stand, at times seemingly alone, and God was with me.

I will also mention a demonstration of painless childbirth that I have had since coming to Idaho. Perhaps it may help some sister who is looking through the *Journal* for a demonstration of this kind, as I was before my baby came. Good help being scarce here, I did my housework up to the time I was confined, and was in perfect health. I awoke my husband one morning at five o'clock, and at half past five baby was born, no one being present but my husband and myself. It was quite a surprise to the rest of the family to see me sitting by the fire with a new baby on my lap. My son got the breakfast, of which I ate heartily; at noon I joined the family in the dining room. I was out on the porch the second day, around the yard the third day, and have been perfectly well ever since, which has been now over three years. To one who had previously passed through agony untold, with a physician in attendance, this seemed wonderful. I hope this will interest some one who is seeking the truth, and I wish to express my sincere love for our beloved Leader, who has given us the *Key to the Scriptures*.— E. C. C., Lewiston, Idaho.

Saved from Insanity and Suicide: A few years ago, while under a sense of darkness and despair caused by ill health and an unhappy home,

---

*Science and Health with Key to the Scriptures, "Fruitage."

Science and Health was loaned me with a request that I should read it. At that time my daughter was given up by [physicians] to die of lingering consumption, supposed to have been inherited.

My own condition seemed even more alarming, as insanity was being manifested, and rather than go to an insane asylum, it seemed to me the only thing to do was to commit suicide. Heart trouble, kidney complaint, and continual headaches caused from female trouble were some of the many ailments I had to contend with. My doctor tried to persuade me to undergo an operation as a means of relief, but I had submitted to a severe operation ten years previous, and found only additional suffering as a result, so I would not consent.

When I began with *Science and Health*, I read the chapter on "Prayer" first, and at that time did not suppose it possible for me to remember anything I read, but felt a sweet sense of God's protection and power, and a hope that I should at last find Him to be what I so much needed, a present help in time of trouble. Before that chapter on "Prayer" was finished, my daughter was downstairs eating three meals a day, and daily growing stronger. Before I had finished reading the textbook she was well, but never having heard that the reading of *Science and Health* healed any one, it was several months before I gave God the glory. One by one my many ailments left me, all but the headaches; they were less frequent, until at the end of three years the fear of them was entirely overcome. Neither myself nor my daughter have ever received treatments, but the study of the Bible and *Science and Health,* the Christian Science textbook by Mrs. Eddy, has healed us and keeps us well.—E. J. B., Superior, Wisconsin.

THE SCRIPTURE OF THE UNIFICATION CHURCH

Dual Characteristics of the Universe and of Human Beings*

The beginning of Sun Myung Moon's Divine Principle *relates the principles of creation. Dual characteristics are built into everything in the world, reflecting the nature of God. The yin-yang explanation shows Moon's concern to combine Christianity and Asian thought, especially in their Korean forms.*[8]

Let us begin by pointing out the common elements which are found universally throughout the natural world. Every entity possesses dual characteristics of *yang* (masculinity) and *yin* (femininity) and comes into existence only when these characteristics have formed reciprocal relationships, both within the entity and between it and other entities. For example, subatomic particles, the basic building blocks of all matter, possess either a positive charge, a negative charge, or a neutral charge formed by the neutralization of positive and negative constituents. When particles join with each other through the reciprocal relationships of their dual characteristics, they form an atom. Atoms, in turn, display either a positive or a negative valence. When the dual characteristics within one atom enter into reciprocal relationships with those in another atom, they form a molecule. Molecules formed in this manner engage in further reciprocal relationships between their dual characteristics to eventually become nourishment fit for consumption by plants and animals.

---

*Divine Principle 1.1.1.1.

[8] All excerpts from *Divine Principle* are taken from its third edition (New York: HAS-UWC Press, 1996). Copyright © 1996 the Holy Spirit Association for the Unification of World Christianity. Used by permission.

Plants propagate by means of stamen and pistil. Animals multiply and maintain their species through the relationship between males and females. According to the *Bible*, after God created Adam, He saw that it was not good for the man to live alone. Only after God created Eve as Adam's female counterpart did He declare that His creations were "very good." Let us take human beings as an example. A human being is composed of an outer form, the body, and an inner quality, the mind. The body is a visible reflection of the invisible mind. Because the mind possesses a certain structure, the body which reflects it also takes on a particular appearance. This is the idea behind a person's character and destiny being perceived through examining his outward appearance by such methods as physiognomy[9] or palm reading. Here, mind is the internal nature and body is the external form. Mind and body are two correlative aspects of a human being; hence, the body may be understood as a second mind. Together, they constitute the dual characteristics of a human being. Similarly, all beings exist through the reciprocal relationships between their dual characteristics of internal nature and external form.

---

[9] *physiognomy:* the study of external physical characteristics to determine the character or destiny of an individual.

The Purpose of the Creation of the Universe*

Why did God create the world—or, as one modern philosopher has asked in a nonreligious mode, Why is there something rather than nothing? Sun Myung Moon states here that God created the universe for God's own enjoyment.

It is recorded in the *Bible* that after God completed each day of creation, He saw that it was good. This suggests that God wanted His creations to be object partners embodying goodness that He might take delight in them. How can the creation give God the greatest joy?

God created human beings as the final step in creating the universe. He created them in His image, in the likeness of His internal nature and external form, and gave them sensibility to all feelings and emotions because it was His intention to share joy with them. After their creation, God blessed Adam and Eve: Be fruitful and multiply, and fill the earth and subdue it; and have dominion over the fish of the sea and over the birds of the air and over every living thing that moves upon the earth (*Gen.* 1:28). These are the *three great blessings:* to be fruitful (mature and ready to bear fruit), multiply, and have dominion over the creation. Had Adam and Eve obeyed this divine mandate and built the Kingdom of Heaven, there is no doubt that God would have felt the greatest joy as His sons and daughters rejoiced in the world of His ideal.

How can God's three great blessings be fulfilled? They can be realized only when the four position foundation, which is the fundamental foundation of creation, has been established. The three great blessings are fulfilled when the whole creation, including human beings, completes the . . . foundation with God as the center. This is the Kingdom of Heaven, where ultimate goodness is realized and God feels the greatest joy. This is, in fact, the very purpose for which God created the universe.

The ultimate purpose of the universe, with human beings at its center, is to return joy to God. All entities have dual purposes. As was explained earlier, every entity has dual centers of

---

*Divine Principle 1.1.3.1.

movement, one of internal nature and another of external form. These centers pursue corresponding purposes—for the sake of the whole and for the sake of the individual—whose relationship is the same as that between internal nature and external form. These dual purposes relate to each other as cause and result, internal and external, subject partner and object partner. In God's ideal, there cannot be any individual purpose which does not support the whole purpose, nor can there be any whole purpose that does not guarantee the interests of the individual. The infinite variety of beings in the universe form one vast organic body interwoven by these dual purposes.

The Spiritual Fall and the Physical Fall of Adam and Eve*

Duality of being and action leads to duality in the human fall. Moon's emphasis on the key role of sexual intercourse in the fall itself (largely unknown in Jewish, Christian, and Islamic traditions) ties into his prescription for the salvation of the world by the propagating of a true, heavenly family on earth.

God created human beings with two components: the spirit self and the physical self. The human Fall likewise took place in two dimensions: the spiritual and the physical. The fall which took place through the sexual relationship between the angel and Eve was the *spiritual fall,* while the fall which occurred through the sexual relationship between Eve and Adam was the *physical fall....*

(The Spiritual Fall:) God created the angelic world and assigned Lucifer (*Isaiah* 14:12) to the position of archangel. Lucifer was the channel of God's love to the angelic world, just as Abraham was the channel of God's blessing to the Israelites. In this position he virtually monopolized the love of God. However, after God created human beings as His children, He loved them many times more than He had ever loved Lucifer, whom He had created as His servant. In truth, God's love toward Lucifer did not change; it was the same before and after the creation of human beings.... Lucifer, feeling as though he were receiving less love than he deserved, wanted to grasp the same central position in human society as he enjoyed in the angelic world, as the channel of God's love. This was why he seduced Eve, and this was the motivation of the spiritual fall.

Everything in the universe is created to be governed by God through love. Thus, love is the source of life, the key to happiness, and the essence of the ideal to which all beings aspire. The more one receives love, the more beautiful one appears to others. When the angel, created as God's servant, beheld Eve, the daughter of God, it was only natural that she looked beautiful in his eyes. Moreover, when Lucifer saw that Eve was responding to his temptation, the angel felt the stimulation of her love to be deliciously enticing. At this point, Lucifer was seducing Eve with the mind to have her, regardless of the consequences. Lucifer, who left his proper position due to his excessive desire, and Eve, who wanted to open her eyes and become like God (*Genesis* 3:5–6) before the time was ripe, formed a common base and began give and take action. The power of the unprincipled love generated by their give and take led them to consummate an illicit sexual relationship on the spiritual plane.

All beings are created based on the principle that when they become one in love, they exchange elements with each other. Accordingly, when Eve became one with Lucifer through love, she received certain elements from him. First, she received feelings of dread arising from the pangs of a guilty conscience, stemming from her violation of the purpose of creation. Second,

---

*Divine Principle 1.2.2.1–2.

she received from Lucifer the wisdom which enabled her to discern that her originally intended spouse was to be Adam, not the angel. Eve was in the position to receive wisdom from the Archangel because she was immature and her wisdom was not as seasoned as that of the Archangel, who was already in a state of angelic maturity.

(The Physical Fall:) Perfect Adam and Eve were supposed to have become an eternal husband and wife in God's love. But Eve, who in her immaturity had engaged in the illicit relationship with the Archangel, joined with Adam as husband and wife. Thus, Adam fell when he, too, was still immature. This untimely conjugal relationship in satanic love between Adam and Eve constituted the physical fall. . . . Eve then seduced Adam with the hope that by uniting with him, her intended spouse, she could rid herself of the dread and once again stand before God. This was Eve's motivation which led to the physical fall.

Once Eve had united with the Archangel through their illicit sexual relationship, she stood in the position of the Archangel with respect to Adam. Thus, Adam, who was still receiving God's love, appeared very attractive to her. Seeing Adam as her only hope of returning to God, Eve turned to Adam and tempted him, playing the same role as the Archangel had played when he had tempted her. Adam responded and formed a common base with Eve, and they began give and take action with each other. The power of the unprincipled love generated in their relationship induced Adam to abandon his original position and brought them together in an illicit physical relationship of sexual love. When Adam united in oneness with Eve, he inherited all the elements Eve had received from the Archangel. These elements in turn have been passed down to all subsequent generations without interruption.

The Restoration of Humanity*

Fallen humans cannot restore the creation to achieve its purpose. Only with a new group of humans, a new human family sprung from True Parents, can the Kingdom of Heaven come about. Notice the emphasis on moral perfectionism, often a hallmark of new religious movements.

We dwell in ignorance of history, uncertain about its origin, the direction in which it is heading, and its final destination. Concerning eschatology, or the doctrine of the "Last Days," many Christians believe literally what is written in the Bible. . . . One pertinent question for Christians is whether these events will take place literally or whether the verses are symbolic, as are many parts of the Bible. To address this issue, we should first understand such fundamental matters as the purpose of God's creation, the meaning of the human Fall, and the goal of the providence of restoration.

[1.1] We have discussed how God's purpose in creating human beings was to rejoice with them. Thus, our purpose of existence is to bring joy to God. What must we do to bring joy to God and fully manifest our original value? Created beings other than humans are endowed with the innate nature to grow to maturity naturally and become object partners which bring God joy. Human beings, on the other hand, can become true and authentic object partners who bring joy to God only through their free will and free actions. . . .

The relationship between God and a person who has attained individual perfection can be

---

* *Divine Principle* 1.3, Introduction.

compared to that between the mind and the body. The body is the dwelling place of the mind and moves according to the mind's direction. Likewise, God abides within the mind of a fully mature person. Such a person becomes a temple of God and leads his life in harmony with His Will. . . . Living in oneness with God, he acquires a divine nature. Thus, it is impossible for him to commit sin or to fall. A person who has perfected his individual character embodies total goodness and fulfills the purpose of creation. If a person embodying total goodness could fall, this would lead to the illogical conclusion that goodness contains the seed of its own destruction. Moreover, if human beings, who were created by the all-powerful God, could fall even after becoming perfect, we would have reason to doubt the omnipotence of God. God is the absolute and eternal Subject. To give Him true joy, His object partner must necessarily also be eternal and absolute. For these reasons, a person who has perfected his individual character can never fall. Had Adam and Eve reached perfection, being thereafter unsusceptible to sin, they would have borne good children and founded a sinless family and society in complete concordance with God's blessings. They would have founded the Kingdom of Heaven, which consists of one great family with the same parents. . . .

Regardless of the purity of the people of this society, if they were living in primitive circumstances like cavemen, this could not be considered the Kingdom of Heaven which both God and human beings desire. God gave us the mandate to have dominion over all things. Hence, to realize the ideal of creation, people of perfected character should advance science, harness the natural world, and create an extremely pleasant social and living environment. This will be the Kingdom of Heaven on earth. Once people have attained full maturity and enjoyed life in God's earthly Kingdom, then when they shed their physical bodies and pass into the spirit world, they will form the Kingdom of Heaven in heaven. Accordingly, God's primary purpose of creation is to build the Kingdom of Heaven on earth.

Salvation through the Second Messiah, the True Parent*

This short reading presents the essence of the Unification teaching of salvation, achievable by following the Second Messiah, the True Parent who will begin a new, perfect human family that will usher in the Kingdom of Heaven.

The *providence of restoration* refers to God's work to restore human beings to our original, unfallen state so that we may fulfill the purpose of creation. As discussed in Part I, human beings fell from the top of the growth stage and have been held under Satan's dominion ever since. To restore human beings, God works to cut off Satan's influence. Yet, as was explained in Christology, we must have the original sin removed before we can sever Satan's bonds and be restored to the state before the Fall. This is possible only when we are born anew through the Messiah, the True Parent. To explain further: we first need to go through a course to separate Satan from ourselves. We do this in order to restore ourselves in form to the spiritual level which Adam and Eve had reached before the Fall—the top of the growth stage. On this foundation, we are to receive the Messiah and be reborn, and thereby be fully restored to the original state of human beings before the Fall. Finally, by following the Messiah, we should continue our growth to maturity where we can fulfill the purpose of creation.

---

*Divine Principle 2, Introduction.

The Advent of the Second Messiah as a Korean*

In Unification thought, which now explicitly identifies Sun Myung Moon as the Second Messiah, this Messiah "returns" by being born as a human. He finishes the work that Jesus began and founds the Kingdom of Heaven on earth by means of propagating a "True Family." The first part of this reading defends Moon's knowledge of the end times against traditional Christian teaching that it is hidden from human knowledge. The second part advances the idea that when the Second Messiah comes, he will come from Korea.

Jesus clearly foretold his return. Yet he added that no one knew of the day and hour of his return, not the angels, not even himself (*Matthew* 24:36). Hence, it has been commonly thought unwise to speculate about the date, place, and manner of the Second Advent. Nevertheless, we can deduce from the words of Jesus, "But of that day and hour no one knows . . . but the Father only," and the verse, "Surely the Lord God does nothing, without revealing his secret to his servants the prophets" (*Amos* 3:7) that God, who knows the day and hour, will surely reveal all secrets about the Second Advent to His prophets before He carries out His work. . . .

[2.6.3.2] As Jesus explained through the parable of the vineyard, when the Jewish people, like the tenants in the parable who killed the son of their master, led Jesus to the cross, they lost their providential mission. Which nation, then, will inherit the work of God and bear its fruits? The Bible suggests that this nation is in the East.

The Book of Revelation describes the opening of a scroll sealed with seven seals . . . (*Revelation* 5:1–5). The Lion of the tribe of Judah signifies Christ; it is he who will open the seven seals in the Last Days. "After six of the seals are opened: Then I saw another angel ascend from the rising of the sun, with the seal of the living God, and he called with a loud voice . . . saying, 'Do not harm the earth or the sea or the trees, till we have sealed the servants of our God upon their foreheads.' And I heard the number of the sealed, a hundred and forty-four thousand" (*Revelation* 7:2–4). This indicates that the seal of the living God will be placed on the foreheads of the 144,000 in the East, where the sun rises. These chosen ones will accompany the Lamb at his return. We can thus infer that the nation which will inherit the work of God and bear its fruit for the sake of the Second Advent is in the East. There Christ will be born and received by the 144,000 elect of God. Which among the nations of the East is chosen to receive the Lord?

[3.3] Since ancient times, the nations in the East have traditionally been considered to be the three nations of Korea, Japan, and China. Among them, Japan throughout its history has worshipped the sun goddess Amaterasu-omikami. Japan entered the period of the Second Advent as a fascist nation and severely persecuted Korean Christians. China at the time of the Second Advent was a hotbed of communism and would become a communist nation. Thus, both nations belonged to Satan's side. Korea, then, is the nation in the East where Christ will return.

---

*Divine Principle 2.6, Introduction; 2.6.3.2–3.

GLOSSARY

Book of Mormon the main scripture of the Church of Jesus Christ of Latter-day Saints; it relates the story of the coming of ancient Israelites to the Americas and the creation of golden plates of sacred writings.

Divine Principle the main scripture of the Unification Church, written by Sun Myung Moon.

Doctrine and Covenants the third canonical writing of the Church of Jesus Christ of Latter-day Saints; it contains revelations on doctrine and "official declarations" on ending polygamy and admitting blacks to the priesthood.

Holy Writings the scriptures of Baha'i, written by the Bab, Baha'u'llah, Abdu'l-Baha, and Shogi Effendi.

new religious movements religious groups that arose since the nineteenth century and now have sufficient size, longevity, and cultural impact to merit academic study.

Pearl of Great Price the second canonical writing of the Church of Jesus Christ of Latter-day Saints; it is a selection of Joseph Smith's testimony and his translations of sacred writings.

Science and Health with Key to the Scriptures the scripture of the Christian Science Church, written by Mary Baker Eddy. "Science and Health" explains the principles of healing; "Key to the Scriptures" interprets several biblical passages in Christian Science terms.

QUESTIONS FOR STUDY AND DISCUSSION

1. How adequate is the term *new religious movement,* in your view? What are its strengths and weaknesses?

2. What are the main similarities and differences between Baha'i scriptures and the *Qur'an*? In what sense are the Baha'i *Holy Writings* a successor to the *Qur'an*?

3. Critique this statement: "The *Book of Mormon* is, among all world scriptures, the most American."

4. The Church of Jesus Christ of Latter-day Saints has given the *Book of Mormon* an unofficial subtitle: "Another Testament of Jesus Christ." What do you think was the church's reason for doing so? What might this subtitle be intended to imply about the *New Testament*?

5. Discuss the origin and growth of the Christian Science scripture from "Science and Health" to its supplement by "Key to the Scriptures" and the testimonial section "Fruitage."

6. Discuss the main teachings of the *Divine Principle*. How is it based on, and how does it depart from, the teachings of mainstream Christianity? Would you say that the Unification Church is a Christian church? Why or why not?

SCRIPTURES IN FILM

Perhaps because of their controversial nature, the stories of new religious movements are not often captured in feature films. One exception is the Latter-day Saint church, which has its own motion-picture operation (nicknamed "Mollywood"). *The Book of Mormon Movie* (vol. 1 of 2; 2004, rated PG), directed by Gary Rogers, tells roughly the first half of the *Book of Mormon*. The portrayal of this book is selective but literal. Viewers accustomed to typical Hollywood production values may be disappointed in the cinematic quality of this film, but it is worthwhile watching as an example of Mormons explaining their scriptures through the medium of film.

SUGGESTIONS FOR FURTHER READING

Scholarship on scripture in new religious movements is slim, because academic inquiry into the nature and use of their scriptures has hardly begun. For primary sources on new religious movements, many of which deal with scriptures, see especially Dereck Daschke and W. Michael Ashcroft, *New Religious Movements: A Documentary Reader* (New York: New York University Press, 2005). On the *Book of Mormon,* see Terryl L. Givens, *By the Hand of Mormon: The American Scripture That Launched a New World Religion* (New York: Oxford University Press, 2002). Students of religion should concentrate on the scriptures themselves. Published editions of these scriptures are listed in the footnotes in this chapter, and access to most of these scriptures is available on the World Wide Web by way of the website accompanying the present book, which is located at Wadsworth's religion site: http://religion.wadsworth.com.

INDEX

(Note: Boldface entries indicate pages where subjects are defined in a glossary section.)

Abraham
  in Islam, 143, 150, 161, 162
  in Judaism, 37, 42, 46–47, 49, 69,
  in Latter-day Saint Church, 181, 196
  in Unification Church, 207
Abrahamic monotheisms, 7, **19**
Adam. *See also* Eve
  in Christianity, 115
  in Islam, 146
  in Judaism, 53–54
  in Latter-day Saint Church, 196, 197
  in Unification Church, 206, 207, 208, 209
Ahura, 23, 24, 25, 26, 27, 28, 29, 30, 31, 32, 33, 34
Alms
  in Christianity, 120
  in Islam, 139, 148, 160, 163, 164, 165, 170
  in Judaism, 33, 34
Angel
  in Christianity, 90, 94, 102, 108, 110–111, 114, 119
  in Islam, 129, 133–136, 138, 144–146, 148, 149, 151, 166, 167, 169, 173
  in Judaism, 46, 48, 54, 57
  in Latter-day Saint Church, 189, 191, 193, 196
  in Unification Church, 207–208, 210
  in Zoroastrianism, 23, 24, 35
Apostle
  in Christianity, 85, 89, 118, 119, 122, 125, **126**
  in Islam, 159, 164, 165, 166, 167
Arabia, Arabs, 95, 129, 131, 134, 137, 148, 151, 154, 156, 161, 167
Ark, 9, 41, 49, 72, **79**
Authentic writing, 17, 25, 85, **126**, 164, 169, 208
Avesta, 22, 23, 24, 25, 26, **34**, 35
Ayah, 133, **173**

Baha'i
  scripture in, 177–180
  scripture selections from, 183–188
Baptism
  in Christianity, 82, 84, 115, 123, **126**
  in Latter-day Saint Church, 191, 197, 198
Bible, Christian. *See also* New Testament. 1, 2, 4, 6, 7, 11, 14, **126**
  in Baha'i, 183
  in Christian Science, 200, 201, 202
  in Islam, 129, 164
  in Latter-day Saint Church, 177, 178, 179, 180, 197
  in Unification Church, 205, 206, 208, 210
  selections from, 90–117
Bible, Jewish. *See also* Tanakh. 36–46, 60–61, 72, 74, 76, **79**
  selections from, 46–73
Bibliolatry, 9, **19**
Bibliomancy, 9, 10, **19**
Birth, 9, 28, 90, 118, 131, 166, 178
Bishop, 89–90, 113, 118–119, 121, 125
Bismillah, 132, 141, 148, **173**
Book of Mormon, 1, 176–183, **211**
  selections from, 192–195
Buddhism, 4, 7, 8, 17

Canon, 5, 7, 8, **19**, 25, 42, 44, 45, 88, 89, 90, 117, 118, 119, 178, 179, 180, 182
Challenge verses, 136, **173**
Child, children, 9
  in Baha'i, 186, 187
  in Christian Science, 200
  in Christianity, 90, 92, 99, 104, 106, 107, 109, 112, 113, 114, 120, 125
  in Islam, 138, 139, 141, 144, 147, 149, 153, 155, 158, 160, 164, 166, 167, 170
  in Judaism, 37, 41, 42, 49, 50, 51, 54, 57, 58, 59, 61, 65, 66, 70, 74, 75, 77, 79

213

Child *continued*
  in Latter-day Saint Church, 194, 196, 199
  in Unification Church, 207, 209
Christianity, 1, 3, 4, 6, 7, 9, 14, 15, 17, 19, 23, 29
  and Baha'i 184, 185
  general description, 83
  and Islam, 141, 147, 148, 149, 150, 164
  and Judaism, 37, 38, 43, 53, 59, 61, 79
  and Latter-day Saint Church, 196
  and new religious movements, 177, 178, 179, 180, 181, 183
  scripture in, 83–90
  scripture selections from, 90–117
  and Unification Church, 207, 210
Christian Science
  scripture in, 177–183
  scripture selections from, 199–205
Church of Jesus Christ of Latter-day Saints
  scripture in, 1, 176–183
  scripture selections from, 189–199
Circumcision
  in Christianity, 97, 118, 120
  in Judaism, 69, 78
Commentary, **19**, 40, 131, 173, 181
Confession, 24, 50, 51, 72, 117, 159, 170
Confucianism, 4, 7
Covenant. *See also* Testament
  in Bahai', 186, 187
  in Christianity, 84, 116, 126
  in Islam 167
  in Judaism, 49, 50, 69, 71, 78, **79**
  in Latter-day Saint Church, 195
Creation. *See also* Earth, World
  in Baha'i 186, 188
  in Christianity, 121
  in Christian Science, 203, 204
  in Islam, 137, 142, 144, 145, 146, 168, 172
  in Judaism, 45, 52, 53
  in Latter-day Saint Church, 190
  in new religious movements, 180, 181
  in Unification Church, 205, 206, 207, 208, 209
  in Zoroastrianism, 24, 26, 27, 29, 30, 33

David
  in Christianity, 90, 97, 119
  in Judaism, 42, 43, 45, 49, 50, 55, 64, 65
Day of Atonement, 72

Deacons, 113–114
Death, 1, 12, 15
  in Baha'i, 185
  in Christianity, 83, 85, 88, 89, 91, 92, 93, 102, 103, 115, 116, 119, 120, 122, 126
  in Christian Science, 201, 202, 203
  in Islam, 129, 130, 133, 134, 136, 138, 140, 142, 145, 148, 149, 150, 151, 159, 164, 165, 169
  in Judaism, 58, 59, 60, 71, 72, 75
  in Latter-day Saint Church, 193, 194, 196
  in new religious movements, 180, 182
  in Zoroastrianism, 33
Decalogue, 57, 71, **79**
Devil. *See also* Satan
  in Judaism, 53
  in Christianity, 102, 103, 114, 125
  in Islam, 144, 145
Divine Principle, 177, 179, 180, 181, 182, 183
  selections from, 205–210, **211**
Divorce. *See also* Marriage
  in Christianity, 90, 104, 107–108
  in Islam, 140 154, 155
  in Judaism, 50
Doctrine and Covenants, 179, 181, 182, 183, **211**
  selections from, 195–196, 197–199

Earth. *See also* Creation, World
  in Baha'i, 185, 186, 187, 188
  in Christianity, 85, 86, 95, 96, 103, 104, 105, 109, 110, 111, 112, 113, 115, 119, 122, 125
  in Christian Science, 202, 203
  in Islam, 130, 132, 136, 137, 138, 141, 142, 143, 144, 145, 146, 147, 149, 150, 151, 152, 153, 154, 156, 159, 168, 169, 171
  in Judaism, 46, 49, 52, 53, 57, 58, 64, 65, 67, 71, 74, 79
  in Latter-day Saint Church, 191, 193, 194, 197, 199
  in Unification Church, 206, 207, 209, 210
  in Zoroastrianism, 26, 28, 30, 32, 33, 34
Eddy, Mary Baker, 177, 179, 181, 183, 199, 201, 203, 204, 205, 211
Eucharist, 116

Eve. *See also* Adam
  in Christianity, 115
  in Islam, 146
  in Judaism, 54
  in Unification Church, 206, 207, 208, 209
Evil, 9, 17
  in Baha'i, 186, 187
  in Christian Science, 201, 202
  in Christianity, 91, 100, 104, 105, 106, 118, 120, 121, 122
  in Islam, 131, 138, 144, 149, 154, 156, 163, 165, 168
  in Judaism, 50, 55, 56, 75
  in Latter-day Saint Church, 189, 191, 196
  in Zoroastrianism, 24, 26, 27, 29, 30, 31, 32, 33, 34
Ezra, 38, 39, 43, 44, 45, 50, 51

Fast, fasting
  in Baha'i, 185–186
  in Christianity, 105, 118, 120
  in Islam, 140, 161, 162, 164, 169
  in Judaism, 79
Fatihah, 131, 158, **173**
Fight, fighting. *See also* Jihad, War 11, 48, 59, 89, 96, 148, 156–157, 166–167, 170
Fire. *See also* Hell
  in Islam, 137, 151, 152, 155, 156, 157, 163
  in Zoroastrianism, 28
Forgive, forgiveness
  in Bahai', 185, 187
  in Christianity, 105, 113
  in Christian Science, 202
  in Islam, 138
  in Judaism, 71
Fravashi, 30, **34**

Gathas, 24, 25, 30, **34**, 35
Genre, 4, **19**, 86, 87
Gentiles, 85, 95, 97, 105, 106, 124
God, gods, 8, 12
  in Baha'i, 184, 185, 186, 187, 188
  in Christianity, 83–118, 121, 122, 125, 126
  in Christian Science, 200, 201, 202, 203, 204
  in Islam, 129–168, 171–173
  in Judaism, 37, 38, 40, 42, 43, 45–58, 60, 61, 63, 64, 66, 68, 69, 71, 74–80
  in Latter-day Saint Church, 190–197, 199
  in new religious movements, 177–183
  in Unification Church, 205–210
  in Zoroastrianism, 26, 27, 29, 33, 34
Good, goodness 11, 13, 17
  in Baha'i, 186
  in Christianity, 84, 89, 96, 98, 101, 104–107, 109, 110, 113–115, 117, 121, 122, 126
  in Christian Science, 200, 202, 204
  in Islam, 136, 139, 140, 144, 147, 149, 150, 153, 154, 155, 156, 157, 160, 161, 162, 167, 168, 173
  in Judaism, 41, 42, 43, 47, 52, 53, 54, 55, 65, 72, 76, 77, 78, 79
  in Latter-day Saint Church, 191, 197
  in new religious movements, 178, 182
  in Unification Church, 206, 209
  in Zoroastrianism, 24, 26–29, 30, 31, 32, 33, 34
Gospel, gospels
  in Christianity, 84, 85, 89, 90, 117, 118, 119, 121, 123, 124, **126**
  in Islam, 149
  in new religious movements, 181
  in Latter-day Saint Church, 191, 197, 198, 200

Hadith, 6, **173**
  description of, 164
  selections from, 164–167
Heaven. *See also* Hell
  in Baha'i, 185, 187, 188
  in Christianity, 86, 89, 93, 94, 95, 100, 102–106, 109, 111–113, 115–117, 122, 125
  in Christian Science, 202, 203
  in Islam, 5, 135, 137, 138, 144, 147, 151, 160, 166, 172
  in Judaism, 50, 52, 53, 56, 57, 58, 71, 75, 76
  in Latter-day Saint Church, 190, 191, 192, 193, 195, 198, 199
  in Unification Church, 206, 208, 209, 210
  in Zoroastrianism, 23, 29, 32, 33, 34
Hell. *See also* Heaven
  in Christianity, 91, 104, 112, 125
  in Islam, 135, 136, 143, 145, 146, 151, 166, 167, 168, 170
  in Judaism, 75
  in Zoroastrianism, 23, 29, 32, 33, 34

Hinduism, 4, 7, 8, 15, 17, 18
Historical-critical method, 14, **19**
Holy Writings, 178, 180, 182, **211**
Husband. *See also* Wife
   in Christianity, 90, 99, 103, 107, 108, 109, 113
   in Islam, 155, 165
   in Judaism, 54, 59, 65, 66, 78
   in Unification Church, 208
Hymn, 8, 24, 27, 28, 35, 41, 99

Icon, 9, **19**
Islam, 1, 2, 4, 6, 7, 9, 15, 17, 19
   and Baha'i, 184, 185, 187
   general description, 129
   scripture in, 129–134
   scripture selections from, 134–163
   and Zoroastrianism, 23, 25, 29
Isnad, 164, **173**
Israel
   in Christianity, 84, 88, 93, 95, 96, 100, 111, 112
   in Islam, 138, 139, 147, 149
   in Judaism, 37, 42, 43, 45, 47, 48, 49, 50, 51, 55, 57, 58, 60, 63, 64, 66, 68, 69, 70, 71, 73, 74, 76, 78, 79
   in Latter-day Saint Church, 191, 192, 195, 196, 197

Jerusalem
   in Judaism, 36, 37, 40, 41, 43, 45, 49, 51, 61, 62, 65, 69, 74, 75, 79
   in Christianity, 89, 94, 95, 96, 97, 103, 105
   in Islam, 138, 139, 159
   in new religious movements, 181, 197
Jesus, 1, 17
   in Christianity, 82, 83, 84, 85, 87, 88, 89, 90, 91, 92, 93, 94, 95, 96, 97, 98, 99, 100, 101, 102, 103, 104, 105, 107, 111, 112, 113, 114, 115, 116, 117, 118, 119, 120, 123, 125, 126
   in Islam, 143, 147, 148, 149, 150, 171
   in new religious movments, 176, 177, 178, 179, 180, 181, 182, 184, 189, 193, 195, 196, 197, 198, 199, 200, 201, 210, 211
Jew, Jewish. *See also* Judaism. 4, 7, 11, 12, 17
   and Christianity, 84, 85, 87, 88, 90, 93, 94, 95, 97, 100, 107, 110, 115, 126

   and Islam, 139, 149, 159, 164
   and Latter-day Saint church, 192, 193
   and Unification Church, 207, 210
Jihad, 156, 164, 166, 167, **173**
Jinn, 131, 141, 143, 144, 145, 163, 170, **173**
John the Baptist, 3, 7
   in Christianity, 82, 83, 85, 86, 87, 89, 90, 92, 99, 112, 113, 116, 118, 119, 125
   in Islam, 149
   in Latter-day Saint Church, 192
Judaism. *See also* Jew. 1, 4, 6, 7, 9, 14, 17, 19
   and Christianity, 84, 86, 87, 88, 95, 97, 102
   general description, 37
   and Islam, 147, 150, 153
   scripture in, 37–45
   scripture selections from, 46–74
   and Zoroastrianism, 23, 29
Judgment
   in Christianity, 102, 104, 110, 112, 125
   in Islam, 137, 143, 145, 150, 151, 156, 158, 160, 166
   in Judaism, 56, 57, 63, 75
   in Latter-day Saint Church, 193, 195
   in Zoroastrianism, 23, 32, 33, 34

Kethuvim, 38, 39, 41, 43, 45, 79
Kosher, 73

Law, 4, 6, 12, 18
   in Christianity, 91, 92, 93, 96, 97, 99, 101, 103, 104, 106, 107, 110, 116, 118, 124
   in Christian Science, 200, 202
   in Islam, 157, 164
   in Judaism, 37, 38, 40, 42, 45, 46, 50, 53, 57, 58, 63, 73, 75, 76, 79, 80
   in Latter-day Saint Church, 197, 198
   in Zoroastrianism, 23, 24, 27, 28, 29, 35
Lectionary, 41, **79**, 87
Letters, 38, 40, 78, 79, 84, 85, 86, 89, 90, 118, 119, **126**, 132, 180, 204
Love, 4
   in Baha'i, 184, 187, 188
   in Christianity, 86, 100, 101, 105, 106, 108, 109, 110, 113, 115, 119, 120, 125
   in Christian Science, 202, 204
   in Islam, 149, 152, 157, 171
   in Judaism, 37, 43, 51, 55, 57, 58, 61, 62, 63, 64, 75, 79

in Unification Church, 207, 208
in Zoroastrianism, 31

Marriage. *See also* Divorce.
   in Baha'i, 185, 187
   in Christianity, 107, 108, 109
   in Islam,140, 154, 155, 157,
   in Judaism, 50, 78
   in Latter-day Saint Church, 198
   in Unification Church, 177
   in Zoroastrianism, 31
Martyr, 164, 166
Martyrdom, 164
Mary, the mother of Jesus
   in Christianity, 84, 90, 94, 100, 114, 123, 124
   in Islam, 147, 149, 171
Mary Magdalene, 94, 100, 114, 123
Matn, 164, **173**
Mecca, 132, 135–139, 141, 142, 144, 145, 147, 150–153, 156, 159, 160–163, 165, 169
Medina, 132, 137, 138, 139, 142, 143, 147, 148, 157, 159, 160, 162, 163
Meditation, 9, 10, 17, 19
   in Christianity, 88
   in Christian Science, 201, 202
   in new religious movements, 179
   in Zoroastrianism, 25
Mercy
   in Baha'i, 187, 188
   in Christianity, 104, 108, 121
   in Islam, 136, 143, 153, 157, 161
   in Judaism, 63
   in Zoroastrianism, 34
Messiah
   in Judaism, 49, 57
   in Christianity, 84, 88, 90, 99
   in Islam, 149
   in Unification Church, 181–182, 209, 210
Mezuzah, 41, 42, 51, **79**
Miracles, 91, 120
Money, 59, 106, 113, 154
Moon, Sun Myung, 177, 179, 182, 205–207, 210–211
Moses
   in Christianity, 84, 97, 99, 100, 101, 103, 116, 124
   in Islam, 139, 143, 147, 150, 169

   in Judaism, 40, 42, 45, 46, 47, 48, 49, 51, 58, 66, 70, 71, 72, 73, 74, 75, 78, 79
   in Latter-day Saint Church, 181, 196
Mosque, 12, 131, 139, 163
Muhammad, 6, 7, 41, 129, 130–140, 142–144, 146, 148–149, 156–157, 159, 161, 164, 167, 169–171, 173
Muslim, Muslims. *See also* Islam. 1, 7, 9, 11, 15, 25, 129, 130, 131, 132, 133, 134, 138, 141, 142, 148, 154, 163, 164, 165, 169, 170
   and Baha'i, 184, 185

Narrative, 4, 18, **19**, 45, 52, 130, 180, 181
Nevi'im. See also Prophets. 38, 39, 42, 45, **79**
New Religious Movements, 6, 7, 10, 11, 13, 17, 176–180, 182, 199, 208, **211**
New Testament, 11, 38, 43, 79, 83, 84, 85, 86, 87, 88, 89, 118, 119, 125, **126**
   and Islam, 131, 149, 150
   and new religious movements, 181, 192
   selections from, 90–117

Old Testament, 7, 38, 84, 87, 117, 118, 119, **126**
Oral tradition, 5, 13, 15, **19**, 25, 45, 98, 133, 182

Palestine. *See also* Israel. 42, 46, 47, 90, 111
Parable, 98–99, 100, 141, 152, 210
Passover, 41, 47, 70, 87, 94, 95, 116
Paul (Christian apostle), 18, 84–86, 89, 97, 99, 107–108, 114–115, 118–119
Peace. *See also* Fighting, War. 12, 17
   in Baha'i, 184, 188
   in Christianity, 91, 101, 104, 107, 112, 124
   in Islam, 141, 156, 162, 165, 171
   in Judaism, 37, 48, 55, 60, 61, 69, 75, 76, 78
   in Zoroastrianism, 26
Pearl of Great Price, 178, 181, 189, 196, **211**
   selections from, 189–192, 196–199
Peter (Christian apostle), 86, 87, 89, 90, 91, 92, 94–97, 112–113, 118–119, 124, 125, 192
Pilgrimage
   in Baha'i, 185, 187
   in Islam, 144, 148, 161, 162, 165

Pray, prayer
  in Baha'i, 185, 186, 187, 188
  in Christianity, 105, 114, 115, 117, 120, 125
  in Christian Science, 201, 202, 203, 205
  in Islam 135, 139, 147, 142, 148, 149, 156, 159, 160, 161, 163, 164, 165, 166, 169, 170, 171, 173
  in Judaism, 41, 55
  in Latter-day Saint Church, 190, 191
  in new religious movements, 179, 181
  in Zoroastrianism, 26, 27, 29, 31
Priest, priesthood, 8, 22
  in Baha'i,184
  in Christianity, 87, 88, 92, 93, 96, 103, 113
  in Judaism, 45, 46, 49, 50, 51, 60, 66, 67, 69, 71, 72, 73
  in Latter-day Saint Church, 191–192, 197, 199
  in Zoroastrianism, 23, 24, 25, 27, 28
Prophet
  in Christianity, 87, 90, 94, 95, 101, 103
  in Islam, 129, 132, 135, 136, 137, 138, 139, 140, 142, 143, 144, 145, 146, 147, 148, 149, 150, 155, 156, 157, 159, 160, 161, 163, 164, 165, 166, 169, 170, 171, 173
  in Judaism, 43, 67, 68, 79
  in Latter-day Saint Church, 181, 194
  in Zoroastrianism, 23, 24, 25
Psalm, 43, 49, 55, 76, **79**, 87, 93
Pseudonymous (writings), 85, 86, **126**

Qiblah, 159–160, 169, 170, **173**
Qiblih, 188
Qur'an, 1, 4, 5, 6, 7, 9, 11, 13, 15, 17, 128–133, **173**
  in Baha'i, 178, 179, 180, 185
  and the *hadith*, 164, 166, 167
  selections from, 134–163

Resurrection
  in Baha'i, 185
  in Christianity, 94
  in Islam, 147, 149, 150, 151
  in Judaism, 57
  in Zoroastrianism, 33, 34
Revelation
  in Christianity, 122
  in Islam, 130, 133, 134, 135, 142, 146, 147, 156, 164, 167, 173
  in Judaism, 38, **79**, 80
  in Latter-day Saint Church, 192, 197, 198, 199
  in new religious movements, 179, 182
  in Zoroastrianism, 27

Sabbath
  in Christianity, 94, 97
  in Judaism, 41, 53, 58, 71, 73, 78
Sacrifice, 4, 6, 10
  in Christianity, 92
  in Islam, 162
  in Judaism, 47, 63, 67, 70, 71, 74, 76
  in Zoroastrianism, 22, 23, 24, 27, 33
Saoshant, 31, **34**
Satan. *See also* Devil
  in Christianity, 98, 102, 103, 107, 125
  in Islam, 134, 144, 145, 146, 153, 154, 165, 170
  in Unification Church, 209, 210
Science and Health with Key to the Scriptures, 177, 179, 180, 181, 182, 183, 199, 201, 202, 203, 204, **211**
Scripture, 1, 2, 3, 4, 5, 7, 9, 11, 15, **19**
Shema, 51, **79**
Shi'ite, 130, 131, 167, 168, 170, 178, 184, 185
Sikhism, 4, 10
Sin
  in Christianity, 83, 92, 104, 108, 112, 115, 116, 117, 120,
  in Christian Science, 199, 200, 201, 202, 203
  in Islam, 134, 144, 146, 153, 154, 169
  in Judaism, 42, 53, 66, 67, 71, 72, 76, 78, 79
  in Unification Church, 209
  in Zoroastrianism, 31
Slave, slavery
  in Christianity, 85, 92, 96, 109, 115
  in Islam, 140, 154–155, 157, 160, 164, 171
  in Judaism, 46, 58–59, 69
Smith, Joseph, 178–181, 183, 189, 191–192, 195–196, 211
Spirit
  in Baha'i, 184, 187

in Christianity, 84, 90–92, 95–97,
    99–101, 104, 108, 110, 111, 115,
    118, 120, 122–124
  in Islam, 145, 147
  in Judaism, 55
  in Latter-day Saint Church, 192, 196,
    198, 199, 200, 201, 202, 203, 205,
    207, 209
  in Zoroastrianism, 26, 27, 28, 29, 34
Struggle, 11, 29, 78, 156, 164, 173, 194
Sunni, 130, 131, 167–169, 184
Surah, 131–138, 141, 144–145, 148,
    150–151, 157–163, **173**
Synagogue, 37, 41
Synoptic, 85, **126**

Tafsir, 131, **173**
Talmud, 6, 40, 41, 74, 75, 76, 77, **79**
  selections from, 75–78
Tanakh, 38, 46, 61, **79**
Taoism, 4, 7
Tao Te Ching, 6, 13
Tefillin, 42, **80**
Testament. *See also* Covenant.
  in Christianity, 83, 84, 85, 86, 87, 88, 89,
    90, 99, 100, 102, 110, 114, 117,
    118, 119, 125, **126**
  in Islam, 131, 149, 150
  in Judaism, 38, 43, 79
  in new religious movements, 177, 181
Tilawah, **173**
Torah, 37, 38, 39, 40, 41, 42, 45, 50, 74,
    75, 76, 77, 78, 79, **80**

Unification Church, 2, 17, 177, 178, 179,
    180, 181, 182, 183, 205, 211
  scripture in, 177–180
  scripture selections from, 205–210

Vendidad, 24, 32, **35**

War, 11, 17
  in Christianity, 111, 118
  in Islam, 140, 156, 166, 167
  in Judaism, 60, 61
  in Latter-day Saint Church, 189, 194
Wife, wives. *See also* Husband, Woman
  in Christianity, 90, 104, 107, 108, 109,
    113, 114

  in Islam, 139, 140, 143, 146, 149,
    154–155, 161, 166, 171
  in Judaism, 46, 59, 53, 54, 58, 59, 60, 65,
    68, 69, 75, 76, 77, 78
  in Zoroastrianism, 31
Woman, women, 9, 11, 17
  in Christianity, 85, 91, 94, 96, 100, 101,
    103, 104, 107, 108, 110, 111, 113,
    114, 115, 123, 124
  in Islam, 129, 139, 140, 149, 151, 154,
    155, 157, 158, 164, 165, 167
  in Judaism, 41, 43, 50, 51, 52, 53, 54, 59,
    61, 62, 64, 66, 68, 75, 77, 78
  in new religious movements, 177, 186.
    187, 196, 203
  in Zoroastrianism, 28, 32, 33, 34
World. *See also* Creation, Earth. 1, 2, 3, 5, 6,
    10, 11, 12, 13, 14, 15, 17, 18, 19
  in Baha'i, 183, 184, 185, 186, 187, 188
  in Christianity, 83, 85, 86, 88, 89, 92, 94,
    96, 99, 100, 102, 104, 108, 109,
    111, 112, 114, 116, 118, 122, 123
  in Christian Science, 199, 200, 203
  in Islam, 131, 134, 136, 138, 144, 149,
    154, 160, 163, 166,168, 169, 170,
    171, 172
  in Judaism, 37, 38, 40, 41, 42, 46, 52, 56,
    68, 75, 76
  in Latter-day Saint Church, 189, 190,
    193, 196, 197, 198
  in Unification Church, 177, 205, 206,
    207, 209
  in Zoroastrianism, 26, 27, 29, 30, 31, 32,
    33, 35

Yashts, **35**
Yasna, 23, 24, 25, 26, 28, 29, 30, 31, **35**
Young, Brigham, 195

Zarathushtra, 23, 24, 25, 26, 27, 28, 29, 30,
    31, 32, 35
Zoroastrianism, 2, 4, 6, 7, 17, 23, 24, 25,
    30, 31
  general description, 23
  scripture in, 23–26
  scripture selections from, 26–34